FROM SENEGAL TO SOUTH CAROLINA

A Comprehensive Study of a People in Crisis

by

WILLIAM BERNARD BOYD

To: Brothers Lance Sr. & Lance, Jr.

Thank you for your support!
Respectfully,
Wm. Bernard Boyd
6/19/2021

CONTENTS

ACKNOWLEDGEMENTS

I acknowledge professor and author William L. Baker of Howard University (Washington, D.C.) for his encouragement and support as I undertook and completed this project. He is a fellow veteran of the U. S. Military (Marine Corps) that via his spirit and wit is an enhanced and savvy person. I would be remiss if I didn't acknowledge Dr. Percial M. Thomas of Johnson C. Smith University, a person of character, professionalism, and compassion who has played a vital role in my life. Thank you....

Thank you, my new comrade and long lost Wolof brother Ismael Bocar Ba of Senegal, West Africa. After 400 years of separation by greed, scandal, and strife, we have finally re-united (thanks for inviting me to return home).

I thank my fellow South Carolinian Mrs. Wanda Ezozo for providing me with such a timely re-typed copy of this manuscript, for which I am very grateful. A note of appreciation is due to Dr. Itibari M. Zulu of the Ralph J. Bunche Center for African American Studies at UCLA for his astuteness and advice in publishing this work.

DEDICATION

This book is dedicated in loving memory to my shipmate, and dear friend, Senior Chief Petty Officer Vernon Foster, QMCS, United States Navy. May your attention to duty, courage, valor, heroism, compassion, leadership, and infinite knowledge be the arcs that guide your soul into eternity. Navigator!

This book is also a token of my appreciation to my family for all the years of enduring the hardships of my life, and never once giving up on me.

To all of my extended family and friends, thank you for your love, patience, and tolerance, as I've grown.

To my dear sisters Rosetta and Helen... with eternal love.

This book also recognizes the late Yolanda D. King, daughter of the Rev. Dr. Martin Luther King, Jr., whom I share the same date of birth, 11-17-55, and had the distinct honor and priviledge of meeting.

W. Bernard Boyd

INTRODUCTION

The purpose of this study is to provide a realistic view of the plight of African-Americans in American society and to denote critical circumstances and obstacles they have endured. Moreover, this study will allow the facts to be told by the chief components and central figures in the topic discussed. I began this research in 1978, and after twenty-five years of acquiring the appropriate tools, and temperament vitally necessary to attempt such a project, the opportunity presented itself based on a course in Historiography to meet the requirements for the Bachelor of Arts degree in History.

I grew up in the South, thus I feel a strange kinship for the region, and more importantly, I feel obligated to reveal the humiliations inflected upon African-Americans while struggling to survive in America.

The main oppression has come from the people who are the majority in the American society, and in their attempt to maintain dominance in the land they have oppressed others. I believe we can never totally eliminate the prejudices that the concept of "race" carries, but we must present the facts and live with its truths. Therefore, by having lived amid racial oppression, I feel I have the legitimacy to talk about it and present valuable facts that must not be just another closed page in history.

To the general reader, the "CRISIS" that presently confronts people of color in America has a very long and tragic origin. Yet, this history has a close and most unexpected bearing in society today. Thus, it emerges as a remarkable legacy of a people who were doomed and expected to become extinct via their massive importation and severe inhumane treatment they were forced to endure.

This account of history is fascinating as it explores past and present stages of the evolution of people in American society. Let us know that in order for man to know where he is going, it is the upmost importance for him to know from where he has come. Hence, this is a subject so often evaded because it underscores man's cruelty to man (perhaps due to the lack of respect for God's most treasured creation, man).

From generation to generation, and generations to come, this study will explain the struggle and reveal what it means to be free. Much has been written about African-

Americans who live in the Americas, their heritage, and present identity. Nevertheless, as our history slowly emerges from the past, it begins to look like the most cruel torture man has ever perpetrated.

Most importantly, the resentments felt by African-Americans are justified and valid. African-American people have a very unique story to tell, however, it is often overlooked due to a lack of knowledge or understanding of the facts and their grim origins. To accurately tell our story or even to express our point of view, we will generally insult some people. Some will be insulted because our system of government has benefited from centuries of exploitation of African-American people.

Nevertheless, it is extremely important to discuss here, the true feelings and emotions of those who were there and affected most in our plight toward freedom. In order to remove any doubt of the extent of the brutality and inhumanity, this study will employ the parties involved. In order to feel the pain and suffering of a people who are being oppressed. I believe no one other than the people involved can tell of their experiences with credibility.

Thus, this study will allow readers to experience first-hand and onsite eyewitnesses of the plight of African-American people, in their own words. My hope is that I will say something that will motivate some young person to move ahead and pursue their dreams. More importantly, I feel this is a reasonable service. In the words of the famous poet and the son of former enslaved parents, Paul Lawrence Dunbar, said, "You don't have time to sit down on that rock and ponder, you have to get up and keep moving."

Collectively, we will achieve success through positive self-empowerment and perseverance toward excellence!

I have heard the footsteps of Harriett Tubman as she fled plantations of the South carrying her people to the safe sanctuary of the Northern borders. I have heard the thunderous voice of William E. B. DuBois, bolting out that "the Black Man will not be satisfied with one jot or one tittle less than the human rights afforded him by God." I have felt the urgency of Malcolm X as he echoed the sentiments of Denmark Vesey exclaiming he is willing to protect himself "By Any Means Necessary." I have heard the voice of the Reverend Dr. Martin Luther King, Jr. as his voice roared out like the lion of Judah saying: "We as a people will get to the promised land." And I have read the words of the prophet Ezekiel (39:1) saying:" Behold, I am against thee 0'GOG, thus saith the Lord. I will give thee unto the ravenous birds of every sort, and unto the beast of the fields to be devoured."

Lord, make me an instrument of thy peace; where there is hatred, let me sow love; where there is injury, pardon; where there is doubt, faith; where there is despair, hope; where there is darkness, light; and where there is sadness, joy. O' divine Master, grant that I may not seek to be consoled, as to console; to be understood, as to understand; to be loved, as to love; for it is in giving, we receive; for it is in pardoning, we are pardoned; and it is in dying, that we are born to eternal life. Amen!

There has been many people (including white), who have tried to help African-American people achieve social, political, and economic equality in America. Some of these people have included my fellow South Carolinians Ronald McNair (astronaut), and the Rev. Jesse Jackson. Others who have sought to bring about cultural parity have included: Marcus Garvey, the Rev. Nat Turner, Denmark Vesey, Paul Cuffy, Harriet Tubman, Peter Salem, Salem Poor, Sojourner Truth, Cinque, A. Phillip Randolph, Gen. Benjamin 0. Davis, Seaman Dory Miller, Rosa Parks, Mary McLeod Bethune, Henry 0. Tanner, Josephine Baker, Paul Robeson, Jackie Robinson, Blanche K. Bruce, Arthur Ashe, P. B. S. Pinchback, Ira Aldridge, Huey P. Newton, Bobby Seale, Eldridge Cleaver, James Brown, Hiram R. Reveals, George Washington Carver, Maxine Waters, Sydney Portier, Dr. Percial M. Thomas, Billie Holiday, Jim Brown, Pres. Jimmy Carter, Benjamin Bannaker, Bill Russell, Phyllis Wheatley, Paul Lawrence Dunbar, Medgar Evars, Jessie Owens, Stevie Wonder, Elijah Muhammad, Curtis Mayfield, Sammy Davis, Jr., Kareem Abdul-Jabbar, Muhammad Ali, Malcolm X, Frank Sinatra, Walter White, lnez Rainey, Thurgood Marshall, Lerone Bennett, Jr., Professor Cornell West, Dr. Alvin F. Poussaint, Robert Massey, Jeff Brown, Eddie Robinson,.... (Obviously, this list is far from complete. Here is the story of millions, and millions more, and it is my story).

LEAGACIES OF OPPRESSION

At the dawn of the 20th century, professor William Edward Burghardt Dubois of Harvard University stated: "The problem of the twentieth century is the problem of the color line- the relation of the darker to the lighter races of men in Asia and Africa, in America, and the Islands of the sea."1 Long after the death of this social pioneering genius, Dr. DuBois' prognosis stands true to his clairvoyant vision of yesterday.

As we enter the 21st century, we must continue to ask ourselves these same questions. "How does it feel to be a problem?"2 We people of color are a problem for America. We were a problem in America yesterday and we will still be that same problem in America tomorrow. The problem that still perplexes people of color's oppressor is," What to do with the children of their fore parents slaves?"3

In 1963, the Centennial year of the Emancipation Proclamation, Black people launched a series of massive demonstrations to protest against the unfair conditions that had followed them out of slavery. These conditions consisted of: Unfair Labor Laws, Equal Housing, Equal Job Training, Fair Employment opportunity, Equal protection under the Law, Equal Rights, An end to public segregation in schools and public facilities, Voting Rights, Police Brutality, Federal Employment, Last Hired and First Fired pratices, Church Burnings, and Lynching. Under the guidance of the Rev. Dr. Martin Luther King, Jr., the roads toward freedom were paved with hostility from the oppressors. Indeed, one need not make any miscalculations about the roads in which we have traveled towards freedom, because they have literally been filled with blood, which was too much to bare. Clearly, people of color in this society have suffered from a consciousness of thought from the oppressor certainly equalling that of a total genocidal attitude.

The origins of these genocidal ideas can be traced back to early Nineteenth Century Southern governing officials in the United States. "In 1837, South Carolina led the way in the attitudes of genocidal oppression. Then Governor, George McDuffie, told the South Carolina General Assembly:" the (Negroes) were destined by providence for slavery and this was made evident not only by the color of his skin, but also by "Intellectual Inferiority" and natural improvidence of this race." They were, he indicated, "unfit for self government of any kind, and in all respects; physically, morally, and politically, inferior to millions of the human race." The Charleston, S .C. lawyer William Drayton, said much the same thing the same year in a pamphlet attacking Abolitionists.

In August of 1963 200,000 civil rights activist gathered in nation's capital for a demonsration, the 'March on Washingtom'. They gathered to protest unfair conditions and call for human rights, equal rights,voting rights and end to segregation in public schools and public accommodations, egual job oppertunity and just labor laws.

1

He said "personal observation must convince every candid man that the Negro is constitutionally indolent, voluptuous, and prone to vice. That his mind is heavy, dull, and un-ambitious; and the doom that has made the African in all ages and countries, A Slave, is the natural consequence of the inferiority of his character." Later that same year South Carolina State Senator John C. Calhoun made his famous speech in defense of slavery before the Senate of the United States, and showed how important racial doctrines really were in the new and militant defense of servitude which had developed in the 1830's. "I hold that in the present state of civilization, where two races of different origins, and distinguished by color, and other physical differences, as well as intellectual, are brought together, the relation now existing in the Slaveholding states between the two, is, instead of an evil, A good - A positive good." Calhoun further suggested that "the Negro is an inferior race and if freed he would dwell as an inferior class of people who could not rise."[4]

It was thus in tandem with the concept of slavery as a "positive goods" that the doctoring of permanent black inferiority began its' career as a rationale, first for slavery itself, and later for post Emancipation forms of racial oppression. The attitudes that underlay the belief that Blacks were doomed by nature itself to perpetual slavishness and subordination to whites were not new, nor was the doctoring itself if considered a popular belief that lacked intellectual respectability.

But, when asserted dogmatically, and with an aura of philosophical authority by leading Southern spokesmen and Northern supporters in the 1830's, it became for the first time the basis of a worldview, an explicit ideology around which beneficiaries of white supremacy could organize themselves and their thoughts.

In their efforts to justify slavery as a necessary system of race relations, the proslavery theorists of the 1830's and 1840's had developed an arsenal of arguments for Negro inferiority that they repeated Ad Nauseam. Heavily emphasized was the historical case against the Black man based on his supposed failure to develop a civilized way of life in Africa. As portrayed in proslavery writings, Africa was always the scene of savagery, cannibalism, devil worship, and every evil known to man. Also advanced was an early form of biological argument, based on real or imagined physiological and anatomical differences - especially in the cranial (Brain) characteristics and facial angles which allegedly explained mental and physical inferiority."[5]

The most fervent of the Scientific Rationalists for the American system of racial subordination was Dr. Josiah C. Nott, Leading "Ethnologist" of this era. In 1845, Nott wrote to James Henry Hammond, a vigorously proslavery South Carolina planter and political leader. Abolition, He wrote, is one of those unfortunate questions which present one face to the philosopher and another to the mass - reason or religion can never decide it - the results of Emancipation. The Negro question was the one I wished to bring out and I embalmed it in Egyptian Ethnography, etc. He liked to describe his field of study as "The Nigger business", or "Niggerology." The fullest extent of his racism and how he hoped to see it implemented came out in one of the sections he wrote in "Types Of Mankind."

He describes, the Caucasian as having in all ages been the rulers. Their destiny, therefore, is to conquer and hold every foot of the globe where climate does not interpose an impenetrable barrier. No philanthropy, no legislation, no missionary labors can change this law; it is written in man's nature by the hand of his creator. As for the "Inferior Races," they would serve out their purposes and become extinct."

There has always been attempts to show how the anatomical evidence of Negro inferiority could be correlated with the Biblical description of the "Curse On Canaan"- God's condemnation of Canaan, and his allegedly black descendents to be "Servants unto Servants." These Pluralist ideas responded to the Southern desire to place the Negro as low as possible on the scale of creation, not only because this was a way to justify slavery, but also because it did so in a manner that allowed the whites to retain their beliefs that "All Men", meaning now all members of the "Caucasian species"- were created equal."6

Ironically, when confronted or asked about their racist and oppressing fore parents, the general response of the people who are the recipients of the benefits of centuries of oppression, and dehumanization, denies any knowledge of these facts. Moreover, these beneficiaries refuses to accept the responsibility for the genocidal affects on the people that their fore parents left in their wake. Now when asking the offspring of these racist oppressors about the acts and atrocious deeds of their fore parents; such as, "what ever happened to the million of Indians that use to inhabit these lands?" They reluctantly and wittingly respond, "Well I don't know, or, well I guess they put them somewhere." My immediate thought is yes, you put them somewhere all right. You put them in the ground just like your racist fore parents said they would. Moreover, these beneficiaries like to say they are "not responsible" for what their fore parents did, or "I wasn't there, "or" Why do you want to dwell on the past?" Well, I say I wouldn't want to dwell on the past too much either if I had been the beneficiaries of hundreds of years of murder, genocide, stealing, raping, robbing, lying, cheating, deception, deceit, castrating, colonizing, conquering, exploiting, on and on, from one end of the earth to the other. Literally, these oppressive people reared their faces out of the caves of the Caucasus Mountains' and killed off people, in order to preserve their own way of life.

History has proven it was not as much a question of whether or not the Black Race was inferior. But rather, it was the necessity of the Caucasian Race to suppress or oppress the people of color in order to achieve their own self-interest. Thus, after the Negro had been beaten down and exploited for hundreds of years via slavery, the question then arose "what do we do with them now?"

The Negro had been artificially introduced into the United States as "a slave," and it was only the protection of servitude that had allowed him to survive until Emancipation "exclaimed most Southern Whites. These were all the philosophies of pro-genocidal racists of the era of post Emancipation." The Anglo-American looks upon every acre of our present domain as intended for him and not for the Negro." There was an expectation of Anglo expansion into every corner of the nation, with the disappearance of the Negro as an inevitable corollary. The Reverend J. M. Sturtevant wrote in detail exactly how Black extinction in the United States would occur. He conceded that "White prejudice against Black equality was insurmountable." Although most Americans believed slavery was economically, socially, politically, and morally wrong, the fear of a growing and assertive Negro population was a barrier to acceptance of the governments Emancipation policy. Sturtevant assured those who could not decide what they disliked more, slavery or the Negro and that Emancipation would be a safer and easier way to dispose of both.

He concluded with a high degree of assurance that "The result of Emancipation must not be the Amalgamation of the races, not an internecine war between them, but the inevitable extinction of the weaker race by the competition of the stronger." After Emancipation, the Negro would enter into direct competition with the whites, and because of the superiority of the Whites, the Negro would be pushed into A "Lower Stratum." The consequence is inevitable. He will either never marry, or he will, in an attempt to support A family, struggle in vain against the laws of nature, and his children, many of them at least, die in infancy.... Like his brother, the Indian of the forest, He must melt away and disappear forever from the midst of us." For antislavery racists this desire for homogeneity led logically to a defense of Emancipation as a step toward genocide by natural causes. In the Nineteenth Century South, egalitarian ethos seemed to require the Negro be regarded, not merely as a client, but as a creature, not quite human."[7]

In 1859, two years after the Supreme Courts decision in the Dread Scott case denying American citizenship to all Negroes, Abraham Lincoln noted that some northern Democrats were openly asserting that when the Declaration of Independence spoke of "All Men," this did not include Negroes. Although a believer in black inferiority, Lincoln was not willing to go so far as to continence denoting the Negro" from the rank of a man to that of a brute."[8]

Lincoln wanted to return or re-colonize the African to another land after emancipation to South America. There will be a full discussion devoted to the position held by President Lincoln in regard to slavery in the later chapters in this study.

However, it is important to say at this juncture that the attitude of genocide held by most proslavery advocates toward the African was the predominate school of thought of the day. More importantly, if we are what we have been becoming, then this country has inherited the belief that a totally (Caucasian) America is yet best suited in order to fulfill the intent of its' so-called founders. Moreover, this is why I still believe there is so much more work to be done here if we as a "Human Race" will be able to co-exist. We are going to have to somehow destroy the myth that America belongs to one race of people only, because we all belong here on God's earth.

PHILOSOPHIES AND PREDICTIONS: TOWARDS EXTERMINATION AND EXTINCTION

The image of African American people that many Caucasian people currently hold is directly the result of what was handed down to them by their ancestors. Furthermore, the idea of a Utopian society is what we all would like to achieve. However, realistically the means of the so-called founding fathers did not justify the end. It was the surrealistic desires of the pro-slavery advocates and later these pro-genocidal advocates that has shaped much of the thinking pervasive today in American society. "Southern humanitarians envisioned the eventual whitening of America as coming through an amicable and painless process of voluntary migration allegedly beneficial to both races, another group of free-soil theorists manifested a more callous attitude toward the future of the people of color. Before the Civil War, spokesmen saw the oppressor pushing his slave counterpart to the wall and predicted freedom would be accompanied by the disappearance of the African, not so much because he would be happy to move southward, but because he would be pushed out or otherwise eliminated in an "Unequal Economic Struggle"[1]

In 1857, George M. Weston, an economist, put it in plain terms when he stated: "When whites want the rooms which the Africans occupies, the whites will take it, not by rude force, but by gentle and gradual peaceful processes. The African will disappear...but at all events he will disappear." Weston compared the fate of the African to the Indians. Who were then expected to become extinct shortly, and denied the disappearance of the inferior races in the presence of more vigorous stocks was a catastrophe, it was rather the beneficent result of "laws which nature manifests throughout not only the animal but vegetable world as well. The only thing prevented African "extinction" was the artificial protection provided by the institution of slavery which was "no scheme of nature" but a violation of all moral and natural laws."[2]

Horace Bushnell, a Congressional Clergyman and Theologian, predicted the African race would not survive because of competition with whites. Within "Fifty Years" of Emancipation, he predicted, "Vices which taint the blood and cut down life will "penetrate the whole stock, and begin to hurry them off, in a process of premature extinction, as we know to be the case with another "barbarous" people [the Indians], now fast yielding to the infection of death.

Bushnell believed, the day of emancipation would be "Glorious", especially for whites".... as to the poor herd who may yet be doomed to spin their brutish existence downward into extinction, it will be a relief to know, the first day of conscious liberty gave them one bright spot, in the compass of a sad and defrauded immortality." The extents of these genocidal beliefs were practiced and preached about in white churches. Reverend Bushnell told his congregation, "I know of no example in human history where an inferior and far less cultivated stock has been able, freely intermixed with a superior, to hold its ground.... it will always be seen that the superior lives the other down, and finally quite lives it away. And finally indeed, since we all must die, why should it grieve us, that a stock thousands of years behind in the scale of culture, should die with few and still "fewer children" to succeed, till finally the whole succession remains in the more cultivated race."[3]

Another racist who predicted African extinction in America was Theodore Parker. Although he was willing to fight for African freedom, Parker was unwilling to concede a permanent African future in America. Unlike Bushnell he kept such opinions largely to himself, revealing them only in private correspondence; but his public depiction of the destiny of Anglo-Saxons to expand their domain at the expense of the inferior races implied that Blacks would have a difficult time after emancipation. In illustrating this the "Curious Law of Nature" dictates "The stronger replaces the weak," Parker describes how one kind of New England grass inevitably drives out another. "Thus, he continued, "moving easily to another sphere of natural competition, "The White man kills out the Red Man and the Black Man. When slavery is abolished the African population will decline in the United States, and die out of the South....

He also wrote in 1857: "There are inferior races of men which have always born the same ignoble relation to the rest of man and always will. For two generations, what a change there will be in the condition and character of the Irish in New England! But in twenty generations, the Africans will stand Just where they are now if they have not disappeared."

Elsewhere Parker suggested African blood might be absorbed into the Anglo-Saxon amalgam through intermarriage. But whether it was miscegenation or merely competitive failure, it would lead to the Negro's disappearance as a distinct American race, he was fairly certain he would vanish. And, given his negative view of the essential African character, there is no reason to believe he shed any tears over the prospect, however outraged he may have been by the immorality of slavery."[4]

Predictions of African extinction as an acceptable, even desirable, consequence of emancipation continued to be made during the Civil War by men who rejoiced at the impending annihilation of the slavery system.

In 1862, Charles Francis Adams, Jr., who was in the Army in South Carolina, wrote to his father that in his opinion, the Black race "will be destroyed the moment the world realizes what a field for white emigration the South affords. The inferior will disappear... before the more vigorous race."[5]

Dr. Samuel Bradley Howe, the famous New England physician, philanthropist, and reformer suggested in 1863 the likely result of Emancipation as far as the North was concerned, was "the colored people in whom the Negro nature prevails will tend to move toward the North while the weaker and lighter ones will remain and die out among us." Slavery, Howe pointed out, "had fostered and multiplied a vigorous Black race, and engendered a feeble mulatto breed."

Many of both types had drifted northward, "in the teeth of thermal laws," to escape servitude; but the complete destruction of slavery would "remove all these disturbing forces and allow fair play to natural laws, by the operation of which, it seems to me, the colored population will disappear from the Northern and middle states, if not from the continent, before the more vigorous and prolific race." He went so far as to suggest that it would be "the duty of statesmen to favor, by wise measures, the operation of these laws and the purification and elevation of the natural blood." More specifically, he recommended "mulattoes," who was the same, as "hybridism" ought to be met and lessened as far as might be by wise statesmanship and enlightenment of public opinion. Howe's suggestion that the free operation of "natural laws" might lead to the extinction of the African in the entire continent as well as in the North implied he was not entirely convinced of "the permanent foothold" doctrine as put forth, and thought it quite possible the U.S. was destined to be all white.

For Howe, this mixture of blood was clearly one of the principal evils of the slave system, and he believed mulattoes had gone so far as to be "widespread among the whole population of the United States," which meant it had already impaired "the purity of the national blood taken as a whole." His observation of mulattos seemed to theorize: they appear highly susceptible to disease and infertility: "... without the continuance of mulatto breeding, in the South, and fresh accessions of population... mulattoes would fade out from the blood of the Northern states. "With freedom and protection of their legal rights; with an open field of industry, and opportunities for mental and moral culture, African people will not seek relationships with whites, but will follow their natural affinity, and marry among themselves."

And once given the right of choosing the soil and climate most congenial to their nature," those in the North would migrate to the South, where they have a curious fate in store for them. Drawn by natural attractions to warmer regions, they will co-operate powerfully with whites from the North in reorganizing the industry of the South; but they will dwindle and gradually disappear from the people of this continent. But surely, history will record their blameless life as a people; their patient endurance of suffering and of wrong; and their sublime return of good for evil to the race of their oppressors."

In Howe's opinion, therefore, most of the African population, perhaps all of it, was doomed to disappear because inherited weaknesses would put them at a disadvantage in the inevitable competition. The touch of romantic racialism appended to his prediction of African extinction- his reference to the Blacks' "patient endurance of sufferings and of wrong" suggested how little the "natural" Christian virtues attributed to blacks would actually avail them in the long run.

His condescending accepts the romantic racialist stereotype also came out in his description of the Canadian Fugitive Slaves: as 'a little effeminate, as though a portion of the girt had been left out of their composition." "... with their African blood" he maintained, "they may have inherited more of womanly than of manly dispositions; for Africans have more of womanly virtues than fiercer people have. Indeed, it may be said that among the races, Africa is like a gentle sister in a family of fierce brothers." Romantic racialism had in fact set the Black man up for a kill, in a sense, by denying him the very qualities he would need to survive."[6]

Some people felt the disappearance of the Negro would come through the mixing of the races and the creation of a mulatto breed would be the ideal human being would exemplify both Characteristics of the African and the Caucasian races.

"Praise of the Mulatto" as a superior human type was occasionally forthcoming in antislavery writings of the late 1850's. C. G. Parsons, for example, wrote in "Inside Slavery": The mulattoes are the best specimens of manhood found in the South. The African mothers have given them a good physical system, and the Anglo-Saxon fathers a good mental constitution. But it was not until wartime that emancipation raised the specter of the widespread miscegenation in the minds of Northern Negro-phobias that a pair of deadly serious romantic racialists actually carried the doctoring to its logical extreme and openly defended intermarriage as a way of taking the rough edges off the overly aggressive Anglo-Saxons.

One was Moncure Daniel Conway, an abolitionist of Southern origin who immigrated to England during the Civil War, partly because he was disgusted with the mixed motives and equivocation with which the North had approached the slavery question. Writing to a British audience in 1864, Conway argued:

Each race is stronger in some direction than all others but for that strength it has suffered loss in other directions." The European was distinguished for his "intellect and energy" but deficient in "simple goodliness, kindliness, and affectionateness"; and it was precisely here that the African excelled. In considering the desirability of miscegenation, therefore, Conway concluded "the mixture of Blacks and Whites is good, and that the person so produced is, under ordinarily favorable circumstances, healthy, handsome, and intelligent.

Under the best circumstances, I believe such a combination would evolve a more complete character than the unmitigated Anglo-Saxon." And it was inevitable, in his opinion, such a mixture would take place in America; for the nation was "bound by fate" to "rear a new race" which would also be a better one."[7]

The African was the subject of many a study in an attempt to determine the exact distinctions between the races. The idea that the African was a natural Christian was set forth in detail, with many of the implications inherent in such a notion, in a series of lectures given in Cincinnati, Ohio, in 1837 and 1838 by Alexander Kinmont, a leading Midwestern exponent of Swedenborgianism. Kinmont, who conducted a school where scientific education was harmonized with a classical literature and define revelation, sought in his "Twelve Lectures on Man" to combine ethnology and religion in a new system. His efforts excited great interest in Cincinnati, then the center of Western intellectual life. In response to the widespread praise for his ideas, Kinmont prepared his lectures for the publication but died before they appeared in print in 1839. Kinmont began from the premise not unlike other racists, contending that Africans, in both "their physical and mental condition, are naturally and originally distinct" from whites. He maintained further it was "the effect of a particular providence, or, to speak in the dialect of science, an express law of nature, each peculiar race of men should occupy those limits, which have been assigned and none other."

Thus, the enslavement and forced migration of Blacks was not only a violation of the Christian morality but also a "sad error" that went in the teeth of natural law. But unlike the scientific proponents of polygenesis, Kinmont did not accept the notion Africans constituted a lower order of beings. Although the "original" differences between the races were not caused by "any combination of causes, natural or artificial, with which we are acquainted," and were "obscure," they were nevertheless compatible with the religious doctoring of the unity and fraternity of the human race. Whites and Blacks manifested different traits because this was part of what Kinmont saw as "God's Plan" for the gradual fulfillment of man's intellectual, moral, and spiritual potentialities. The present epoch, he indicated, was obviously of the Caucasians, a race that excelled all others in "intellectual expansion", and it was the divinely appointed mission of the whites to develop the arts and sciences.

But such intellectual advancement was not the last word in human aspiration. Africans, even in their present unfulfilled state, possessed some very desirable traits sadly lacking in Caucasians- "Light-Heartedness" a "natural talent for music" and, above all, "willing to serve, the most beautiful trait of humanity, which we, from our innate love of dominion, and in defiance of the Christian religion, brand with the name of "Servility," and abuse not less to our own dishonor than to their injury."

Hence, the Caucasian, with all his gifts, was almost constitutionally unable to be a true Christian: "All the sweeter graces of the Christian religion appear almost too tropical and tender plants to grow in the Caucasian mind; they require a character of human nature which you can see in the rude lineaments of the Ethiopian."[8]

Among others who conducted studies of amalgamation of the races were Mrs. A. M. French- one of the humanitarians who went to Port Royal, South Carolina, to teach the ex-slaves who fell under Union control after the capture of some of the Sea Islands in late 1861- was impressed from the beginning by the religious sensibilities of the Africans. "In some of the deep things of God we may learn from some of them," she wrote, "for they have religious experiences deep in the heart...." Moreover, she opposed amalgamation on the ground that "there is not in the Caucasian race the warmth of the soul to adapt him to the African. There is not the Colored adaptation to him" "It is far better that the races are distinct" she concluded, and added that the pure African was unquestionably superior to the mulatto."[9]

Nevertheless, the question of inferiority is still promulgated by this society strictly on the basis of the color of the skin. For centuries, and in some respects today, ...the closer one is to resembling the oppressor, the more accepted he is by the society at large. These are the children of fore parents who professed racial dominance and oppression through their belief in God that it was their will to be superior at all cost. They believed through their racist Christian belief, and imperialist inheritance, that it was through their natural selection that they could conquer, dominate, and consume, all other races. The whole dirty business of slavery was based on the premise that the Negro was a thing to be used and not a person to be respected. To put the matter in its proper perspective and to accurately identify the position held by the bondsman, it can be summed up in this paraphrase, but never totally, due to its cruelty.

"Unconditional submission" was the only footing upon which slavery could be placed. The slave must know his master is to govern absolutely and he is to obey implicitly, he is never, for a moment to exercise either his will or judgment in opposition to a positive order. The master felt they had to implant in the slave a consciousness of personal inferiority. This sense of inferiority was deliberately extended to his past. The slave owners were convinced that in order to control the African, the slaves 'had to feel that his African ancestor tainted them, and their color was a badge of degradation.

Also it was necessary to make them stand in fear and to impress upon Africans their helplessness; to create in them a habit of perfect dependence upon their masters, impress upon him a sense of his innate inferiority, and develop in him a sense of complete dependence. To leave no doubt in the mind of the captured he was literally at the mercy of his master's disposal.

Out of greed, propelled by hatred and the belief it was their God given right to inflict a sense of "nothingness," except to serve the oppressor, upon the [Negro], the oppressor went to the fullest extent to achieve his end. Absalom Jones, a Negro sergeant in the union army is remembered for saying each morning he wakes up and realizes the white man hasn't slaughtered him, he kisses the ground. Out of the desire to remain in control of people of all races the oppressor will go to any lengths. The killing, burning at the stake, lynching, maiming, to oppress in order to intimidate and remain in power with the aim to pass this position of power, rule and authority on to the next generation of their lineage, was their intent.

"Uprooted from their native homelands and forced through the horrors of the voyage to America known as the "Middle Passage," Africans arrived as strangers in a strange land. Africans became Pilgrims in America not in the sense that they came in search of new beginnings in a new Eden, or a New Jerusalem. But rather, Africans came to America in the confusion of their new environment. The majority of the new arrivals had been uprooted from an area of the West African" coast stretching from Senegal to the Niger River."[10]

"When European voyagers first encountered West Africans in the Fifteenth Century, they were much taken by their creative achievements. The bronze work created in Benin was considered then, as it is now, to be some of the finest craftsmanship of the period, and Europeans of the Renaissance Era could appreciate it's brilliance. Europeans also did not find the Africans architectural hierarchy unfamiliar, accustomed as they were to their lords living in grand houses and their peasants living in thatched cottages. In both cultures people ate using their hands, assisted by a knife and sometimes a spoon, and the smoking of tobacco after a meal was a shared pleasure. From this exchange and others it is clear neither the European nor the African, regard the other as primitive."[11]

"The creativity of African people was evident long before they were brought to the North American continent. European explorers were in awe over the advancement of African civilizations, and they returned home with wonderous stories of a Black-skinned people who were more advanced in their knowledge of Astronomy, Navigation, Mathematics, Architecture, Literature, and Agriculture than anyone they had ever encountered. They spoke of the mighty empires, the power and emotion in the art, the elaborate government and ornate cities, the detailed codes of law and the ingenious methods Africans used to irrigate their crops, keep time, and embalm their dead.

The first noted European historian and philosopher Herodotus, a Greek, remarked in the Fifth Century "Africa was the greatest civilization in human history."[12]

"Most of us might not dare believe a French nobleman and adventurer, Count Constantine DeVolney, made the following observation in 1787. He wrote: "How astonished... when we reflect to the race of Africans, at present our slaves, and the object of our extreme contempt, we owe our arts, sciences, and even the very use of speech, and when we recollect in the midst of those nations who call themselves the friends of liberty and humanity, the most barbarous of slaveries is justified; and it is even a problem whether the understanding of Africans be of the same species with the white men." Further research by Count Volney revealed "Civilization had been first conceived on the borders of the upper Nile River, in Africa, among a black race of men."[13]

"Europeans have long considered Africa to be a strange and mysterious land. Many called it the "Dark Continent." But to Africans and the enlightened Europeans who came to know it, Africa was a land kissed by the Gods. Africa is the home of the Nile, the worlds longest river; the Sahara, the worlds largest desert; and Mount Kilimanjaro, one of the world highest mountains. It is the home of Egypt and Timbuktu, cradles of civilization, commerce, medicine, mathematics, and knowledge. It is the birthplace of all life, the land where human life began some four million years ago.

Before the Europeans came, my people were known by their indigenous names. They were: the Ashanti, the Fulani, the Ibo, the Bambara, the Mende, the Ewe, the Akan, the Kimbundi, the Zulu, the Bantu, the Sans, the Hausa, and the Teso. Africans called their empires: Songhai, Benin, Mali, Dahomey, Katsina, and Kane-Bornu. Before my people spoke English, French, Portuguese and Spanish - languages of their European conquerors- they spoke: Twi, Fula, Hausa, Shona, and a thousand other African languages. This was before the invasion of the Europeans. Before Africa was theirs, she belonged to the Black man.

They called our lands "The Gold Coast" "The Ivory Coast" "The Grain Coast" "and soon The "Slave Coast," labeling them according to the riches they could exploit. They carved Africa into pieces among themselves, claiming its' wealth and exerting their military and political power. It would not be until the 1990's, through armed struggle and resistance that Africa would again be ruled by Africans. If you want to know the Africa of our Ancestors, look to Africa from the beginning of civilization - The Africa before the arrival of the Portuguese and other European invaders."[14]

Map of africa

THE EUROPEAN-AFRICAN
TRANSATLANTIC SLAVE TRADE

The slave trade begins in the early l430's when Prince Henry of Portugal became known throughout Europe as the Navigator and urged his mariners to chart a new course to explore the shores of Africa, allowing Portugal to trade for gold, silk, spices, ivory, and African slaves. From the start, Africa was prominent in the navigators grand scheme, for the continents goods and slaves were already well known in Europe."[1]

Slavery existed in Africa (as it did in most all civilized societies) before the arrival of Europeans. Enslaved Africans were often prisoners of war, thieves, and debtors. But the treatment of slaves, particularly, those who were viewed as servants to a family, was far different and, in general, far more humane than the chattel slavery of the Americas and the islands. Historians say that in the African system, slaves, though of inferior status, had certain rights while their owners had definite and often onerous duties toward them. Slaves were used to till the earth for their owners, and were, in return, fed and clothed. Many of the groups, notably Mandingos treated their slaves very well" they are remarkably kind to, and careful of their slaves ... whom they treat with respect, and whom they will not suffer to be ill-used. This is a forcible lesson from the "wild and savage Africans" to the more polished and enlightened Europeans, who treat them i.e., (their slaves), as if they were" a lower order of creatures, and abuse them in the most shocking manner."[2]

"For the Portuguese sea merchants, slaves would ultimately prove to be the most profitable form of commerce. The earliest seeds of the slave trade were sown when the first Portuguese boat pulled ashore in West Africa. As the Africans approached the boats with curiosity, strange looking occupants, the Portuguese sailors, suddenly fell upon them, seizing the nearest of the onlookers and bundling them into a boat to be ferried off into the unknown. This happened time and time again before the Africans learned to conceal themselves when a European vessel was sighted or to launch the first attack. Many of the first Portuguese ships lost along the coast fell prey to the retaliating Africans. Shortly a stalemate was reached, and the Portuguese realized if they hoped to gain some share of Africas' wealth, they would have to establish formal trading ties with Africa. Between 1456 and 1462, Portugal sent official diplomatic missionaries to open trade relations with West African states. This encounter resulted in the successful exchange of goods, and the peaceful purchase of slaves."[3]

"They came, they said, as friends - to trade for ivory, spices, and gold. They returned a few years later, this time wanting something more" Black Gold." men, women and children to work on the lands they had just conquered. In 1435, the Portuguese established trading posts along the coast of Senegal, West Africa. With the Columbus 'discovery' of a new world in 1492, and the introduction of sugar cane in the Spanish West Indies, this turned slave trading into big business. The great sugar plantations needed cheap labor. At first the Spanish enslaved the native Arawak Indians. When slavery nearly decimated the native population, Spain turned to what it deemed the next best alternative - Africa - where there seemed to be an inexhaustible supply of laborers"[4]

The trade for men was never easy nor simple. In the early days, traders sailed from port to port, kidnapping Africans and trading for goods until they had enough to make the voyage profitable. However, they soon abandoned this for more efficient ways of securing captives - hiring African middlemen to raid villages deep in the interior or by pitting African kings against each other, convincing them to sell their captives as slaves."[5]

Africans who were already Christians did not preclude their enslavement by Europeans however; and the argument put forth by many advocates of the TransAtlantic slave trade. Hence, slavery was an opportunity to convert the "African Heathens" by transporting them to Christian lands - was never set against the fact that many Africans had embraced that faith while still in their homelands."[6]

"Charles Ball, a slave during the Nineteenth Century, came into contact with many African who had been brought to America. His grandfather had come from Africa as a child and Ball had heard many stories from him. Thus he recorded the story of one slave who was brought from Africa to America.

"We were alarmed one morning just at the break of day, by the horrible uproar caused by mingled shouts of men, and blows given with heavy sticks upon large wooden drums. Enemies, who attacked us with clubs after fighting for more than an hour, surrounded the village, those of us who were not fortunate enough to run away were made prisoners. It was not the objective of our enemies to kill us. The heavy blow of a club knocked me down, and when I recovered from the stupor that followed, I found myself tied fast with the long rope I had brought from the desert... We were Immediately led away from the village through the forest and were compelled to travel all day as fast as we could walk...We traveled for three weeks in the woods-sometimes without any path at all. I had never seen white people before and they appeared to me to be the ugliest creatures in the world. Then we came in sight of what appeared to be the most beautiful object; this was a large ship anchored in the river.

The surprise attack of an African Village

3

Captured victims of an African Village led away to be traded

Once on board, the prisoners were taken below the deck and chained together in what was called the ships galley. It was here that they were kept throughout the long voyage from Africa to America. And it was here that millions died from the conditions on board the ships. The ships doctor made the most of the room and wedged them in. They had not so much room as a man in his coffin, either in length or breadth. It was impossible for them to turn or shift with any degree of ease. At the time we came into the ship, she was full of Black people, who were all confined in a dark and low place, in irons. The women were in irons as well as the men. About twenty persons were seized in our village at the time I was; and among these were three children so young they were not able to walk or to eat any hard substance. The mothers of these children had brought them all the way with them and had them in their arms when we were taken on board the ship.

When they put us in irons to be sent to our place of confinement in the ship, the men who fastened the irons on these mothers took the children out of their hands and threw them over the side of the ship into the water. When this was done, two of the women leaped overboard after their children. The third was already confined by a chain to another woman and could not get into the water, but in struggling to free herself, she broke her arm and died a few days later of a fever. One of the two women who were in the river was carried down by the weight of her irons before she could be rescued. But the other was taken up by some men in a boat and brought on board. This woman later threw herself over-board one night when we were at sea.

The weather was very hot whilst we lay in the river and many of us died every day; but the number brought onboard greatly exceeded those who died, and at the end of two weeks, the place in which we were confined was so full no one could lie down, and we were obliged to sit all day and all the time for the room was not high enough for us to stand. When our prison could hold no more, the ship sailed down the river; and on the night of the second day after she sailed, I heard the roaring of the ocean as it dashed against her sides.

After we had been at sea some days, the irons were removed from the women and they were permitted to go upon deck, but whenever the winds blew high, they were driven down amongst us. We had nothing to eat but Yams, which were thrown amongst us at random, and of these we had scarcely enough to support life. More than one third of us died on the passage, and when we arrived in Charleston, S.C., I was not able to stand. It was more than a week after I left the ship before I could straighten my limbs.

I was bought by a trader with several others, brought up the country and sold to my present master. I have been here five years. Another man had not taken his food and refused taking any. They then whipped him with a cat, but this was also ineffectual. He always kept his teeth so fastened it was impossible to get anything down.... In this state he was for four or five days, when he was brought up as dead and thrown overboard."[7]

Few can imagine the horrors that awaited my people aboard these slave vessels. The filth, the stench, the loss of life, the disease, the packing of men in spaces so tight they could neither turn, nor stand, nor squat, nor sit, is beyond human comprehension. Yet, such were the conditions my people were forced to bare during the hellish journey from Africa to the new world- the journey known as the "Middle Passage" or the "Maafa". (The Massive Disaster).

For fifty days or more, my people were forced to live like animals, caged in spaces as tight as coffins. Captains shared two schools of thought. "Tight packers" herded as many Africans aboard the ships as possible, arguing that the net receipts from sales of slaves would offset the number who died on board. Loose packers preferred to give their captives "breathing room", trusting more would survive under sanitary conditions. So great was the profit from the sale of the enslaved, most European captains filled their vessels to the top, adding a second platform, if necessary, barely twenty inches above the heads of those below, to accommodate more. Crammed in suffocating heat, held fast by chains bolted to the floor, forced to lie in their own waste, breathing air rancid with vomit, disease, and sickness - my people suffered unimaginable horrors. There, amid huge rats that gnawed through wood and flesh, men went mad; on the floors covered with blood and excrement, pregnant women gave birth, there the living awoke, chained to the dead."[8]

The daily routine brought little relief. Meals- Horse beans pounded to a pulp and served with slabber sauce, a mixture of flour, water and palm oil came twice a day, once if rations ran short, that they washed down with a half or perhaps a full pint of water, the total allotment for the day. Next came the dancing of the slaves- a cruel form of exercise and amusement conducted by the slave ship captains to keep their human cargo in salable condition. The crew played the bagpipe or forced my people to beat out a rhythm as the enslaved Africans, ankles rubbed raw from the friction of the leg irons. But the few hours above decks ended quickly, and each evening my people again were herded below. Nighttime became a horrible nightmare.

The cries of my people rose, when the utterance of sorrow filled the air. An enslave woman interpreted her people's lamentations and anguish, describing the noise and their howling as "owing to their having dreamt they were in their own country and finding themselves, when awake, in the hold of a slave ship." It was this journey that brought millions of my people from Africa to the West Indies, North America, South America, and the countries of Europe.

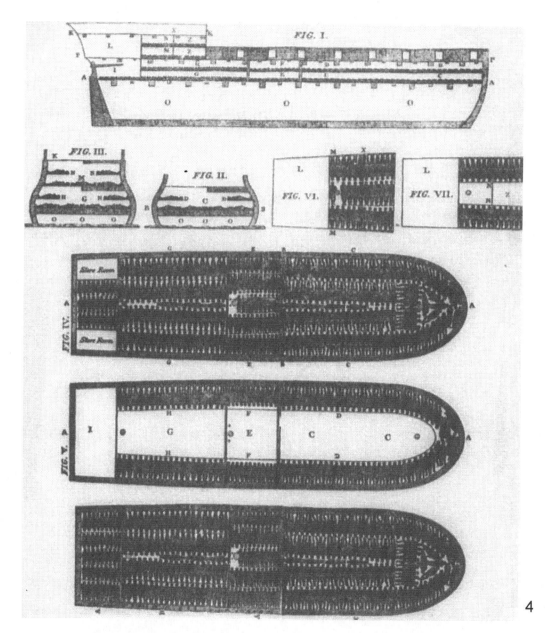

Organization of human cargo aboard slave ships.

4

We do not know how many died during the voyages. Those who endured suffered a horror unmatched in history- a horror words can only begin to describe."[9]

"By the late 1600's, European slave traders had become the scrooge of Africa. They would travel up key rivers like the Gambia or the Congo, and raid villages with their cannons and rifles. They would attack at dinnertime or just before sunrise. They would set fires to parts of a village and force men, women, and children to run from fear of being burned to death, into their own captivity. If you were a woman, you would be sexually abused. Rape, public and private, gang and individual, was a primary form of dis-empowering a powerful proud people. It was usually the first act after all were rounded up and shackled and yoked. African men shackled, yoked, held at gunpoint, could only look on as their mother, daughter, sister, wife, relative, and friend, were put through some of the most degrading acts a human could do to another.

Children were sexually violated in the most brutal ways, often leaving them bleeding to death or racked with trauma, not to mention syphilis and gonorrhea. For the white men, often poor illiterate outcasts, Christianity and their male dominated culture had so distorted sexuality that the madness of rape and sexual abuse was looked upon as a reward, as proof of their manhood as evident they at least had power over something, the African.

For the women of Africa to be attacked was never a question of age, looks, size, or what shade of brown you were. If you were one of the fortunate ones not raped or sexually abused, you were still beaten, shackled, and deprived of any privacy. The violence was consciously intended to announce that you were no longer in control of any part of your life for the rest of your life and the lives of your children now and to come."[10]

As stated earlier in the study, "the institution of slavery had long existed on the continent of Africa, mostly as a way to deal with prisoners of war, debtors, and malefactors. In Africa, slavery was considered to be primarily a condition of servitude, more humane than indefinite imprisonment or outright killing. Now, with the new trading alliance between Europe and West Africa, the vast numbers of captives, who had been once marched across the desert, were diverted to the coast and herded aboard European vessels, particularly those of Portugal and Spain. When the first captured Africans stepped aboard a Portuguese vessel, they embarked on a journey that would be repeated over a thousand times over the next four centuries.

The agony of the "Middle Passage"-the sea voyage from West Africa to the European colonies in the Americas, became notorious for the millions who died during its' course. How many Africans traveled to the Americas in these reeking death ships of the "Middle Passage"? Conservative estimates range from 80 to 115 million based on surviving custom records in both Europe and America. Considering loss and damage of records and theft of slaves or whatever estimate one accepts, the reckoning in human lives was staggering, and almost incomprehensible.

By 1500, roughly sixty years after the Portuguese reached the West coast of Africa; five thousand Africans per year were exported as slaves. A hundred years later this number had almost doubled, and by 1700 the number had soared to thirty-six thousand per year"[11]

The English were not as involved in the early evolution of the slave trade as were Portugal, Spain, Italy, and the colonies of North America. The islands active role as a slave trader began with the ascendance of Elizabeth the first to the English throne in 1558, and by the middle of the Eighteenth Century, England had become the worlds primary slave trading power. The Europeans soon started to feel at home in Africa by 1668. They described it as a well kept city, the city of Benin, of remarkable architecture, thriving commerce, and industry."[12]

The trade in flesh was an evil act that would haunt Africa and her descendant for over 400 years. It disrupted cultures, depopulated the continent, provoked wars, and took from Africa the brightest and the strongest. No doubt those who participated in the trade lived to regret their involvement. In a letter to the King of Portugal in 1526, King Affonso of the Congo, an African baptized and educated by white missionaries, wrote" We cannot reckon how great the damage [of the trade] is, since the merchants are taking everyday our Natives, Sons of the land, and the Sons of our Noblemen, and vassals, and our relatives…We beg of your Highness to help and assist us in this matter, commanding your factors [buying agents] that they should not send either merchants or wares, because it is our will that in these kingdoms there should not be any trade of slaves nor outlet for them; King Affonso's plea fell on deaf ears. The trade was underway, and once it began, it would be hundreds of years before it was halted."[13]

In its' simplest terms, the slave trade had begun because Native Americans did not make strong enough slaves. Weakened by overwork and despair, huge populations were swiftly felled by European diseases which they had no previous exposure. The English colonists experimented with slavery by buying twenty Africans who had arrived on a Dutch slave ship in Jamestown, Virginia, in 1620. At the time, the English identified the Africans as "Indentured Servants", which implied the Africans might expect to be free after a certain period.

Some of these Africans were freed, and a few went on to establish thriving plantations of their own. But, as history would demonstrate, this was generally the exception to an increasingly harsh rule."[14]

It is estimated that more than 115 million people were taken from the continent of Africa during the years of the slave trade. These millions were, of course, the youngest, the strongest, the most capable of bringing the greatest profit, first to the slave trader, and later to the slave owner. The Africans were scattered throughout South America, the Islands of the West Indies, and the United States. Africa's citizens became the laboring backbone for much of the Western Hemisphere.

But it was in the United States that a system of slavery evolved that was more cruel and total than almost any other system of slavery devised by one group against another. No other country where Africans were enslaved destroyed African culture to the extent it was destroyed in the United States. Today there still exists, in South America, and the Caribbean Islands, African religions, music, and languages that came over on the slave ships. Yet, only fragments of Africa remain among the Africans of the United States, thus, the slavery instituted by the founders of America has few comparisons for its far-reaching cruelty."[15]

Bound in chains, slaves were loaded aboard wooden vessels to voyage sometimes lasting from four to six months without knowing their fate or destinations. Those who were considered to be in bad health were either killed by the Europeans before sailing, or thrown overboard at sea to be eaten by sharks. In the beginning, it is said to have been "Only A Trickle" of "Human Souls" transported across the seas. But as the economic demand for these soon to be exploited human beings grew, history would record the most tragic epoch in the annals of all humankind. God only knows the true severity that my people must have been treated and the untold number of senseless beatings that occurred and the losses of family members taken away by this brutal and greedy desire to gain wealth. The stinch and filth from being overcrowded for weeks and months led to many attempted take-overs aboard these slave ships, and historians believe many Africans committed suicide rather than scum to the apparent tragedy awaiting these victims.

More importantly, the Atlantic Ocean is a very sickening phenomenon, particularly during the winter months between October and March. Swells comes over the top of the ships and current causes rolls of sometimes over 60 feet. Finally, God only knows how many "Human Souls" were lost through heart attacks brought on by fear.

It would seem that the irony of this dreadful era is evidence of perhaps Christians committing these atrocious acts against other Christians. But is this true? Well Caucasians have always claimed to be Christian people.

However, their acts as a whole appear to be quite the contrary and empirically a pseudo-Christian variety, in that only particular laws of Moses apply to them, or a total lack of the laws altogether.

For example, in the book of Revelations Chapter 13, verse 9 says: If any man have an ear, let him hear: He that leadeth into captivity shall go into captivity. He that killeth with the sword must be killed with the sword. Also, Exodus Chapter 21 and verse 16 says "He that stealeth a man, and selleth him, or if he be found in his hand, he shall surely be put to death."

Moreover, the Lord spoke unto Moses saying tell the children in Exodus 20 verse 13 "Thou shall not kill." And Exodus 20 verse 14 "Thou shall not steal." Well, in accord with the laws, statutes, and commandments of God as given to Moses, Abraham, and all true Israelites, The Caucasian has regressed all these laws.

Therefore, in the words of Jesus Christ in St. Johns 8:42 saying: "if God were your father you would love me: For I proceeded forth and came from God; neither come of myself but he that sent me. Verse 43: "Why do ye not understand my speech, even because ye cannot hear my word? Verse 44: "Ye are of your forefather the "Devil", and the lust of your father you will do. He was a murderer from the beginning and abode not in the truth. Because there is no truth in him."

The Caucasian people say they believe in the teachings of Moses but when it comes to following the laws of Moses, they don't. Therefore, prevailing themselves to not be of the teachings of the "LAW" they profess to believe, and through their own actions, have demonstrated themselves to be of the following of "Satan."

Coincidently, American writer Thomas Paine a leader of the American Revolution, published an article in the Pennsylvania Journal and Weekly Advisor entitled "African Slavery in America", saying (March 8, 1775):

"That some desperate wretches should be willing to steal and enslave men by violence and murder for gain is rather lamentable than strange.... The managers of this trade themselves, and others, testify that many of these African nations inhabit fertile countries, are industrious farmers, enjoy plenty and live quietly, adverse to war, before the Europeans debauched them with" liquor," and bribed them against one another, and these inoffensive people are brought into slavery, by stealing them, tempting kings to sell subjects, which they have no right to do, and hiring one group to war against another to catch prisoners. By such wicked and inhumane ways the English are said to enslave toward one hundred thousand Africans yearly; of which thirty thousand are suppose to die by barbarous treatment in the first year; besides all that were slain in the unnatural wars excited to take them.

So much innocent blood have the managers and supporters of this inhumane trade to answer for to the common Lord of all."[16]

"The slave trade was not a statistic, however astronomical. The slave trade was about people living, lying, stealing, murdering and dying. The slave trade was a Black man who stepped out of his hut for a breath of fresh air and ended up, ten months later, in South Carolina with bruises on his back, and a brand on his chest.

The slave trade was a Black mother suffocating her newborn baby because she didn't want him to grow up a slave. The slave trade was a kind captain forcing his suicide-minded passengers to eat by breaking their teeth, though, as he said, he was "naturally compassionate." The slave trade was a bishop sitting on an ivory chair on a wharf in the Congo and extending his fat hand in wholesale baptism of slaves who were rowed beneath him, going in chains to the slave ships. The slave trade was a greedy king raiding many villages to get slaves to buy brandy, and later being kidnapped and sold into slavery himself.

The slave trade was a pious captain holding prayer services twice a day on his slave ship and later writing the famous song, "how sweet the name of Jesus sounds". The slave trade was deserted villages, bleached bones on slave trails and people with no last names. The slave trade was Caesar Negro, Angelo Negro and Negro Mary."[17]

According to my good friend and brother Mr. Ismael Bocar Ba of Dakar, Senegal, West Africa of the Wolof group: "There was never any slave trade in Senegal, the encounters between European traders and Africans are considered swindling, kidnapping, or right out stealing of the people by the Europeans. He told me in a personal interview that in his school in Senegal they studied how European traders would come saying they wanted to trade "Beef" for gold, people, and other goods. But the traders actually had dog meat, thus the traders were ran out of the country."

"Records in the Danish state archives indicate that the earliest Danish trading vessel to touch the West Coast of Africa arrived on or about the middle of the 17th century. Some of the vessels returned to Denmark with gold, ivory, and tropical fruits. Mariners told glowing tales of African kingdoms, internal wars, exciting adventures, and exotic vegetation. These stories stirred the imagination of the Danes, investors as well as adventurers. During the second half of the 17th century, attempts were made to gain a foothold on the West African coast alongside other European powers (the Portuguese had built forts there as early as 1482).

When the Danes arrived on the Guinea Coast, they found the area divided into kingdoms. To the Danes, the most important group with whom they had to deal was the Fetu at Elmina and Accra.

The Fetu gave them a choice of three places. The Danes picked an abandoned fort or "castle," Amanfro (later called Fredericksburg), which they got it for 50 benda of gold to be divided among Fetu leaders. They also got some fortifications at close by Cabo Corso with permission to build stone buildings. Fredericksburg was situated 1130 yards east of Cabo Corso. Since it was not possible to build a harbor to load and unload their vessels. Because of very dangerous anchorage and very heavy seas, they had to stay aboard their ships until the Africans came to pick them up in their canoes. The Danes worked closely with the Fetu and other neighboring groups such as the Akwamu and the Akim. The Danes paid monthly rent and had to give presents to the local leaders. They also paid the Fetu duty on all goods imported from Europe. The Fetu chieftains received the first piece of every kind of good.

The Danes had their "ups" and "downs" during the latter part of the 17th century and at times, they were mostly "downs." The Dutch harassed them at every turn and finally attacked the Danish fortification at Fredericksburg, plundered it, and burnt it down."[18]

"There was much fighting between the Danes and the Dutch, and much brutality. "After the loss of Fredericksburg, the Danes concentrated their holdings and activities at Christiansburg. They were weakened by the losses caused by the Dutch as well as by devastating illnesses among the Danish survivors. Christiansburg was built on bought land on a cliff close to the coast with consistently rough seas, and it was even more difficult to land by Christiansburg than by Cabo Corso.

Danish historians say their ships carried but a fraction of the total number of slaves transported. In retrospect, it was neither worth the stigma nor the trouble. It did not produce profits and it cost many Danish lives. As it was, the Danish colonies had been able to buy their slaves cheaper from the Dutch, the British, or the interlopers. It was not until the latter part of the 17th century that the Danish king and the West India and Guinea Company tried to reactivate the Guinea trade with a positive emphasis on slave trading. To quote directly from archive sources: "Suddenly it seemed a good idea to send Danish ships with Danish merchandise to Guinea and from there with slaves to the West Indies and from there on home to Denmark with West Indian goods...

"The necessity to get black labor for St. Thomas in the West Indies that the Danish West India and Guinea Company had taken over spoke strongly for using the three concerned routes and make the slave trade the main point in the company's activities, and "there were no moral scruples at this point. Everybody involved wanted to make a profit..."

In trying to explain the involvement of the Danish Court and the Danish West India and Guinea Company in the slave trade, Danish historians point to a widely held concept of many monarchs and capitalists of the 17th and early 18th centuries that trading in slaves meant huge profits.

It was believed to be the best way to bail out near bankrupt colonial companies that were operating in the red and showing no dividends or returns to stockholders.

"It was during the governorship of Johan Lorentz (1694-1702) when St. Thomas began to be administered as a normal, well-ordered colony the directors were able to carry out a plan for direct participation in the slave trade with ships owned by the company. It was not until 1733, after the company had suffered a number of severe losses at sea, and about the time it began negotiations for the purchase of St. Croix from France, it was ready to let the slave trade fall back into private hands...."The sea losses, mentioned, are important because, occurring as they did within a period of four or five years, they almost broke the financial back of the Danish West India and Guinea Company. The records show the losses occurred when the company was becoming more and more involved in the slave trade. Actually the company had assigned large, well-equipped ships to the business in the hope of developing substantial profits.

Danish archivists tells us that on April 25, 1699, the Christianus Quintus sailed from Christiansburg, West Africa, for St. Thomas with a load of 549 slaves, 295 men, 254 women plus 61 elephant tusks which weighed a total of 2,371 pounds. The ship also carried gold and gold dust at a value of 2,488 rix dollars. On July 29, 1700, the Fredericus Quartus left Christiansburg for St. Thomas with 542 slaves and 7,185 pounds of ivory. After this, there were frequent sailings of these two specially equipped slave ships carrying substantial loads of slaves, ivory, and gold to St. Thomas. Prospects looked good. Tragedy struck in 1705 and it happened to one of the largest ships in the Danish slave fleet. After considerable delay due to the internal wars raging, the Cron-printzen left Christiansburg for St. Thomas with a load of 820 slaves, 460 men and 360 women, the largest number of slaves ever to leave on one Danish ship from Guinea for St. Thomas. Before the departure, smallpox broke out, and many died on board.

From Christiansburg, The Cron-printzen went to Principe, an island in the Gulf of Guinea, to get provisions, but here a fire started in the ship's gunpowder room and the ship exploded. Only five men were saved. Other ship tragedies occurred in 1709-1710. According to Danish Archives: "From November 28, 1708 to April 1, 1709 the violent and blood-thirsty chief of the Akwamu, Aquando, had laid seige to the provincial capital at Accra. During this period, he ruined four African towns: Orsu, near Christiansburg, and Labadi, Tossing and Ningo, further towards the east, destroying inhabitants of Accra by the thousands and taking many prisoners. The Accras fled to Christiansburg and asked for protection but the factory stayed neutral and watched the Accras being killed and captured in large numbers.

'It was under these conditions that the two big company ships Christianus Quintus and Fredericus Quartus arrived in Christiansburg on April 16 and April 25, 1709, respectively. There was a large amount of gold at the fort and 8,000 pounds of ivory but because of the closeness of war, a considerable delay occurred in the loading of the ships.

"Finally on October 2, 1709, both ships departed for St. Thomas. The Fredericus Quartus had 435 slaves onboard, the Christianus Quintus, 334. The large load of gold was divided equally between the two ships. "But the voyage was haunted with bad luck. First the winds were against the ships. They got lost and bypassed St. Thomas. They got into the western part of the Caribbean Sea where the stream forced them south. The slaves were put ashore on the coast of Nicaragua and after mutiny aboard; the crew plundered the gold boxes. On March 7, 1710, they left the ships in lifeboats. "The Fredericus Quartus burned the following night. The Christianus Quintus went ashore where the waves splintered her..."

Two very revealing narratives dealing with the slave conditions at the Guinea "factories" and aboard the slave ships appeared in the year 1788.

Both books were written by ship doctors, one Danish, and the other British. Both men wrote from a wealth of first hand experience, and what they had to say had a profound effect on the public at the time.

The Danish work was authored by P. E. Isert who had been chief physician in the Danish "factory" in Guinea and who had served for several years as surgeon aboard slave ships on the Atlantic crossing. Isert presented a vivid and detailed description of the handling of slaves from the time they were received and "processed" at Christiansburg, West Africa, until they reached their destination, St. Thomas, West Indies.

"As the slaves were brought in by tribal captors," noted Isert, "they were sold on a barter basis to the factors of the forts and then housed and guarded by their new owners in sheds or warehouses, known as barracoons, until the arrival of the slave ships."

In the Dutch and British barracoons, those purchased, "were set aside for branding with a hot iron on the breast or the shoulder with the identifying mark of the company or the individual purchaser."

Whenever possible, the Danes tried to avoid or dispense with this "branding process." In most cases the entire cargo was consigned to one proprietor only, the Danish West India and Guinea Company in St. Thomas, so there was little need to separate or differentiate the cargo.

In the event, the Danes had to "brand," the operation was performed carefully with pieces of silver wire, heated just hot enough to blister without burning the skin.

The British work was written by Alexander Falconbridge, entitled: "Account of the Slave Trade on the Coast of Africa." Because the British traffic in slaves was on a much greater scale than the Danish, the horrors, the brutality, and the sickness occurred under the British flag made the Danish effort seem trivial by comparison. Regardless of nationalities, there was an overall similarity in the settlements, the manner, and the techniques of the building of the trading, and the methods of preparations for the "Middle Passage", the movement of slaves across the Atlantic.

The horrors of the "Middle Passage" from the Guinea Coast to the West Indies showed no preference. Captives, whether they be persons of authority uprooted from the great groups of Accra, Dahoney, Ashanti, Loango, El Mila, Malabo, and others; kings, queens, warriors, statesmen, were crammed into the tightly confining holds of the slave ships with many wretched captives already accustomed to servitude and slavery. Victims, the mighty and the lowly, all were exposed to the humiliation of the "Middle Passage" and suffered terribly. They were led and jammed into spaces that were impossible to sit or stand in; no light, air, sanitation, wracked by frightful diseases, it was little wonder many died in transit.

In his narrative, Voyage From Guinea to the Caribbean, P. E. Isert, the Danish physician tells of the indignities African women slaves were subject at the hands of the ship's officers and crewmen during the crossing from Africa to St. Thomas.

Many of these officers and crewmen were outcasts at home, convicts released from the Copenhagen jails, bankrupts, or plain rejects from a Danish society eager to get rid of them. With most opportunities closed to them at home, it was little wonder they were willing to go to the coast of Africa where they, and other European outcasts and wretches could lead a life of indolence, with little or no restraint at all. There they might indulge nearly every human passion with utter freedom, whether it is confirmed drunkenness or unrestrained intercourse with African girls. They knew the deadly climate was likely to calm them, so it was a short life and a merry one' for many of these outcasts and wretches. It was little wonder that the degree of bestiality and debauchery aboard the slavers on their way to St. Thomas reached its' heights. The monotony of a long voyage, bad foods, access to rum casks, captive African women, naked and defenseless, all were factors that led to uncontrolled orgies. Nor was this bestiality and debauchery limited to the Danish slavers. Slave history is full of similar "orgies" on the ocean crossings and no nation was exempted, the "Orgies and Debauchery" aboard the slave ships continued into the 19th century.

This bestially seemed to increase after slavery had been declared illegal by most of the European nations and the traffic had been taken over by a group of desperate and brutal men who ran the blockade. Captain Richard Drake, a notorious slave smuggler, gives the following account of a voyage on the illegal Brazilian slaver, Gloria: once off the coast of Africa, the ship became half-bedlam and half brothel. Our Captain and his two mates set an example of "reckless wickedness." They stripped themselves and danced with the slave wenches (women), while our crazy cook played the fiddle. There was little attempt at discipline, and rum and lewdness reigned supreme...."

As a result of all this ghastly business on the slave ships, particularly during the 18th Century, the graveyards of St. Thomas hold many forgotten sailors and ship officers, debilitated by scurvy and debauchery on the "Middle Passage."[19]

According to Danish archives, Paul E. Isert had been a chief physician in the Danish settlement in Guinea (Christiansburg), and had served for a time on a slave ships traveling between Africa and the Danish West Indies, St. Thomas, and St. Croix. Isert wrote a series of letters from the African Guinea Coast and the West Indies slave markets to family and friends in Denmark telling of his experiences.

Between 1783 and 1787, Isert wrote a series of remarkable letters to family and important friends in Europe. He described the flora and fauna of the Guinea Coast in detail, and the problems and human patterns of European and native behavior in the little known Danish settlement there.

In one of his letters from Christiansted, St. Croix, to his father in Denmark, dated March 12, 1787, Isert described an uprising on a slave ship in which he was almost killed, he said: " I am still alive, dear father, after another long sea voyage, but I have been very close to death. We left the coast of Africa, October 7, 1786, aboard the ship, Christiansborg with the West Indies slave markets as our destination. Try to imagine the commotion aboard a slave ship, built originally to carry 200 people and now crammed with 452 slaves, kept in line by 36 Europeans. Imagine the sight of these unhappy people, prisoners of war, or for some other reason, who have been sold to Europeans and are now being taken in chains from their native lands and homes to a country they do not even know".

It is impossible they can expect something good from the future, since the Europeans are using such violent means in dealing with them. In their homelands, the most terrible rumors circulated about the use of slaves in the West Indies that these captive people are terrified. "A slave once asked me if the shoes I was wearing had been made of African skin.

He could see, he said, that they had the same color. Others believe that we eat Africans and make powder from their bones. They cannot believe they are only to be used for field labor, since from their experiences, field labor takes such little time and occupy so few hands.

Therefore, they did not believe what the Europeans said about going to a wonderful country. They use any and every opportunity to run away or to kill themselves. They fear death less than slavery. One has to use the greatest forethought to prevent them from ending their days. Captains on French ships do not allow them to carry a ribbon of linen, fearing they will hang themselves with it, which several have done.

'The terrible treatment these unhappy people suffer under barbaric skippers and crews, often cause them to conspire against the powers that be. Usually these conspiracies take place in the harbor before departure, or during the first days while the ship is still close to the African coast. "During my stay in Guinea, I have seen several such sad examples. In 1785, the slaves aboard a Dutch ship rebelled the day they were to leave for the West Indies. They overpowered and killed every European, except for a young ship's boy who had saved himself by climbing up the mainmast. "Before the whites succumbed completely, they had succeeded in firing several distress guns, heard on shore.

Canoes with soldiers and armed free-Africans were sent to help them. As soon as the rebelling slaves saw them coming and knew they would be overcome, they decided to kill themselves. One of them ran into the powder room carrying a lighted torch. The ship exploded. The oncoming canoes fished up little more than thirty Africans and the ship's boy. The rest, more than 500 slaves, disappeared in the waves."

Less lucky were the Africans aboard an English slave ship the same year (1785), also at the Gold Coast. They killed all Europeans, hauled anchor and let the ship drift ashore. When they came into the surf, they jumped overboard and swam ashore. To their distress, soldiers were waiting for them, took them prisoners, and sold them once again to the Europeans...

'"Now, dear father, let me tell you about the 3rd slave rebellion, the one I experienced. "It was the 2nd day after our departure from the African Coast. I was on deck talking with some of the Akras, since I understood their language. Suddenly I noticed everything had gotten very quiet. Usually there is a lot of noise and commotion aboard. This sudden quiet disturbed me. I proceeded quickly to the rear of the ship to see if the guards were at their posts, particularly the key lookout on the quarterdeck. This is a strategic area where small cannons are mounted. These cannons command a full view of the ship and are fired every evening as a warning to the slaves.

When I reached about halfway to the quarterdeck, the door was opened by the first mate, which came out to meet me. At that moment, a cry sounded out from the slave deck, the worst cry one can imagine. I had heard such a cry before. It was a signal for attack, common among the Africans during battle. "The slaves closest to me were chained in pairs, the hand of one coupled to the foot of another. Rising suddenly around me, some of them hit me in the head with their hand irons. I fell down among those who had not risen because of the heavy chains on their feet. Since these slaves were so locked, they could hardly move, I crawled away between them and reached for the quarterdeck door.

The officers inside wanted to let me in, but they knew if they opened the door the many standing Africans outside, who were able to maneuver despite their chains, had the power to tear the door apart. It was a case of letting me, one European, be killed rather than permit the Africans to become master of the door." The rebelling slaves did not let me stay by the door very long, but forced me down to the floor. Then many hands dragged me by the feet, passing me from one to another, toward the open deck where one slave waited with a knife.

"In a frenzy, he cut me across the forehead, the temples, through my ear and way down in my throat. There he was having trouble plunging the knife in since, very fortunately, I was wearing a thick silk scarf." "Meanwhile some of the ship's guards had gained control of the lookout station above the quarterdeck and had trained guns on the rebels. At that moment, my salvation came. A bullet, bred from the quarterdeck, penetrated the chest of my executioner. He fell backwards. Other hands, holding me down, let go. I was freed. The cannon shots cleared a way to the quarterdeck. I barely had the strength to crawl towards the quarterdeck door, while a fountain of blood marked my way, since my right temple artery had been sliced through.

Near the quarterdeck door, I fainted. When I regained consciousness, I found myself on a couch. The captain of the ship, himself, was wetting my head with some hot wine. It all seemed like a bad dream. I tried to stand up, but I could not. My head was heavy as lead. The cloth bandages were soaked with blood."

"Because of the many blows that I had received from the slave irons (one of them had knocked a hole in my head), my wounds were deep and very inflamed. As the muscles of the temples had been cut, my teeth had locked and I could hardly open my mouth. I had to be given liquid foods to sustain me...."

"Several hours passed before the revolt was brought under control. Those who hadn't participated in the uprising were sent below deck. The others had jumped into the ocean."

'The ship's officers lowered the boats to try to fish up as many of the slaves as possible. It was surprising how some coupled pairs, having only one free arm and one free leg, had managed to keep their heads above water. Some faced death with such stubbornness that they pushed the rescue roped away and drowned by their own free will. There was a coupled pair, where one wanted to be rescued, the other one not, and the one who wanted to die, forced the other one under." By counting, we found that we had lost 34 Africans. Among the Europeans, there was nobody dead, only two wounded."

"About me, even though my condition had looked rather bad, I recovered from my wounds, and the day I arrived in the West Indies, two months after the rebellion, I was healed. If you ask me why the Africans were so frantic to kill me. I found out later. As I had been last to board the ship, they believed I was the principal owner of the slaves. They thought by sending me into the next world first, it would be a simple matter to get rid of the others. Afterwards, during the voyage, they came to like me. In the mornings when I went down to see them and gave them medical care, they received me with a strong clapping of the hands, which among these people is a sign of approval just as we do in the theatre. "Without the unfortunate uprising, we would have had a very lucky voyage, since only seven Africans died from sickness, a very low percentage when you consider the large number of persons we were carrying. Some ships lose as much as 50 percent of their human cargoes between Africa and the West Indies.

"On our ship the greatest cleanliness was undertaken. Every second day the slaves would come up on deck to get fresh air and exercise. Our canvas air-stacks were so arranged as to catch the maximum amount of wind and send it below. Before the Africans were sent back down, the holds were thoroughly smoked out."

"We gave them plenty of well cooked portage, beans, and fresh fish, which we were lucky to catch in abundance especially as we got close to the Equator...."

"Shortly After our arrival in St. Croix, the slaves were prepared for sale. They were given extra rations. Limbs and bodies were washed and oiled. Then, in groups, our Africans were paraded ashore before many spectators."

"The sales-day arrived. Our entire human cargo was transferred to a large auction-house. At designated moments a door was flung open. An army of planters stormed in and furiously grabbed male and female Africans they had noticed and visually selected during the previous days. The whole affair happened with such speed and fury I was startled. One can imagine the fright of the Africans."

"Before four hours had passed, the greater part of the slaves was sold. Only 48 remained, most of them invalids or older Africans. They were sold the next day for 750 Kroner each. The total amount derived from the auction was more than 364,000 Kroner.

"The more that one sees of slavery, the more it sickens the spirit of a moral and decent person. One can only have deep pity for the miserable victims of a cruel owner, and there are many such owners."

"I saw one poor slave tied to a pole and whipped until it seemed that his flesh was coming apart. And all because of some simple misdemeanor that enraged his master."

"None will treat their slaves more barbarically than free Mulattoes, or those mixed with European and African blood. Such a female mulatto in my neighborhood owned a slave woman who had broken something by accident. To take revenge on her, the cruel owner tied the hands of her offending slave and hung her up on a spike in the wall. Taking her dress off, this beast of a woman slowly stung her with a needle, all over her body, so the poor human being was crying out something terrible. The cruel mulatto woman continued this cruel torture for more than an hour, until merciful neighbors came running and begging for the slave woman." "These cruel slave owners created the reason for most of the crimes committed by slaves. They demanded that Africans be servile and not run away; but they gave them every reason for doing so."

"I always feel saddened to watch these unhappy people being driven to work like cattle. Thirty or forty of them, with picks on their shoulders, move forward with one or two bombas cracking their whips in the air. If a slave forgets himself for a moment, he right away tastes the lash of the whip."

"I often asks myself when I see these groups of wretched people and the bombas driving them: Oh, poor human beings, what were you before? And what are you now... In a letter from St. Croix, Danish West Indies, dated March 12, 1787, to his father in Copenhagen, Denmark, Isert expressed an idea that was later to dominate his thinking and actions; his deep seated conviction that carrying slaves from Africa to the Western Hemisphere and the West Indies was a great historical blunder, commercial as well as moral. "Why did our forefathers not have the sense to found plantations right there on the fertile continent of Africa; plantations for sugar, coffee, coccao, cotton, and other articles had become so necessary in Europe?"

"Had we gone to Africa with the leaf of the olive tree in our hands rather than weapons of murder, willingly would the natives have given us access to the best and most fertile parts of their lands, areas which for untold years had been lying desolate.

Why was not our approach more Christian, more intelligent and humane? Why? "Those African people would have helped us in freedom and for low wages would have given us greatness and riches with no offense against nature, or our personal and national consciences."

"Why did we have to uproot vast numbers of people from their homelands, subject them to agony, torture, humiliation, and death; transplant them to alien continents, Caribbean Islands, big and small? Why?"

"Great plantations could be founded where free Africans would do the work, but under good conditions. At the same time, they would be educated, and the terrible slave trade with all its immoral aspects would not be necessary."

Dr. Paul E. Isert spent several weeks in St. Croix. In his letters to his family in Denmark, he described the beauty of the island, its lush rain forests and lowering plants, and its good roads, its well-organized plantations, and hospitable people.

Dr. Isert found St. Croix almost as hot as Guinea but more pleasant because of the constant trade breezes. He noted the pearl-hens (Guinea fowl) imported from Africa adapted well to St. Croix as they did in Guinea. On a visit to St. Thomas (April, 1787), he described the thriving commerce there: "All nations are doing business here, with the North Americans most active. They seem to supply the island with most of the basic foodstuffs and in return are the island-merchants best customers for the European manufactured goods. The traders, and the Americans are more prompt in meeting their payments than the Europeans. Many local merchants thrive on illegal trade with Porto Rico and islands in the Spanish Main. Payments received are mostly in Spanish dollars, but there is a considerable amount of outright barter."

When Dr. Isert returned to Denmark, he told them of his experiences in Africa. He described in detail the horror and agony he had personally witnessed on the slave ships carrying their human cargoes to the West Indies. He gave them information on the slave system as it operated in the Danish West Indies. Above all else, he offered his plan to put an end to the evil trade with a minimum of economic dislocation.

Dr. Isert's plan did not fall on deaf ears. He enlisted the powerful support of Count Ernst Schimmelmann, the Minister of the Treasury for the Danish Government. A deeply religious and compassionate man, Count Schimmelmann had assumed the leadership of the Danish liberals in their light to end the system of slavery and particularity Denmark's involvement. More than any other Dane, Ernst Schimmelmann was responsible for the Danish law of March 10, 1792, putting an end to the traffic of slaves between Africa and the Danish West Indies, with a cut-off date in the year 1803."[20]

"In November of 1788, Dr. Isert returned to Guinea, West Africa, to begin his experiment of establishing plantations in Africa. Isert planned to plant cotton on the fields from the mountains to the coast. This new experiment had the consent of both African chieftains and his noblemen and thought it would be to their advantage to cooperate with the Danes. They worked out an agreement that Isert should found plantations adjacent to their villages so long as they did not disturb land already in use by the Africans. A formal decree was formed by the Danish King before hand and was signed by members of the African chiefs Count Attiambo, the powerful leader of an African group friendly to the Danes. Isert named the colony Frederiksnopel after the then Crown Prince of Denmark. White craftsmen began to build more storehouses and friendly Africans, working for wages, cleared the woodland. "The first seeds sown were for kitchen vegetables, cotton, indigo, and tobacco. Isert had brought seeds from Denmark expecting them to thrive well in the African mountains, and with some domestic animals from Europe.

"From the beginnings everything seemed to develop well. The Africans were extremely friendly and helpful, and in his initial report to Denmark from Frederiksnopel, Guinea, dated January 1789, Isert wrote warmly and optimistically about the progress being made. "Five days later, Paul Erdmann Isert was dead! "Earliest report reaching Denmark from officials in Christiansburg, Guinea, attributed his death to fever. Later reports indicated that slave traders and conniving settlement officials had murdered Isert in a plot. "That Dr. Isert was sick seemed very unlikely, since in the report dated only five days before his death, Isert was not only filled with optimism, but he had placed large orders for European goods and equipment.

There was no lack of strength or inspiration in his report. Evidence continued to grow that Isert's initial successes, and what they reported for the future, had so disturbed the slave traders and their official supporters that they plotted to killed him.

Isert's ideas began to work in practice by creating an attractive social and economic alternative to slavery for both blacks and whites, clearly represented a massive threat to the lucrative slave trade, which its powerful exploiters could not tolerate, so they killed him! When Isert died, his ideas fell apart, thus there was no one with his zeal and missionary spirit to take over.

"During the period that followed Isert's death, there were several attempts made to carry out his ideas and found plantations in Africa. 'Unfortunately, these plantations and their great potentials collapsed as soon as their creator died. There was never anyone to take over who had the interest, knowledge, or energy to carry on. Nor did anyone have Isert's religious fervor, missionary zeal or ability to understand and get along with others. Isert's untimely death was a monumental disaster."[21]

"The term middle passage arose in reference to the voyages of slave-laden vessels from the African coast to the slave markets in the Americas. The voyages lasted from eight to ten weeks and sometimes longer. They occurred in the Torrid Zone where equatorial heat, drawn out calms, and sudden storms added to the suffering of the slaves. Unbearable conditions, intensified by overcrowding, caused massive elimination of the sick and the weak among the human cargoes.

In his book, Slaveships and Slavery, George Francis Dow tells us: "The cruelty and horror of the middle passage can never be told in all its gruesome details. It is enough to recall that the ships were always trailed by man-eating sharks."

"Between decks where the slaves were stored" wrote an 18th-century commentator, "there can hardly a man fetch his breath by reason there riseths such a funk in the night that it causeth purifications of the blood and breadth disease much like the plague."

A 19th- Century observer noted: "Were the Atlantic Ocean dried up today, one could trace the pathway between the slave coast of Africa and America by a scattered roadway of human bones."

The mortality rate of slave cargoes was directly related to the care and cleanliness of the quarters in which the bulk of the slaves were stored. So the proper stowage of slaves, particularly at night, was of most importance to a successful crossing from the African Coast to the Americas.

On a "Well-Run" slave ship, the process of stowing the slaves for the night began at sundown. One of the best descriptions of the process is in the account of Captain Theodore Canot, as told by Brantz Mayer:

"The second mate and the boatswain descend into the hold, whip in hand, and arrange the slaves in their regular places; those on the right side of the vessel facing forward and lying in each other's laps, while those on the left are similarly stowed with their faces toward the stern. In this way each African lies on his right side, which is considered preferable for the action of the heart."

"In allocating places, particular attention is paid to size, the taller being selected for the greatest breath of the vessel, while the shorter and younger are lodged near the bows."

The Danes always claimed organization and treatment aboard the Danish slave ships were better than on the British slave ships. Treatment on the latter was suppose to be the worst possible, not only because of the tendency of the British to overcrowd their ships but because of the notorious brutality of the British Captains, officers and crews.

The end result, mortality-wise, depended almost entirely on the organization and management aboard individual slave ships regardless of which national flag was flown. Statistics in the Danish State Archives demonstrate this clearly. There are extremes represented by the Danish slaver Acras with a death percentage of 43.3 percent, while the Danish slaver Ada reported less than 1 percent.

Close to the end of the monopoly period of the Danish West India and Guinea Company, precise records were kept of the movement of slaves to St. Croix on Danish vessels. The total was 6513. The death rate was 1056. On slave ships that were poorly organized and overcrowded, Africans were jammed into the holds with little regard for stowage. "They were literally piled one on top of another and the unsteady motion of the ship, combined with foul air and great heat made the place simply horrible...."

Invariably, epidemics broke out under such conditions. According to the British ship doctor Alexander Falconbridge: "when the sea was rough and the rain heavy, it became necessary to close the air vents. Fresh air being thus excluded, the Africans storage area grew intolerably hot. The confined air, rendered noxious by the effluvia exhaled from their bodies and by being repeatedly breathed, soon produced fevers and fluxes which generally carried off great numbers of them...."

"Frequently, I went down among them until the hold became so unbearably hot that I could not stay. Excessive heat was not the only thing that rendered the situation intolerable. The floor of the hold was so covered with blood and mucus which proceeded from them in consequence of the flux, that it resembled a slaughter house."

"It is not in the power of the human imagination to picture a situation more dreadful or disgusting. Numbers of the slaves having fainted, they were carried on deck where several of them died and the rest, with great difficulty, were restored....

Upon going down in the mornings to examine the condition of the slaves, I frequently found several dead, and among the men, sometimes a dead and living African fastened by their irons together. When this was the case, they were brought upon the deck and laid in the grating when the living African was disengaged and the dead one thrown overboard.

"An exertion of the greatest skill and attention could afford the diseased African little relief so long as the causes of the diseases, namely, the breathing of a putrid atmosphere and wallowing in their own excrements, remain. When once the fever and flux get to any height at sea, a cure is scarcely ever affected...."

"By constantly lying in the blood and mucus flowing from those afflicted with the flux, others contracted it," continued Dr. Falconbridge. "Few were able to withstand the fatal effects of it. The utmost skill of the surgeon was here ineffectual."

From the very beginning of the slave movement from Africa to the West Indies and America, mention is made of the ruinous effects of the flux on slave cargoes and ships' crews. Whether it is the 16th, 17th, 18th, or 19th centuries, the record is they're showing a constant dread of the Flux (an early name for the amoebic dysentery, an ulcerative inflammation of the colon. It may reach the liver by the portal blood stream, producing abscesses on that organ. Today we know this acute form of dysentery is caused not by "foul air" and "excessive heat" but by the organism Entamoeba Histolytica found in bad water and rotted food. (I. P.) and its devastating effects.

Sir John Hawkins, the great sea captain and the first Englishman to engage in the slave trade between the Guinea Coast and America in the year 1563, limited the number of his crew "for fear of the Flux and other inconveniences whereunto men in long voyages are commonly subjected to...."

Another quote, typical of the 18th century, taken from a narrative: The journal of Capt. Thomas Phillips, printed in London, in 1764, Declared: "This distemper which my men as well as the Blacks mostly die of, was the "White Flux," which was so violent and inveterate no medicine would in the least check it; so when any of our men were seized by it, we esteemed him a dead man, as he generally proved....'"

So severely were Africans affected with the Flux at times, declared Falconbridge, after being landed, obliged by the pain and virulence of the complaint to stop almost every minute to seek relief?

Falconbridge described in detail one of the deceptions practiced by a ship's captain: "A Liverpool captain boasted of having cheated some "Jews" by the following stratagem: "A lot of slaves afflicted with the Flux being landed for sale, he directed his ship's surgeon to stop the extremity of each of them with Oakum. Thus prepared, they were taken to the place for sale, where being unable to stand but for a short time, they were permitted to sit.

"The "Jews", when they examined them, obliged them to stand in order to see if there be any discharge, and when there was no appearance of such, they considered it a symptom of recovery. A bargain was struck and the slaves were bought. But it was not long before the discovery of the cheat followed, for the excruciating pain, which the prevention of the discharge occasioned, could hardly be borne by the sick ones.

The obstructions were removed and the deluded buyer: were speedily convinced of the imposition...." Falconbridge did not mention if this incident occurred in St. Thomas, but it is probable it did.

The records of the period tell us that a group of "Jews" and surgeons conducted a "rehabilitation" farm on the eastern end of St. Thomas to care for many of the disparately sick slaves. After intensive care with the help of experienced "Bush Doctors" as well as full utilization of medical knowledge available at the time, they had a considerable number of remarkable recoveries.

Journals of slave ship captains and doctors from the 18th and early 19th centuries show marked agreement in one area. Of all calamities that might occur on the passage from Africa to the West Indies and America, the calamity most dreaded was an outbreak of smallpox.

So unmanageable and so catastrophic were the effects of this virulent disease every well-organized slaver carried preventative medicine on board in the form of potent poisons. Ship captains, doctors, and experienced staff men did not hesitate at first sign of the disease try to isolate and destroy the affected person or persons. Acting quickly and disparately, they hoped to stop the spread of the deadly "Pox" to the rest of the ship.

In the Adventures of an African Slaver, Capt. Theodore Canot vividly describe two experiences, the first aboard the slave ship San Pablo:

"We had been several days buffeting a series of adverse gales when word was brought to me after a night of weary watching, several slaves were ill of small pox. The news appalled me. I called the officers into my cabin for consultation.

"The gales had lasted nine days and with such violence that it was impossible to take off gratings, release the slaves, purify the decks, or rig the wind-sails.

When the first lull occurred, a thorough inspection of the (800) slaves had been made, and a death announced. As life had departed during the tempest, a careful inspection of the body was made, and it was this that first disclosed the pestilence in our midst. The corpse was silently thrown into the sea and the malady kept secret from the crew and Africans.

"When breakfast was over on that fatal morning, I was determined to visit the slave deck myself, and ordering an abundant supply of lanterns, descended to the cavern, which still reeked horribly with the human vapor, even after ventilation. Here I found nine of the Africans infected by the disease.

"We took counsel as to the use of laudanum in ridding ourselves speedily of the sufferers a remedy used secretly in desperate cases to preserve the living from contagion. It was quickly resolved the disease had already gone too far, when nine were prostrated, to save the rest by depriving the nine of life. Accordingly, these wretched beings were at once sent to the forecastle as a hospital.

'The ship's hold was then ventilated and limed yet before the gale abated, our sick list was increased to 30. The hospital could hold no more. Twelve of the sailors took infection and 15 corpses had been cast into the sea. All reserve was now at an end. Body after body fed the deep.

"When the wind and waves had lulled so much as to allow the grating to be removed from our hatches, our consternation knew no bounds when we found nearly all slaves were dead or dying. There was no time for languor. Twelve of the stoutest survivors were constantly drenched with rum to neutralize them, still we were forced to aid the gang by reckless volunteers from our crew, who, arming their hands with tarred mittens, flung the fetid masses of putrefaction into the sea."

"At length death was satisfied, but not until the (800) beings we had shipped in high health had dwindled to 497 skeletons..."

In another instance, Captain Canot described how quick and desperate action aboard the slaver La Estella stopped an epidemic from spreading:

"We made land at Porto Rico and were swiftly passing its beautiful shores, when the inspector called my attention to the appearance of one of our attendant slaves, whom he had drilled as a sort of cabin boy. He was a gentle, intelligent child and had won the hearts of all the officers.

"His pulse was high, quick and hard; his face and eyes, red and swollen. On his neck I detected half a dozen rosy pimples! He was sent immediately to the forecastles free from contact with anyone else and left there, cut off from the crew till I could guard against pestilence. It was smallpox!

"The boy passed a wretched night of fever and pain, developing the malady with all its horrors. It was likely I slept as badly as the sufferer, for my mind was busy with his doom. Daylight found me on deck in consultation with our veteran boatswain, whose experience in the trade authorized the highest respect for his opinion.

Hardened as he was, the old man's voice was husky as he whispered the verdict in my ear. I guessed it before he said a word.

As I went after the quarterdeck, all eyes were bent on us, for everyone conjectured the malady and feared the result, yet none dared asked a question. "I ordered a general inspection of the slaves, yet when a favorable report was made, I did not rest content, and descended to examine each one personally, and it was true, the child alone was infected.

"For half an hour, I trod the deck to and from restlessly, and caused the crew to subject themselves to inspection. But my sailors were as healthy as the slaves. There was no symptom indicated approaching danger. I was disappointed again. A single case- a single sign of peril in any quarter- would have spared the poison.

"That evening, in the stillness of the night, a trembling hand stole forward to the afflicted boy with a potion that knows no waking. In a few hours, all was over, life and the pestilence were crushed together...."

Narrative after narrative records the scourge of smallpox aboard the slavers. Time and again the horror repeated itself. In the Revelations of a Slave Smuggler, Captain Richard Drake, an African trader for over 50 years (1807-1857), describes a smallpox epidemic aboard the slave ship Boa Morte, Captain Pierre Le Clerk: "The captain's illness turned out to be smallpox and two of the crew soon come down with it. It was impossible to keep the disease from the slaves and the ship turned out to be well named."[22]

"We soon began to feed corpses to the sharks and one day hauled 60 bodies out of the hold. The crew revolted at this work and we had to rely on gangs of slaves to drag the dead heaps from among the living."

Sharks followed the slave ships from the time they left the African coast. Whether attracted by the pungent smell of the "slaver" or the daily ration of bodies were thrown overboard, the records of the time repeatedly note the presence of these scavengers.

The voyage took weeks, even months, until the vessel finally arrived at its destination. Sometimes fate intervened to add horror and destruction to human misery. In his diary covering the year 1793, Johan Nissen tells of two overcrowded slave ships finally reaching the entrance of St. Thomas's harbor only to be destroyed by a dreadful hurricane in which all lives were lost, officers, crewmen, and the entire cargo of slaves."[24]

"The cruelty and wanton barbarity of the these acts of murder and rape of innocent people is apparent of such a heinous and atrocious nature; a total disregard and degrading to humanity among mankind and morally evil.

These profiteers, not having the fear of "God" before their eyes, were being moved and seduced by the instigation of the "DEVIL."[23]

"Such could be said of Captain James De Wolfe who admittedly threw the living as well as the dead overboard his slave ship to the sharks when diseases threatened the lives of his crew and his human cargoes. De Wolfe was a man of force and indomitable energy with no nice ethical distinctions...."

At age 26 he owned his own vessel, The Little Watt. In 1790, he married Nancy Bradford, daughter of Governor William Bradford of Rhode Island, an intimate friend of George Washington.

James De Wolfe's earliest voyages as a sea captain were made to the Coast of Guinea where he traded for slaves. Rhode Island merchants of highest commercial and social standings backed him. Apparently he had no qualms of conscience and often went to southern ports to personally supervise the sale of his cargoes.

According to George Howe, the Rhode Island historian, the profits were enormous: "the operation of the De Wolfe family was almost fool proof. Molasses from the De Wolfe plantation in Cuba reached Bristol, Rhode Island in De Wolfe vessels, was turned into "Rum" at the De Wolfe distillery there, and exported with other trade goods again in De Wolfe's ships to the slave coast of Africa. There the cargoes were exchanged for slaves, and the human freight brought back for sale at the starting point in Cuba.

Captain James De Wolfe's distillery on Thames Street, Bristol, Rhode Island, converted 300 gallons of molasses every day into 250 gallons of rum. The cost of distillation was 10 cents a gallon. He paid the U. S. Treasury an import duty of 5 cents on every gallon of molasses but received a drawback, when he exported it as rum...." Before the age of thirty, Captain James De Wolfe had "accumulated wealth enough to make him independent for the rest of his life...."

Captain James De Wolfe's principle trade was in slaves in the West Indies and when, in 1804, South Carolina threw open her ports to the importation of slaves because of a threatened national prohibition, De Wolfe leaped to aid and ten of the 202 vessels that entered Charleston between 1804 and 1808 belonged to him. In 1821 he was elected to U. S. Senate."[24]

Another illness that played havoc among human cargoes crowded in the holds of slave ships was the dreaded disease Ophthalmia. This disease, once started, spread so fast and with such frightening consequences that in a matter of days whole cargoes of Africans went blind.

One of the most dramatic cases of an Ophthalmic epidemic encompassing an entire ship of slaves, crewmen, and officers occurred aboard the French Slaver, Le Rodeur, in the year 1819. A youthful passenger, a twelve year old boy in a diary intended for his mother recorded the epic tale. So tragic and heart rending was his poignant tale that it later received widespread attention.

Like other European nations, the French had been very active in the slave trade during the 17th, 18th, and early 19th centuries. The principal French fort and slave factory was Fort Louis, located at the mouth of the River Senegal. There was another important French factory on Goree, an island near Cape Verde.

From these collecting centers, as well as other non-French trading centers on the African coat, thousands of slaves were carried on French slavers to the French possessions, particularity to the sugar plantations in Hispaniola, Guadeloupe, Martinique, and other areas in the French colonial empire.

Young Jacques B. Romaigne begins his eyewitness account with a description of the ship: "The slaver, Le Rodeur, of 200 tons burden, sailed from the port of Havre for the river Calabar on the coast of Africa. She arrived there and anchored at Bonny, March 14, 1819. During a stay of three weeks, she obtained a cargo of 160 Africans and sailed for Guadeloupe on April 6th, 1819..."

Jacques B. Romaigne, who wrote the account of the epidemic, was the son of a planter from Guadeloupe who had spent time with relatives in France. His holiday over, he was returning to Guadeloupe as a passenger on Le Rodeur, under the special care of the captain. To quote from his diary: "The Africans were confined closely to the lower hold and this brought on a disease called Opthalmia which produced blindness."

"The sailors, who slung down provisions from the upper hold, report that the disease is spreading frightfully and today, at dinner, the captain and the surgeon held a conference on the subject. The surgeon declared from all he could learn, the cases were already so numerous as to be beyond his management. "The captain insisted that every slave cured was worth his value and that it was better to lose a part, than all. The result of the conservation was that the infected slaves were to be transferred to the upper hold and attended by the surgeon."

"All the slaves and some of the crew are blind. The captain, the surgeon and the 1st mate are blind. There are hardly enough men left out of our 22 to work the ship. The captain preserves what order he can and the surgeon still attempts to do his duty, but our situation is frightful.

"All the crew are now blind but one man. The rest work under his orders like unconscious machines, the captain standing by with a thick rope, which he sometimes applies, when led to any recreant by the men who can see.

"My own eyes begin to be affected. In a little while, I shall see nothing but death. I asked the captain if he would not allow the Africans to come up on deck. He said it was no use, the crew, who were always on deck, were as blind as they; if brought up, they would only drown themselves, whereas if they remained where they were, there would, in all probability, be at least a portion of them salable, if we had ever the good fortune to reach Guadeloupe.

"We were blind, stone blind, drifting like a wreck upon the ocean and rolling like a cloud before the wind. The captain was stone blind, yet had hopes of recovering his sight, while most of the others were in despair.

"A guard was continually placed, with drawn swords, at the storeroom to prevent the men from getting at the spirit-casks and dying in a frenzy of intoxication. Some were cursing and swearing from morning till night, some singing abominable songs, some kissing the crucifix and making vows to the blessed saints.

"A few lay all day long in their hammocks, apparently content to starve rather than come aboard for food. For my part, I snatched at anything I could get to eat. Cookery was not thought of. I thought myself fortunate when I was able to procure a cup of water to soften a biscuit as dry and as hard as a stone.

"Mother, your son was blind for ten days, although now so well to be able to write to you. I can tell you hardly anything of our history during that period. Each of us lived in a little dark world of his own, peopled by shadows. We did not see the ship, or the heavens, or the sea or the faces of our comrades.

"Then there came a storm. No hand was upon the helm, not a reef upon the sails. On we flew like a phantom ship of old that cared not for wind or weather, our masts straining and cracking; our sails bursting from the bonds, with a report like that of musketry; the furious sea one moment devouring us up, stem and stern, and the next casting us forth again, as if with loathing and disgust. "The wind, at last, died away and we found ourselves, rocking without motion, on the sullen deep...."

"It was at this time that a sail was sighted, and the one man who had the use of his eyes steered Le Rodeur toward her. The oncoming vessel turned out to be a drifting derelict with all sail set, though men were wandering her deck. The young Romaigne tells what followed in a most dramatic fashion:

"We heard a sound upon the waters. Our hearts burst with hope. We held our breath. The sound continued. It was like the splashing of a heavy body in smooth water. A cry arose from every lip on deck and was echoed by the men in their hammocks below and by the slaves in the hold."

"Our cry was answered! We shouted again, our voices broken by sobs and our burning eyes deluged with tears. Our captain was the first to recover his self-possession. We heard him speak to the approaching ship with the usual challenge: "Ship Ahoy! Ahoy! What ship?" 'The St. Leon of Spain. Help us for god's sake!'

"We want help ourselves,' replied our captain.". "And from the Spaniard:' we are dying of hunger and thirst. Send us on board some provisions and a few hands to work the ship and name your own terms..."

"Answered our captain: "we can give you food, but we are in want of hands ourselves. Come on board of us and we will exchange provisions with you...."
"And from the Spaniard: Dollars! Dollars! We will pay you in money, a thousand fold, but we cannot send men. We have Africans on board. They have infected us with Ophthalmia, and we are all stone-blind...!"

"At the announcement of this horrible coincidence, there was a silence among us, like that of death. It was broken by a fit of laughter on our ship, in which I Joined. Before our awful merriment was over, we could hear by the sound of curses, which the Spaniards shouted against us, when the Saint Leon drifted away. The vessel, in all probability, lost at sea. She was never heard from again....

"The man who preserved his sight the longest, recovered the soonest. To his exertion alone we owe that we are now within a few leagues of Guadeloupe, this 21st day of June 1819.

"I am almost well. The surgeon and eleven more are irrecoverably blind. The captain has lost one eye. Four others have met with the same calamity. Five are able to see, though dimly, with both. Among the slaves, 39 are completely blind and the rest blind of one eye or their sight otherwise injured…"[25]

African slaves ... were generally from the following groups or places in Africa: Mandingo, Kanga, Loango, Congo, Amina, Papaa, Ibo, Bibi, Karabari, Watje, Kassenti, Selungo, Fida, Ashanti, Bantu, and Fulah...." Upon Arrival to their new lands as slaves, these human beings were subjected to various initiation ceremonies which included severe beatings in the form of lashes across the back and shoulders to atone for so-called "Evil-Doings" in African countries from whence they came. These ceremonies had no relationship to religion but was meant to provide the newcomers with "God-parents" who would "help them to adjust to their new surroundings as slaves."

Most of the Africans had been captured in inter-group warfare and came from all levels of African societies. These Africans presented a mix company of rich and poor, high and mighty, and lesser persons in status.

The condition of slavery and bondage had done for these uprooted African societies what death does for all men; it had flattened them to a common level, Kings, Queens, children of princes, nobles, and tradesmen. Slavery had set them in a kind of rigid equality.

Some Africans of noble birth found it impossible to adjust themselves to their reduced circumstances. An African Queen, full of memories of her former greatness, refused to submit herself to her mistress: "I was much greater in Africa than you are here. I had many more slaves than you have here. Now you expect me to be your slave? I would rather starve to death..." She carried out the determination, completely indifferent to harshness or leniency, and died a lingering death." Some Africans absolutely refused to work and had to be dealt with in a firm manner. This high degree of strong will and refuse to bend was most prominent among the Karabari, Ibo, Bibi and Amina Africans.

On the other hand, a more willingness to accept their position of servitude was known among the Africans of the Watje, Kassenti, Congo, Selungo, Fida, and Papaa. The price of these Africans from the latter groups was higher as a result of this Africans from Accra, men and women from Dahomey, Ashanti, Sherbros, Fellaths, and Bambarras were much in demand. They were strong and durable and, once acclimated, fit well into the slave economy. Africans from the Mandingo were known for their speed in adjusting and acquiring skills. They made excellent artisans and craftsmen and were eagerly sought after at the slave auctions. So were the Africans from the nations of Kassaos, Fi and the Sherbroo Bottom at the bottom, so they were finely built, intelligent men and women. This was particularly true of the Foulah women from Timbo, not only were their courage and resistance a byword of the slavers, but of all the African women, they were most desired by the Europeans.

'The tragic trade in human flesh, to be as great as it was, needed organization, and that organization was supplied by many of the so-called civilized nations of Europe, and to a lesser degree the so-called "interlopers"- ship captains and adventurers eager to get a "piece of the action."[26]

An African chief sells prisoners of war to European slave merchants. Slavery was common in Africa; it was used as a punishment for crimes or making war. However, African slavery protected the basic rights of the prisoner and allowed him to own property, marry (even a member of the owner's family), and eventually gain his freedom. Slavery in the New World would be very different.

4a

SLAVERY AND THE OLD SOUTH

A black slave stepped upon the ground that would be the District of Charleston in early 1670. The 220-ton frigate CAROLINA, six months out from the Island of Barbados, entered the waters forming what is now Charleston Harbor. The ship sailed up a shallow river to a point overlooked by a heavily wooded bluff, and they're about twenty white Barbadians disembarked as part of the first permanent English-speaking settlement in South Carolina. Although no one recorded the name, the Barbarians had brought with them black slaves to work in the colony.

Slavery was present from the beginning in South Carolina, uniquely among the North American colonies, where in all other cases it was introduced only after their founding. And for the next two centuries, South Carolina would maintain its preeminence. From the arrival of the whitemen in the Seventeenth Century to the U. S. prohibition of slave importation in 1807, over one-forth of all African enslaved persons bought and sold into the United States (at least 132,918 people) entered through Charleston or one of South Carolina's lesser ports. Hence, among the current African American population of the United States in the late twentieth century (roughly one in four) has an ancestor who was sold as a slave in Charleston.

There is no reason to think these figures would have displeased the men from Barbados as the Carolina found slippage between the trees at the riverbank. They had come to South Carolina intending to grow rich on a slave economy, just as had their fathers on the small island they left.

Barbados, a piece of "sixpence thrown down" upon a sailor's map of the Eastern Caribbean as one contemporary chronicler described it, was at the time of the Carolina settlement the most densely populated, the richest, and the most lethal of the English Colonies in the New World. Established less than fifty years before the Carolina expedition, Barbados also was the first English colony to introduce the gang-labor system of Black slavery into the New World.

Rather than encouraging the immigration of a free peasantry, the early settlers chose to import African slaves to work the sugar fields, which they were clearing on this once rain-forested Caribbean Island. Barbarians, as this first generation of Englishmen called themselves, became known throughout the Caribbean as hard masters.

They imposed their will upon their new African laborers by frequent floggings, brandings, and mutilations; and by thus coercing large gangs of slaves to repeat monotonously the same tasks for ten or eleven hours - slashing the sugarcane with curved knives, grinding the canes between heavy stones, then boiling out the dark molasses to produce crystallized white sugar - the Barbadians became rich.

By mid-century, Barbados was controlling nearly half the refined sugar sent to the European market, and it had become the first English settlement to form a plantation ruling class. Within two generations, this island, with a population in 1660 of forty thousand blacks and whites had produced a planter elite of about sixty-two families who controlled local politics, held the most arable land, and owned the most slaves. Practically all the European visitors to the island in the 16th century remarked upon the display of wealth and extravagant conscription of the Barbadian elite-behavior to be repeated, as several scholars of the South have noted, by their South Carolina descendants.

There was a unity of two ruling classes in the Caribbean and in South Carolina with the same show of finery, sometimes even to the point of ostentatious ness, evident in both their choice of clothing and their lavishly furnished country estates; and the same easy munificence among the ruling males in bestowing honorary militia titles upon one another, such as "Captain" or "Major." And there was also transport to Carolina with the same unhesitating brutality, and absolute conviction slavery represented, a most profitable economic system known to Western man.

The slave-generated wealth of Barbados came at an appalling cost in African lives. Throughout the 17th century, the island had one of the highest mortality rates for blacks in the Western Hemisphere, and whether from disease, malnutrition, or torture, more died annually than were imported to work the great sugar plantations. Unlike their English contemporaries in Massachusetts, Barbarians seldom looked inward to their consciences, and so long as the supply of African slaves seemed illimitable, their economy appeared untroubled. What concerned the masters was the lack of arable land on which to expand their slave economy. Barbados is only 21 miles long and 14 miles wide, and with practically all of it under cultivation and concentrated within a few families, economic advancement, particularly for younger men, was limited. Accordingly, a group declaring themselves the Corporation of Barbados Adventurers wrote to England on August 12, 1663, offering to establish a colony in the unsettled lands south of Virginia, an area that had become known as "Carolina in Ye West Indies."

The Barbadians promised the Eight Royal Proprietors to expect not only "the aptness of the people here "for establishing a new plantation economy in North America but also a "Number of their Negroes and other servants fit for such labor."

For six years, the Proprietors and the Adventurers negotiated their terms, but ultimately the barbarian's proposal financially enticed the English proprietors. A mainland colony could be supplied and populated much more cheaply from the existing plantations at Barbados than from Europe; accordingly, the proprietors conceded to the Corporation of Barbados Adventurers the exclusive right to settle Carolina with grants of 150 acres to each Adventurer, with an additional 150 acres granted him for each servant transported.

The philosopher John Locke, secretary to one of the proprietors, devised an elaborate constitution for the new colonists, a copy the Barbadian Adventurers carried with them. Among other stipulations, it promised religious freedom to all residents of the colony, whether black or white. In late 1669, three ships carrying colonists sailed from Barbados, of which only one, the Carolina, bearing its black slave with an unrecorded name, succeeded in reaching the new colony on the South Atlantic coast.

The grant of 150 acres to the master of each servant transported to Carolina was the device by which the Barbarians turned their tiny encampment into a slave colony. Early on, the Corporation of Barbados Adventurers had obtained a written concession from the royal proprietors by which it was made explicit in granting 150 acres for every "able man servant" transported to Carolina, the proprietors affirmed "we mean Africans as well as Christians." Within a year of the first settlement, more than a hundred other colonists arrived from Barbados, bringing their black slaves with them. John Locke, reporting back in England to the royal proprietors of news he had received from Carolina, noted the arrival in June 1671 of the colony's new governor from Barbados. "Sir Jo Yeamans intends to stay all the winter," Locke wrote. He has brought Negroes and expects more."

The white masters marked out the boundaries of what they anticipated would become a world port upon a narrow and sandy peninsula extending into the ocean bay, and, in honor of the English monarch Charles II, named their settlement Charles Town. (The spelling was changed to Charleston after the American Revolution). Carolina attracted white Immigrants from the other English islands in the Caribbean from England, and from Ireland, but the early Barbadians dominated both public and private wealth. Their importation of African slaves matched, and then eventually surpassed, the number of free immigrants and landholdings among the Barbarian families increased proportionately.

Nor did the Carolina plantation owners from Barbados limit themselves to enslaving only Africans. The bondage of Native Americans was practiced throughout North America, but Carolina within a few years of its' settlement gained the distinction of enslaving more Indians than any other of the Thirteen Colonies.

By the early 18th century, the Barbadians had established a lively trade in Native American slavery, having captured and sent thousands in shackles down to Charles Town for export to the Caribbean islands for use as hunting or fishing guides, and importing black laborers from these same islands to be used as agricultural slaves in Carolina. These practices, along with the Carolina colonists' immediate attempts to circumvent the religious freedoms proposed in the colonial constitution, alarmed the royal proprietors and their philosopher secretary. "The Barbadians," remarked John Locke in England, "endeavor to rule all."

The small community that the Barbadians ruled continued to grow in slave and free population until by the mid-1700 it was the fourth-largest city of the colonies. Charles Town, which by 1740 was the capital of a colony with at least thirty thousand black slave inhabitants, succeeded even beyond the ambitions of the planters from Barbados. The city exported indigo, rice, and later, cotton on a world scale, and the peninsula began to be crowded with two and three-story houses erected in the distinctive Charlestonian architecture or walled gardens, piazzas, and elaborately designed private doorways concealed from the street. Many were town houses built by owners of plantations farther in the Carolina interior, who escaped the tropical heat or the tedium of rural winters by retreating for holidays to Charles Town. The influence of these English-speaking settlers from Barbados was succeeded by a wave of French Huguenots and these Protestant immigrants became numerous enough to support three French-language newspapers and a French theatre. And, in delayed fulfillment of John Locke's insistence that the Barbarian founders practice religious tolerance, Charles Town became a sanctuary from the late 1600s for Sephardim and other Jewish refugees from Europe. The city eventually contained the largest community of "Jews" of any urban settlement in colonial North America.

Charles Town was still smaller in population than Boston, Philadelphia, or New York, but by the eighteenth century this thriving southern port was arguably the most cosmopolitan trading center of North America. Charles Town was also cosmopolitan in its slavery. When each of the groups of white immigrants arrived in the city, they either brought with them or imported their African slaves. The new slave arrivals from the Guinea coast spoke the languages of present-day Angola, Togo, Benin, and Nigeria. Some were Muslims and left evidence that they also spoke and wrote Arabic.

The blacks shipped from the Caribbean into Carolina by their Barbadian or French masters talked among themselves in a form of Creole and were known by both the blacks and white at Charles Town as "the French Negroes."

And distinct among all other languages heard among blacks at the city's wharves and on her crowded streets was Gullah, an emerging amalgam of English and African words having an African-based syntax, used exclusively by slaves on the plantations of the Carolina and Georgia Sea Islands.

To the Charlestonians of European descent, their city, with its complex population and growing wealth, was a new metropolis of the eighteenth century, in succession to the international ports of Amsterdam and London. In both its exercise of law and physical appearance the city could not deny its Caribbean origins. Legal power was encoded in Charles Town's comprehensive slave law enacted within the first generation of the colony's founding and copied almost word for word from an earlier Barbadian statute. This slave law established the legal precedent for slaves prosecution and execution; and also authorized the use of whipping, branding, or the splitting of the noses for black slaves who offer violence against their white masters.

For those who attempted the most feared of crimes, insurrection against the Carolina white ruling class, a trial under punishment of death was to be conducted not within the usual court system of jury men but by a special tribunal of "freeholders."

The streets of Charles Town as well as its laws made immediately apparent to any new visitor to this slave city was not a typically developing North American port. Unlike the brick walkways of New York City or the ballast-stone pavements of Philadelphia or Boston, the principal streets of Charles Town were covered (as they would continue to be into the early twentieth century) with a mixture of sand and finely crushed seashells. It was an inheritance from the city's Caribbean founding, and practically all northern visitors for the next two hundred years remarked on this unique white covering spreading over the urban peninsula; as an obdurate and crystalline reality it permeated even into the interiors of one's pockets and the folds of one's bedclothes, and in the noon day sun the white sand made the streets dazzling and difficult to countenance. But it was a reminder also of the whiteness of Charles Town's growing wealth, stacked in high rows for export at the city's wharves in 500-pound bales of white cotton and 525-pound barrels of white rice, cultivated by black slaves and loaded by them onto ships; and it was a reminder of the whiteness of the city's economic elite, of the hand merchant and planters from Barbados who had sailed here from the Caribbean and accumulated their fortunes in Carolina.

The Barbadian founders of Charles Town left a third inheritance, a black majority. The original land grants were a strong inducement to import as many black slaves as possible into the Carolinas, and the economic success of the gang-labor plantation system meant easy credit to subsequent white arrivals willing to pledge future crops in exchange for immediate ownership of slaves. Possibly as early as the second generation from the Barbadians' arrival, blacks were a majority in the Carolina colony.

The number of slave imports from the Caribbean proved inadequate, and the original Indian slaves died or were sold. As a consequence, Charlestonians began to prefer "saltwater blacks" and importing firms were established at Charles Town to ship blacks directly to the city from the African western coast. White immigrants early in the 18th century noticed the increasingly slim minority that exercised control over the colony's majority inhabitants. "Carolina," noted a Swiss immigrant upon his arrival at Charles Town in 1837, "looks more like an African country than like a country settled by white people."

"White planters and merchants at Charlestown were caught in an economic trap, tightening one hundred years later. Having speculated their lands and crops in exchange for slaves, the whites were obliged each generation to import even more bondsmen to clear additional land and to produce rice and cotton ever more cheaply. But having created a slave majority, the white owners had made their own position physically and demographically perilous. Psychologically, white Charlestonians reacted to their situation by expressing revulsion for the blacks that they shared their narrow peninsula. Privately, they expressed their fears of a possible slave insurrection.

"Is it possible that any of my slaves could go to Heaven, and must I see them there?" The Reverend Francis Le Jau recorded this startling question by one of his female parishioners shortly after his arrival in Charles Town in 1706. Le Jau had come to Carolina as a young rector sent by the Church of England in his private hopes, as he wrote in his journal, of "instructing the poor and ignorant from among the white, black and Indians," As he settled in residence among the wealthy plantation owners who were his sponsors.

However, Le Jau recorded his despair at converting his white parishioners from their received beliefs. "I cannot to this day," he wrote in his diary, "prevail upon some to make a difference between Slaves, Free Indians, and Beasts." Later in the century, the Boston lawyer Josiah Quincy recorded his experience as a dinner guest at the Charles Town mansion of Miles Brewton.

Brewton had been among the first of the city's residents to establish a firm importing African slaves, and at the time of his dinner party he possessed one of the largest fortunes in North America. Upon entering the Brewton mansion with the other guests, Quincy encountered "the grandest hall I ever beheld," and he found the wines served during the meal "the richest I ever tasted." But what particularly interested him was the conversation of his fellow guests at the table; many white Charlestonians, he wrote, expressed "great fear of an insurrection."

Throughout the 18th century, Charlestonians of Brewton's economic class considered a project of cutting a canal across the neck of the harbor's peninsula, thereby making their city an island; such a cannel would give Charles Town " the appeal of Venice" and, its promoters reasoned, also provide a barrier "against a [slave] insurrection."

This engineering feat proved beyond the abilities of the Carolina government, but, with two notable exceptions, Charles Town throughout the 1790's remained free from the threat of a slave insurrection. What was needed for revolt was a messianic leader who could combine Christianity, Islam, and elements of African religion into a moral crusade for freedom and second, the organizational skills to arm the Africans and to deploy against Charles Town the force of their numerical superiority.

The religious leaders for black freedom appeared, surprisingly, among white planters. The Barbadians founders were strong Church of England believers, but despite their dominance, a few dissenters and evangelicals had taken advantage of John Lock's promise of religious tolerance to travel to Carolina. Among them was George Whitehead, a young Anglican evangelist from England who was described by contemporary accounts as preaching with extraordinary "Flame and power." Whitehead arrived at Charles Town in the spring of 1740, and immediately he began preaching to large crowds in the city to give up their patronage of "jewelers and dancing masters." Nor did he limit his criticisms only to Charles Town residents' well-known fondness for opulence.

Considering himself a "crying voice, to bid the world repent," Whitefield later published an open letter addressed to the inhabitants among other Southern colonies, of "North and South Carolina." In his letter, Whitefield castigated slaveowners who were "monsters of barbarity," Whitefield cautioned the Carolinians that they were fortunate that the slaves had "not more frequently risen up in arms against their owners." He wrote that he heartily prayed to his God that the blood of white people not be so split; but should African rise up and take the lives of their owners, he wrote, "All good men must acknowledge the judgment would be just."

Whitefield subsequently returned to England, but he left a strange convert in Hugh Bryan, a wealthy forty-one-year-old rice planter who lived sixty miles from Charles Town. Bryan had supported Whitfield in the evangelical work in Carolina that became known in the other colonies as the "Great Awakening", and after the evangelist's departure, Bryan's thoughts at his South Carolina plantation turned increasingly to religion. A recurrent quotation in his journals became a passage from JOB: "Who can bring a clean thing out of an unclean?" Undeniably, a sense of personal sin was becoming linked in Bryan's mind with the historical transgressions of African slavery. He later wrote in his journal: Bathe my soul in the fountain of his blood, and take away all my guilt, so I shall rejoice in thee forever.

Neighbors near Bryan's plantation began complaining in late 1741 to the Charles Town authorities of the "great assemblies of African" whom he was heard leading in shouts, singings, and exhortations. A group of travelers passing by Bryan's plantation in December 1741 reported hearing "a Moorish slave woman... singing a spiritual near the water's edge." Bryan himself was reported to be filling the minds of his plantation African with "a parcel of Chant-phrases, Trances, Dreams, and Revelations." At some time probably in the late fall or early winter of 1741, Bryan retreated into the woods, announcing his intention to live there several days, "barefoot and alone with his pen and ink to write down his prophecies."

Bryan returned from the woods bearing "a whole Volume of his prophecies," which he claimed to have received there from "many Days' intimate converse with an invisible spirit." He promptly sent this only copy of his revelation to colonial officials at Charles Town. It could not have been comforting reading. In his book, Bryan prophesied the coming "Destruction of Charles Town and Deliverance of the Negroes from their servitude." He claimed to have had a vision of Charles Town being destroyed by fire and sword." News of his prophecies spread privately like a secret fire among other Carolina white and Africans, and there were rumors Bryan had spent his days in the woods collecting and distributing weapons for use by his "African hosts" in the coming revolt. Bryan himself insisted only that his message was the same as it had been since the autumn of 1741: "The cry is repent, turn you, now is the accepted time."

Reaction from Charles Town was swift. Sheriffs were dispatched to arrest Bryan and the few other planters attracted to his revivalism. Miles Brewton, the wealthy Charles Town merchant who entertained so lavishly, was directed to buy and store gunpowder at guarded sites around the city for its defense. The colonial government as an act of public safety destroyed the books of prophecies of Bryan.

Bryan subsequently recanted, in early 1742, in an open letter addressed to Brewton and other public officials, confessing his earlier preaching to have been a "Delusion of Satan." No reason other than satanic influence was given for his actions, and Bryan therefore begged as a repentant sinner that "Your Honors will the more easily pardon me in this thing." Whether his conversion came from fear of imprisonment or fear for his soul, his display of deep contrition was probably what led the colonial authorities to spare him.

The authorities also were amused by the report that Bryan in imitation of Moses, had waded into the Atlantic surf with a walking staff, commanding the waters to part for his black and white followers to walk with him toward freedom. He had nearly drowned. He was allowed to return to his plantation, and his slave ownership, and for the remainder of a lengthy life in South Carolina, nothing more was heard from him as a religious prophet. But the documental fervor among the participating slaves in the religious revivals of the 1740's, and as well the undeniable alarm felt by the Charles Town officials, demonstrate that both races anticipated a time close at hand when a messianic figure--probably by necessity a black man--would rise up to lead the slaves into revolt. Charles Town authorities had reacted in 1741 to Bryan's brief conversion with such alarm because less than two years earlier South Carolina had experienced its most serious slave insurrection to date.

Gathering by prearranged plan, a group of about twenty slaves had met by the banks of the Stono River, within twenty miles of Charles Town early on Sunday morning, September 9, 1739. Under the leadership of an Angolan known only by the English name of Jemmy, the group broke into a country store, seized arms and gunpowder, and beheaded the white owners. Raising the shout of "Liberty!" and displaying a large banner, the original group recruited other slaves from neighboring plantations and announced their intention to fight their way to Spanish Florida, where they would be received as free men. Now numbering perhaps about one hundred, the group set out on the main road south to St. Augustine.

The sympathetic slaves hid some plantation owners in their path; some whites were captured but spared because of their earlier kindly treatment of blacks; and some masters were shot or hacked to pieces on the spot. By sheerest coincidence, the armed slaves happened to meet the same Sunday the lieutenant governor of the colonial South Carolina, traveling on horseback on the same road on his way to open the legislative session at Charles Town. After a narrow escape, this official succeeded in raising an alarm among white plantation owners, many of whom were attending Sunday morning Anglican Church services. A group of from twenty to one hundred planters was mustered, and the rebellious slaves were confronted at a river crossing. In an exchange of gunfire, whites killed or wounded at least fourteen blacks, but a large body of slaves crossed the river and continued southward.

Many blacks did not succeed in crossing the river and were captured, interrogated, and given an "easy death."

In the following days, the Charles Town militia arrived and, according to local reports, "killed twenty odd more, and took about forty captive." By the end of the month, the Stono Rebellion was officially declared at a close, and there is no evidence that any of the Africans ever succeed in reaching Florida and their freedom. The African leader Jemmy apparently was executed, along with most of his followers.

Despite its success in crushing the Stono River Rebellion, the colonial government knew it had reasons to worry. For the first time, a charismatic slave leader had risen to organize Africans in South Carolina along national or religious lines for a violent revolt against slavery. In a period of a week, these rebels had fought two pitched battles against their armed masters and the local militia, inflicting almost as many casualties on whites as they themselves suffered. And despite the public assurances that autumn by the Charles Town government that The Stono River Rebellion was at an end, a few surviving members of the rebel band were still at large and wasn't apprehended until months after Christmas 1739.

The Stono River Rebellion had demonstrated at least the possibility of organizing a widespread slave revolt, but to later South Carolina blacks, it was also a generational memory to expect no mercy from their white masters should a revolt fail. The old Barbabian slave code, adopted in South Carolina in 1696 and revised several times since, was applied with particular severity to the rebels the white planters succeeded in catching. According to one account, the planters, celebrating and drinking heavily along the twenty-five-mile road back to Charles Town, took prisoners and "Cut off their heads and set them up at every mile post they come to."

South Carolina appeared to be free from any other major organized slave revolts through out the 1700's. The American Revolution temporarily interrupted the African Slave Trade, but the city known as Charleston after the war emerged with its fortunes and its trading connection intact. The last decades of the Eighteenth Century were the beginnings of the economic "golden age" of Charleston, the city becoming perhaps the third most populous and certainly the richest urban settlement in the United States. Charleston resumed its role as the preeminent North American port for the purchase of slaves, and in the enjoyment of its slave-generated wealth, the city deserved its description by the evangelist George Whitefield as a heaven for "jewelers and dancing masters" and hell for sober-minded men."

This small society of rice and cotton planters at Charleston, "Henry Adams later wrote of the city, "with their cultivated tastes and hospitable habits, delighted in whatever reminded them of European civilization."

With the close of the war, British luxury items were once more welcomed in Charleston, and Adams added, English visitors to the city "long thought it the most agreeable in America." Charleston underwent a post-revolutionary war building boom, with mansions rising at the farthest tip of its civic peninsula in an exclusive residential district then known as "White Point", which twentieth century tourists would know as the "Battery" and as the heart of the city's historical district. Taverns and other public houses of this period regularly advertised wide selections of syllabubs and Madeira wines, and, in imitation of London's famous recreational park, Charleston even boasted an identically named Vauxhall Gardens for the exhibition of fireworks, concerts of the 18th century music, and the display of animal oddities.

Despite this luxury, the jaws of an economic trap, having traveled from the Caribbean, were tightening upon this port city: the African enslaved continued to be purchased on credit in order that even more slaves could be bought. But, given the protection of slavery by the newly ratified U. S. Constitution, the rising world market for cotton and rice, and the expansion of gang-labor plantations into the Southern frontier, white Charlestonians either chose to ignore the consequences of their trap or were oblivious to it. Incidents such as the Stono Rebellion and the straying of souls such as Hugh Bryan were considered unfortunate aberrations.

Slave ships with their human cargoes continued to dock monthly in Charleston's harbor, and their arrivals and points of origin were reported regularly in the Charleston Courier and South Carolina Gazette. Most of these slaves were sold at curbside auctions, along such major thoroughfares as Meeting Street, or Queen Street, All within the sight of the rising steeple of St. Philip's Anglican church, the original house of worship of the city's Barbadian founders.

On the afternoon of September 24, 1783, the South Carolina Gazette reported the safe arrival at Charleston of two ships, the Polly and the "Eagle," bearing a cargo of 104 slaves from the African coast and the Caribbean. The cargo of slaves were scheduled to be sold within a week "at Mrs. Dewee's, No. 43, Queen Street." The importation and sale of these blacks was being handled by a recently established merchant, Captain Joseph Vesey."[1]

South Carolina had the largest and most widely developed Slave Trade of any of the other colonies. This was owing to the charter of her settlers, her nearness to the slave markets, and the early development of certain staple crops, such as rice, which were adapted to slave labor. Moreover, this colony suffered much less interference from the home government than many other colonies; thus it is possible here to trace the Slave Trade... in a typical planting community.

As early as 1698 the slave trade to South Carolina had reached such proportions that it was thought that "The great number of Negroes which of late have been imported into this colony may endanger the safety thereof." And the immigration of white servants was encouraged by a special law, which reduced this disproportion, but nevertheless, Africans continued to be imported in such numbers as to afford considerable revenue from a moderate duty on them."[2]

In 1740, an insurrection under a slave named Cato, at Stono, South Carolina, had caused such a widespread alarm that a prohibitory duty of 100 pounds was immediately laid on the colony. Later the slave trade to the colony increased; but there is no evidence of any effort to restrict or in any way regulate it before 1786, when it was declared that "The importation of slaves into this colony is productive of "evil consequences" and "Highly Impolitic," and a prohibitive duty were laid on them. Next to South Carolina, Virginia had probably the largest slave trade."[3]

Due to the growing influx of slaves to the new colonies and the fears of escapes, murders, and threats of insurrections of the slaves, there grew a need in someway to get greater control over the bondsmen. Hence, by 1712, Slave owner Willie Lynch had delivered his famous speech to other slaveholders of the South by saying: "Gentlemen, I greet you in the year of our Lord one thousand seven hundred and twelve. First, I shall thank you. I am here to help you solve your problems with slaves.

Your invitation reached me on my modest plantation in the West Indies, where I have experimented with some of the newest and still the oldest methods for control of Slaves. Ancient Rome would envy us if my program were implemented. As our boat sailed south on the James River, named for our illustrious king, whose version of the Bible we cherish, I saw enough to know that your problem is not unique. While Rome used cords of wood as crosses for standing human bodies along its' highways in great numbers, you are here using tree and rope on occasion. I caught a whiff of a dead slave hanging from a tree a couple of miles back. You are not only losing valuable stock by hangings, you are having uprisings, slaves are running away, your crops are sometimes left in the fields too long for maximum profit, you suffer occasional fires, your animals are killed. Gentlemen, you know what your problems are; I do not need to elaborate. I am not here to enumerate your problems I am here to introduce you to a method of solving them. In my bag here, I have a foolproof method for controlling your black slaves. I guarantee every one of you that if installed correctly it will control the slaves for at least (300) three hundred years.

My method is simple, any member of your family or your overseer can use it. I have outlined a number of differences among the slaves; and I take these differences and make them bigger. I use fear, distrust, and envy, for control purposes. These methods have worked on my modest plantation in the West Indies, and it will work throughout the South.

Take this list of differences and think about them. On the top of my list is "age", but it is there only because it starts with an "A". The second is "color" or shade, there is intelligence, size, sex, size of plantations, status on plantations, attitude of owners, whether the Slaves lives in the valley, on a hill, East, west, North, or south. Have fine hair, course hair, or short. Now that you have these lists of differences, I shall give you an outline of action, but before that, I shall assure you that distrust is stronger than adulation, respect, or admiration. The black slave after receiving this indoctrination shall carry on and will become self-generating for hundreds of years, maybe thousands. Don't forget, you must pitch the old black male vs. the young black male, and the young black male vs. the old black male. You must use the light-skinned slaves against the dark-skinned slaves. You must use the female vs. the male, and the male vs. the female. You must also have your white servants and overseer distrust all blacks, but it is necessary that your Slaves trust and depend on us. They must love, respect, and trust us only. Gentlemen, these kits are your keys to control. Use them. Have your wives and children use them, never miss an opportunity. If used intently for one year, the slaves themselves will remain perpetually distrustful. Thank you gentlemen for your attention."4 This was the extent to which the slave owners resorted to in order to gain and maintain control over their bondsmen. Moreover, to a large extent they were successful.

In South Carolina, plantation agriculture did not really develop until the introduction of rice cultivation at the end of the 17th century. Ironically, it is likely that Slaves familiar with its' technology in Africa made possible its' successful cultivation in Tidewater South Carolina, thus accelerating the rapid expansion of Slavery there in the first part of the Eighteenth Century. During the 1780's, the average size of Slaveholdings in the counties surrounding Charleston, South Carolina, was about three times the average holding in the principal plantation counties of Maryland and Virginia. In 1790, the largest Slaveholder, the noted signer of the Declaration of Independence, Charles Carrol, held 316 slaves, while in the Charleston District one planter held 695 slaves, and five other slaveholders held over 300 Slaves apiece.

The African population was chiefly concentrated in the areas of South Carolina and Georgia, where the largest plantations were located. In such counties, blacks in fact outnumbered whites, though South Carolina was the only colony where slaves were consistently in the majority throughout the entire Eighteenth Century.

With the increase in the numbers of Blacks, the fear of lawlessness and insurrections rose, leading to the passage of stringent Slave Codes regulating their activity. While codes varied from colony to colony, generally they provided that Slaves could not carry arms, own property, or leave their plantation without a written pass. Murder, rape, arson, escape, and in some cases robbery, were capital crimes; common punishment for lesser offenses were maiming, whipping, or branding. After insurrection plots were discovered in Charleston, South Carolina, in 1739, South Carolina strengthened its' Slave codes, sharply limiting the assembling of Slaves and prohibiting the sale of liquor to them. These legal restrictions upon slavery and free blacks were employed throughout the period of slavery."[5]

South Carolina is where most of the Slave ships had landed to unload its' cargo of "Human Souls." Later South Carolina would become known as the first state to seceded from the union in order to protest its' harsh stance against the abolition of the evil empire of Slavery and bondage.

Thomas Jefferson, a worried slaveholder, inserted a clause in the Declaration of Independence which indicted the King of England for promoting slavery: "He has waged cruel war against human nature itself, violating its most sacred rights of life and liberty in the person of a distant people who never offended him, capturing and carrying them into slavery in another hemisphere, or to incur miserable death in their transportation thither...." This clause was struck out in deference to slaveholders and slave carriers who had grave doubts about the meaning of the sentence: "All Men Are Created Equal...."[6]

"An irony of ... one of history's greatest paradoxes: The American Revolution. Consider the background of that great event. A colony with a half-million slaves decides to go to war in support of the theory that all men are created equal and are "endowed by their creator with certain inalienable Rights that among these are Life, Liberty, and the Pursuit of Happiness." Consider the prologue. A bold African Cyrspus Attucks decides to strike a blow for liberty and becomes the first martyr of the Revolution.

Consider the climax, Black men, some slaves, enter the lines and sign the Declaration of Independence with their blood. "It was not", Harriett Beecher Stowe said, "for their own land they fought, not even for a land which had adopted them, but for a land which had enslaved them, and whose laws, even in freedom, oftener oppressed than protected them." "Bravery, under such circumstances, has a peculiar beauty and merit."

Behind the Revolutionary rhetoric, behind the bombast, behind the living and dying and bleeding is the irony: black men toiled and fought so that white men could be free. This fact was not lost on the Revolutionary generation.

It worried good men and women so much that they made African freedom an "inevitable corollary" of American freedom. James Otis and Thomas Paine, the great propagandists of the Revolution, thundered against British tyranny and slaveholder tyranny. Abigail Adams told her husband John Adams: "It always appears a most iniquitous scheme to me to fight ourselves for what we are daily robbing and plundering from those who have as good a right to freedom as we have."[7]

"The nation's third president, author of the Declaration of Independence, and rutting statesman would pinion slave child Sally Henning captive beneath him for thirty-eight years, never to set her free in his lubricious heat by night, and writing talent by day. Had he wanted to, he could have killed Sally and faced no consequences. He could have done anything to any of them, for they were but chattel about whose forebears he had apparently learned nothing from the work of Herodotus or Diodorus.

Comparing them by their faculties of memory, reason, and imagination, it appears to me that in memory they are equal to whites; in reason they are much inferior; as I think one could scarcely be found capable of tracing and comprehending the investigations of Euclid; and that in imagination they are dull, tasteless, and anomalous.

They secrete less by the kidneys, and more by the glands of the skin, which gives them a very strong and disagreeable odor.... they are at least as brave, and more adventuresome. But this may perhaps proceed from a want of forethought, which prevents their seeing a danger till it is present.... Their grief is transient. "The differences between the races", exclaimed Jefferson, "is fixed in nature...."

And is this difference of no importance? Are not the fine mixtures of red and white, the expressions of every passion by the greater or less suffusions of color in the one, preferable to the eternal monotony, which reigns in the countenance, that immovable veil of black which covers all the emotions of the other race? Add to these, flowing hair, a more elegant symmetry of form, their African own judgment in favor of the white, declared by their preference of them, as uniformly as is the preference of the Oranootan-orangutan for the African woman over those of his own species, wrote Jefferson.

In another place and time the middle-aged Thomas Jefferson's sexual exploits and plundering of Sally Hemmings would have been described as rape. She had begun with him as a child, 14. And even well into her maturity she would have no choice in the matter. He was the father of American liberty, who had indeed taken plenty with a young woman he had selected from a pool of human property he had once described in animal terms. For all practical purposes, Thomas Jefferson was a slaveholder; thus a racist, and- if one accepts that consent cannot be given if it cannot be denied- a rapist.[8]

BILL OF SALE FOR SLAVE

STATE of SOUTH-CAROLINA.

KNOW ALL MEN by these Presents, That *Stephen Tinker of the City New York Mariner*

for and in Consideration of the Sum of *Fifty one Guineas*

to *me* in Hand paid at and before the Sealing and Delivery of these Presents, by *William Gibbons Junior of the State Georgia* the Receipt whereof *I* do hereby acknowledge, have bargained and sold, and by these Presents, do bargain, sell, and deliver unto the said *William Gibbons*

One Negro Man Slave named Ceasar

TO HAVE AND TO HOLD the said *Negro Man Ceasar*

unto the said *William Gibbons his*

Executors, Administrators and Assigns, to *his* and their only proper Use and Behoof for ever. And *I* the said *Stephen Tinker my*

Executors and Administrators, the said bargained premises unto the said *William Gibbons his*

Executors, Administrators and Assigns, from and against all Persons shall and will warrant and for ever defend by these Presents. In witness whereof, *I* have hereunto set *my* Hand and Seal. Dated at *Charleston* on the *Fifteenth* Day of *July* in the Year of our Lord One Thousand Seven Hundred and Eighty *five* and in the *Tenth* Year of the Independence of the United States of America.

Signed, Sealed and Delivered,
in the Presence of

Stephen Tinker

Tho.ˢ Ham Sun.ʳ

5

A field hand returning from laboring   7

As Africans became more and more discontent with their conditions under the slavery regime, plots of revolt and insurrections became more widespread. Denmark Vesey, Gabriel Posser, and Nat Turner were cast in the same mold. In August of 1800, Denmark Vesey won a lottery and purchased his freedom. From that date until 1822, he worked as a carpenter in Charleston, South Carolina. He accumulated money and property and was respected by fellow Africans and white. He was, by his own admission, satisfied with his own condition; yet he risked everything in a bold effort to free other men. Offered a chance to immigrate to Africa, Vesey balked. He said, a witness reported, "That he did not go... to Africa, because he had not a will, he wanted to stay and see what he could do for his fellow creatures." There burned in Vesey's breast a deep and unquenchable hatred of slavery and slaveholders. A brilliant, hot-tempered man, he was the slave of a slave trader. He traveled widely and learned several languages; he learned also that slavery was evil and that man was not meant to slave for man. Vesey reached a point, it is said, where he could not bare to have a white person in his presence.

The conspiracy this firebrand conceived is one of the most elaborate on record. For four or five years, he patiently and persistently played the role of an agitator. Men, he said, must not only be dissatisfied; they must be so dissatisfied that they will act. Denmark Vesey was interested in action. He told the enslaved their lives were so miserable that even death would be an improvement.

Vesey buttressed his argument with quotations from abolitionists, Toussaint L' Ouverture and the Bible. He would read to the slaves "from the Bible how the children of Israel were delivered out of Egypt from bondage." But he warned that God helped those who helped themselves. It was necessary to strike the first blow. Always, everywhere, the words of Joshua were on his lips.

 "And they utterly destroyed all that was in the city, both man and woman, young and old, and ox, and sheep, and ass, with the edge of the sword."

This "Volcanic man" witnesses say, never rested. If he saw slaves bowing to whites in the street, he would rebuke them. When the slaves replied, "But we are slaves," Vesey would comment with biting sarcasm "You deserve to be slaves." If he were asked, "What can we do?" He would tell the story of Hercules and the man whose wagon was stuck at the bottom of the hill. The waggoner began to cry and pray; Hercules told him, Vesey would say,' to put the whip to the team and his shoulder to the wheel"

Always, everywhere, Denmark Vesey was teaching. "I know Denmark Vesey," a slave said; "On one occasion he asked me, what's new? I told him nothing. He replied, "We are free, but the white people here won't let us be so; and the only way is to rise up and fight the whites."

Another witness said: "if it had not been for the cunning of the old villain Vesey, I should not now be in my present situation. He employed every stratagem to induce me to join him. He was in the habit of reading to me all the passages in the newspaper that related to St. Domingo (Haiti), and apparently every pamphlet he could lay his hands on, that had any connection with slavery."

Ridiculing, taunting, and threatening, Vesey gained a vise hold on the minds of Africans in Charleston's surrounding areas. Many slaves feared him more than they feared their masters. One man said he feared Vesey more than he feared God. Having reached this point, Vesey switched from the role of agitator to the role of organizer. Around Christmas in the year of 1821, he chose lieutenants and perfected his organization. He was then in his early fifties, a vigorous big-bodied man with a keen insight into human nature. "In the selection of his leaders," said the judges, "Vesey showed great penetration and sound Judgment." He enlisted slave artisans and class leaders in the Methodist church. He did not disdain the darker arts. A valuable functionary in his own organization was Gullah Jack, an African-born sorceress who was considered invulnerable. If Gullah Jack could not convince a potential recruit, the talents of Blind Phillip were available. Phillip reportedly could see ghosts and other invisible phenomena. Timid recruits were carried to his house. Phillip would run his unseeing eyes over them and inquire: "why do you look so timorous?" The abashed recruits, thunderstruck that a blind man should know how they looked, would refrain silent. Blind Phillip would quote scriptures, "Let not your heart be troubled."

The chief lieutenant of this remarkable organization was Peter Poyas, a "first-rate ship carpenter" who displayed an organizing ability bordering on genius. Ice water ran in Peter Poyas' veins he was undoubtedly the coolest gambler in the history of American slave revolts. Like a good poker player, Peter was a blend of caution and recklessness. Characteristically, he volunteered for the most difficult and important assignment, the surprise and capture of the main guardhouse. The plan called for Peter to advance alone, surprise the sentinel and quietly slit his throat.

Vesey recognized Peter's talents and gave him large responsibilities. Peter was in charge of organization; he decided who should be approached and who shouldn't. It was Peter who pinpointed the greatest danger to a slave revolt; house servants. He told one of his recruiting agents to "take care and don't mention it to those waiting men who receive presents of old coats, etc., from their masters, or they'll betray us, I will speak to them."

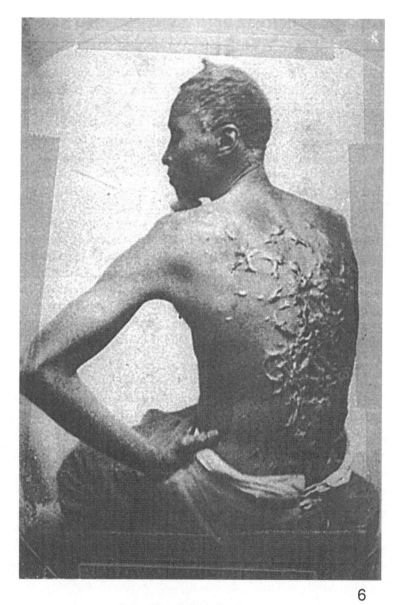

6

The Reality of Slavery

Vesey and peter perfected a cell-like organization. Each leader had a list of recruits and an assignment. Only the leaders knew the details of the plot; the average recruit knew nothing except the name of his leader and vague outlines of the plan. If a single recruit was arrested, he was not in a position to endanger the whole plot.

For four out of five months, the Vesey organization recruited slaves from Charleston and the surrounding areas. Whole plantations were signed up. Weapons were constructed. A Barber was hired to make Caucasian disguises. It has been estimated that some 9,000 slaves were recruited. Plans were discussed at secret meetings in Vesey's house. On Sundays July 16, 1822, the slave army was to strike at six points, taking possession of arsenals, guardhouses, powder magazines, naval stores. All whites were to be killed. Vesey's house on the eve of the insurrection was a beehive of activity. Under the cover of darkness, agents slipped in conferred and slipped out. One conspirator left an interesting account of a cell meeting. "I was invited to Denmark Vesey's house," he said, "and when I went, I found several men met together, among whom was Ned Bennett, Peter Poyas, and others, whom I did not know.

Denmark opened the meeting by saying he had an important secret to communicate to us, whom we must not disclose to anyone, and if we did, we should be put to instant death. He said, "we were deprived of our rights and privileges by the white people... and it was high time for us to seek our rights, and that we were fully able to conquer the whites, if we were only unanimous and courageous, as the St. Domingo people were." He then proceeded to explain his plan, by saying "that they intended to make the attack by setting the governor's mill on fire, and also some houses near the water, and as soon as the bells began to ring for fire, that they should kill every man as he come out of his door, and that the servants in the yard should do it, and that it should be done with axes and clubs, and afterward they should murder the women and children, for he said, God had commanded it in the scriptures." And at another meeting at Denmark's, Ned Bennett and Peter Poyas and several others were present in conversation, some said, they thought it was cruel to kill ministers and the women and children, but Denmark Vesey said, he thought it was for our safety, not to spare one white skin alive for this was the plan they pursued in St. Domingo."

On Saturday in the last week of May, the disaster Peter tried to prevent, materialized, an unauthorized slave, William Paul, attempted to recruit a house servant. Within five days, the authorities were in possession of the bare outlines of the plot. There followed one of the most extraordinary poker games in the history of slave conspiracies.

At one end of the town, the mayor and other city officials worked feverishly in frantic effort to crack the plot. In another room, at the other end of town, Vesey and his aids worked feverishly in a frantic effort to spring their trap.

The city officials and Vesey were working under certain difficulties; neither side knew what cards the other side held. The city officials did not know the names of the leaders or the details of the plot; but Vesey did not know this. With incredible boldness, he continued to hold meeting and walked the streets as though nothing had happened.

For two weeks, the game continued. The two rooms buzzed with activity, tension mounted. Word comes through the grapevine that city officials were getting close, two of the top leaders-Peter Poyas and Mingo Hart- were under suspicion. A weak organization would have crumbled at this point; men and leaders would have scurried to the hills. But the Vesey organization didn't work that way. Peter and Mingo ran not to the hills but to the mayor's office. They were indignant; their honor, their fidelity had been questioned and cleared. The authorities were confounded; guilty slaves didn't act that way. Peter and Mingo were released and the cops-and-robbers game continued. Vesey, in his room on Bull Street, read the signs and moved D-Day up. Then on the Friday before D-Day, another slave went over to the enemy. This slave, unlike the others, knew what he was talking about. He was privy to the plans and he knew the names of some of the leaders. Thoroughly alarmed now, the officials beefed up the guard and alerted the militia. Vesey and most of the leaders were arrested, tried and hanged. They behaved nobly, eyewitnesses say.

Only the leader confessed; the rest remained silent in the face of abuse, threats, promises, and torture. Peter Poyas, the official report said, was splendid in defeat. His only anxiety, the report said, was "to know how far the discoveries had extended; and the same emotions were exhibited in his conduct. He did not appear to fear personal consequences, for the whole behavior indicated the reverse.... His countenance and behavior were the same when he was sentenced; and his only words were, on retiring, "I suppose you will let me see my wife and family before I die?"' and that not in a supplicating tone. When he was asked, a day or two after, was it possible he could wish to see his master and family murdered, who had treated him so kindly, he only replied to the question with a smile.'"

So cool, so carefree was Peter that he spurned last minute pleas for additional information. "Do not open your lips," He said to other leaders. "Die silent, as you shall see me do. "It was said that" such words, considering the circumstances under which they were spoken, were worthy of a Son of Sparta or of Rome, when Sparta and Rome were at their highest levels as breeders of iron men."9

In America, in the French, English, Spanish, Dutch, and Danish Colonies, the Slaves were given a new conception of themselves to the different lights of their captors. This process, whether it took place in liberal Brazil or harsh South Carolina, was a painful, mind-reversing operation in which two or three out of every ten died.

In one form or another, every Slave from Africa went through a" breaking in" period. During this period, which varied from one to three years, the Slave was taught pidgin English or French or Spanish. He got a new name and began to look at himself and others in a different manner. Yahweh took the place of Olorum; Legba became St. Peter; the mass or hymnal replaced voodoo. The strain was too much for tens of thousands. Some died from old and new diseases; some refused to give up Shango and wasted away; others ran away and died of exposure; still others committed suicide; drowning was popular in liberal Brazil. Charles S. Johnson has given an excellent description of the" breaking-in" process in South Carolina."[10]

In the early days of the plantation regime, when gangs of fresh Africans were purchased, they were assigned in groups to certain reliable slaves who incited them into the ways of the plantation. These drivers, as they were called, had the right of issuing or withholding rations to the raw recruits or the inflicting of minor punishment. They taught the Slaves to speak broken English and to do plantation work, which required little skill.... At the end of the year the master or the overseer for the first time directed the work of the new African who now had become tame, assigning him to special tasks of the plantation work along with the other seasoned hands who had long since learned to obey orders, to arise when the [horn] blew at "day clean," to handle a hoe in listing and banking, to stand still when a White man spoke."[11]

"For over Two Hundred years, black, brown, and yellow men and women were held in bondage in America. During these years a social system as coercive as any yet known was erected on the framework of the most implacable race consciousness yet observed in virtually any society. A curtain of cotton rang down on some "Four Million Human Beings." It became a crime to teach these men and women to read and write. It became a crime to give them a "Bible." Behind this cotton curtain Four Million Human Beings were systematically deprived of every right of personality. Vice, immorality and brutality were institutionalized. The sanctity of the family was violated. Children were sold from mothers; and fatherhood, in effect, was outlawed. The "Rape" of a Slave woman, a South Carolina court held is "an offense unknown to common or civil law." The "father of a slave," another court ruled, is unknown to our law."[12]

"To be A Slave." To be owned by another person, as a car, house, or table is owned. To live as a piece of property that could be sold, a child sold from its' mother, a wife from her husband. To be considered not as human but a thing that plowed the fields, cut the wood, cook the food, and nurse another's child. A 'thing", whose sole function was determined by the one who owned you.

9

Enslaved labor in the Antebellum South.

"To be A Slave." To know, despite the suffering and deprivation, that you were human, more human than he who said you were not human. To know joy, laughter, sorrow, and tears, and yet be considered only the equal of a table.

"To be A Slave." Was to be a human being under conditions in which that humanity was denied. They were not Slaves. They were people. Their condition was Slavery. They who were held as "Slaves" looked upon themselves and the servitude in which they found themselves with the eyes and minds of "Human Beings," conscious of everything that went on around them. Yet, Slaves are often pictured as little more than dumb, brute animals, whose sole attributes were found in working, singing and dancing. They were like children, and Slavery was actually a benefit to them ---this was the view of those who were not Slaves. Those who were Slaves tell a different story."[13]

"Plantations and planters varied. There were small farmers with two or three slaves, planters with ten to thirty slaves, and big planters who owned a thousand or more slaves. Almost half of the bondsmen, however, lived, worked, and died on the plantations. Of much more pointed social relevance is the fact that the plantations, and its fleecy flower, king cotton, gave tone and direction to the whole society."[14]

"Twice a year the regimented slave was issued a clothes ration. A South Carolina planter described a typical allowance in his plantation manual. In the fall, each man would get two shirts of cotton twilling, a pair of woolen pants and a woolen Jacket. In the spring, two shirts of cotton and two pair of cotton pants. "Children had to go to the field at six on our place, maybe they don't do nothing but pick up stones and tote water, but they got to get used to being there."[15]

"The hands worked steadily and "with the exception of ten or fifteen minutes, which is given them at noon to swallow their allowances of cold bacon they are not permitted to be a moment idle till it is too dark to see, and when the moon is full, they often labor till the middle of the night. Some slaves said that it seemed that the fields stretched from one end of the earth to the other. Men, women and children worked in these fields. Male and female, the quick and the halt worked traditional hours of slavery - from can (see) to can't (see). Overseers and drivers, armed with whips, drove the work force. The overseer sometimes carried a bowie knife and a pistol. He often rode a horse, accompanied by a vicious dog. Fear, toil, the lash, hard words, a little ash cake and bacon" - such was life for most slaves, day in and day out, season after season with half day off on Saturdays "perhaps", and a whole day on Sunday. "Come day, go day, God send Sunday is all I pray." On a South Carolina plantation a slave elder leader named Sinda prophesied the end of the world, and an interesting, and significant circle of elders, who occupied a position in slave society roughly equivalent to the position of the elders in West African society.

The religion that was taught to the slave was censored which dealt always on the duties of the patients and obedience.

Other South Carolina slaveholders had no objection to his slaves hearing the gospel if they heard it in its "original purity and simplicity," Which implied Ephesians, 6:5 usually: "Servants, be obedient to them that are your masters...." Most slaves, with few exceptions rejected this version of Christianity. Their God was the God who delivered the "Israelites." "Didn't my Lord deliver Daniel, and why not every man."[16]

When the slave preachers would elect to preach the truth about the God of Abraham many inhuman atrocities would result as a consequence. Here is just one of the slaves' testimony of these atrocious acts that occurred in response to the bondsman's desire to seek a God to help ease the pain of his being in bondage.

Testimony: "It happened at Greenville, in the County of the same name, in South Carolina via a slave a preacher in the State of Georgia. His master told him if he continued his preaching to his fellow slaves, he would for the next offense give him 500 lashes. The slave (George) disregarded his master's threat and continued to preach to them. Upon his master having discovered the fact, George being dreadfully alarmed lest the threatened punishment should be carried into effect, fled across the Savannah river, and took shelter in the barn of a Mr. Garrison, about seven miles from Greenville. There he was discovered by Mr. G. Who shot at him with a rifle, on his attempting to run away, without effect. Mr. G., who endeavored to knock him down with the butt end of the piece, unsuccessfully, then pursued him. George wrenched the rifle out of his hands and struck the pursuer with it. By this time several persons were collected. George was secured, and put into Greenville jail. The facts having transpired, through the news people of his master came from Greenville to claim him as his property, but consented, upon being required to do, to receive 550 dollars as his value, with which he returned home. Shortly after this, George was burnt alive within one mile of the courthouse at Greenville, in the presence of an immense assemblage of slaves, which had been gathered together to witness the horrid spectacle from a district of twenty miles in extent. The manner in which George was burnt was as follows: A pen of about fifteen feet was built of pine wood, in the center of which was a tree, the upper part of which had been sawn off. To this tree George was chained; the chain having been passed around his necks, arms and legs, to make him secure. The pen was then filled with shavings and pinewood to his neck. A considerable quantity of tar and turpentine was then poured over his head. The preparations having been completed, the four corner of the pen were fired, and the miserable man perished in the flames. For several years later some of his burnt bones could still be seen fastens to the tree stump in which he had been fastened."[17]

According to Professor Samuel Byuarm Professor of Sociology in Charlotte, North Carolina, countless authorities such as this took place in the Four Hundred years of captivity and bondage. To place the matter in its' proper perspective, many people of color have endured life long humiliating and dehumanizing acts at the hands of the oppressor.

People of color in the land of the oppressor, have most of the time lost all hope of living in a world of rational behavior. We, to a large extent, have conceded to the acts of the oppressor who continue to enact atrocious means to further promote his own superiority, and to further demean any type of existence for people of color in this society. We find ourselves victims of scandalous means predicated on greed, and outlandish attempts, to further promote an unequal society. The oppressors have found a way to keep the people of color at bay, largely by the assignations of all of the people who made any attempts to speak up for us creating further disarray and further disillusionment for us.

In America, the oppressor has hid his shameful face behind the transparencies of his lies. One can concede to some of the thoughts of the slaves in that the oppressor is, in fact, the "Devil" himself, because he has broken every law of "Moses" in the Bible, which says "Thy shall not kill" "Thy shall not steal," "He that stealth a man and selleth him, or if he be found in his hands, he shall surely be put to death."

The status of the African in America has been labeled as "A Prophetic Return To Egypt."

In Deuteronomy Chapter: 28 verse 68, we find the prophetic statement made by God that the African Hebrews would be returned to Egypt again. But this time, by way of ships... and there they would be sold unto their enemies for bondmen and bondwomen. "It is certain that this prophecy fell upon only one people on the face of the earth, the people of Africa-the victims of the greatest, most cruel, vicious, and horrifying slave trade in the annals of history.

In their quest to escape the onslaught of destruction that came upon Jerusalem in 70 A.D., by the Roman General Titus, the African Hebrews fled westward and southward into northern and central Africa. This invasion of Jerusalem and the conquest of the region caused the final dispersion of all the remnants of the Black Northeast African trade people. This flight into Northern, Central, and Western Africa placed the African Hebrews in position for the fulfillment of the prophecy "The Great African Slave Trade." This brought about the final phase of the chastisement and the disbursement of the people of Africa into Europe and the lands of the Americas, "New World." The African Slaves were transported to the new world (A Second Egypt) in the bottom of slave ships, under the most inhumane conditions. These people were stretched out face to face in two lines, and in the space between their feet were others lying on their backs. The ships were packed to the brim. On board, the most frequent sicknesses were scurry, dysentery, and the "Pian" a skin disease. The high mortality rate led to a large number of suicides. Floors of the compartments were covered with so much mucous from the dysentery cases that the scene resembled a slaughterhouse. God's prophecy upon Israel to "bring thee into slavery again with ships" was fulfilled.

Over 115 million people were either taken as captives or killed in the slave wars. About one-third of the Africans taken from their homes died on the way to the coast and at embarkation stations, and another third died at sea, so that only one third finally survived to become laborers in the new world. The great captivity in the Americas not only enslaved the people of Africa/Eden physically, but it also served as a means to remove all former knowledge, history, language, and culture from the minds of the slaves. A great international religious conspiracy was formulated to destroy the truth of their relationship with the true and living God.

The African/Edenic people have been the most abused, exploited, and oppressed people in all of history and only God can bring about their redemption and salvation. God said, "No man shall buy you." No man shall intercede on the behalf of the African/Edenic people except he that is sent by God Almighty himself to break the bonds of slavery. -Deut. 28:68"[18]

"That a large number of bondsmen were worked severely during the colonial period is beyond dispute. The South Carolina code of 1740 charged that "many owners do confine the Slaves so closely to hard labor, that they have not sufficient time for natural rest." In the Nineteenth Century, conditions seemed to have improved, especially in the older regions of the South. Unquestionably, the antebellum planter who coveted a high rank in society responded to the subtle pressures that others did not feel. The closing of the African Slave Trade in 1805, and the steady rise of Slave prices were additional restraining influences. "The time has been,' wrote a planter in 1849, "that the farmer could kill up and wear out one African to buy another, but it is not so now. [Slaves] are too high in proportion to the price of cotton, and it behooves those to make them last as long as possible."[19]

"On a North Carolina plantation a temporary overseer assured the owner that he was " A whole Hog Man Come Rain Or Shine," and boasted that the Slaves had not been working like men but like horses. "I'd rather be dead than to be a "Nigger" on one of these big plantations," he exclaimed. There were numerous cases of collapses in the fields, numerous cases of sunstrokes, and fainting in the fields. Hot weather and heavy labor caused the deaths of many, many, many [Slaves] in the harvest fields."[20]

Neither public opinion nor high prices prevented some of the bondsmen from suffering physical breakdown and early deaths because of overwork. The cotton growers deliberately worked their Slaves to death every seven years with the intention of replacing them for profit. In the "Race For Wealth"... all were enlisted, and few proprietors managed their estates according to the code of the patricians."[21]

"Few Southerners familiar with these conditions would have challenged the assertion made before a South Carolina court that hired Slaves were "commonly treated more harshly than those in the possession of their original owner(s)."[22]

"Some planters avoided night work as much as they felt they could, but Slaves rarely escaped it entirely. Night work was almost universal on the cotton plantations when the crops were being picked, grinned, and packed. Moreover, among the smaller planters and Slaveholding farmers there was generally no appreciable relaxation of this normal labor routine. Their production records, and their diaries and farm journals and the testimony of their Slaves, all suggest the same "Dawn to Dust" regiment that prevailed on the large plantations.

This was also the experience of most Slaves engaged in the non-agriculture occupations. Everywhere, then, masters normally expected from their Slaves, in accordance with the standards of their time, a full stint of labor, "From Day Clean To First Dark."[23]

In order to accurately feel the despair of the Slaves, all one has to do is to listen to their pain and sufferings. Then you will began to envision exactly what their cries and prayers were. Here is still another testimony of the cruelty suffered by my people during our captivity at the hands of our captors and oppressors.

Slave Testimony: "When I git's to thinkin' back on them Slavery days I feel like risin' out O this here bed and tellin' everybody bout the harsh treatment us colored folks was given when we was owned by poor-quality White Folks. My master was mean and cruel. I hate him! The God Almighty has condemned him to eternal Fiah. Of that I is certain. Even the cows and horses on his plantation was scared out O' their minds when he come near 'em. Oh, Lordy! I can tell you plenty bout the things he done to us poor Niggers. We were treated no better than one O' his hound' dogs. Sometimes he didn't treat us as well as he treated them. I pray to the Lord not to let me see him when I die. He had the "Devil" in his heart.

His name was Jim Rankin an' he lived out on a plantation in Marion County, South Carolina. I was born and raised on his place. I spec' I was 'bout twelve years old at the time O' the war. Old man Rankin worked us like animals. He had a right smart plantation an' kept all his Niggers, 'cept one houseboy, out in the field a-workin'. He'd say, "Niggers is meant to work. That's what I paid my good money for 'em to do." He had two daughters an' two sons. Them an' his poor wife had all the work in the house to do, 'cause he wouldn' waste no Nigger to help 'em out. His family was scared O' him as we was. They lived all their lives under his whip. No Sir, No Sir, There warn't no meaner man in the world than old man Jim Rankin.

My pappy was Allen Rankin and my mammy was Ca'line. There was twelve of us chillum, nine boys an' three girls. My pa was born in Mississippi, and sold to master Rankin over at Columbia, South Carolina. My Ma' had to leave her family. But she warn't long in gittin' her another man. Oh Lordy!, the way us Niggers was treated was awful. Master would beat, knock, kick, and kill. He did everything he could except eat us. We was worked to death. We worked all day Sunday, all day, and all night. He whipped us till some of us just lay down to die. It was a poor life. I know it ain't right to have hate in the heart, but - God Almighty - it's hard to be forgivin' when I think of old man Rankin. If one O' his Niggers done something to displease him, which was mos' everyday, he'd whip him till he'd mos' die, an' then he'd kick him round in the dust. He'd even take his gun an'; before the Nigger had time to open his mouth, he'd jus' stan' there an' shoot him down.

We'd git up at dawn to go to the fields. We'd take our pails 0' grub with us an' hang 'em up in a row by the fence. We had meat an' pork an' beef an' greens to eat. Many a time when noon-time come an' we'd go to eat our vittles, the master would come a-walkin' through the fields with ten or twelve 0' his ol' houn' dogs. If he looked in the pails an' was displeased with what he seem in 'em, he took 'em an' dumped 'em out before our very eyes an' let the dogs grab it up. We didn't get anything to eat then till we come home late in the evenin'.

After he left we'd pick up the pieces of grub that the dogs left an' eat 'em. Hongry - Hongry - Hongry We was so Hongry! We had our separate cabins, an' at sunset all of us would go in and shut the door and pray to the Lord that master Jim would not call us out. We never had much clothes, 'ceptin what was give to us by the master or the mistis'. Wintertime, we never had 'nuf to wear nor 'nuf to eat. We wore homespun all the time. The master didn't think we needed anything, but jus' a little. We didn't go to church, but Sundays we'd gather 'round an' listen to the mistis' read a little out 0' the Bible. The master said we didn't need no religion and he finally stopped her from readin' to us. When the war comes, master was a captain of a regiment.

He went away and stayed for a year. When he comes back home from the war he stayed for two weeks. The night before he was a-fixin' to leave to go back, he come out of the house on the front porch to smoke his pipe. He was a-standin', leanin' up against the railin' when somebody sneaked up in the darkness an' shot him three times. Oh, my lord! He died the next morning. We never knowed who done it. I was so glad they shot him down.

Sometimes the cavalry would come an' stay at the house an' the Mistis' would have to tend to 'em an' see that they got plenty to eat an' fresh horses. I never saw no fightin'. I stayed on the plantation till the war was over. I didn't see none 0' the fightin'.

I don't 'member nothing 'bout Jefferson Davis. Lincoln was the man that set us free. He was a big general in the war. I 'member a song we sung, then. It went kinda like this: Free at las', Free at las', Thank God Almighty! I's Free at las', Mmmmm, Mmmmm, Mmmmm. When the mistis' tole us we was free my pappy was already dead by then - my mammy packed us chillum up to move. We traveled on a cotton wagon to Covington, Louisiana. We all worked on a farm there 'bout a year.

Then all 'cept me moved to vaudeville, Louisiana, an' worked there on a farm in the year of 1870, I got the call from the Lord to go out and preach. I preached the word of the Lord and traveled from one place to another. I only had seen the Ku Klux Klan once. They was a paradin' the streets of Brookhaven. They had a Nigger that they was a-goin' to tar and feather. Slavery days were bitter, and I can't forget the sufferin'. Oh God! I hates 'em. God Almighty never meant for "Human Beings" to be treated like animals. Us Niggers has a "SOUL" and a heart and a mind. We ain't like a dog or a horse. "Masters like mine ought never been allowed to own Niggers. I didn't 'Spect nothing out '0 freedom here in this place 'cept peace and happiness and the right to go my way as I pleased. I pray to the Lord for us to be free, always. That's the way God almighty wanted it."24

It was not until 1833 that Abolitionists produced evidence in a pamphlet refuting in detail all known arguments for the inferiority of all people of color. The pamphlet affirmed that Africans seemed at least equal, according to their advantages, to whites, and went on to provide examples of individual distinction among Negroes of the past, pointing to achievements in literature, law, science, mathematics, and statesmanship. Moreover, "Africans are as capable...of the finest sensibilities as we are; as capable of self-government, and eminent attainment in knowledge, usefulness, piety, and respectability." Accentuated was the great achievements of ancient "Ethiopians" and contended that the supposed indolence of contemporary inhabitants of Africa was due entirely to a "Natural Abundance" that made work unnecessary, and that where African lived in a [tropical] environment, as in Senegal, they were as industrious as any people on Earth."25

Slave Testimony: "In 1862 Rosa Barnwell, of South Carolina proposed to give a very brief account of her life in bondage, and also of scenes which I have witnessed, showing the cruel affects of slavery. No one who has not been in slavery knows the real curse of it. A northern person cannot tell half how bad it is. I was born in Charleston, S.C. I was a slave for more than twenty years. My mother was of Indian descent, and a free woman, but was kidnapped by a man named Leo Edwards, and doomed to a life of servitude. She had twelve children, one of whom was sold to Texas. God alone knows her fate. Five others now sleep between the sod, while the rest are still in slavery, and I alone have escaped to a life of freedom, through the mercy and goodness of God.

The person who claimed me as their slave owned two plantations. During the life of the old man the slaves were treated relatively well. After his death the plantations came into the possession of his son. Then came a change. The hands were obliged to go to work at 4 o'clock in the morning, and if they did not finish their task, had to stay till eleven at night. The overseer was a very cruel man, who applied tie lash freely, at all hours of the day. The slaves had for their weekly allowance a peck of corn and a half a peck of sweet potatoes, and were never allowed a piece of meat, unless they should take sometimes a hog on their own account, for which they were severely whipped. I will mention some cases of whipping which came under my notice.

One old man who was a blacksmith, was told to finish off some ploughs. After working until nine o'clock he stopped without finishing his task. The young master became very angry with him and began to beat him unmercifully. After he had finished, the poor old man said, "well master Robert, have you treated me so? The master coolly replied, "Well, I'll only have to meet you at the bar of God." The old man died in twenty-four hours."[26]

Slave Testimony: "Solomon Bradley, a colored man testified in regard to the punishment of slaves in South Carolina:

Q: What do you know of the modes of punishment upon the plantations?

A: They are more cruel here than anything I ever saw in my life. I was born in North Carolina, in the northern part of the state, and the people are not treated there so hard. If a master wants to flog a man and the man can break away while he is punishing him, there is no attempt made to renew the punishment.

Q: How long have you lived here?

A: More than five years; my owner hired me to the contractors for building the railroad between Charleston and Savannah and I was employed in the construction of the road both at my trade of blacksmithing and in getting out and laying the ties. I am acquainted with the road during its entire length and with the plantation on its route.

Q: Can you speak of any particular cases of cruelty that you have seen?

A: Yes sir; the most shocking thing that I have seen was on the plantation of Mr. Farrarly, on the line of the railroad. I went up to his house one morning from my work for drinking water, and heard a woman screams awfully in the dooryard. On goin up to the fence and looking over I saw a woman stretched out, face downwards on the ground her hands and feet being fastened to stakes. Mr. Farrarly was standing over her and striking her with a leather trace belonging to his horse carriage harness. As he struck her the flesh of her back and legs was raised in welts and ridges by the force of the blows.

Sometimes when the poor thing cried too loud from the pain Farrarly would kick her in the mouth. After he had exhausted himself whipping her he sent to the house for sealing wax, and a lighted candle and melted the wax droppings it upon the woman's lacerated back. He then got a riding whip and, standing over the woman, picked of the hardened wax by switching at it. Mr. Farrarly's daughters were looking at all this from a window of the house through the blinds. This punishment was so terrible that I was induced to ask what offense the woman had committed and was told by fellow servants that her only crime was in burning the edges of the waffles that she had cooked for breakfast. The sight of this thing made me wild almost all that day. I could not work and I prayed the Lord to help my people out of their bondage. I felt I could not stand it much longer.

Q: Have you seen any other cruel punishments?

A: Yes, whippings and irons and the stocks, but not quite so bad as what Mr. Farrarly did. I have seen a woman in the family way punished by making a hole in the ground for her stomach when she was stretched out for whipping.

Q: Solomon, you are in uniform - do you belong to the South Carolina regiment?

A: Yes sir.

Q: Did you volunteer or were you drafted?

A: I volunteered. I heard they wanted men for the third regiment and I had to go. I was Chief Cook then on board a steamer "Cosmopolitan" and getting good pay, but I could not stay there.

In such times I used to pray to the lord for this opportunity to be released from bondage and to fight for my liberty, and I could not feel right so long as I was not in the regiment. Q. Are you married? A. Yes sir, I have been married since I came here. I was married before, eight or nine years ago but my wife and two children were sold away and I never expect to see them again."[27]

Slave Testimony: "My father was born a slave. He was fourteen years old before he had a shoe on his foot. And across the hills of South Carolina you could track him. They had big snows in the winter, and he wrapped his feet in gunnysacks. He said you could track him through his blood in the snow as he went out to bring the cow's home during those snowy nights. In the morning he'd get up and run the cows up from where he slept all night to warm his feet, warm his hand with the warmth of their bodies. He was fourteen years old before he had his first pair of shoes. My grandmother was half Indian. Course the Indians are stubborn, supposed to be. And being half Indian and then being a slave also, she was stubborn. She said that her master was a very cruel man. Since she was stubborn, he's taken her by the ears to the corner of a house, and just bangs her head against the corner until she'd bleed.

She'd come out covered in blood. She died in the insane hospital in Columbia, South Carolina. You couldn't find three square inches on her head where there wasn't a scar when she died. And well, you find naked places all through her head where she was beaten until she is beaten into unconsciousness. Sometime she comes to herself under a tree; Master had knocked her out. In her later years it was discovered that during one of the forays the skull was crushed into her brain. The older she got, the worse it got. Thus she died at the age of seventy-seven, right there in Columbia (South Carolina), hospital."[28]

"Many Slaves created machinery and other inventions that would make the work a little easier for them on the plantation. "Because of the menial positions Africans held in society, most of the inventions served domestic needs, such as farm and kitchen utensils, trouser leg straighteners, cosmetic products, and ironing boards. Even when their breakthroughs proved beneficial to society as a whole, Black inventors were shunned by bigoted White. The Reconstruction Era saw a burst of patents filed by Black inventors. Between 1871 and 1900 more than three hundred patents were awarded to Blacks. The 1790 U. S. Patent Act should have opened the door to free Black inventors. Despite this, few of them even attempted to patent their creations. Enslaved Blacks had even fewer options. Until 1858 slavery laws made the inventions of the slaves the property of their enslavers. It may never be known just how many inventions credited to whites were actually created by their African captives."[29]

Just how many slaves created significant tools and other inventions during their years of bondage is unknown. Neither is the fate of these creative people known in their entirety except their eventual deaths. However, here is one of these inventors whose fate was recorded and is traced from his beginnings. "Henry Boyd (1802-1866) used his carpentry skills and one invention to buy him and his family out of Slavery.

His invention, the Boyd Bedstead, was constructed in such a way that its' wooden bed rails could be screwed into both the headboard and the footboard, creating a stronger structure. Boyd was born into Slavery in 1802. At a young age he was apprenticed to a cabinetmaker. He began saving his money, hoping to earn enough to buy his freedom. Armed with a general pass from his Slaver, he went to work in Salts work, working double time for double pay. He cut wood by day and tended to a boiling Salt kettle by night until he saved enough money. Many Black men who were carpenters used their skills to escape bondage. They knew, for example, that cabinetmakers were afforded a higher status and were more in demand than general carpenters, so they sought out that skill. A free man in 1826, Boyd went north to seek his fortune. What he encountered were shops owners who would not hire a Black man. He eventually teamed with a white carpenter and began building houses. He soon earned enough money to purchase his brother and sister.

By 1833 Boyd was worth more than Three Thousand Dollars. Three years later he opened his own company, using his bed frame design as its' foundation.

Boyd never received a patent for his bed design, though he did try to have it protected by having a white man apply for the patent. To ensure that his customers were getting the real thing, Boyd stamped his name on every frame he made. By 1843, he was among the most successful furniture makers in the furniture making business. He had a staff of twenty-five to fifty employees and owned steam powered machines. The majority of his customers seemed to come from the South and the ever-expanding West. Nevertheless, arsonists' torched Boyd's plant twice, thanks to insurance, he rebuilt. But in 1863, when no insurance company would insure his business because of the risk, he retired, and died three years later."[30]

Over the years the thought has often occurred to me that if Slavery was so "Evil" in the eyes of so many people during its' era, then why didn't someone who was in a position of authority put an end to it sooner? Why not George Washington? Why not John Adams? Why not Thomas Jefferson, or John Quincy Adams or James Monroe? Moreover, the question also in my mind is that "if Abraham Lincoln came to the office of the President of the United States in 1860, then why was it not until 1863 that the Proclamation for Emancipation of the African in America issued? In my mind, this only meant three more years of genocide through rape, lynching and forced free labor. If Lincoln was such a friend of the African, then why wasn't slavery eradicated the moment he gave his inaugural address in 1860?

Having been a student of history for the better part of thirty years these are questions that have perplexed me persistently. Historians generally have given me mixed views of our sixteenth president, Mr. Abraham Lincoln. Yet this has led me to be still in search of the truth. According to historian Benjamin Quartes, "Lincoln was opposed to slavery because it was contrary to the ideals of the Declaration of Independence. He held that the "all men created equal" phrase in the Declaration included the Colored man. Obviously slavery was at variance with the fundamental American principle which said Lincoln, until recently '"was held sacred by all, and thought to include all." To Lincoln there was no reason in the world "why the Negro; is not entitled to all the natural rights enumerated in the Declaration of Independence, the right to Life, Liberty, and the Pursuit of Happiness. "I hold that he is as much entitled to these as the White man."

However, it must be noted that while Lincoln supported Negro freedom, he was no advocate of Negro equality. "I have no purpose," wrote he in 1858, "to introduce political and social equality between the white and black races." Lincoln did not believe that the Negro was on a par with the White man in mental endowment, and he supported laws forbidding intermarriage. He was not an advocate of Negro voting or Negro office holding or of Negroes serving on juries. Lincoln believed in equality of opportunity for all Americans but he did not fully sense that a denial of any basic right was, in effect, a denial of equal opportunity for advancement. Lincoln opposed slavery, and for many reasons. One was its effect on the white worker. Lincoln held that slavery was contrary to the best interest of the wage earners in the North, who was forced to compete with unpaid laborers.

"The masses of white men," said he in a Cincinnati speech in 1859, "are really injured by the affect of slave labor in the vicinity of the field of their own labor."

It has also been said that Lincoln opposed slavery on moral grounds, as an evil. "It was," he said, "a contradiction of a basic law of God-that of freedom," writes Benjamin Quarles. "We live in an ethical world, one that holds us accountable. Hence, said Lincoln, "A man who did not wish to be a slave should not proceed to enslave anyone else; those who deny freedom to others, deserve it not for themselves, and under a just God, can not long retain it."[31]

There are, on the other hand, different views of the "Great Emancipator" Abraham Lincoln. While he has been greatly revered as the savior of African-American people, he has, indeed left behind skeletons that must be examined and dissected in order to know the real truth.

Well, who then was Abraham Lincoln? According to the great historian Lerone Bennett, Jr., "In his interest, in his associations, in his habits of thought, and in his prejudices, he was a "White man." "During the first years of his administration, Lincoln was ready and willing at any time to deny, postpone, and sacrifice the rights of black people to promote the welfare of white people. Why? Because of racism! Moreover, because black people were not "the special objects of his consideration."

Speaking to his cabinet and white people everywhere, Lincoln said "you and yours were the objects of his deepest affection and his most earnest solicitude. You are the children of Abraham Lincoln. "We, are at best, only his step-children; children by adoption, children by forces of circumstances and necessity." Lincoln was above all else a white man in that none of his public acts, either before or after he became president, exhibited any special tenderness for the African race, or any extraordinary commiseration of their lot.

He invariably, in his own words and deeds postponed the interests of the blacks to the interests of whites and subordinated one to the other." Lincoln had no intention of extending to blacks "the privilege of governing...white men," and that it was "as a white man, and in the interest of white men" that he opposed the extension of slavery.

The case against "The Great Emancipator" myth, then, is clear, and quite compelling:

1. As an Illinois citizen, as a lawyer, legislator, congressman and politician, Lincoln supported the enslavement of the four million Africans and opposed abolitionists who wanted to free them.
2. As an Illinois citizen, as a lawyer, legislator, congressman and politician, he personally supported the infamous Fugitive Slave Law and asked his neighbors to go out into the streets and hunt down fugitive slaves and return them to slavery.
3. As president, he ordered the return of fugitive slaves to slave masters, supported proslavery generals who returned slaves to slave masters, and struggled to keep from destroying the institution of slavery.

In all of this time, he did not "aid, directly or indirectly, the movement to abolish slavery, until the voice of the people was heard demanding it in order that the Union might be saved." Even then, he continued to oppose immediate emancipation, going to his death arguing for the pro-position that men and women should be judged not by the content of their character but by the color of their skin."

These are unimpeachable facts, asserts Dr. Bennett. More importantly, then the question arises that "if Abraham Lincoln was such a proslavery advocate then who in fact freed the slaves?" Well in the view and mind of Dr. Bennett, it was History, itself; the movement and the orchestration of the dominant forces of the age-freed the slaves, which is another way of saying that events and forces created the conditions and the men and women who used time and the social forces to make the only history it was possible to make.

Blacks were not freed by one individual or one social force, but to an extent freed by an intersection of individuals and social forces in a climate favorable to social change. This climate was created not only by the development of social forces but also, and most importantly the development of individuals who anticipated changes that would only become possible later and who planted seeds and prepared the ground in the 1830's and 1840's, while Lincoln was sleeping, for a crop that could only be harvested in the 1860s.

What we reproach Lincolnologists for is that they remove Lincoln, and themselves, from history, from the Black men who fought at Bunker Hill and the Black majority in South Carolina and the Black men and Women who were hunted down, like beasts, on the streets of Springfield.

According to Bennett, we will never understand anything about Abraham Lincoln, or ourselves, if we don't put Lincoln, and ourselves, back into that history within the perspective of two complementary and contradictory facts.

First of all, and most important of all, there has never been a real emancipation for African-Americans in the United States. The second fact, which contradicts the first and fulfills it, is that the real emancipation of African-Americans started not with Abraham Lincoln but with the first revolt on slave ships and will not end until somebody sign a document ending the Republic's never-ending, never-dying struggle with the only American question, a question bigger than money or property or sex, the question that defeated Washington, Jefferson, Lincoln, Woodrow Wilson, Roosevelt, Eisenhower, Reagan, not to pursue the matter further, the question of slavery, race, equality, all.

The poet Vachel Lindsey was wrong. That wasn't Abraham Lincoln walking at midnight- that was old John Brown and Harriett Tubman and the ghosts of the slaves, who are still rattling their chains in the Republic and demanding the wherewithal, the forty acres of land and (mechanical) mules, that separate freedom Lincoln-style from the actual freedom that the document mentioned but nowhere provided for or even defined.

And perhaps I should say here, by way of introduction, that almost all major historians have approached Lincoln and the Civil War from a White perspective. With few exceptions, historians have approached Lincoln from the perspective of how and why the war could have been avoided and how and why the issue of slavery could have been compromised. Which means, to be blunt, that almost all historians have approached this story from the standpoint of how and why my ancestors could have been kept in slavery longer-for ten, fifty or even a hundred years longer.

Greatfully, says Dr. Bennett, I write unapologetically from a different perspective, which may be the only perspective, truth being, as Jean-Paul Sartre and W. E. B. Dubois said, the perspective of the truly disinherited. Early in the war, while Lincoln and almost all senators and congressmen were operating from a white perspective, Wendell Phillips said in a speech published in the August 9, 1861, issue of the "Liberator" that the only perspective from which to view this war and Lincoln and Robert E. Lee was the perspective of the slave.

"Today," Phillips said, "belongs to the Negro. Today belongs to the slave. Whatever question we discuss today, we should discuss as the slave looks at it- from no other standpoint." It is from that standpoint that Bennett approached his writings from which I have relied upon, because his assessment in my opinion is the most indisputable and credible. For example, his discussion of a conscious and lucid slave aware of his objective interests, and with enough information to evaluate himself and all others in terms of his immediate demands to include immediate emancipation, arming of the slaves, the destruction of the political and economic power of the slaveholder class, the redistribution of land for Blacks and an educational crusade for blacks and whites.

9a

"General Moses," John Brown had called her. Before she died at 93, Harriet Tubman had led 300 slaves to freedom, directed Union raiding parties during the Civil War, and built a home for ex-slaves who were too old or too ill to work.

"In the whole of this conflict," Phillips said, "I have looked only at liberty, - only at the slave. "In the whole of this book," Dr. Bennett writes, I have looked only at freedom, only at the slave who hastened the war and welcomed it, believing that it was the coming of the Lord of history and that the graces of Gettysburg were the stern and the just wages of 250 years of Black slavery.

Bennett, and I, along with hundreds of millions of others around the world, has assumed, more importantly, that slavery was a crime against humanity. Like Apartheid in South Africa, and the concentration camps in Germany, and that all participants, Lincoln and Lee above all, must be evaluated on the basis of what they did and didn't do to end an American Holocaust that raises questions of personal and collective responsibility that have not been settled in this republic.

Slaves of the South were trusting Lincoln and they thought that he was their friend. Contrarily, what the slave victims believed and wanted was not Lincoln's concern, and the gravest charge against Lincoln that one can place against him is that he betrayed the trust of four million slaves who, not having reliable information, believed Lincoln was their friend because their enemies said that Lincoln was the enemy of the Slaves.

Plainly, Lincoln never pretended to be a racial liberal or a social innovator. He said repeatedly, in public and in private that he believed in white supremacy. Not only that, Lincoln had profound doubts about the possibility of realizing the rhetoric of the Declaration of Independence and the Gettysburg Address on this soil; and he believed until his death that blacks and whites would be much better off separated, preferably with the Atlantic Ocean or some other large and deep body of water between them. If, as Benjamin Quarles said, Lincoln became Lincoln because of the African, it could be argued that never before in history did a man give so little and so grudgingly to his historical fathers.

The man's personality, his way with words and his assassination, together with the psychological needs of a racist society, have obscured these contradictions under a mountain of myths, which undoubtedly would have amused Lincoln, who had a wonderful sense of the ironic and ridiculous.

Therefore, based on the Lincoln records of no solid quotation on Black Liberation and Equal Rights is most conclusive proof against Lincoln and the myth as the great emancipator. On the contrary, there is overwhelming evidence that Lincoln was a wiley and determined foe of equal rights and Black liberation. "Indeed" as author Kenneth M. Stampp said, "it may be said that if it was Lincoln's destiny to go down in history as the Great Emancipator, rarely has a man embraced his destiny with greater reluctance than he."

9b

Africans aboard the Amistad seize control.

Most historians focus on the eventful hero, praising him for events that happened on his watch, although in some cases, and in Lincoln's case in particular, the events happened not because of his intervention but despite his intervention. And we can appropriate here the words Lincoln himself used about Stephen A. Douglas and the Kansas-Nebraska Act and say that the slaves were freed not because of the Proclamation and its author but in spite of both. His Emancipation Proclamation was ineffective said antislavery leader John F. Hume.

The Lincoln story on the level of race is the story of a historical failure. For, in the end, Hume wrote, it was not Lincoln's policy but 'the policy of Salmon P. Chase, Charles Summner, Thaddeus Stevens, Horace Greeley, Henry Ward Beechers and other advocates of radical cure, with whom the president was in constant opposition, that prevailed... and with a decisiveness that proves it to have been feasible and sound from the beginning." If the Emancipation Proclamation was intended to eradicate slavery altogether, it was too narrow; if to free the slaves of Rebels only, it was too broad. His reconstruction proposals and his colonization efforts all failed. Indeed, if we take his official action from first to last, it is a question whether the president, owing to his extreme conservatism, was not more of an obstructionist than a promoter of the Anti-slavery cause."[32]

"Lincoln was a symptom of a larger and deeper problem that has never been addressed in America. Four scores and seven years of private and public lying, of sanctioning genocide and blatant racism, of approving violations of the Constitution and the Declaration of Independence, of winking at violations of democracy and free speech in the south not only for Blacks but also for whites, had weakened the moral fiber of the Republic and its leading men, including Washington, Jefferson, Madison, and Lincoln."[33]

"In 1836, the year Abraham Lincoln called for a White-only suffrage, a white attorney named Salmon Portland Chase stood in the door of a Cincinnati, Ohio, building and faced down a mob trying to lynch a white abolitionist editor.

In 1838, the year Illinois state legislator Abraham Lincoln voted to tax "slaves and servants of color," an untutored slave named Frederick Douglas escaped from slavery in Baltimore and began the fifty-seven-year career that made him one of the benefactors of the century.

In 1839, members of the Liberty party joined the antislavery process along with the heroic slaves who killed the captain and took over the slave ship Amistad in one of the slave mutinies that Lincoln feared.

1848 was a good year, bringing with it the Free Soil Party that Lincoln deplored. So was 1849, the year Harriett Tubman, afterward called "the Moses of Her People," escaped from slavery in Maryland, at a time when Congressman Lincoln was pressing a gradual emancipation plan and a fugitive slave law for the District of Columbia?

On and on it came, a great black carpet of moving forms and energies with squares of white and brown and yellow, history's stepchildren at history's door. The Reverend Nat Turner, David Walker and John Brown were among that number. So were Douglas, Tubman, Zebina Eastman and the Illinois activists who fought the battles Lincoln evaded. White and Black, nonviolent and violent, politicians and preachers and guerrillas, all marched in the great procession which was helped even by its enemies, even by Stephen Douglas, who pulled the scab off the gangrenous Missouri Compromise and forced a national CRISIS- even and especially by Confederate soldiers who vetoed an easy victory and thereby made emancipation necessary and inevitable, no matter who occupied the White House. And don't leave out the white Dreamers, the Jeffersons and Lincolns, who said all, meaning some, who said humans meaning whites, and played into the hands of the liberators.

Lincoln, who was no friend of John Brown and the Black and White men who died with Brown, tried at first to push the procession back. Failing that, he tried to divert the marchers into the side of the road of gradualism and colonization. But when it became necessary to free the slaves to save the Union and to stop the slaughter of husbands, brothers, fathers and friends, conservative white people raised their voices, and the procession become irritable, pushing a protesting Lincoln on before it into glory. From first to last, Lincoln was more of a follower than a leader in the procession."

That's the way it happened, more or less, in the long lens of a history that never forgives and never forgets and is always, as the slaves said, signifying and calling somebody's name. And the spectacle of Abraham Lincoln the Separatist, Colonization's and Racist marching in the front ranks of the emancipation procession he had opposed all his life causes us to meditate on the irony of a history that conspired in these years to make an Illinois white supremacist the signer of the Emancipation Proclamation, as it had conspired in another time to make a Virginia slaveholder the author of the Declaration of Independence, and with the same results."[34]

"To recapitulate, then, Abraham Lincoln was a man who defined himself and chose himself as a White man. Secondly, and more concretely, he was a man who defined himself and chose himself as a racist committed to the subordination of non-whites. Thirdly, he was a man who defined himself and chose himself as a colonizationist and who was reduced, out of anguish and out of fear of the future and the human condition, to projecting a world without the African-American whom he wanted to eliminate, not by actual murder, but by the symbolic murder of banishment.

9c

Joseph Cinque, leader of the Amistad slaves. He told his comrades: "Brothers . . . our hands are now clean for we have striven to regain the precious heritage we received from our fathers . . . I am resolved that it is better to die than be a white man's slave, and I will not complain if by dying I save you."

To answer the question them "Who was Lincoln?" The answer to that question on a first level of approximation is that he was a tragically flawed figure, marked by Black fear and Indian fear and limited by his commitment to the white supremacy ethic. Socially, he was the archetype of the poor white that makes good and marries the "frivolous" daughter of the rich plantation owner and slave master. Politically, he was the archetype of the sensitive, suffering, ineffectual fence figure-in America, in the Third Reich, in Algeria, in South Africa who is born on a fence and lives and dies on a fence, unable to accept or reject the political evil that defines him objectively.

History knows its own, hides its own, and selects its own, creating men with needs that meet the needs of the time; and it is an open question whether history chose Lincoln because it was preparing a history of halfness that would end slavery formally without ending slavery in fact or whether Lincoln chose that history because history had given him that halfness and because the halfness was in him and of him and the true expression of his objective being. Whatever the result was the same. The son of the luckless and virtually illiterate Thomas Lincoln and the doomed Nancy Halts Lincoln, born in a log cabin, halfway between the rich white slave-owners and the Indians and slaves, and distinguished only by his dark white skin, entered the ranks against the slaves and the poor whites, choosing the party of the aristocracy and privilege.

Lincoln chose the big money crowd because he perceived early in the game that the money people were generally Whigs and that political power sooner or later followed economic power. A number of informants said Lincoln started out as a Jacksonian but was converted by his bosses and mentors. From that point onward, he surrounded himself with conservative supporters and partisans of the slave system. Some, like his closest friend, Joshua Fry Speed, and his future wife, Mary Toddy were slaveholders or products of slaveholders. All believed the Negro was inferior and supported the Illinois Black Laws and the hunting and capturing of fugitive slaves in and around Springfield.

Not only did the Lincoln circle believe in Negro inferiority, but there was a doubt about democracy and the term plasm of the poor whites. Lincoln himself had, like most Whigs, deeply ingrained doubts about the potential of the (White) masses, and in some of his associates in Sagamon County loathed Catholics and the impoverished immigrants from Ireland and other countries.

Lincoln was a republican not a democrat, he believed not in government of the people but in government of the "best (white) citizens," "men of property and education who had a reverence for (and a stake in) law and order."[35]

"Abraham Lincoln was fascinated - and horrified-by the color black and couldn't get enough of imitation whites imitating the imitation Blacks he wanted to banish from his white American Eden.

Attracted and repelled, tempted and threatened, he loved "n----r jokes" an "n----r shows " but feared real Black people, real Black violence and the darkening of white America. It will be said, of course, that Lincoln was "friendly" to Negro servants and suppliants, but "the friendliness of Lincoln toward colored people was, "as Lincoln authority J. G. Randall said, 'a Southern (White) type of friendliness and no one can read the record without realizing that he had an almost obsessional fear of Black violence and slave insurrections.

The threat of blackness, the temptation of blackness, the magic of blackness, and the blackness of blackness: Lincoln seemed to have been obsessed by the subject. It was in response to blackness, and as a relation to blackness, that he created his identity, making color the center of his world and making what he considered the opposite of blackness, that is to Say, whiteness, his main value. And so while living a double life and psychologically, putting on blackface in his imaginary minstrel life and manipulating the mask of whiteness on the political stage, he constructed a personal myth of black inferiority based on the presence or absence of color.

If there was one notion he was committed to, it was that the Negro race was inferior to the white race because of its color. If there was one thing he was certain of, it was that he was better than Black people because of the whiteness of his skin. Certainly, he said, over and over again, "the Negro is not our equal in color...."

Moreover, Lincoln was a white man and lived as a white man. Although Lincoln may have been saffron-brown or dark complexioned or "a long black fellow" and whatever his family background, he had a mountain-size color problem. George Frederickson, who does not agree with Dr. Bennett's' thesis, said that in view of "Lincoln's unequivocal statement that Blacks are inferior in color...It seems reasonable to conclude that Lincoln sensed in the attitudes of white Americans, and probably in himself as well, a strong distaste for Negroid physical features and a powerful preference for white pigmentation as the human norm." Concerning which three points can be made. First of all and most important of all, color in the Western World is not a physiological characteristic it is a historical or, better, a political characteristic.

Secondly, color, however defined, is not the cause of racism it is the excuse or justification. Thirdly, "a strong distaste for Negroid physical features" didn't bother Thomas Jefferson and other slaveholders who showed, according to all available statistics, "a powerful preference" for non-white norms.

Nothing gave Lincoln more pleasure than minstrel shows. He was especially fond of Negro minstrel performances. He had an insatiable fondness for Negro minstrelsy and seemed to extract the greatest delight from the crude jokes and harmless fun of the blackface and red lipped performers."

The minstrel shows Lincoln loved were conceived in cupidity and dedicated to the proposition that all Negroes were created unequal, frozen for all time in timeless "Jim Crow" archetypes of shuffling, mindless buffoons. Cunningly created to give whites a sense of disdain for blacks, the shows were written by racists, performed by racists and watched by racists. This was not, as Lincoln admirers contend, "harmless" fun. This was sadistic fun with political overtones that poisoned the social atmosphere, fastening the chains of the slaves and providing ideological support for the inhuman Black Laws that Lincoln supported.

Form followed function in these shows, which were essentially variety shows for white people presented by white men in Black face, "their painted lips leering," Ken Emerson wrote, "like gashed watermelons as they laughed at their own racist jokes." Sex defined the postures and presentations, which were based in many cases, Lott said, on phallic and homoerotic images. It was a visual art, a voyeur's art that made it possible for Lincoln and other whites to visit Slave Row (and Harlem and the South Side) while remaining white and insular and smug. It was also a sadistic art, which encouraged "murderous fantasies" about the death and disappearance of Blacks.

There was a suspiciously large amount of dying in minstrel shows, and Lincoln and other minstrel fans, including Walt Whitman and Mark Twain, spent a lot of time shedding tears over the untimely end of Old Black Joes "gone whar de good N---rs go," to that great plantation in the sky. More than racial cruelty was involved in all this. For this "generic death drive," as Lott said, "was ultimately rooted in the most pressing racial questions of the day." In and through the minstrel drama, minstrel fans "repeatedly wished away the existence of Blacks altogether." And it seemed to Lott and others that "what was being symbolically eliminated and put to rest was the whole lamented business of slavery in the United States, by means of the elimination of Black People themselves."

On this level, Blackface constituted a disguised wish for "the elimination- by extinction, expulsion or magic-of the Black Race" a disguised wish directly linked to the politics of Lincoln and other whites who favored colonization. Perhaps the worst example of the "metaphorical murder" of the genre Lincoln loved is the verse, cited in popular songs of the Nineteenth Century, in which Stephen Foster joked about a boat that sank, drowning five hundred Blacks "I Jump'd aboard the telegraph and trabbled down de ribber, De lectrik fluid magnified, And kil'd five hundred Nigga. Oh, Susanna, do not cry for me. This was not entertainment; this was genocide in black face, and there was a direct link between this political theatre and the sexual, racial, and economic anxieties of Lincoln and other nineteenth century whites. It was, at any rate, no accident that Lincoln and other devotees of the politics of burnt cork made Daddy Rice's "Jim Crow" the biggest hit of the 1830's "Weel a-bout and turn a-bout and do just so. Every time I weel a-bout I jump jim crow."

Wheeling about and turning about and jumping just so, Daddy Rice, the White man who was called "the Negro par excellence," shuffled across the stage at New York's Bowery Theatre in 1832 in Blackface and gave America its first international hit song. By 1838, as I have pointed out elsewhere, Jim Crow was wedged into the language as a synonym for Negro. A noun, an adjective, a "comic" way of life. By the 1850s when Lincoln launched his campaign to colonize real Blacks, the Jim Crow song, the Jim Crow train, the Black-faced minstrel and the White-faced auditor were so mixed up in the American mind that it was impossible to tell where the lyrics ended and the whips and chains began.

Cultural historians say the minstrel show was the beginning of the American entertainment industry, menacing that it was the beginning of the white entertainment industry, meaning that it was the beginning of the white performer's burden of going to the "neighborhood, "however named, and stealing and marketing watered-down and distorted versions of Black songs and rhythms. Lincoln, who was virtually a minstrel show groupie, was there at the beginning. On one occasion, a literary man tried to find out if Lincoln while in St. Louis had attended a lecture by the celebrated English writer William Makepeace Thackeray.

One of Lincoln's Springfield, Illinois, friends sent a message back that if Lincoln "was in St. Louis and the wonderful Mr. Thackeray was billed to lecture in one public hall and Campbell's or Rumsey's Negro Minstrels were to hold forth in another hall on the same evening, it would have been folly to look for Lincoln at the lecture. Instead of the latter the 'n----r show' would have caught him every time."

It was a minstrel show or as he and his friends said indelicately "a n----r show" that caught Lincoln on his visit to Chicago two months before he was nominated for president of the United States. Whitney said that when, on March 23, 1860, he was presented three tickets to Rumsey and Newcomb's Minstrels he asked him if he would like to go to a "n----r show" that night. Lincoln "asserted rapturously" saying: "of all things I would rather do tonight that suits me exactly…."

The "piece d' resistance" of the show, Whitney reported, was a performance of a new song, an "Ethiopian 'walk round" called "Dixie's Land." One of the verses went like this: Sugar in de gourd an 'stony batter, De whitegrowfat an 'de niggahs fatter; Look away- look away- lookaway- Dixie land. Rumsey and Newcomb's Minstrel, Hooley and Campbell's Late George Christy's Minstrels, Barney Williams, the Ethiopian Serenaders, Dombey & Sons, Brudder Bones: Abraham Lincoln knew them all. And the question we have to ask ourselves, once again, is who must Abraham Lincoln have been in order to imagine that he was an Oreo minstrel, black on the outside and white on the inside, chocolated and transformed and pulled out of his whiteness by Ersatz Negro melodies and rhythms?

The answer, once again, is that he was in this regard, as in everything else, a quintessential racist, torn apart by his attraction to the Blacks he wanted to subordinate and banish, partly because he had projected his fears and desires and otherness onto them. The historian Benjamin Quartes, who tried to save Lincoln from himself, said Lincoln "like most whites...Believed that the Negro as such was funny." Lincoln also believed, as Quarles also noted, that the Negro as such was inferior and was not "on a par with the white man in mental endowment."

Lincoln was as active as any racist of his time in perpetuating Negro stereotypes. The words n----r, darkey and colored boy came easily to his lips. It appears from the admittedly incomplete record that Lincoln used the N-word at least as often as the Mark Fuhrmans of today. He might have used it even more, for unlike Fuhrmam who tried to hide his hand on official occasions, Lincoln used the word openly on platforms and in the Illinois State House and the White House.

The N-word was used freely by Lincoln throughout his political career. During the Lincoln-Douglas Debate held in Ottawa, Illinois, Lincoln denied that he wanted "to set the niggers and white people to marrying together" and said, in passing, that there was "no danger that the people of Kentucky will shoulder their muskets, and, with a young nigger stuck on every bayonet, march into Illinois and force them upon us.

"Although white writers have tried to cover up the true Lincoln and his frequent use of the N-word. Writers like Carl Sandburg and Paul Angle refuse to accept the evidence of their eyes and blame incompetent reporters for putting bad words in Lincoln's mouth. But nobody was putting bad words in Lincoln's mouth when he was making statements that although he supported the Fugitive Slave Law he personally had "no taste for running and catching niggers."

Before, after and during the Lincoln-Douglas debates, in public and in private, Lincoln used and abused the N-word. In the Carlinville, Illinois, speech, he used the word twice, and it is surprising that historians who are always praising Lincoln's skill in opening speeches never mention the Carlinville speech, which started, according to the Carlinville Democrat, with this sentence: He said, "the question is often asked, why this fuss about niggers?" The answer, Lincoln said, was that the extension of slavery posed a threat to white workers. "Sustain these men and Negro equality will be abundant, as every white laborer will occasion to regret when he is elbowed from his plow or his anvil by slave niggers." Carl Sandburg and others suggests that Lincoln was misquoted, and it is odd that a different reporter heard the same word when Lincoln told a crowd in Elwood, Kansas, a year later, "people often ask, why make such a fuss about a few niggers?"

On the question of Popular Sovereignty, Lincoln asked, "was it the right of emigrants in Kansas and Nebraska to govern themselves and a gang of niggers, too, If they wanted them?" However, Lincoln had not the boldness to say that the right of people to govern niggers was the right of people to govern themselves. Other racists felt that it was the right of the White man to "breed and flog niggers" and that it was a "sacred right of self-government." In the same period, Lincoln made it clear that he was opposed not to slavery but to the extension of slavery to the territories. Why was he opposed to slavery in the territories? He didn't want the West, he said, "to become an asylum for slavery and niggers."

The N-word went to Washington with Lincoln. Lord Charnwood said congressmen and other officials "were puzzled and pained by the free and easy way in which in grave conservation he would allude to "the nigger question" or question, others said, whether it was advisable to "touch the nigger." Still others were pained by the free and easy way he interrupted official conferences to tell stories about "darkey" preachers or "darkey" arithmetic. Colleagues told Lincoln that this was cruel, racist and sadistic, but he ignored them and even managed to imply, as almost all modern Lincoln interpreters imply, that there was something wrong with men who didn't like a good "darkey" joke.

Twentieth-century historians have created an extremely sympathetic portrait of the jokester president, but contemporaries, even sympathetic contemporaries, repeatedly criticized his joke-making, particularly in periods of national mourning over massive Union reverses and disasters. Lincoln's choice of fables was often a deadly offense and his humor often "miscarried" or "backfired." When shortly after the national disaster of the first Bull Run, the president interrupted state business to tell a visiting crony the latest jokes, a high ranking officer who specialized in making cannons stormed out of the White House, "declaring that Lincoln was a fool and had got closeted with a damned old hoosier from ills. And was telling dirty stories while the country was going to hell." N-words, N-shows, N-jokes, Cuffie, Sambo, Aunty, colored boy: these phenomena have a name and a meaning. No interpretation of Lincoln that fails to take them into account by naming them and him is valid."[36]

"None of Lincoln's public acts, either before or after he became president, exhibits any special tenderness for the African race, or any extraordinary commiseration of their lot. On the contrary, he invariably, in words and deeds, postponed the interests of the blacks to the interests of the whites, and expressly subordinated the one to the other. When he was compelled, by what he deemed an overruling necessity, founded on both military and political considerations, to declare the freedom of the public enemy's slaves, he did so with avowed reluctance, and took pains to have it understood that his resolution was in no wise affected by sentiment."[37]

By omissions and evasions, by half-truths and quarter-truths and lies, by selective quotations and suppressed quotations, by begging the question and forgetting the question and ignoring the question, by committing all the logical fallacies in the book, and by inventing new ones, by all the methods, and others, and by the biggest attempt in recorded history to hide a man, Lincoln defenders have managed to turn a separatist into an integrationist and to fool all the Black people and all the white people, save one or two, all the time.

Lincoln said repeatedly in private and public, in Springfield and in the White House, that he was a white supremacist and that he wanted to deny Blacks equal rights because of their race and deport them to a tropical climate with people of their own color and kind."[38]

"Post Lincoln-assassination reverses affected almost everyone, including Frederick Douglas, who said eleven years after the assassination that Lincoln was a racist but soften his view in a collection of reminiscences published twenty-three years after the event."[39]

To further prove this point let us continue to investigate and dissect the Great Emancipator. "Everybody, or almost everybody, tells us that Lincoln said in Chicago in July 1858 that we should stop all this quibbling about this race or that race and get on with the business of realizing that the Declaration of Independence, which Lincoln called the "White man's" Declaration of Independence. Almost nobody tells us that he said in the same speech that the interest of white people made it necessary to keep Blacks in slavery and that God himself was a fellow white conspirator, having, as Lincoln put it, "made us separate."

There is finally the mother of all Lincoln Quotes. - The Last Best Hope of Earth quotations from the "We Cannot Escape History Peroration" of the 1862 Annual Message to Congress. Lincoln reached levels of eloquence unsurpassed by any other human being in a futile attempt to persuade Congress to pass Constitutional Amendments calling for, among other things, a federally funded plan to deport Blacks."[40]

"Lincoln wanted Congress to "Ethnically Cleanse" the United States of America by buying the slaves over a thirty-seven-year period and sending them "Back To Africa." And that included the ancestors of the distinguished African-Americans who are always recruited to recite words that call for the deportation of their great-great grandmothers and great-great-grandfathers. According to Lincoln, "It is the eternal struggle between these two principles-right and wrong. It is the same spirit that says, "you work and toil and earn bread, and I'll eat it". No matter in what shape it comes, whether from the mouth of a king who seeks to bestride the people of his own nation and live by the fruit of their labor, or from one race of men as an apology for enslaving another race, it is the same tyrannical principle.

This same tyrannical principle was endorsed by Lincoln, saying that "it was necessary to maintain the divine right of slaveholders in the South and to join with them in "running and catching niggers" who escaped from people who believed in the divine right of kings and slaveholders."

Finally, and definitively, everybody tells us that Lincoln said that, "As I would not be a slave, so I would not be a master." They don't say that the same man made hundreds of thousands of slaves, and it was closer to the truth when he said "There is something worse than to be a slave. It is to make other men slaves or to support others who are making other men slaves." All major historical Lincoln biographies have systematically wrenched out of context Lincoln's words to make him say the precise opposite of what he really said. The fallacy of the isolated quote is linked in spirit and intent with the fallacy of detached data, which wrenches Lincoln out of his social and historical context and presents a lifeless abstraction who tells jokes and loves everybody, except the slaves, but has no connection with the violent and racist system of slavery and Jim Crow that stained his soul and the soul of the nation. Here was a man who supported, voted for and helped manage the worse system of slavery in human history, but scholars routinely write six-hundred page books without mentioning these facts in context."[41]

"What then was the problem? You know what the problem was. The problem-Lincoln tells us so a thousand times-was "Race." Abraham Lincoln supported slavery in the South because he saw the slavery through the lenses of a White man, and because the institution of slavery contained and postponed racial problems that threatened his white dream. If someone asks, condemning him, how else could Lincoln have seen the slaves, the answer is that he could have seen the slaves through the lenses of a "Human being...." But, to repeat, one of the tragedies of American History-and Historiography-is that "Racism" made it impossible for America's greatest icon to leap over the barrier of his skin and make a "Human" connection.

The evidence on this point is overwhelming, and the main witness-Abraham Lincoln, is unimpeachable. Let us track the evidence and the main witness: In 1855 when asked to clarify his position on slavery, Lincoln said frankly, "I now do no more than oppose the extension of slavery." Lincoln said this so often and so loud that it is astounding that some people, even some historians, claim to misunderstand him. He said it in CAPITALS in 1854: "I wish to MAKE and to KEEP the distinction between the EXISTING institution, and the EXTINCTION of it, so broad, and so clear, that no honest man can misunderstand me, and no dishonest one successfully misrepresent me." "We have no right to interfere with slavery in the states. We only want to restrict it to where it is." "I will say here, while upon this subject, that I have no purpose directly or indirectly to interfere with the institution of slavery in the states where it exists. I believe I have no lawful right to do so, and I have no inclination to do so."

"I expressly declared in my opening speech, that I had neither the inclination to exercise, nor the belief in the existence of the right to interfere with the States of Kentucky or Virginia in doing as they pleased with slavery or any other existing institution." Now I have upon all occasions declared as strongly as Judge (Stephen) Douglas against the disposition to interfere with the existing institution of slavery." "We must not disturb slavery in the states where it exists, because the constitution, and the peace of the country, both forbid us." "I have declared a thousand times, and now repeat that, in my opinion, neither the General Governments nor any other power outside of the slave states, can constitutionally or rightfully interfere with slaves or slavery where it already exists." "He asserted positively, and proved conclusively by his former acts and speeches that he was not in favor of interfering with slavery in the States where it exits, nor ever had been."

To be sure that we have made a thorough examination of this corpse, let us re-read the Abraham Lincoln autopsy report.

Abraham Lincoln proved conclusively by his former acts and speeches that he was not in favor of interfering with slavery where it existed, nor ever had been. This statement covers every act and speech of Lincoln's life from his birth in 1809 to the speech he delivered in Greenville, Illinois, on September 13, 1858, in his forty-ninth year and provides most conclusive proof that he had never been in favor of interfering with slavery in the slave states. In all of his speeches, he was not opposed to slavery in Alabama, Georgia, South Carolina, Louisiana, Arkansas, Texas, Maryland, Missouri, Florida, Delaware, Tennessee, North Carolina, Virginia, and Kentucky. What, then, was he opposed to? He was only opposed to the extension of slavery to the territories, to places, Frederick Douglas said, where it was most likely not to go.

This is a pivotal point, one that has been masked by rhetoric and imperfect analysis. For to say, as Lincoln said a thousand times, that one is only opposed to the extension of slavery is to say a thousand times that one is not opposed to slavery where it exists. Based on this autopsy record and findings on the words right out of his own mouth, we can say that the "Great Emancipator" was one of the major supporters of slavery in the United States for at least Fifty-Four of his Fifty-six years.

As we read the autopsy record of what Lincoln said and did, we are struck not only by the contradiction between his words and deeds but also by the contradiction between his premises and conclusions. For it was no more possible for him to be for slavery and against its extension than it is to be for cancer and against its growth.

There was, thus, a deeper and more ominous reason for Lincoln's difficulty on this issue- a reason that rejects the strategic weakness of his whole position on slavery. He was committed-out of racism, out of fear of the unknown-to the cancer itself, believing, as he said publicly, that the cure was worse than the disease and that the enslavement of Blacks was a white "Necessity."

To come right out with it, Lincoln didn't want slavery to end if it meant free Negroes in the United States. Until somebody came up with a magic wand that would make slaves and Negroes disappear, he was content to support the Missouri Compromise, which served as a fence-Lincoln's metaphor- to contain slaves and Negroes in the slave states.

Lincoln, to this writer, appears to be just another "Bigoted" White man who spoke with a "Fork-Tongue," just like the Native-American Indians said he does. In one instance he says that he hates slavery: "I am naturally anti-slavery. If slavery is not wrong, nothing is wrong. I can not remember when I did not so think, and feel." Lincoln also said, "I have always hated slavery, I think as much as any abolitionist." What is failed to be documented about these great Lincoln one liners is that they were always followed by the words: "YET or BUT." Take for example, the statement, "If slavery is not wrong, nothing is wrong." However, when one reads farther you see that It is followed by, as Dr. Bennett explains, the weasel-worded sentence: "And "YET" I have never understood that the presidency conferred upon me an unrestricted right to act officially upon this judgment and feelings."

The presidency had nothing to do with it, for the sentence that followed the 1858 declaration of private citizens Abraham Lincoln said: "I have always hated it (slavery), but I have always been quiet about it until the new era of the introduction of the Nebraska Bill began."

It was quite a technique that Lincoln practiced to perfection. What the left hand gave rhetorically, the right tongue took away practically. The problem, however, was deeper than that. For the difference between what a person says he believes, as Lincoln said, between a horse chestnut and a chestnut horse. This is elementary in law and love affairs, and it is surprising that so many Lincoln enthusiasts forget that a self-serving statement from a person must be tested not only by the statements of other witnesses but also, and more importantly, by what the person does.

Almost all Lincoln defenders violate this rule by making a rhetorical leap from assertion to conclusion. Lincoln, we are told, said he hated slavery. Therefore, he hated slavery. This leap from saying to doing and from wish to fulfillment without the sayer or the wisher doing anything to make the saying and the wishing real is another defining fallacy of Lincoln studies, hiding both the studier and the studied. Lincoln said he hated slavery; he may even have believed that he hated slavery-but there is no evidence that he always hated slavery or that he even had strong feelings about Negro slavery.

No one understood this better than John Hume, who heard Lincoln speak during the Lincoln-Douglas debate and who said that Lincoln "was sentimentally opposed to slavery, but... was afraid of freedom.... He was opposed to slavery more because it was a public nuisance than because of its injustice to the oppressed Black man, whose condition, he did not believe, would be greatly, if at all, benefited by freedoms".

Beyond all this, it is necessary to restore some dignity to language. John Brown hated slavery. He hated slavery so much that his body vibrated like the strings of a violin when he heard the word. Wendell Phillips hated slavery. He hated slavery so much that he seceded from the United States, refusing to practice law or exercise any other function under a government that sanctioned slavery. Harriett Tubman hated slavery. She hated slavery so much that she risked her life repeatedly in guerilla strikes in slavery land. Lincoln was not in their league, either as a hater or lover, and it is a debasement of language and logic to compare his YEA-NAY to their nay. After all, he was forty-five years old when he made his first public statement against (the extension of) slavery in October 1854.

Four years later, in his forty-ninth year, Lincoln said that slavery had always been "A Minor Question" to him until the passage of the Kansas-Nebraska Act. Astonishing. A grown man actually said that. A grown man actually said in the United States of America on July 17,1858, that the question of slavery had been a "Minor Issue" to him and that he thought it was in the "course of ultimate extinction" in the years of Nat Turner, in the years of the escape of some twenty thousand slaves, in the years of the Amistad, in the years of the fight over the right to petition in Congress and the right to deliver the mail in South Carolina, in the years when thousands of Black Men and Women were tortured and lashed and murdered in the South and Illinois and scores of white men and women were jailed in the South for distributing books and saying that all men were created equal."[42]

"To get at Lincoln's true position on slavery, one must situate him first in a historical space in relation to his principal protagonists-not the slaveholders nor even the Confederates, but the slaves. Lincoln was fond of saying, as we have seen that he "had no right and no inclination to keep the slave masters from doing exactly as they pleased with "their" slaves." What did this mean in human terms? What did Lincoln's moral default mean to a runaway slave captured, tortured, and burned at the stake or a woman raped by an overseer or a grown man being lashed by another man who called himself a slave master and who were backed up by the state of South Carolina, the United States of America and politicians like Abraham Lincoln?

The meaning, not to mince words, was that Abraham Lincoln was, by his own words, the "de facto" enemy of the slave. For by repeatedly endorsing the "right" of slave owners to do what they pleased with their slaves, Lincoln was personally and unambiguously endorsing one of the most racist and violent social systems in human history. The key word here and elsewhere is system. The slave system Lincoln supported was a totalitarian system that controlled and conditioned blacks and whites, making men and women in its own image. That system banished freedom of speech, freedom of assembly and freedom of association for blacks and whites in slave states. It "suppressed, free inquiry and discussion, denying by law and by violence in the slave states the right to express other than support for slavery, in private conversations, in print, in the pulpit, and in courts of Justice."

The system searched ships, invaded the mail, banned books and newspapers with sections critical of slavery, raped black women, whipped black men, silenced or exiled white preachers, murdered and tortured black and white resisters. This was the system that Lincoln supported. This was the system that he wanted to last for a long time; and what we are concerned to emphasize here is the internal logic of the slave and racism system, how it had to create Jeffersons and Lincolns in its own image, and how it had to lead to the rotting bones on the slopes of Gettysburg.

Behind the cotton curtain of this system, four million of Abraham Lincoln's fellow "Human Beings" were systematically violated and robbed of their labor and the meaning of their lives. Every one of the Four Million slaves was... a "Human Being", a father like Lincoln, a mother like Mary Todd Lincoln, a child like Robert Todd Lincoln. Every slave was a member of a family, like the families of the people who defended Lincoln's moral default, and every one of them was being violently and systematically destroyed by a system Lincoln was supporting.

To awe these slaves, to beat them into submission and steal their labor and the meaning of their lives, the slave South turned itself into a police state with slave patrols, pass systems and guards at key installations. Behind the inhumane violence stood the power of the United States Government, the massed might of the Church and the University, and all of the presidents from Washington to Lincoln. "Let Us Understand Each Other." We are talking here about the attempted destruction of a whole people for racial reasons. We are talking here about "Genocide." Which is precisely by United Nations definition- the attempted destruction of a whole people or a part of a people because of its race. We are talking here-let there be no misunderstanding- about a crime against "Humanity."

To be fair, one should say that Lincoln, like Jefferson, like Clay, like all of the prototypes and after types in Algeria, South Africa, and Germany, frowned on the autrocities of the system. But to single out isolated atrocities is a trick and a trap, for the system itself was an autrocity that engendered, mandated, demanded violence wherever it existed, producing and reproducing violent men. And although overt violence was not always visible, every relationship between a slave and a slave master or a white representing or supporting slave-masters was an act of violence, not because it was accompanied by force but because it unfolded in a historicity (violence past requiring violence present and violence future) of violence that defined them both, a violence that was written in words, things, institutions, whips, chains, plantations, roads, dogs and even principles, especially the principles articulated by Lincoln, who was always quoting principles, not to free the existing slaves but to justify the violence that kept Blacks in slavery. The overt violence of the system was, thus, only a reflection of a fundamental violence that defined everything and corrupted everything, even and especially the Declaration of Independence.

It is this original violence that gives meaning to the carnival of the violence reported in every slave state and even in free states like Illinois. Solomon Northrup, a free Black who was kidnapped and sold into slavery, said "The crack of the lash, and the shrieking of the slaves (could) be heard from dark till bedtime... any day almost during the entire period of the cotton-picking season."[43]

"Never having opposed slavery where it existed and never having assisted the Abolitionist Movement in any way, Abraham Lincoln came late to the battle, his trumpet giving an uncertain sound. All through the 1830's and 1840's, in the midst of the greatest moral "Crisis" in the history of America, he remained silent and inactive. Evaluating Lincoln's "first considerable literary effort," the Lyceum Address of 1838, Roy P. Basler, one of the pillars of the Lincoln establishment, chided Lincoln for "completely ignoring the greatest moral issue of the day-The Abolition of Slavery."[44]

"While Lincoln slept, thousands of Black and White Americans rose in rebellion and risked stiff fines and prison terms in order to oppose slavery and help runaway slaves. In the beginning of this crusade and for a long time afterward, as I have indicated elsewhere, pioneer Black abolitionists like Samuel E. Cornish and James Forten educated themselves and their white colleagues, most of who were stuck in reformist-gradualist holes. Building on that platform in the 1830s, in the wake of the slave rebellion of Nat Turner and the founding of William Lloyd Garrison's "Liberator" and "The American Anti-slavery Society," Black and white activist created a militant Abolitionist Movement that goaded and provoked a slumbering people into facing "The Greatest Moral Issue of the day."

The Abolitionist accomplished this feat by creating a mass movement remarkably similar to the Freedom Movement of the 1960s. Like the demonstrators of the Sixties, the militant abolitionists pioneered in nonviolent direct action, staging sit-ins and freedom rides. They, like their modern counterparts, marched, demonstrated, and picketed. In the end, the militant abolitionists discovered that the issue of Black freedom is a total issue that raises total questions about the meaning of America. The end result was that the freedom movement of the 1860s, like the Freedom movement of the 1960s, branched out into the issues of Women's rights, sexual freedom, and economic democracy."[45]

"All across the North now, as the future Gettysburg orator stuck his head in the sand along with other Whigs, men and women mobilized against the American government. And it is impossible to take his measure if we don't compare him directly with white men who demonstrated more vision, more courage, and more morality in his own times and on his own terrain.

In Ohio in these years, Salmon P. Chase defended fugitive slaves, attended Black meetings, and created the ideological infrastructure of the political antislavery movement. In Massachusetts, Charles Sumner helped inaugurate the struggle for integrated education.

In Illinois, Owen Lovejoy defied the state and the Federal Government and assisted every slave who came to his door. In a house speech, he told the nation: "Owen Lovejoy lives at Princeton, Illinois, three quarters of a mile east of the village; and he aids every fugitive that comes to his door and asks.... Thou invisible demon of slavery... I bid you defiance in the name of my God." What was Lincoln doing all this time? He was, as usual, sitting on the fence, telling everybody how much he loved the Declaration of Independence and expressing regrets that it was not, unfortunately, applicable to the real world, or real Blacks in Illinois, or South Carolina."[46]

"Lincoln's failure to respond to the defining moral "Crisis" of his age foreshadowed one of the most agonizing questions of the modern world: What is the duty of an oppressor or a member of an oppressing group when his group is responsible for a situation of total oppression? What should an oppressor or a person identified with the oppressing group do in a situation of collective evil sanctioned by the violence of the state? Since there is no possibility of acting morally short of a destruction of the situation, which makes him or her illegitimately, privileged, no matter what he or she does, where should the oppressor or the person identified with the oppressing group stand? Should he or she abandoning all others stand with the oppressed, as Wendell Phillips and John Brown did, or should he or she stand with his group, whatever the evil? Abraham Lincoln said slavery was evil, perhaps the greatest of all evils. Yet he consciously and deliberately chose whiteness, slavery, man hunting, and evil. What does that tell us about his morals, and ours? American moralists, who are famous for choosing their victim's -and their morals- and who have 20/20 vision in Germany, Russia, and China but are struck blind and dumb in the face of the moral failure of Lincoln or Robert E. Lee, never get around to posing these questions. One reads their books in vain for some light on the moral dilemmas four hundred years of Slave Trade and two hundred years of slavery, concentration camps, and apartheid prisons have bequeathed to us."[47]

"Congress passed the Fugitive Slave Law on Wednesday, September 18,1850. What happened next was a national crime, never exasperated, seldom if ever discussed. A Liberator dispatch from Pittsburgh, published on October 4, 1850, said, "nearly all the waiters in the hotels have fled to Canada. Sunday, thirty fled; on Monday, forty; on Tuesday, fifty; on Wednesday, thirty.... They went in large bodies armed with pistols and bowie knives, determined to die rather than be captured."

The same thing happened in Illinois, where Lincoln and others urged citizens to go out into the street and help marshals capture men, women and children and return them to slavery.

Appalled by the moral myopia of whites like Lincoln and terrified by the increasing boldness of slave catchers backed by the power of the United States Government, abolitionists, Black and White, told Blacks without authenticated papers to flee for their lives because there was not enough morality in the United States to keep men from capturing them and returning them into slavery.

Harriet Tubman spoke for slaves all over America when she said that she "wouldn't trust Uncle Sam with (her) people no longer" and that the Fugitive Slave Law made it necessary to take fugitive slaves directly to Canada without stopping in the United States.

Unquestionably the high/low point of the official U. S. Racism, the law denied runaway slaves the right of trial by jury. Under its provisions, a Black person charged with the "crime" of escaping from slavery could not even testify on his own behalf in star chamber proceedings which gave the judge ten dollars if he ruled in his/her favor. This was a legal obscenity and a personal threat to every Black, slave or free; for any Black, even a Black who had lived in a Northern community for years, could be accused, tried and hustled off to slavery or the auction block before his family or friends could intervene.

Viewed from the vantage point of the slave, the Fugitive Slave Law was a hysterical response that doomed the system it was designed to defend by, first, nationalizing slavery and, secondly, by personalizing slavery, forcing every White, under pain of severe penalties, to choose between being an accomplice of slaveholders and slave catchers or a rebel against the Constitution and the United States Government. Lincoln readily accommodated himself to this dilemma, choosing slaveholders and slave catchers in beautiful language that is still admired by people who have already decided in their own lives for or against fugitives, Black or White. Other whites, some more conservative than Lincoln, said nothing could make them dirty their hands by complying with this law."[48]

"After forty-five years of silence and yea and nay, Abraham Lincoln, who would go down in history as the greatest antislavery fighter of all time, finally found his voice and stood up in public and made a speech about slavery? This was an extreme act for Lincoln; and in 1854, as in 1863, he was pushed and pulled into glory. The triggering mechanism in 1854 was the passage of the Kansas-Nebraska Act, which not only reopened the question of the extension of slavery to the territories of the West but also, and more importantly on a personal level, made it possible for Lincoln to revive a political career that was in terminal arrest.

By a paradoxical act of political poetry, the architect of this act, which virtually repealed the Missouri Compromise, ending the age of compromises, was Lincoln's old nemesis, Senator Stephen Arnold Douglas of the state of Illinois. Douglas was a racist, and a virulent racist at that, but one should give the devil his due and say at once before passing on that the friends of freedom owe almost as much as they owe Lincoln.

By ripping the Band-Aid off the festering sore of slavery and by opening or threatening to open the West and perhaps even the North to slavery, Douglas and the forces allied with him unwittingly made it possible to ignore the question everybody had been trying to ignore since slave owner Thomas Jefferson attended by a favorite slave- Robert Hemings, the brother of his future mistress, Sally Hemings-sat down in a room in Philadelphia and wrote a document that said "All Men Were Created Equal."

From that day in 1776 until 1863, the domestic politics of America had revolved around a series of compromises- the Compromise of 1787, the Compromise of 1820, the Compromise of 1850- that tried to settle a problem that could not be settled with words, the problem of the huge and growing gap between the words Jefferson wrote and the reality America lived. Following Jefferson, Henry Clay, John C. Calhoun, and Daniel Webster, all of who solved the "Problem" forever, Douglas came forward in 1854 with a tricky formula that proposed once again to solve the "Problem" forever. Douglas called his magic wand "Popular Sovereignty." Under it provisions, White settlers in a new territory could decide whether they wanted slavery by voting it up or down in a referendum.

If Douglas hoped by this to solve the white problem, he was mistaken. For popular sovereignty made almost everybody mad and set in motion forces that led directly to the Civil War. Future consequences apart, Douglas's folly had immediate consequences, destroying the foundations of Lincoln's beloved Whig Party and forcing the political realignment that gave birth to the Republican Party. Lincoln's party, the only party really that he ever had, died because it tried to evade the biggest "Problem" of the day, and the fact that Lincoln supported it so long and never really left it is additional evidence, if additional evidence is needed, of his limited historical vision.

Beyond its effect on social forces, the Kansas-Nebraska Act had enormous personal consequences, awakening Abraham Lincoln from his long deep sleep and reactivating the feud between him and Stephen A. Douglas. For eighteen years, every since they sparred for the first time in the Illinois legislature, the two men had been circling each other warily, like boxers, bobbing and weaving. During these years, they had competed for offices, honors, and hands of at least one woman. Mrs. Lincoln apart, Douglas had taken almost every match, outdistancing his less charismatic rival and going on to Washington where he became one of the leading men of the nation. He was on his way to the presidency when hubris and the hope of political and economic gain led him into the dead-end trap of the Kansas-Nebraska Act, which made it possible for anti-slavery forces, led by Senator Chase and Senator Sumner, to frighten and inflame the North.

Antislavery leaders had been trying unsuccessfully since the Compromise of 1850 and passage of the Fugitive Slave Law to arouse the North by stressing the threats to Negro right and the basic guarantees of the Constitution.

But the majority of Northern Whites, Lincoln above all, remained remarkably unconcerned about the Negro rights and the threats to the Constitution until Douglas came forward with a double-edged gift that seemed to be a direct threat not to Blacks but to White farmers lusting after Western land and big entrepreneurs chafing under the restrictions of the slave power."[49]

The whole argument- and Lincoln's and Douglas's fate- revolved around the being of the Negro, not because Lincoln or Douglas had any particular interest in the Negro but because neither could defend his personal or political interest without defending or attacking Negroes. That point has somehow eluded modern interpreters, but Lincoln understood it clearly, and said it clearly: "If we admit that a Negro is not a man... it is right to allow the South to take their peculiar institution with them and plant it upon the virgin soil of Kansas and Nebraska. If the Negro is not a man, it is consistent to apply the sacred right of popular sovereignty to the question as to whether the people of the territories shall or shall not have slavery; but if the Negro, upon soil where slavery is not legalized by law and sanctioned by custom, is a man, then there is not even the shadow of popular sovereignty in allowing the first settlers upon such soil to decide whether it shall be right in all future time to hold men in bondage there."[50]

To Lincoln, who repeatedly defined the phrase in a moralistic context that included the Negro's morals, intellect, courage, working habits, "and funny bones," the difference was biological. Not only that, God was involved in it. This was the theology of a little-noticed section of his July 10, 1858, speech in Chicago. Responding as usual to Douglas, he said: "I protest, now and forever, against that counterfeit logic which presumes that because that I do not want a Negro woman for a slave, I do necessarily want her for a wife (sic). My understanding is that I need not have her for either, but as God made us separate, we can leave one another alone and do one another much good thereby."[51]

Although Lincoln believed that Blacks were inferior and actively opposed equal rights, some commentators, even some Black commentators, say he was not anti-Negro. Conceding his bias, these analysts say Lincoln was not a vicious or malevolent man and that he was personally decent. The argument, in other words, is that he was a moderate and that he was only a little bit prejudiced.

Does this change the equation? NO! For one can't be a little bit prejudice, anymore than one can be a little bit pregnant. And you can't say that a person is a supporter of White Supremacy ethic but that he is not all that bad because he does not lynch Black Men and take the bread out of the mouths of Black children and women; for these vitalities, to paraphrase Fanon, are already on the horizon and are implicit in active commitment to a system of White Supremacy that requires the harming and liquidation of a certain number of Blacks and the appropriation of their bread and resources.

Given this record, it is no wonder that abolitionists were less than enthusiastic about Lincoln's election in November 1860. Frederick Douglas said the Republican victory was a step in the right direction but that the president-elect, based on his white-dress rehearsal in Illinois, was questionable. "With the single exception of the question of slavery extension," Frederick Douglas said, "Mr. Lincoln proposes no measure, which can bring him into antagonistic collision with traffickers of human flesh, either in the States or in the District of Columbia.... Slavery will be as safe, and safer in the Union under such a president, than it can be under any president of a Southern Confederacy."

Wendell Phillips agreed, saying Lincoln was "not an abolitionist, hardly an anti-slavery man." To emphasize that point, Phillips questioned an imaginary Lincoln in a public speech: "Do you believe, Mr. Abraham Lincoln, that the Negro is your political and social equal, or ought to be? Not a bit of it. "Do you believe he should sit on juries? Never. "Do you think he should vote? Certainly not. "Should he be considered a citizen? I tell you frankly, no. "Do you think that when the Declaration of Independence says, 'All men are created equal,' it intends the political equality of blacks and whites? No, Sir."

It has been said that the election changed Lincoln and that he went to Washington with a new set of racial ideas and attitudes. But this retrospective alibi overlooks the whole orientation of the man's life. Once again the best authority on the racial views of Abraham Lincoln at that stage in his life is Abraham Lincoln, who interrupted his packing in December 1860 to reply to a letter from editor Henry J. Raymond. Raymond had enclosed a letter from a Mississippi legislator named William Smedes, who contended on the basis of erroneous reports that Lincoln was a wild-eyed abolitionist who made an equal rights speech to a meeting of Negroes. "What a very mad-man your correspondent, Smedes is," Lincoln replied on December 18. "Mr. Lincoln is not pledged to the ultimate extinction (sic) of slavery; does not hold the black man to be the equal of the whites, unqualifiedly as Mr. S. States it; and never did stigmatize their white people (in other words, slaveholders) as immortals and unchristian...." As for the speech to Negroes, Lincoln said: I was never in a meeting of Negroes in my Life..."

Thus, Abraham Lincoln, at the end of his "prelude to greatness." And to understand where he was, and where he was tending, we can do no better than to consult his Peoria Declaration, which pointed both to his past and his future. The gist of the speech, from our perspective and from the perspective of Lincoln, who quoted it repeatedly, was in a paragraph that begins with a blow to the sensibilities of Southern white and an acknowledgment of how hard it was to get rid of slavery "in any satisfactory way."

"When Southern people tell us they are no more responsible for the origin of slavery, than we; I acknowledge the fact. When it is said that the institution exists, and that it is very difficult to get rid of it, in any satisfactory way, I can understand and appreciate the saying. I surely will not blame them for not doing what I should not know how to do myself.

If all earthly power were given to me, I should not know what to do, as to the existing institution." Having made that extraordinary confession, Lincoln conceded that he had a few unsystematic ideas:

"My first impulse would be to free all the slaves, and send them to Liberia to their own native land. But a moment's reflection would convince me, that whatever of high hope, (as I think there is) there may be in this, in the long run, its sudden execution is impossible. If they were all landed there in a day, they would all perish in the next ten days; and there are not surplus shipping and surplus money enough in the world to carry them there in many times ten days.

What then should be done?

"Free them all, and keep them among us as underlings? Is it quite certain that this betters their condition? I think I would not hold one in slavery, at any rate; yet the point is not clear enough for me to denounce people upon." (The authors italics and his remembrance of the very different sentence, "as I would not be a slave, so (I think?) I would not be a master.")

What next? "Free them, and make them politically and socially, our equals? My own feelings will not admit of this; and if mine would, we well know that those of the great mass of white people will not. (Sic) We cannot, then, make them equals. I will not undertake to judge our brethren of the South."

The fundamental racial and political characteristics of Abraham Lincoln are clearly defined in this passage: his sympathetic identification with his White" brethren" of the South, not the Black people of the South; his support of slavery where it existed; his opposition to equal rights for blacks; his belief in gradualism and colonization; and his lack of faith in the ability of African-Americans.

Lincoln Said, "If all earthly power were given to me, I should not know what to do, as to the existing institution of slavers. However, if all the earthly power had been given to the average person, Black or White, conservative or militant, he or she would probably have freed the slaves, if only in the imagination. If all earthly powers had been given to me, I would have freed the slaves immediately and provided forty acres of land and a mule to each head of household. I would have additionally used all earthly power and any means necessary to create conditions to ensure that the sons and daughters of former slaves and the sons and daughters of former slave owners lived together equally and peaceably. That's what I would have done. What would you have done? What would the Lincoln biographer, who always overlooks that sentence, have done? Abraham Lincoln said that if all earthly power had been given to him, he wouldn't have known what to do. Let the record show that he was telling the truth. Earthly power, or what passed for all earthly power, was given to him - and he didn't know what to do."[52]

"Lincoln grew during the war- but he didn't grow much. On every issue vital to Blacks- On emancipation, confiscation, suffrage, and the use of Black soldiers- he was the essence of the White Supremacist with good intentions. Long before Fort Sumter, and even long before his inauguration, he told White Southerners that he had been misunderstood and that he would execute the Fugitive Slave Law "with more fidelity than any Southern (White) man they could possibly find."[53]

"President Abraham Lincoln wrote a letter to an old friend, Alexander Stephens of Georgia, asking: "Do the people of the South really entertain fears that a Republican Administration would, directly, or indirectly, interfere with their slaves, or with them, about their slaves?

If they do, I wish to assure you, as once a friend, and still, I hope, not an enemy, that there is no cause for such fears." In fact, he said, "the South would be in no more danger in this respect, than it was in the days of Washington."[54]

On Thursday, March 21, 1861, seventeen days after Lincoln's Inaugural Address, Alexander H. Stephens, now vice president of the Confederacy... defined the Confederacy as the first state founded on a Racist-Fascist foundation of racial supremacy. In a speech delivered at Savannah, Georgia, on March 21, 1861, Stephens, a contemporary report said, "avowed, in very explicit terms, not only that slavery was the cause of the revolt, but that the insurgents had taken their position of armed hostility to the government in direct opposition to the opinions and the purposes of the founders of the republic, the framers of the Constitution, including those from the slave states."[55]

The "Corner-Stone" of the confederacy was the idea that "African slavery as it exists among us" is the proper status of the Negro in our form of civilization." This was in contrast to the ideas of the White founding fathers, which said the same thing in fact while saying that all men were created equal. Stephens and the people that he represented were tired of Jefferson and Lincoln and their word games: Stephens wrote," Our new government is founded upon exactly the opposite ideas; its foundations are laid, its corner-stone rests, upon the great truth that the Negro is not equal to the White man; that slavery, subordination to the superior race, is his natural and moral condition. This, our new government, is the first in the history of the world based upon this great physical, philosophical, and moral truth." Few modern scholars notice the similarities between the "Third Reich" and the "Confederacy," and almost no one arraigns it or its leaders for "Crimes" against Humanity."[56]

"The Firing on Fort Sumter changed all plans and pleas, and we ought to pause for a moment to adjust to the new climate. Abraham Lincoln was fifty-two years old in that month, Frederick Douglas was forty-four, Wendell Phillips was fifty, Thaddeus Stevens was sixty-nine, and Charles Sumner was fifty. There were 27,000,000 white in America, according to the 1860 census, and 4,441,830 Blacks. The overwhelming majority of Blacks were slaves, 3,953,760, compared to 488,070 free Blacks.

Blacks were in the majority in South Carolina, Mississippi and probably Louisiana. The largest Black population in the free states was in Pennsylvania (56,949), New York (49,005), and Ohio (36,673). There were only 7,628 Blacks in Illinois, and about one thousand in Chicago, which has an African-American population of more than one million today."[57]

"As the war continued and as Northern casualties mounted, the same damn three fellows and their allies put events to use and mobilized public pressure Lincoln couldn't ignore. Delegation after delegation waited on the president and demanded that he free the slaves and arm them.

Lincoln parried the pressure with heat and conviction, citing constitutional, political, and military reasons to justify his anti-emancipation stand. Lincoln usually expressed his opinion of emancipation in a trouble but polite tone, but he could be pushed across the border of politeness.

When Edward L. Pierce urged Lincoln to adopt a more enlightened policy, he exploded and denounced "the itching to get niggers into our lives." Other White House visitors reported that the mere mention of the word slave made Lincoln nervous. The traditional image of Lincoln is of a harried and large-hearted man fending off "extremists of the left and the right" only to emerge at the precise psychological moment to do what he had always wanted to do. This image clashes, unfortunately, with incontrovertible evidence that sudden, and general emancipation was never Lincoln's policy and that he feared Black freedom for social and economic reasons.

It was not fear of emancipation but the fear of what would happen afterward that palsied Lincoln's hands. He was terrified by the implications of freeing four million Blacks suddenly and generally, and he said repeatedly that it was his considered judgment that" gradual, and not sudden, emancipation, is better for all." Critics said that Lincoln feared amalgamation, black and white competition over jobs, and Black violence. Hofstadter said he was always thinking "primarily" of the interest of White workers, and not the interest of Black workers. But in this case, as in others, the personal and the political, as Hofstadter also said, intersected in Lincoln, who shared and magnified the fears he projected onto poor whites. This explains in part the intensity of his feelings about deporting Blacks, a "fantastic idea" Hofstadter said, that "grew logically out of a caste psychology in a competitive labor market...."

Logically or not, it also grew out of a deep-seated fear of Black violence. Even as a young politician, Lincoln had keen anxiety about a slave revolt and suggested that he would stop opposing the extension of slavery and support the violence of slave owners if slaves rebelled. Lincoln said "We should never knowingly lend ourselves, directly or indirectly, to prevent Slavery from dying a natural death," adding significantly: "Of course I am not now considering what would be our duty, in cases of insurrection among slaves."

Lincoln believed that the "white people" organized as the state of South Carolina and white people organized as the United States gave him the duty and moral right and the moral obligation to violently put down a slave insurrection and keep Blacks in slavery. And why did Lincoln believe or seem to believe that if it came to a shooting between (Black) slaves and (White) slave owners, it would be his duty to shoot the slaves? The answer of course is that Lincoln gave himself the rights-duty-obligation structure by choosing to be white and by establishing an un-transcendable limit of whiteness within himself and his world.

To gain some perspective on this phenomenon, which is passed over in silence by almost all historians, one has to confront Lincoln with the diametrically opposite view of his contemporaries, David Walker, Nat Turner, Henry Highland Garrett, Denmark Vesey, and Wendell Phillips, who anticipated modern analysts like Jean-Paul Sabre and Frantz Fanon, saying that there never was any other violence, except slaveholder violence not only advanced humanity but was itself an expression of the highest octave of humanity.

"I do not shrink," Phillips said in Boston's Music Hall on February 17,1861, "from the toast with which Dr. Johnson flavored his Oxford Port -"Success to the first insurrection of the Blacks in Jamaica!" " Phillips said his support of slave violence was dictated by "the highest of Humanity." adding: "I know what anarchy is. I know what civil war is. I can imagine the scenes of blood through which a rebellious slave population must march to their rights. They are dreadful. And yet, I do not know, that, to an enlightened mind, a scene of civil war is any more sickening than the thought of a hundred and fifty years of slavery. Take the broken hearts; the bereaved mothers; the infant, wrung from the hands of its parents; the husband and wife torn asunder; every right trodden under foot, the blighted hopes, the imbruted "Souls," the darkened and degraded millions, sunk below the level of intellectual life, melted sensuality, herded with beasts, who have walked over the burning marl of Southern slavery to their graves; and where is the battle-field, however ghastly, that is not white, -compared with the blackness of that darkness which has brooded over the "Carolinas" for two hundred years?

What appalled Phillips was not the possibility of Black violence but the continuation, to change Phillips's palette, of the legalized insurrection of slavery and the white violence of slave states like South Carolina.

The difference between Lincoln and Phillips on this issue was fundamental. Phillips said he preferred a Black insurrection "which frees the slave in ten years to slavery for a century." Lincoln preferred slavery for a century or even forever to a Black insurrection that would have freed the slaves in ten. This racial fear played a major role in the formation of his war policy, especially his opposition to immediate emancipation and the use of Black soldiers."[58]

It was an old American failure. Jefferson started it, and it was the duty of Lincoln, it was the duty of a great leader... to tell the people that they couldn't be a whore and a virgin at the same time and love slavery and liberty at the same time."[59]

"The great educator Benjamin E. Mays said that not failure but low aim is sin. Lincoln, especially in the first years of his administration, aimed low, and from all sides, from antislavery advocates and proslavery advocates came a recurring refrain: there was no purpose, no backbone, no "stiffness" in him. Lincoln specialists, who manage somehow to make a virtue out of every Lincoln vice, say he must have been doing something right if everybody, or almost everybody, thought what he was doing was wrong.

This argument assumes that there is no moral difference between being moderately in favor of slavery or moderately in favor of freedom. It ignores, moreover, the fact that the criticism came from cabinet members, conservatives, abolitionists, cronies, and congressional Leaders."[60]

"Since Lincoln seemed to be confused about the nature of the conflict, Joseph Medill of the Chicago Tribune attacked Lincoln's conservative posture on freeing and arming Blacks. In 1862, medial sent a letter to Lincoln telling him, "Mr. Lincoln, for God's sake and your country's sake rise to the realization of our awful national peril. You, the country and I know that this is a slaveholder's rebellion. "Slavery," he told Secretary Chase, "is at the bottom of the whole trouble. The revolt was inaugurated to expand and strengthen the system, to give the oligarchy more domains, more slaves and the unrestricted powers of government to defend and foster the institution.... And until the Administration sees the contest in its true light the blood of loyal men will be shed in vain and the war will come to naught." Lincoln, he said had exhibited "some very weak and foolish traits of character."

Reading the letters and newspapers of that day, one is struck by the unanimity of opinion and by the withering terms friends and foes used to describe Lincoln. He was called a "Wet Rag" by one critic and a "Tortoise" and a "Slow Coach" by another. Iowa Republicans said he reminded them of Phillip II of Spain, "Who did not understand his time any better than Lincoln does. The consensus comparison was Louis XVI, the inept French King who lost his head in the French Revolution. Some said that the war was too much for Lincoln, saying that "a better man and a better president might have won the war in half the time and with half the blood and treasure."[61]

"The new president's racial policy was based on the wildest idea ever presented to the American people by an American president. What Lincoln proposed officially and publicly was that the United States government buy the slaves and deport them to Africa or South America. This was not a passing whim. In five major policy declarations, including two states of the Union addresses and the Preliminary Emancipation Proclamation, the sixteenth president of the United States publicly and officially called for the deportation of Blacks.

On countless other occasions, in conferences with cronies, Democratic and Republican leaders, and high government officials, he called for colonization of Blacks or aggressively promoted colonization by private and official acts.

If Lincoln had completed his second term, his friend Henry Whitney said, he would "have still made more heroic (sic) efforts, looking to that end." Colonization, Whitney said, was close to the heart of Lincoln's policy, for "he was not only of the opinion that this nation could not remain partly free and partly a slave nation; but he was equally pronounced in his belief that the white and African races could not occupy the same nation in peace."

Fredrick Douglas   8

Abolitionist, Activist, Social Pioneer

In 1862, largely at President Lincoln's urging, Congress appropriated $600,000, a sum desperately needed, Hume said, to prosecute the war, to begin the colonization process but balked at the hundreds of millions of dollars Lincoln officially requested in his 1862 State of the Union Address, which ended with the famous words, "We cannot escape history."

Nobody tried harder than Lincoln to escape the history he couldn't escape. For he never gave up this wildly impractical idea-it was, in fact, the only racial solution he ever had- and under his leadership, almost without notice, certainly without the notice of latter-day historians, "Racial Cleansing" became, 72 years before the Third Reich, 133 years before Bosnia, the "Cornerstone" of president Lincoln's policy.

"Almost from the commencement of this administration, Secretary of the Navy Gideon Wells said, "the subject of deporting the colored race has been discussed." On Wednesday, April 10, two days before the firing on Fort Sumter, Lincoln interrupted his war gaming to confer with Ambrose W. Thompson, a shady character who would play a major role in the administration's colonization efforts.

At this conference or at a later conference, Thompson outlined a plan for transporting Blacks to a Panamanian isthmus where his Chiriqui Improvement Company had a contract, he said, to mine coal. Wells and others told Lincoln that Thompson was a hustler and that the contract was questionable at best, but Lincoln bought the idea and asked Secretary Wells to follow up.

"As early as May 1861," Welles told his diary, "a great pressure was made upon me to enter into a coal contract with this company. The president was in earnest in the matter, wished to send the Negroes out of the country."[62]

On all other issues relating to Blacks, on emancipation and the use of Blacks soldiers, Lincoln was slow, tardy, hesitant, but on the issue of separation and Black deportation he was passionate and impetuous, brushing aside all objections, conferring with questionable characters, sending aides abroad and messages to the foreign offices of colonial powers.

In December 1861, he discussed the possibility of sending high-level mission to Chiriqui, and it was evident from the instructions he prepared... that the president was motivated by a sense of extreme urgency."

As one examines the autopsy record, and review the comments of men who worked with Lincoln day by day, one is struck by the repetition of the same phrases: The president "was in earnest." "He was persistent." He was "motivated by a sense of extreme urgency." He "wished to send the Negroes away."

Like most nineteenth-century racists, Lincoln pretended to believe that Blacks had to live in tropical climes, although he knew it required marshals and the massed white population to keep slaves from running away to the Arctic Zone of Chicago, which was founded by a free Black man, Jean Baptiste Pointe DuSable, more than fifty years before the Lincolns arrived in Illinois.

Not only freed slaves but also free Black citizens were scheduled for removal under Lincoln's plan. It "might be well to consider, too," he said in his first state of the Union Address, "whether the free African people already in the United States could not, so far as individuals may desire, be included in such colonization." Whenever Lincoln remembered or whenever he was prompted, he always added the phrase, "so far as individuals may desire." But he knew-he had to know- that his official announcements in favor of Negro removal played into the hands of racist forces who were prepared to do anything to destroy African-Americans.

Many believed that Lincoln's proposal belonged in an "Insane Asylum." Among these was Adam Gurowski, the expatriate Polish count who criticized Lincoln's views from his State Department position. "Those colonizers," he wrote in his diary, "forgot that if they should export 100,000 persons a year, an equal number will be yearly born at home, not to speak of other impossibilities. If carried on a small scale, this scheme amounts to nothing; and on a grand scale it is altogether impossible, besides being as stupid as it is recklessly cruel. Only those persons insist on colonization who hate or dread emancipation." Gurowski said that colonization was harmful to the best interest of Blacks and white, Northerners and Southerners, for "exportation of the four millions of slaves (would deprived) the country of laborers, which a century of emigration cannot fill again. All these fools ought to be sent to a Lunatic Asylum! To export the emancipated would be equivalent to devastation of the South, to its transformation into a wilderness."

Another man who believed colonization belonged in an "Insane Asylum" was Wendell Phillips, who said: "Colonize the Blacks! A man might as well colonize his hands; or when the robber enters his house, he might as well colonize his revolver...." Phillips added: "We are none of us, as a nation, fit for the lunatic asylum, and until we are, we never shall colonize four million of workers."

Both Phillips and Douglas said that the Union needed Blacks not only for the war but also and, perhaps more importantly, for the peace. "The Negro," Phillips said, for 'Two Hundred and Forty-Four Years" has been the basis of our commerce, the root of our politics, the pivot of our pulpit, the inspiration of almost all that is destined to live in our literature." Over and above that, he said, the destiny of America was linked to the destiny of the Negro, who was the only democratic force in that section. Although a handful of Blacks supported colonization for reasons markedly different from the reasons advanced by Lincoln, the overwhelming majority of Blacks repudiated Lincoln's vision. Most agreed with Frederick Douglas, who said "the destiny of the (African-American) ... is the destiny of America....

The allurements of providence seem to make the Black Man of America the open book out of which the American people are to learn lessons of wisdom, power and goodness-more sublime and glorious than any yet attained by the nations of the old or the new world."

So: "We are here, and here we are likely to be. To imagine that we should ever be eradicated is absurd and ridiculous... We shall neither die out, nor be driven out; but shall go with this people, either as a testimony against them, or as an evidence in their favor throughout their generations..."[63]

"It began, if processes of this magnitude can be said to have a beginning, on Monday, December 2, 1861, with the opening of the second session of the Thirty-Seventh Congress, which was the second milestone, after Bull Run, on the road to emancipation, and the beginning of the end of slavery in the United States.

"At this session," a contemporary report said, "the legislation of congress assumed a new aspect. Two positions were taken, which became the basis of the action of the controlling majority in that body on all subjects relating to the troubles of the country."

The first position was that slavery was the cause of the troubles of the country. The second was that "the government was engaged in a struggle for its existence, and could, therefore, restore to any measure which a case of self-defense would justify."

What all this meant, as a practical matter was that the Thirty-seventh Congress, pushed by the Bull Run dialectic and pulled by the demands of constituents had moved to the hard-war position defined earlier by anti-slavery leaders. Because the Thirty-Seventh Congress saw further than Lincoln, and because it probed deeper, it became the emancipating congress and the leader of the Republican Party, Abraham Lincoln, and the American people.

Adam Gurowski said the Thirty-seventh Congress destroyed the foundations of slavery in the United States, changed the direction of the country and "whipped" Lincoln into glory. Furthermore, the Thirty-seventh Congress was one of the greatest legislative assemblies in world history.

Senator Lyman Trumbull of Illinois, a major architect of the Thirteenth Amendment, distinguished himself in the legal struggle against the Fugitive Slave Law and played a decisive role in turning the war against slavery while president Lincoln was trying to save slavery.

It was Trumbull who moved the debate to a new level by giving notice immediately after the organization of the senate "of his intention to introduce a bill for the confiscation of the property of rebels and giving freedom to the persons they hold in slavery." This bill, a milestone in the history of emancipation was announced on Monday, December 2, 1861, and dominated debate in Congress until its passage in July 1862 pushed Lincoln to the brink of reality.

It was on this note that Congress and the Union crossed over into 1862, marching to the sound of different drummers. Lincoln was deaf to the new music, but Stevens heard it and announced it, rising in the House on the twenty-second day of the New Year to speak in favor of his resolution. The burden of his speech was simple: "The Black Man... is really the mainstay of the war," and "must be made our allies" by a policy of "Universal Emancipation."

"Prejudice 'may be shocked," he said, Weak minds startled, weak nerves may tremble, but they must hear and adopt it. Those who now furnish the means of the war, but who are the natural enemies of slaveholders, must be made our allies. "Universal Emancipation" must be proclaimed to all"

The main problem of the Lincoln administration was that "it lacked the determination and the invincible courage that was inspired in the Revolution by the grand idea of Liberty, Equality, and the Rights of Man."

Like Sumner in the Senate, like Douglas and Phillips on the stump, like Garrison in the "Liberator," like men and women all over, like Harriett Tubman, George Washington Williams, Sojourner Truth, and the great men of the state of Illinois, John Jones, Joseph Medial, and Governor Yates, all of whom demanded a new birth of freedom. Congressman Stevens said the basic issue of the hour was the issue Alexander Stephens had defined, the issue Lincoln was trying to avoid, the issue of the concrete meaning of the Declaration. The Confederates, Stephens said, had "rebelled for no redress of grievances, but to establish a slave oligarcy which would repudiate the odious doctoring of the Declaration of Independence, and justify the establishment of an empire admitting the principle of king, lords and slaves."

Stevens was shocked by the failure of Lincoln to address that issue. "Our statesmen, unlike the men of the Revolution, do not seem to know how to touch the hearts of freemen and rouse them to battle. No declaration of the great objects of government, no glorious sound of universal liberty has gone forth from the capital..." Even worse, Stevens said, Union generals were hunting and capturing men and women and returning them to slavery.

"We have put a sword into one hand of our generals and shackles into the other," he said, adding: "Freemen are not inspired by such mingled music."

Stevens was talking, lest we forget, about a moral vacuum in the heart of Abraham Lincoln. The problem, he was saying, without naming Lincoln, was a president who was pursing a mistaken policy of trying to save the old Union instead of fighting for a new birth of freedom. "Oh," Stevens said, "for six months' resurrection in the flesh of stern old Jackson!... He would abolish slavery as the cause in support of the insurrection; He would arm the free people of color, as he did at New Orleans; he would march into the heart of slavedom to put weapons into every freed man's hands... (and) end the war by wholesale hanging of the leaders."

The only solution, Stevens said, was a struggle to give new meaning to the Declaration of Independence: "Let the people Know that this Government is fighting not only to enforce a sacred compact, but to carry out to final perfection the principles of the Declaration of Independence, which its framers expected would long since have been fulfilled on this continent, and the blood of every freeman, would boil with enthusiasm, and his nerves be strengthened for holy warfare."

The war, in other words, was an unparallel "invitation to "strike the chains from Four Million "Human Beings," to create them MEN; to extinguish slavery on this whole continent; to wipe out... the most hateful and infernal blot that ever disgraced the escutcheon of man...." By resurrecting the principles of the Declaration of Independence, Stevens posed a direct challenge to Lincoln, who believed that "the white man's charter" was an abstract document that didn't apply to any concrete situation involving Blacks and Whites. Who was right? Insofar as that question relates to Stevens's statement about what the framers, Jefferson in particular, expected" would have long since have been fulfilled on this continent," I believe Lincoln was right, for Jefferson and Lincoln shared the same dream of deporting Negroes and creating a "White Eden."

But since words have their own logic, the leaders of the Thirty-Seventh Congress were right above Lincoln in calling for the redemption of a compact which bonded all men (and all women) and which could not be repudiated except by adopting the racist formula that tempted Lincoln, the formula that only white men are full men.

All this was clear as anything needed to be to abolitionist leader Wendell Phillips, who went up and down the North, denouncing Lincoln and his generals and calling for total war. Unquestionably the greatest white orator of his time and perhaps of anytime, the abolitionist leader became a force above the government and did more as a private citizen to mobilize people for emancipation, observers said, than anyone in government, including Abraham Lincoln.

From the beginning, Phillips linked 1861 and 1776, the Civil war and the Revolutionary War, the struggle for Black freedom and the struggle for white freedom. From the beginning he identified the slave with John Hancock, emancipation with the Fourth of July. Unlike Lincoln, who celebrated a successful revolution, Phillips recalled a botch revolution. Unlike Lincoln, who celebrated the triumph of the fathers, Phillips said the Civil War was "the inevitable fruit of our fathers' faithless compromise in 1787." The central meaning of the Civil War, he said, was the struggle to fulfill and complete the abortive revolution of 1776."[64]

As the waves of discontent rose higher and higher, and as millions of dollars and tens of thousands of Northern youths disappeared into the bottomless pit of the Virginia peninsula, the Thirty-Seventh Congress rejected the idea of compensating rebels and passed a series of laws that destroyed the foundation of slavery in America.

The first act, an additional Article of War proposed by Charles Sumner, forbade Union officers to return fugitive slaves "to any such persons to whom such service or labor is claimed to be due." There then followed the landmark District of Columbia Emancipation Act, which Sumner called "the first installment of that great "DEBT" which we all owe to an enslaved race." Lincoln opposed what Sumner called "the first practical triumph of freedom "and refused to sign the bill until an old friend could leave the city with his slaves. When Senator Orville Browning of Illinois visited the White House on Monday night, April 14, Lincoln told him that "he regretted the (D.C. Emancipation) bill had been passed... that now families would at once be deprived of cooks, stable boys...."

Once more we are brought face to face with the Lincoln everybody tries to hide, the Lincoln who had reactionary ideas about who would be "benefited by freedom" and who wanted to save slavery, or as much of it as he could, because he didn't want to deprive families- he meant white families, he meant well-to-do white families- of their '"cooks, stable boys etc" and "they of their protectors without any provisions for them." While Lincoln held the District bill, "poor slaves were in concealment, Sumner said, "waiting for the day of freedom to come out from their hiding places." While they waited, Summer went to the White House to urge speed, astonished "that the President could postpone the approval a single night." Another visitor was Bishop Daniel A. Payne of the African Methodist Episcopal Church, who may have been the first African-American to confer with a president on a matter of a public policy. "I am here," Payne told Lincoln, to learn whether or not you intend to sign the bill of Emancipation..." Lincoln didn't tell him, but he finally signed the bill on April 16. By that time, slaveholders with "family servants" who was thought would not be benefited by freedom" had apparently escaped. Moreover, the scores of and perhaps hundreds of slaves who were hurriedly removed from Washington and who spent three more years in slavery, courtesy of Abraham Lincoln.

Among those who hailed the first dawn of freedom was Frederick Douglas, who told Charles Summer: "If slavery is really dead in the District of Columbia... to you, more than any other American Statesman, belongs the honor of this great triumph of Justice, Liberty and sound policy.

When Lincoln signed the bill....he could have noted that the act proved what has been abundantly established: that he was a poor prophet. A little over a year before, he had "guaranteed" a group of proslavery leaders that slavery would not be "molested" in the District as long as he was president. Moreover, Henry Clay once told the Senate that "the actual abolition of slavery in the district is about as likely to occur as the abolition of the Christian religion." Christianity survived, but slavery didn't, primarily because of the Thirty-seventh Congress, which also banned slavery in the territories and authorized the use of Black soldiers. Lincoln followed Congress's lead slow and grudgingly, signing these act with evident displeasure. Lincoln opposed the major emancipating acts of this Congress.

"African-Americans, whose sense of honoring their benefactors exceeded their knowledge of history might name their sons after Lincoln," (but Frederick) Douglas, with a truer appreciation, knew that if (blacks) wish to honor the greatest friend they ever had in public life they should place wreaths on the tomb of Charles Sumner, Thaddeus Stevens, Owen Loverly, Lyman Trumbull, George Washington Julian, James M. Ashley, Henry Wilson, Congressman Stevens of Illinois, and Senators Wade and Chandler, came to the cause.

Today, it is fashionable to defend Lincoln and say that he loved Black people and demanded Black Freedom. However, based on this surgeon's autopsy, and the skilled and precise dissecting that was conducted by Dr. Bennett, I fail to derive with the diagnosis of the former as stated.

Moreover, my dictation and conclusion is parallel with Professor Bennett's in that Abraham Lincoln opposed Black Freedom and didn't like Black People either, except perhaps as servants; e.g., cooks, stable boys, subordinates, and field hands.

To be sure, Dr. Bennett sums up the whole matter of Lincoln's love for the (African-American) in very simplistic terms in that "whether the man really loved us is an interesting question for a psychiatrist or pastor but is irrelevant in weighting his public acts if those public acts were exemplary and reflected a public demand for equal rights in all areas." The men who really loved the African-American were the Congressional members who believed in four basic ideas: "instant emancipation," the confiscation of the land of rebels, the use of Black soldiers and the political equality for the (African-American)." Anybody who supported these propositions, for any reason was the slave's friend. Anybody who opposed them for any reason was the slave's enemy.

The Thirteenth, Fourteenth, and Fifteenth amendments are permanent testimonials to the vision and devotion of Charles Sumner and Thaddeus Stevens who further captured the imagination of the freedmen with the "forty acres and a mule" legend. They also proposed a Civil Rights Bill that would have banned segregation in schools, churches, cemeteries, public conveyances, and places of public accommodation in the 1870's. They believed Blacks were "Human Beings" and called for a new birth of freedom. Although Summer and Stevens have been systematically vilified by a whole generation of historians, who say they forced Black suffrage and equal rights on the white South, thereby precipitating the "Horrors" of Reconstruction.

The truth is that the failure of Reconstruction and America's current racial "Crisis" are direct results of the disastrous Reconstruction plans of Lincoln and Andrew Johnson and the failure to adopt the comprehensive plan articulated by Sumner, Stevens, Douglas, Phillips, and others.

All these men wanted was the punishment for men who committed "Crimes Against Humanity" and who unleashed, for racial reasons, a "Human Holocaust" that cost the lives of 620,000 [souls]."[65]

"It was their sense of "Righteous Indignation" that propelled men like Phillips, Stevens, Sumner, Douglas, and others who all shared the same common denominator. Combined with intense wrath and joy that gave them the weight unprecedented in American History.

Abraham Lincoln and Robert E. Lee did not succeed in their efforts to preserve the Union as it was due to two groups. #1 The Thirty-Seventh Congress- which changed the emancipation agenda. #2 African-American slaves- who broke into the war, like burglars, and imposed their own rhythm on events. Abandoning plantations by the thousands, shouting jubilee songs and demanding a piece of the Civil War action, they helped emancipate themselves-And Lincoln.

In February 1862, Secretary of State Seward said, "We have entered Virginia" and already five thousand slaves have been emancipated simply by the appearance of our forces. And we have landed upon the coast of South Carolina, and already nine thousand ex-slaves (are in our camp). Although the war has not been waged against slavery, yet the armies act as an emancipating crusade. To proclaim the crusade is unnecessary." Lincoln, of course, was one of the last to hear of the "Crusades" of the Union Armies as usual. However, you could see plainly in New Orleans and the areas around Beaufort, South Carolina, where early Union advances brought new opportunities and dramatized Lincoln's lack of policy. Watching Lincoln's hesitant response to the rising pressure of thousands of Black refugees seeking freedom and demanding arms and land, and what Lincoln feared most of all was not their failure but their success."

Gurowski wrote, Lincoln is frightened with the success in South Carolina, as it will "complicate the question of slavery." Further, Lincoln believed that "emancipation would smother the free states." Again in Beaufort South Carolina, shortly thereafter in May, 1862, Lincoln exclaimed, "Slavery is a big job, and will smother us!"

If Lincoln feared Black freedom, other men, more daring perhaps, certainly more sensitive, welcomed it and moved to give it wings. Among their number was an old Lincoln friend, General David Hunter, who on May 9, 1862 declared all slaves in South Carolina, Georgia, and Florida "forever free." Ten days later, Lincoln revoked Hunter's proclamation and returned these one million men, women, and children to slavery. While Lincoln worried about "the public and private inconveniences of emancipation," ordinary citizens assumed the burden of leadership, going in ones and tens to the White House to urge action and emancipation.

The Lincoln administration, in facts created a new form of political theater, attracting a constant stream of delegations with petitions and arguments in favor of the emancipation of Black Americans. From all over America, from New England and the Midwest, from Republicans, Democrats, Preachers, businessmen, and abolitionists came petitions for the freeing of the slaves. There were even petitions from schoolchildren trying to improve the moral vision of the president of the United State. So many petitions came from so many white people that it is hard to understand why so many historians say that Lincoln was waiting for the people to catch up with him. When a delegation of Quakers, including great names like Thomas Garrett and Dinah Mendenhall, came to he White House on Friday, June 20, and told Lincoln that God wanted him to free the slaves, he said that he "had sometime thought that perhaps he might be an instrument in God's hand of accomplishing a great work...." He was not convinced, however, that the time was ripe or that God favored a decree of emancipation. Perhaps, he said, "God's way of accomplishing the end which the moralists have in view may be different from theirs."

Since the Quakers believed that God's way was an Emancipation Proclamation and since Lincoln and apparently Lincoln's God had another way in mind, the question naturally arises of what other way was available. The answer to this question, as to so many others that arose during this period, was apparently McClellan.

At that point, in June of 1862, McClellan and his troops were aimed like a dagger at the heart of the Confederacy, and Lincoln was feverishly awaiting news of the triumphant Unions march into Richmond."

Abraham Lincoln never changed his mind in regard to the immediate emancipation of slaves nor his views of deportation. However, due to the deteriorating military and political situation, especially the hardening of the hearts of Northern whites, appalled by the slaughter of their sons, brothers, and fathers, this forced a change and conversion; or did it?

Almost all Lincoln scholars say the big change came in July 1862, but as we shall see, Lincoln made so many contradictory statements and did many contradictory things in that month. To see this clearly, one need only revisit that famous July with Lincoln, keeping in mind five indispensable rules for anyone dissecting or performing an autopsy on this racist on the road to emancipation.

Rule One: The Emancipation Proclamation was never Lincoln's plan. The Proclamation was forced on him by events and the pressure of black and white activists.

Rule Two: Lincoln wanted to end the war without touching slavery. For at least eighteen months, by his own admission, he did everything he could to ensure that America remained half slave and half free.

Rule Three: When Southern tenacity and the mounting war casualties and his own policies including the appointment of bumbling proslavery generals, doomed that policy, he changed the order to remain the same, proposing the only emancipation plan he ever believed in, gradual, compensated emancipation linked to the sudden deportation of Blacks.

Rule Four: Lincoln was tenacious and even devious in supporting his plan of gradual emancipation and the deportation and in opposing the idea of an immediate emancipation proclamation, which he feared more than slavery. He never changed his mind on that point and continued to fight for gradual emancipation and deportation, even after Republican leaders forced him to adopt a different language. If that meant saying emancipation words and issuing emancipation documents, without following through with emancipation acts, the better to blind his adversaries and to prepare the way for the triumph of his plan, Lincoln was up to it. It was the essence of his art to yield without yielding and to change while remaining the same.

Rule Five: Lincoln's actions in support of emancipation were rebound actions made in response to the initiatives of the real supporters of Black freedom or the overwhelming pressure of events and were designed, at least in part, to counter, sidetrack and even thwart the movement for real emancipation.

Thus, the Emancipation Proclamation itself was, as we have seen, the high point of a brilliant campaign in favor of slavery not freedom, and was design not to emancipate all slaves immediately but to prevent the emancipation of all slaves immediately and to contain the emancipation pressures until conservatives could, as Lincoln said, help themselves."₆₆

"With the passage of the Second Confiscation act, a door slammed shut on one of history's greatest conceits, a confederacy founded on the rock of Negro inferiority and designed, like other conceits of its kind, to last forever.

The Second Confiscation Act didn't end the Confederacy, but it cut off one of the last avenues of escape and forced the beginning of America's confrontation with slavery, slaves, and African-Americans, with implications that are still reverberating in the land.

Seen whole, then, and in the proper perspective, the Second Confiscation Act was one of the great hinges of our history. More sweeping than the Lincoln proclamations, more threatening to the slave interests than anything that come out of the Lincoln White House, this act freed the slaves of all rebels and struck at the roots of the slave system by confiscating the property and plantations of slave-owners, an unheard-of American revolution that Abraham Lincoln thwarted at the last moment by a threatened veto in favor of the Southern plantation system."[67]

"It was in this volatile atmosphere that Lincoln embraced or seemed to embrace the idea of an Emancipation Proclamation, an idea that suggested or seemed to suggest immediate or general emancipation with one stroke of the pen. Although he was thought to have cold feet on the matter of emancipation of African-Americans, with reluctance he said or seemed to say on July 22, 1862, at a cabinet meeting that he was going to issue an Emancipation Proclamation. Being the proslavery advocate that he was Lincoln felt that this was the least that he could do under the circumstances, and no president in his position could have done less.

Moreover, from Lincoln's standpoint, a proclamation had a number of tactical advantages. Most importantly, a Proclamation was a "Gesture" not an Act, unlike the Second Confiscation Act. Announcing that you "Were" going to free 'Four Million" slaves three or four months later made you feel good but didn't free anybody or change anything. A proclamation, moreover, had the advantage from Lincoln's standpoint, of freezing the status quo and making it unnecessary to immediately hire Black soldiers and confiscate Southern mansions. It also provided additional time to make the political and military arrangements that might eliminate the need for any emancipation. Hence, if these arrangements failed and he was actually forced to sign the documents he could draft it so that it would not actually free anybody. At best, war proclamations, as Lincoln said repeatedly, were proclamations that expired with the war and were of "questionable legality" and would end up Finally, in the hands of judges. Finally, Lincoln believed that the Emancipation Proclamation was a war measure of doubtful legality and that it would have no force when the war ended."[68]

"After mentioning emancipation two times on two days in July - July 13 and July 22 1862, Lincoln reversed his field and said in August what he had said before July, that emancipating Blacks would be inexpedient, impolitic and provoking to Kentucky. Another high-level delegation of Midwesterners said he told them that he would rather resign than use Black soldiers to kill white men. A Lincoln crony said he told him "frankly" that he was not going to emancipate the slaves. In August of 1862, Adam Gurowski wrote that "the president, Mr. Lincoln, is indefatigable in his efforts to "save slavery." Moreover, he was indefatigable in his efforts to ship Blacks out of the country.

Since his first days in office, he had maneuvered to fulfill his Illinois dream of ensuring that Blacks left America "in a body," as the Hebrew children left Egypt. His election gave him an unexampled opportunity to make his private fantasy a public reality, and he worked fervently in 1861 and 1862, trying to organize a national campaign to deport Blacks.

To facilitate his plans for the "Racial Cleansing" of America, Lincoln created a Black emigration department, without giving it that name, in the Interior Department and employed James Mitchell, an Indiana minister and American Colonization Society activist who had worked with him on colonization issues in Springfield. Lincoln approved of Mitchell master plan for the final solution of the Black "Problem." In a letter on the relations of the white and African Races in the United States, showing the necessity of the Colonization of the latter. In this official document of the U. S. Governments printed by the Government Printing Office and mailed on May 18, 1862, to "His Excellency Abraham Lincoln" Mitchell said, "that the presence of the Negro race on the North American continent was more dangerous to the peace of the country than the Civil War. For "terrible as is this civil war between men of kindered race for the dominion of the servant, future history will show that it has been moderate and altogether tolerable when contrasted with a struggle between the black and white race, which, within the next one or two hundred years must sweep over this nation, unless the use and prudent statesmen of this generation avert it." The chief danger in the future, Mitchell told Lincoln, was that "we have 4,500,000 persons, who, whilst amongst us, cannot be of us..." Why couldn't they be "of us"? They were, he said, of a different race, a race that threatens the blood stream of the nation and "is giving to this continent a nation of bastards."

SEX: For Lincoln and for almost all his men, the basic problem was sex. On page after page of his government-sponsored diatribe, Mitchell warns against endangering the purity of white blood by "this repulsive 'admixture of blood," the "possible admixture of inferior blood," attempts to engraft "Negro blood on the population" and attempts "to pour the blood of nearly Five Million Africans into the veins of the Republic."

"This was a threat," he said, to the white nation and the purity of white blood. It was a threat to our people, the men of Europe, who constituted "one family, ordered so of God, and by him kept compact and together through the ages gone."

Mitchell saw conspirators everywhere and warned Lincoln against England and France as well as New England idealists who were opposing efforts to colonize Blacks and who were therefore working together to make the white men of America dilute their blood. He even charged that some Blacks were deliberately using sex for political reasons, furthering strategy "predicated on the hope of the African race to rise to the illicit absorption of their blood into the mass of this nation.

The solution: was "perfecting the proposed plans of the (Lincoln) administration" and "the careful and gradual removal of the African race to some desirable and convenient home in the tropical lands of South America or Africa. It was necessary to remove all Blacks, for "our republican institutions are not adapted to mixed races and classified people. Our institutions require a homogenous population to rest on as a basis,'" a view that Lincoln echoed in his "physical difference" theory.

GOD, Rev. Mitchell said, was in his- and Lincoln's plan. GOD ordained in the beginning a separate and distinct subsistence for the great races of men... 'when he determined the times before appointed, and the bounds of their habitation." Rev. Mitchell prayed that "a perpetual barrier" would be "reared between us and that land of the mixed races of this continent- Mexico." Then, mixing metaphors and races, he said, "As Abraham and Lott agreed to separate their conflicting retainers and dependents the one going to the right and the other going to the left, so let these two governments agree to divide this continent between the Anglo-American and mixed races," the Anglo-American taking the Northern road, and Africans and mixed races taking Central America "which nature, in her wisdom, has prepared for them, and which for beauty, fertility and grandeur of scenery, cannot be equaled on the globe..."

The major obstacle to realizing this new Eden was the African-American, a race that "has hardly attained a mental majority" and cannot be expected to rise in a day to the grandeur of the white race that founded empires and laid "the ground work of civil institutions like ours." Rev. Mitchell didn't find it necessary to remind Lincoln that it was the Black race, not the white race, which created the foundations of American wealth, and Lincoln made no mention of that fact when he appropriated Mitchell's idea and told a group of Blacks that "you should sacrifice something of your present comfort for the purpose of being as grand in that respect as the white people."

Lincoln approved of Rev. Mitchell's proposals and promoted him. Mitchell later brought five African-Americans to the White House who would be willing to listen to Lincoln's proposals. This was the first time in history that African-Americans had been invited to the Whitehouse to confer on an official matter. Lincoln, delighted, began his monologue by saying that at a sum of money had been appropriated by Congress, and placed at his disposition for the purpose of aiding the colonization in some country of the people, or a portion of them, of African decent, thereby making it his duty, as it had for a long time been his inclination, to favor that cause..." Lincoln, using the unfortunate tone of a condescending (Great White) father scolding ignorant children."

Why should "the people of your race be colonized, and where? Why should they leave this country?" The reasons Lincoln said going back to the Lincoln-Douglas Debate was the "Physical Difference" between Blacks and Whites. "You and we," he said are different races. We have between us a broader difference than exists between almost any other two races.

Whether it is right or wrong I need not discuss, but this physical difference is a great disadvantage to the both of us, as I think your race suffer very greatly, many of them by living among us, while ours suffer from your presence." Saying that "Africans" were the cause of the problem and the wars" Lincoln said, "But for your race among us there could not be a war," although many men engaged on either side do not care for you one way or the other." Lincoln told the African visitors that "Your race are suffering, and in my judgment, "The Greatest Wrong Inflicted On Any People."

Lincoln didn't seek the opinion of his visitors, he was simply presenting a fact: Whites didn't want Blacks in America and therefore Blacks would have to go. 'There is an unwillingness on the part of our people, harsh as it may be, for you free African people to remain with us." The only solution from his standpoint was a Black Exodus. "It is better for us both," he said twice, "to be separated." Lincoln proposed a Black settlement on Central American land, "rich in coal" and asked his visitors to help him and Black settlers "capable of thinking as white men."

This idea, the idea of millions of African-Americans going to South America or Africa and leaving the land they helped develop in the hands of white people, moved Lincoln, and he asked the visitors "to consider seriously not pertaining to yourselves merely, nor for your race, and ours, for the present time, but as one of the things, if successfully managed, for the good of mankind-not confined to the present generation.

The response was immediate and explosive. Some Blacks said they had as much right as Abraham Lincoln to live in their native land. Others, more subjective perhaps, certainly more inventive, suggested that the easiest way to solve the problem was to remove the real problem, white people. Frederick Douglas attacked Lincoln's logic and his racism, saying that "a horse thief pleading that the existence of the horse is the cause for his theft or a highway man contending that the money in the travelers pocket is the sole first cause of his robbery are about as much entitled to respect as is the president's reasoning at this point. Lincoln's position didn't surprise Douglas. Illogical and unfair as Mr. Lincoln's statements: are, they are nevertheless quite in keeping with his whole course from the beginning of his administration up to this day, and confirm the painful conviction that though elected as an anti-slavery man by Republican and Abolition voters, Mr. Lincoln is quite a genuine representative of American prejudice and Negro hatred and far more concerned for the preservation of slavery, and the favor of the Border Slave States, than for any sentiment of magnanimity or principle of Justice and humanity."

Philadelphia Blacks argued strongly against Lincoln's proposals and said that there were strong "Pecuniary and Political" reasons for their disfavor. "Blacks have produced much of the wealth of this country and we constitute, including our property qualifications, almost the entire wealth of the Cotton States, and make up a large proportion of that of the others."

Therefore: "We believe that the world be benefited by giving the Four Millions of slaves their freedom, and the lands now possessed by their masters. They have been amply compensated in our labor and the blood of our kinsmen. These masters "toil not, neither do they spin." They destroy, consume, and give to the world in return but a small equivalent. They deprive us of "Life, Liberty, and the Pursuit of Happiness." Everyone knew that Blacks were the only people who worked in the South and that the South without Blacks would be a "White Wilderness."

The most serious charge against Lincoln came from Douglas and other Blacks who said the president of the United States was fanning the flames of bigotry and inciting acts of violence against Black Men and Women and their children. "Mr. Lincoln takes care," Douglas wrote, "in urging his colonization scheme to furnish a weapon to all the "Ignorant and Base", who need only the countenance of men in authority to commit all kinds of violence and outrage upon the African people of the country." In pressing this issue, Lincoln, Douglas said, "showed his bigotry "his pride of his race and blood," and "his contempt for Africans."

The same complaint was made by the Blacks of Newtowm, Long Island, who held a mass meeting on August 20, 1862, and adopted resolutions that said, in part, that Blacks were at home and that they had "the right to have applied to ourselves those rights named in the Declaration of Independence." Like Douglas, they said that the president of the United States was serving as a cheerleader for "our enemies", who wish to insult and mob us, as we have, since (the publication of his statement), been repeatedly "Insulted", and told that we must leave the country."

Lincoln's colonization campaign coincided with a wave of violent attacks on Blacks. In a report on "Persecution of Negroes," the New York Tribune said in an August 6 story that the wave of violence "commenced weeks ago in Cincinnati, Evansville, Ind., and Toledo." The Toledo violence was "traced directly," the newspaper said, "to the instigation of emissaries from (New York City)." According to the Tribune report the violence was instigated by Democrats and undercover Confederate agents. "Months ago," the report continued, "when the rebellion seemed at its last gasp, its partners in the loyal States were secretly impelled to get up a diversion in its favor by instigating riotous assaults on the unarmed and comparatively defenseless Blacks of our Northern cities.

In furtherance of this plot, stories were started that thousands of Negroes at Washington, Fortress Monroe, and elsewhere, were being subsisted in idleness at public cost; next, that fugitive slaves were so abundant in Chester County, Pennsylvania, and its vicinity, that they were taking bread out of the mouths of white laborers by working for ten cents a day...." The New York Tribune and other papers proved that these reports were false, citing, among other evidence, the fact that the labor market was so tight that white laborers could find jobs almost anywhere. Neither fact nor logic stopped the assaults.

On Tuesday, August 4, "a serious riot" erupted in South Brooklyn when a mob of white ethnics tried to beat and "Burn to Death" Black Women and children working at two tobacco factories owned by a certain "Mr. Lorillard."

Taking advantage of the temporary absence of the men, the mob chased the women and children to a top door, barricaded the door and set the building on fire. The whites police showed little or no interest in the attack, which was thwarted at the last minute by the return of the men. The Tribune reported on August 6 that the attack was "instigated and carried into effect by Democrats" and that the ringleader was a rum seller.

The wave of attacks got worse after publication of newspaper headlines on the president's proposal for a Black Exodus. A week later, in the same area of South Brooklyn, Whites tried to lynch a Black man on Furman Street. The leader of this mob, the New York Tribune said in an August 21 story, was a man who had deserted from a Brooklyn regiment after the Battle of Bull Run.

"With seemingly no regard for black reaction to this plan" Lincoln stepped up his high visibility campaign to send Blacks away, making the White House the pulpit and national center of the colonization movement. Hustlers, promoters, Zealots, land developers, international adventurers, and colonizers from all over the United States made their way to the White House, and Lincoln received them with open arms. Lincoln had a belief, amounting to conviction almost, that the two races could not dwell together in unity and as equals in their social relations.

Far from being an anomaly, Lincoln's "Ethnic Cleansing" plan was the "Cornerstone" of his military and political agenda and was based on what Randall called a "grand design" for a new White America without slaves- and without Blacks. In support of this "White Dream", Lincoln mobilized the State Department, The Interior Department, The Treasury Department, and the Smithsonian Institution. By the end of August, Lincoln's "Ethnic Cleansing" plan was the official policy of the American Government."[69]

When at last, after the 74,000 nights of American slavery and the Four Hundred years of the Slave Trade and the slaughter of tens of millions of Blacks, when, after all this blood, after the blood of Nealee and Nat Turner and John Brown, and after all the compromises, the Compromises of 1787 and 1820 and 1850, and after all attempts to evade the issue, including his own, had failed-when, after all this, Abraham Lincoln picked up his pen to sign the thing, and he couldn't do it.

It was Thursday, January 1, 1863, and Lincoln was poised before a handful of people in the cabinet room of the White House to sign the promised Emancipation Proclamation.

But at the last moment, something in him, was it his conscience, or his fear of what he called the evils of sudden emancipation, revolt, and when he picked up the pen to do it, his arm trembled so violently that he stopped, overcome suddenly by a superstitious feeling. He "took a pen" an eyewitness said," dipped it in ink, moved his hand to the place for the signing, held it a moment and then removed his hand and dropped the pen. After a little hesitation he again took up the pen and went through the same movement as before." Always superstitious, always on the lookout for supernatural signs, Lincoln paused, awed despite himself. Then a simple explanation came to him; he had, he said, been shaking hands for hours in the New Year's Day reception and it was only natural that his right arm should be paralyzed. Given Lincoln's deep-seated opposition to sudden and general emancipation and his life-long fear-fascination with the Black/White thing, the explanation, whatever limitations, at least consoled Lincoln temporarily, who then shook off the spasm and scrawled his name, saying he didn't want the signature to be "tremulous" because people would say "he had some compunctions."

Nothing testifies to this more powerfully than the document itself, which is often more celebrated than read, or lived. Cold, forbidding, with all the passion and eloquence of a real estate deed, the proclamation doesn't contain a single principle hostile to slavery. As a document, it lends weight to the observation "that when Lincoln freed the slaves, there was no heart in the act." For the Emancipation Proclamation did not in and of itself emancipate anybody. To be sure, it practically re-enslaved some five hundred thousand slaves. As explained by then Secretary of State Seward "we have let of a puff of wind over an accomplished fact." Further Seward said, "I mean that the Emancipation Proclamation was uttered in the first gun fired at Fort Sumpter, and we have been the last to hear it. As it is, we show our sympathy with slavery by emancipating slaves where we cannot reach them, and holding them in bondage where we can not set them free."

The Proclamation argues so powerfully against itself that a number of scholars believe it was a radical move by which Lincoln hoped to buy time and forestall a real act of liberation.

There is evidence, in fact, that he never intended to free the slaves, and that he hoped that events-a stunning Union victory or adoption of his thirty-seven-year gradual emancipation plan-would make the Proclamation moot or enable him to recall it. Critical opinion is almost unanimous on the limitations of the document that freed all Blacks and freed no Blacks. It has been concluded that Lincoln had been literally "WHIPPED INTO GLORY" by the patriots of both Houses of Congress, as the exponents of the noble and loftiest aspirations of the American People, WHIPPED!... Mr. Lincoln into the glory of having issued the Emancipation Proclamation. The laws promulgated by this dying Congress initiated the Emancipation generated the proclamation of the 22nd of September, and of January 1st, 1863..."

Although the document had little immediate effect on the masses of slaves, it saved the Union by making it impossible for foreign governments to intervene on the side of the Confederacy.

Despite that fact or perhaps because of it, the English government frowned on the whole process, saying in the words of Earl Russel that the Proclamation "professes to emancipate all slaves in places where the United States' authorities cannot, exercising jurisdiction, now make emancipation a reality, but it does not decree emancipation of slaves in any States or parts of States occupied by Federal troops and subject to Federal jurisdiction, and where, therefore, emancipation, if decreed, might have been carried into effect." The net effect of all this, Russel said, was that Lincoln made slavery "at once legal and illegal," and made "slaves either punishable for running away from their masters, or entitled to be supported and encouraged by so doing, according to the locality in which they may happen to be."

Englishmen, Americans, Northerners, Southerners, Lincoln friends, Lincoln critics and Lincoln experts, Randall, Hume, Hofstadter, Quarles: almost everyone concedes that Lincoln's Proclamation wasn't much and that it did little if any emancipating. Does this mean that "the greatest moral act of the Nineteenth Century," to quote one enthusiast, was a fraud? Was it, as so many students have said, a gambit in a white game that had nothing at all to do with freedom? Or was it the earnest, equivocating man, torn apart by convicting personal, racial, and political impulses he could neither name, reject, or accept?

To answer these questions, we shall have to begin with a task that almost all Americans shun- we shall have to read one of the most uninspired documents in American history and the only major Lincoln document with not one scintilla of the famous Lincoln panache. The Proclamation, simply called "A Proclamation" begins by quoting the Preliminary Proclamation of September 22, 1862, and then continues:

Now, therefore, I, Abraham Lincoln, President of the United States, by virtue of the power vested in me as Commander-in-chief of the Army and Navy of the United States in time of actual armed rebellion against authority and government of the United States, and as a fit and necessary war measure for suppressing said rebellion, do, on this first day of January, in the year of our Lord, one thousand eight hundred and sixty three, and in accordance with my purpose to do so publicly proclaimed for the full period of one hundred days... order and designate as the States and parts of States wherein the people thereof respectively, are this day in rebellion against the United States, the following: Arkansas, Texas, Louisiana, (except the parishes of St. Bernard, Plaquemines, Jefferson, St.Johns, St. Charles, St. James[,] Ascension, Assumption, Terrebonne, Lafourche, St. Mary, St. Martin, and Orleans, including the City of New-Orleans), Mississippi, Alabama, Florida, Georgia, South-Carolina, North-Carolina, and Virginia, except the fortyeight [sic] counties designated as West Virginia, and also the counties of Berkley, Accomac, Northampton, Elizabeth-city, York, Princess Ann and Norfolk, including the cities of Norfolk & Portsmouth; and which excepts parts are, for the present, left precisely as if this proclamation were not issued.

And by virtue of the power and for the purpose aforesaid, I do order and declare that all persons held as slaves within said designated States, and parts of States, are, and henceforward shall be free; and that the Executive government of the United States, including the military and Naval authority thereof, will recognize and maintain the freedom of said Persons.

And I hereby enjoin upon the people so declared to be free to abstain from all violence, unless in necessary self-defense; and I recommend to them that, in all cases when allowed, they labor faithfully for reasonable wages.

And I further declare and make known, that such persons of suitable condition, will be received into the armed service of the United States to garrison forts, positions, stations, and other places, and to man vessels of all sorts in said service.

And upon this act, sincerely believed to be an act of justice, warranted by the Constitution upon military necessity, I invoke the considerate judgement of mankind, and the gracious favor of almighty God.

In the opinion of the great author Lerone Bennett, Jr., the first thing to notice about this celebrated document is that there is no 'Hallelujah' in it. There is no new-birth-of-freedom swagger, no perish-from-the-earth pizzazz. Without even thinking about it, without even giving it a second thought, the allegedly illiterate slaves came up with twenty or so phrases, Including "Free at Last" that circled the globe and even shook the foundation of the Lincoln Memorial when Martin Luther King, Jr. quoted it one hundred years later.

But the Gettysburg man, who homered, we are told, out of town in Gettysburg, came up to the plate in the last of the ninth with three men on base and two outs in the world series of freedom and struck out semantically and politically. Lincolnians say he missed on purpose, that he was so terrified by the possibility of Black violence and white opposition that he bent over backwards to keep from exciting Blacks and scaring whites. Even if we allow these considerations, the swing was so inappropriate and missed the ball by such a wide margin that it appears to this author, never missed when he was talking about the freedom of white folks but who always sounded like a probation officer when he was talking about the freedom of Black folks.

The document received much criticism in its lack of passion which plainly reflected Lincoln's indifference toward Blacks.

Moreover, the one sentence that is said to have only a touch of feelings was the line that said, "And upon this act sincerely believed to be an act of justices" Well it is said that this sentence was written not by Lincoln but by Secretary of the Treasury Chase, who told Lincoln, in so many words, that the "greatest moral act of the nineteenth century" needed a little morality and a little "Humanity."

More importantly, according to Bennett, "the document also needed a little emancipating." Not only did the document fail to free anyone, but it re-enslaved and /or condemned to continue slavery more than a half million persons. The 556,540 slaves in the border states of Maryland, Missouri, Delaware and Kentucky were excluded, of course. But the most surprising and damaging omissions were the areas controlled by Federal troops, large sections of Tennessee, Louisiana and Virginia, including the cities of New Orleans and Norfolk, "all of which excepted parts," Lincoln said, "are for the present left precisely as if this Proclamation were not issued.

This meant that Lincoln, as Treasury Secretary Chase had already told him, was practically re-enslaving some 500,000 slaves (87,812 in Louisiana, 33,332 in Virginia, and 275,719 in Tennessee), some of whom were already working for wages and enjoying the first fruits of freedom.

The limitations of the document were analyzed with great insight by Horace Greeley who expressed amazement that Lincoln had excepted the 275,000 slaves of Tennessee and the slaves in the lower portion of Louisiana, "two states with more than one hundred thousand of their citizens in open revolt." Over and above that, Greeley said Lincoln had broken faith with the slaves. He had proclaimed unconditionally in September that he would declare free all slaves in states or districts then in rebellion" not such of them as he should at the set time see fit to liberate." This was unfortunate, Greeley said, adding: "We do most profoundly regret that he has not hewed up to the line chalked by himself."

This, Greeley said, suggested trickery, for Lincoln could have been a contender. He could "have stricken the shackles from the limbs of several hundreds of thousands of slaves, and thereby given to those left in bondage to the rebels an earnest that our failure to reach and liberate them resulted from want of power rather than of will. The exemptions will be seized upon by the Rebels to make the slaves believe that the Unionists are trifling with and duping them- seeking to use them in the contest, but not intending to reward them with liberty."

Lincoln never stopped plotting against his Emancipation Proclamation. He never stopped trying to limit it or to change and soften its potential impact.

Seven days after signing the document, he told one of his old Illinois friends, proslavery Democratic general James A. McClernand, that loyal and disloyal slaveholders had nothing to fear and that he was still on their side. "As to the states not included in (the proclamation)," he wrote General McClernand, on January 8, "they can have their "rights" in the Union as of old." It meant their "rights" to hold, buy and sell slaves as in the pre-war constitution. Lincoln wanted the slaveholders of the Confederacy to adopt systems of Apprenticeship for the Colored people, conforming substantially to the most approved plans of gradual emancipation...." Under such gradual plans for emancipation as suggested by Lincoln, this would have continued slavery under another name for twenty or even fifty years.

It is not noted often enough that Lincoln turned the Emancipation Proclamation on its head and made it the principal instrument for keeping hundreds of thousands of men, women and children in slavery for two more years.

During these three years, from 1863 to 1865, the biggest slaveholder in the United States was Lincoln, who used the Proclamation as a shield to protect himself - and slaveholders - from the rising emancipation waves. It will be said in objection that the half million or so slaves in occupied Union areas in the South, especially the slaves in occupied Louisiana and Virginia, were the slaves of the United States, but the man who kept them in slavery and who could have emancipated them at any moment was Abraham Lincoln."[70]

"Lincoln doubted the wisdom of the Emancipation Proclamation for months afterward and told Congressman Julian and others that it had "Done about as much harm as good." When on Sunday, January 25, 1863, Lincoln received a group of abolitionists, including Wendell Phillips, he said he had not expected much from (the proclamation) at first, and consequently had not been disappointed...." The abolitionist urged a strong follow-up campaign, using antislavery generals and governors in the South. Lincoln objected, saying, Suppose I should put in the South these antislavery generals and governors, what could they do with the slaves that would come to them?

What was shocking to abolitionists was that the recent proclaimer of liberty to three million Negroes should at that date thus confess that he was putting forward in the South generals and governors who would not carry it out in good faith by freeing practically as many as possible of those declared free...." Even more shocking, Lincoln seemed to "be genuinely exercised in mind on so rudimentary a question as to "What should be done with a people who had always supported themselves and their masters?..."

Still more unmistakable evidence of Lincoln's orientation can be found in his failure to provide equal pay and equal protection for Black soldiers, who were promised thirteen dollars a month, the same pay as White privates, and were insulted with an offer of seven dollars a month. Many Black Soldiers refused to accept the seven dollars.

When the Massachusetts legislature passed a bill providing the six-dollar difference, the state's Black soldiers refused to accept the money, saying they were fighting for a principle, not money. When advised that it was his constitutional duty to order equal pay, Lincoln sat on the opinion until Congress rebelled. Before Congress rectified Lincoln's error, a brave Black sergeant named William Walker, who participated in a protest against Lincoln's policy, was arrested and charged with mutiny. At his trial, he pleaded in extenuation that "nearly the whole of his regiment acted in like manner as himself," "when the regiment stacked arms and refused further duty.... I did not then exercise any command over them and that "I carried my arms and equipment back with me to my company street."

Ignoring this testimony and pleas from major leaders, including some Union officers, a military court sentenced Sergeant Walker to death. Although Lincoln repeatedly overruled the death sentences of white soldiers, he looked the other way when, on February 29, 1864, at 9 O'clock in the morning, Sergeant William Walker of company A, A South Carolina Volunteer, was "shot to death with musketry" in the presence of his brigade. A biting footnote was added by Massachusetts Governor Andrews, who said that "the Lincoln administration which found no law to pay Walker except as a nondescript or contraband, nevertheless found law enough to shoot him as a soldier."

Quite a few African-Americans wrote Lincoln to protest his policy, but he probably didn't see the letters since "nearly every letter written to President Lincoln during the Civil War by an African-American was routinely, often mindlessly, sent on to the War Department's Bureau of Colored Troops." Lincoln, as every school child knows, was always writing eloquent letters to the mothers of white soldiers, but it appears from this and other evidence that it was his policy to ignore the pleas of black mothers like Hannah Johnson, who wrote from Buffalo, New York, to ask the man she addressed as "Excellent Sir" to stand up "manfully" and retaliate against Confederate officials who were murdering some captured Black soldiers and selling others into slavery."

"My son," Hannah Johnson wrote, "fought at Fort Wagner, South Carolina, but thank God he was not taken prisoner, as many were. I thought of this thing before I let my boy go but then said Mr. Lincoln will never let them sell our Colored Soldiers for slaves, if they do he will get them back quick he will rettallyate and stop it. Now Mr. Lincoln don't you think you ought to stop this thing and make them do the same by the Colored Men they have lived in idleness all their lives on stolen labor and made savages of the Colored people, but they now are so furious because they are proving themselves to be men, such as have come away and got some education. It must not be so. You must put the rebels to work in State prisons to making shoes and things, if they sell our Colored Soldiers, till they let them all go. And give their wounded the same treatment."

All this, she said, might seem cruel, but "their [is] no other way, and a just man must do hard things sometimes, that shew him to be a great man."

Hannah Johnson, who never went to school and who was the daughter of a slave who escaped from Louisiana, must have been a great person to write such truths. All the wisdom of Machiavelli and Malcolm X are in that line, "a just man must do hard things sometimes, that show him to be a great man." For "what," as Merleau-Ponty asked, "is a goodness incapable of harshness? What is a goodness which wants to be goodness? A meek way of ignoring others and ultimately despising them."

Mrs. Johnson had heard through he grapevine that Lincoln was going to take the Emancipation Proclamation back. She begged him not to do it, saying that slavery was "wicked" and "a horrible outrage."

There "is no sense in it, because a man has lived by robbing all his life and his father before him, should he complain because the stolen things found on him, are taken. Robbing the Colored people of their labor is but a small part of the robbery; their "Souls" are also taken, they are made brute's of, often." She added, You know all about this," and closed with an appeal: "Will you see that the Colored Men fighting now are fairly treated. You ought to do this, and do it at once, not let the thing run long meet it quickly and manfully, and stop this, mean cowardly cruelty."

Lincoln never rose to Hannah Johnson's level, and the atrocities continued, reaching a new low in the history of warfare in the massacre at Fort Pillow, a Union Fort near Memphis, Tennessee, which was captured on April 12, 1864, by forces under the command of General Nathan Bedford Forrest: Then followed [the Senate report said] a scene of cruelty and murder without a parallel in civilized warfare.... The rebels commenced an indiscriminate slaughter, sparing neither age nor sex, white or black, soldier or civilian.

The officers and men seemed to vie with each other in the devilish work; men, women, and even children, wherever found, were deliberately shot down, beaten, and hacked with sabres; some of the children not more than ten years old were forced to stand up and face their murderers while being shot; the sick and the wounded were butchered without mercy, the rebels even entering the hospital building and dragging them out to be shot, or killing them as they lay there unable to offer the least resistance."

According to official records, General Forrest and his soldiers slaughtered men, women and children for hours and continued the bloody work the next morning. All around were heard cries of "No quarter" "No quarter!" "kill them damn niggers; shoot them down!" ...No cruelty which the most fiendish malignity could devise was omitted by these murderers. One white soldier who was wounded in the leg so as to be unable to walk, was made to stand up while his tormentors shot him.... a mere child, whom an officer had taken up behind him on his horse, was seen by (Brigadier General James) Chalmers, who at once ordered the officer to put him down and shoot him, which was done....

The huts and tents in which many of the wounded had sought shelter were set on fire... while the wounded were still in them....one man was deliberately fastened down to the floor of a tent, face upwards, by means of nails driven through his clothing and into the boards under him, so that he could not possibly escape, and then the tent set on fire; another was nailed to the side of a building outside the fort, and then the building set on fire and burned.

Pressured by blacks and congressional leaders, Lincoln promised retaliation but never did anything. Neither General Forrest nor General Chalmers nor any of their men was ever called to account for "a scene of cruelty and murder without a parallel in civilized warfare."

Given the position of Hannah Johnson, and the victims of Fort Pillow, we can now answer the question posed earlier as to whether or not the Emancipation Proclamation was a fraud. The answer is that it was certainly a fraud to the slaves, who were led to believe, on the basis of erroneous information, that "Father Abraham" had freed them from the slave owners only to discover that Lincoln had made the former slave owners their guardians and keepers.

In 1864, Frederick Douglas denounced 'the swindle by which our government claims the respect of mankind for abolishing slavery- at the same time it practically re-establishing that hateful system in Louisiana." On January 25, 1865, in a speech printed in the Liberator, February 10, Frederick Douglas said that the system of forced labor inaugurated in Louisiana by General Banks, with Lincoln's approval, "practically re-enslaves the Negro, and makes the proclamation of 1863 a mockery and delusion."

Wendell Phillips echoed the same theme, saying in a letter to the 1864 Cleveland convention opposing Lincoln's recombination that Lincoln's "model of Reconstruction puts the Black race into the hands of the unchanged white race, makes the freedom of the (African) a sham, and perpetuates slavery under a softer name."

The question of whether Lincoln was a player or a pawn in the game of emancipating the African-American is an interesting inquiry in Lincoln's history denotes Dr. Bennett. However, the ultimate result, etched in the stones and whirring machines of contemporary Atlanta, New Orleans, Charlotte, New York, and Los Angeles, was that the only people who could say, "FREE At Last!" after the Civil War was the White People-Northern industrialists and their allies. That's what Andrew Johnson meant, more or less, when he said that the Emancipation Proclamation freed more White People than Black People. In the days and months following the signing of the Emancipation Proclamation, the invisible slave telegraph told slaves all over the South that a man named Abraham Lincoln had signed a document that made them free forever. The message was wrong, but the slaves, who had no way of knowing this, exploded in an unprecedented human upheaval.

There had never been anything quite like it, John Eaton said, a slave population "rising up and leaving its ancient bondage, forsaking its local traditions and all the associations and attractions of the old plantation life, coming garbed in rags or in silks, with feet shod or bleeding, individually or in families and larger groups." Eaton said it was like "the oncoming of cities."

For in the end, it was the slave who made the Lincoln of history and not the Lincoln of history who made the slave. It was the slave-going in the thousands and tens of thousands to find president Lincoln's soldiers and singing the praises of a new Father Abraham, like the one in the Bible, who had issued a document "freeing" them forever- it was the slave who created the historical halo around the head of "the great emancipator." And it is shocking to realize that Lincoln, who knew that the slaves were risking their lives to get closer to a false freedom, did nothing to meet them halfway.

Told once that South Carolina slaves believed he was a magic man who would solve all their problems, Lincoln bolted from his chair and "walked in silence two or three times across the floor," saying finally: "It is a momentous thing to be the instrument, under Providence, of the liberation of a race of people."[71]

"To W. E. B. Dubois, the miracle was not Lincoln but the slaves who exploded in an American Apocalypse. Because of Lincoln's limits and limitations in the document, the first Black Jubilee was limited to pockets in the South and never became general. But it was, for all that, breathtaking." It was all foolish, bizarre, and tawdry," Dubois wrote, "Gangs of dirty Negroes howling and dancing; poverty-stricken ignorant laborers mistaking war, destruction and revolution for the mystery of the human "Soul"; and yet to these Black folk it was the Apocalypse. The magnificent trumpet tones of Hebrew Scripture, transmitted and oddly changed, became a strange new gospel. All that was Beauty, All that was Love, All that was Truth, stood on the top of these mad mornings and sang with the stars."[72]

"To this bleak picture, one should add in all justice that Lincoln said later that the Proclamation and the arming of Black soldiers constituted the heaviest blows yet against the rebellion. "Abandon all the posts now possessed by Black men," he told two visitors on August 19, 1864, "surrender all these advantages to the enemy, and we would be compelled to abandon the war in three weeks."

Lincoln continued to fight a strange rearguard action against the Emancipation Proclamation and the Thirteenth Amendment. Reading the documents of his last days, it is difficult not to feel sorry for him, as he slowly and grudgingly walked toward the future, repeatedly casting nostalgic glances over his shoulder at the lost dream of deportation and the all-white cities on the prairie."[73]

During Lincoln's Gettysburg Address, in which he paid tribute to fallen soldiers of the war, before, during, and after the speech, which allegedly defined democracy in America, Wendell Phillips and others said publicly that racism made it impossible for the man who made the speech to conceive of a Democratic State in the United States of America. While speaking one month after Gettysburg, Phillips denounced Lincoln's amnesty plan and said, according to a liberator report of January 1, 1864, "that Lincoln was a "Bigot" whose conditioning made it impossible for him to look at Blacks the same way he looked at whites.

Mr. Lincoln does not believe in a nation half slave and half free. But he is a colonizationist, and he does not believe in a nation half black and half white. Hence, prejudice makes it impossible for him to do justice to the Negro." On February 5, 1864, Phillips said "Lincoln does not recognize the Negro as a man; he does not remember the Negro as a soldier; he does not blot out races; he does not forget them; he does not tell of rights he talks of benefits."

Viewed from this vantage point, which is also the vantage point of the slave, the fundamental problem of the Gettysburg Address is that Abraham Lincoln didn't mean a word he said. Not A Word! Take for example the first sentence of this famous speech:

Four score and seven years ago our fathers brought forth on this continent, a "NEW" nation, conceived in liberty, and dedicated to the proposition that all men are created equal. Abraham Lincoln didn't believe that.

No discerning person believed that Abraham Lincoln believed on November 19, 1863, that George Washington and Thomas Jefferson believed on July 4, 1776, that they were conceiving a nation dedicated to the proposition that the slaves at Monticello and Mount Vernon were equal to George Washington and Thomas Jefferson in the same way that George Washington and Thomas Jefferson were equal to George III. Hell No!

Well, so much for the first sentence. Moreover, Lincoln misquoted phrases in his speech by leaving out pivotal words such as "All." For example: A government by "All" the people" is what Theodore Parker said, who called for a democracy, that is, a government of all the people, by all the people, for all the people." Only Lincoln could turn a revolutionary slogan into a conservative slogan and become an immortal by eliminating the dangerous word All. And he didn't even believe that.

On November 19, 1863, there were 402,406 Blacks and 291,300 whites in the state of South Carolina. Did Lincoln believe on November 19, 1863, in government of the people et cetera in South Carolina? Hell NO! Did Lincoln believe on November 19, 1863, that it was the duty of white people to create a new birth of freedom" in South Carolina by giving the vote to the Black majority? Hell NO! Did Lincoln believe that it would ever be possible to create a government of the people et cetera with the Black majority and the white minority of South Carolina? HELL NO!

If he didn't believe that, then what in the world did Abraham Lincoln think he was doing and saying at Gettysburg? The answer is shocking: "He was just "rapping", celebrating something that had never existed before men and women who had never believed in it and who would have stoned him to death if he or anybody else had seriously suggested that they either live or die for it.

In a satirical take-off on people like Lincoln who were always talking about their "fathers", Frederick Douglas asked, "Who were your daddies?" And why are you relying on them to justify what they did not do and what you are not doing for freedom either?"[74]

Unquestionably; and it was during the same period that Benjamin Banneker, a forefather that Lincoln excluded, sent a letter to Thomas Jefferson, calling him and other white fathers to account for the betrayal of the Revolution, saying: Look back, I entreat you and remember how 'pitiful' it is to reflect that although you were so fully convinced of the benevolence of the Father of Mankind, and of his equal and impartial distribution of these rights and privileges, which he hath conferred upon them, that you should at the same time counteract his mercies, in detaining by fraud and violence, so numerous a part of my brethren under groaning captivity and cruel oppression, that you should at the same time be found "Guilty" of that most criminal act", which you professedly detest in others..."

Speaking thus of fraud and violence and accusing Jefferson and the white forefathers of criminal culpability, one of the fathers, a rejected father, calls us back to a desecrated shrine and makes us all witnesses to a national tragedy perpetrated by a small and ruthless minority. For the awkward fact is that the famous "WE THE PEOPLE" preamble, as Supreme Court Justice Thurgood Marshall pointed out, didn't even apply to the vast majority of the American people at that time-Women of all races, African-Americans, Hispanic Americans, Native-Americans, and Lincoln's real fathers, poor and property-less whites, many of whom were semi-slaves called indentured servants.

The same indictment, the same "Crimes", and the same implicit criticism of Lincoln's Golden age inform Frederick Douglas's July 4, 1852, oration at Rochester, New York, an oration many Blacks consider the greatest of all Fourth of July speeches. Speaking sixty-one years after Banneker wrote his letter and eleven years before Lincoln went to Gettysburg, Douglas was pitiless in his denunciation of the "Crime" Lincoln called a blessing.

The theme of the speech was "Hypocrisy": "What to the American slave is your Fourth of July? I answer, a day that reveals to him, more than all other days in the year, the gross injustice and cruelty to which he is the constant "Victim."

To him, your celebration is a sham; your boasted liberty, an unholy license; your national greatness, swelling vanity; your sounds of rejoicing are empty and heartless; your denunciation of tyrants, brass fronted impudence; your shouts of liberty and equality, hollow mockery; your prayers and hymns, your sermons and thanksgivings, with all your religious parade and solemnity, are, to him, mere bombast, fraud, deception, impiety, and "Hypocrisy"- a thin veil to cover up "Crimes" which would disgrace a nation of savages...." Frederick Douglas continued, "You invite to your shores fugitives of oppression from abroad, honor them with banquets, greet them with ovations, cheer them, toast them, salute them, protect them, and pour out your money to them like water; but the fugitives from your own land you advertise, hunt, arrest, shoot, and kill. You glory in your refinement and your universal education; yet you maintain a system as "Barbarous" and dreadful as ever stained the character of a nation- a system begun in avarice, supported in pride, and perpetuated in cruelty...."

Here, then, in graphic detail, are Washington, Jefferson, and Lincoln, turned upside down and viewed from the perspective of the slave, who experienced a nation conceived not in liberty but in compromise and "Hypocrisy" and whose testimony is unimpeachable because it is written in "Blood." The details of this compromise were well-known to Lincoln, he had stated in an earlier speech that the nation was conceived in compromise because "the fathers" were forced by the "necessities" to make a temporary deal with the "Devil."

Further, Lincoln said in his Fourth of July speech in Chicago that this compromise was not only necessary but good, for-you remember the words- "We could not get our constitution unless we permitted them (Blacks) to remain in slavery.

It was in the context of Lincoln's statement that "a house divided against itself cannot stand," that John Hope Franklin asked in another July the Fourth speech, "Who divided this house?" The answer, Dr. Franklin told an audience at the Chicago Historical Society on July 4, 1990, was that the house was divided in large part by Lincoln's fathers." Who divided this house?

The house was divided by George Washington, who was at least as diligent in maintaining control over his wealthy wife's slaves as he was in prosecuting the war against Britain. It was divided by Thomas Jefferson, who not only graciously acquiesced in the deletion of the antislavery clause from the Declaration of Independence but also pleaded unsuccessfully with his protégé Edward Coles, not to set his slaves free and migrate to Illinois but to remain in Virginia and uphold the institution of slavery. Who divided the house? The house was divided by James Madison, the author of the Constitution, who was not only responsible for the style in which slavery was written into the documents but who also helped enact the laws of the First and Second Congresses that respectively barred African-Americans from becoming naturalized citizens and prevented them from becoming members of the United States militia.

Further, it was divided by all the other slaveholders and their accessories, who believed in the obscene incongruity that they could establish a prosperous social order from the exploitation of a labor force without its consent and with no thought of just compensation for it....The house was divided by Benjamin Franklin, whose fears seemed to be limited to the possible Africanization of the country if too many Africans were imported....

The house was also divided in Dr. John Hope Franklin's view by the Abolitionists who were from his standpoint, a negative catalyst and who, from Dr. L. Bennett's standpoint, were a positive catalyst who drove Southerners mad and made it impossible to create a permanent compromise between slavery and freedom.

According to Dr. Lerone Bennett, this brilliant analysis throws new light on the last part of the first sentence of the Gettysburg Address "dedicated to the proposition that "All Men" are created equal," and brings us to the center of the piece. For Lincoln at Gettysburg was America at its best- and worst. Here, give or take a face or a date, was Thomas Jefferson, attended by a favorite slave, writing the Declaration of Independence. Here was Woodrow Wilson, segregating the toilets in Washington, D. C., and setting out to make the world safe for democracy. Here was Nobel Laureate William Faulkner, saying that man would prevail and promising to go out into the streets and shoot Black men and Women to keep Mississippi safe for white folks. Cotton Mather in Salem, Sheriff Clark at Selma, Custer at Little Big Horn, LBJ in the Vietnam quagmire, Ronald Reagan in the white city on the hill; they were all there in spirit at Gettysburg, where Abraham Lincoln carried the American sin, the disassociation of words and reality, of affirmation and act, of principle and practice, to its highest pinnacle.

This political schizophrenia defined and defines the white founding fathers and all those, Lincoln foremost among them, who followed and follow in their path.

The white fathers' dilemma was obvious; They were murdering and robbing Indians and Blacks, and they were in love with words that condemned people who murdered and robbed Indians and Blacks. The solution to this dilemma was clear; they had to give up the words or the murders and robbers. But since they couldn't- or wouldn't-live without the slaves or the Indians' land or the pretty words, they split themselves and reality into two parts, cutting the words off from reality and telling themselves and others that principles were one thing and practice was another and that there was nothing in the Bible or the Declaration of Independence or the Constitution that required white men to respect the rights of Blacks, Indians or Women."75 This Plutocracy reigned well into the Twentieth Century and until the crusade of the late Dr. Martin Luther King, Jr. in 1968, and there yet lies evidence of it today.

To tell the truth, America was reinvented not by Lincoln but against Lincoln. It was reinvented not by his acts but the acts he opposed.

It was reinvented not by the words he said at Gettysburg but by the event-words of the Civil War, by the event-words of Nat Turner and John Brown and the abolitionists by the Thirty-seventh Congress, by the Thirteenth, Fourteenth and Fifteenth Amendments, by the sacrifices of Union Veterans, including the two hundred thousand Blacks without whom the prize could not have been won, by the Black Freedom movement, which continued the process of Emancipation in the Twentieth Century that Lincoln tried to stop in the nineteenth.

In the process of reinventing America, a process that is going on right now, the men and women who opposed Lincoln and Lincoln's ideas, most notably Republican leaders like Sumner, Stevens and Phillips, and Black protestants like Douglas, W. E. B. Du Bois, Thurgood Marshall and Martin Luther King Jr., were more important than Abraham Lincoln. Dr. William E. B. Du Bois gave us further insight on the matter when he asserted that : It was the rise and growth among the slaves of a determination to be free and an active part of American Democracy continually to look into the depths.... This great vision of the Black man was, of course, at first the vision of the few, as visions always are, but it was always there; it grew continuously and it developed quickly from wish to active determination.

One cannot not think of democracy in America or in the modern world without reference to the American Negro. The democracy established in America in the Eighteenth Century was not, and was not designed to be, a democracy of the masses of men and it was thus singularly easy for people to fail to see the incongruity of democracy and slavery. It was the Negro himself who forced the consideration of this incongruity, who made emancipation inevitable and made the modern world at least consider if not wholly accept the idea of a democracy including men of all races and colors."[76]

The situation Lincoln faced in November 1863 was clear and pressing. The logic of war and the intransigence of white Southerners, not Lincoln's purpose and plans, was going to bring about a situation that he considered worse even than slavery itself-the immediate freeing of four million Blacks in a land he, Clay and Thomas Jefferson considered the White man's land.

The new Black citizens would constitute a majority in some Southern states and an overwhelming presence in others. Before Lincoln went up to Gettysburg, he didn't have a single rational idea about how to deal with that new birth of freedom.

Clearly, according to Dr. Bennett, the new birth of freedom Lincoln invoked at Gettysburg was a white variation on an old theme. Did the Gettysburg orator, Lincoln, believe that African-American men-not to mention women- were equal to white men with no ifs, ands, or buts, on the day he said those words at the cemetery in Gettysburg? That answer is NO! The proof is everything he said and did before he spoke at Gettysburg and everything he said and did after he spoke at Gettysburg.

Did Lincoln believe on November 19, 1863, that it would be possible to achieve equality in America for African-Americans, not to mention poor whites, with all deliberate speed? Hell No! Same answer, same proof. Was Lincoln committing himself on this day to a crusade for the far-off goal of equality in America for Blacks, and was he asking his audience and the widows of the white Northern and Southern brothers who died there to join him in that crusade? NO!

Crusades for Black rights were not Lincoln's style, never. Never in his whole life did Abraham Lincoln ask any white to grant any Black equal rights in the United States of America. Whites may view the speech as passionate and kind. However, when viewed from the perspective of the slave, it is very cold, and abstract when it comes to human rights. Its' primary concern is self-government and overlooks the biggest issue of that day. The Gettysburg Address, for all its artistry and eloquence, does not directly address the prickliest issues of its historic moment," Or of any historic movement since the Slave Trade.

If you like feel good words and if you have no interest in slaves, slavemasters, oppression, and liberation, there is much to admire in the Gettysburg Address, especially in the inner sentences-" We cannot dedicate-We cannot consecrate-We cannot hallow this ground." But there is no point in praising the document's aesthetic values, its thirteen alliterations and two antitheses, unless you are a professor who wants to teach students and politicians how to alliterate and equivocate. And I have always found it ominous that there is not a single concrete image in the whole speech, not a single concrete Confederate or Union soldier, not a single concrete slave or concrete slave master, not a single drop of red blood or Black hope, in contrast, say, with the speech of Jesus, which was always full of salt, bread, wolves and sheep, generations of vipers, and dens of thieves."[77]

Abraham Lincoln wanted to return the former slaves to their masters after the Civil War and many saw this as a very disastrous measure right from the start. Congressman Thaddeus Stevens who was so instrumental in the initiatives of the Thirty-Seventh Congress which forced Lincoln into signing the Emancipation Proclamation believed that; "To trust the tender mercies of their former masters and to the protection of State legislation, without giving them any voice in making the laws, is simply to turn them (Negroes) over to the torture of their "Enemies."

To turn them loose unaided and unprotected is wholesale "Murder." This is simply what happened to the newly freedmen and women as the result of Lincoln's plan for Reconstruction of the South after the Civil War.

The Great Abolitionist Wendell Phillips described the condition of the African-American in the post Civil war South when he said; There stands the Negro man, naked, homeless; he does not own a handful of dust; he has no education; he has no roof to shelter him....

"That man made the South a paradise," and when it was done, he shouldered his musket with us, and saved it to the nation. Look at him! The gratitude of republics! Disfranchised, naked, homeless, poor, we give him back to the White man who "Hates" him, to dictate the terms of his existence!"[78] This was the mistake of the Federal government lead by one Abraham Lincoln, which led to mass lynchings and other unparallel murders in any so-called civilized society.

Lincoln spoke at Gettysburg on Thursday, November 19,1863. When, nineteen days later, he unveiled his own post war plan, he made it clear that 'all' meant the same thing to him that it has always meant;"All White People." Thus, in his Proclamation of Amnesty and Reconstruction, issued on Tuesday, December 8, 1863, Lincoln became the first American president to explicitly draw the color line by officially defining a national program based on the exclusion of Black voters. It can be said in Lincoln's defense, of course, that the white founding fathers were the real fathers of the color line, but a different point is involved here.

For the slavery that condemned the Compromise of 1787 made it possible for the white founding fathers to hide behind "State's Rights" and the "Three-Fifths" of other persons language they wrote in the Constitution. This, however, didn't stop Black founding fathers from voting in several of the original states, and nobody told South Carolina that it had to disenfranchise Black.

The Civil War changed the "Three-Fifths" [clause] and made it necessary for a president to issue an official order defining the racial space of new persons who had been defined legally as citizens by events and an ultraconservative attorney general. But the language that served George Washington would not serve the presidents of a country without slavery. What was needed now was a language that included all whites and excluded all Blacks in states like South Carolina and Louisiana where most of the people were Black.

Abraham Lincoln led the way in 1863 by proposing a national policy of reconstructing a Southern state as soon as one-tenth of the male voters of 1860 took a future loyalty oath and organized a government that renounced slavery. Lincoln didn't say a word about race, but every word he said was a race word. In a classic formulation, followed by subsequent "Jim Crow, regimes, Lincoln grandfathered all whites in and grandfathered all Blacks out. For as everyone knew, there were no Black voters in Confederate states in 1860 when it was a criminal offense for a Black man to present himself at the polling place.

What about the slaves, who constituted a majority of the population in South Carolina, Mississippi, and Louisiana? There were no rights for them or any other Blacks in the Lincoln plan. For them and for their children, it was not yet Jubilee. No rockets red glare for them.

To be sure, as Dr. Bennett exclaims, "This was mind-Boggling. To turn the unprotected former slaves over to unreconstructed slave owners and Confederates who hated them and feared them and blamed them for their defeat was more than malice to some, it was a license for murder or mayhem. Lincoln didn't seem to see Blacks and did not seem to realize that the "deeply afflicted people" in the South were not the former slave owner but the former slaves and that the causes of their affliction were the former slave owners to whom he proposed to leave "the vital matter" of Black freedom."[79]

"From 1861 to 1863, Lincoln, by his own admission, struggled to keep from touching the institution of slavery. From 1863 to 1865 he struggled to keep from touching the social system that caused the Civil War. What about slavery? As in the first days of the war, he wanted to touch slavery least of all and last of all. He said everywhere that he would not re-enslave the minority of slaves who had enjoyed actual freedom. What Lincoln said clearly here was that the overwhelming majority of slaves who had not enjoyed actual freedom could, as far as he was concerned, be kept in slavery or quasi slavery, depending on the whims of the court. The only problem, from his standpoint and the standpoint of the slave owners, was the Thirteenth Amendment. It was not certain at this time that it would be ratified, and it was, unfortunately, Lincoln's death, and not his life, that speeded ratification. Lincoln wanted ratification of the Thirteenth Amendment to be "Gradually or Prospectively" as he called it. Moreover, another way was to use the devices all colonial powers use and that Lincoln repeatedly recommended; transitional periods of apprenticeship and slavery under the new names of serfdom or sharecropping.

Then also, what was at stake here, in modern terms, was reparations for the victims of "History's Greatest Crime," the "Four Hundred-Year" ordeal of the "Slave Trade" and the "Two Hundred Year" ordeal of "Slavery." The whole economic empire of the West, including the gold that made capitalism possible and the capital that financed the Western movement, all of it, the docks and streets of Boston and New Orleans and Charleston, the books and finery of Monticello and Mount Vernon, Wall Street and Canal Street and Scarlet O'Hara's house, the one in the movies and the manors on Peachtree Street, "All of it was founded on the 'blood and bones' of the slaves."

None knew of the debt owed to the former slaves better than a former slave herself, Sojourner Truth, who called for land reform and federal subsidies integrated into a comprehensive plan of a magnitude never attempted in this country. "America" she said "owes to my people some of the dividends. She can afford to pay, and she must pay. I shall make them understand that there is a debt to the Negro people they can never repay. At least then they must make amends."

When Wendell Phillips thought of the enormity of the "Crime" and the staggering "Debt" owed to African-Americans, he was overcome with horror and remorse.

"This nation,' he said in a Boston speech, reprinted in the Liberator, February 5, 1864, "owes the Negro not merely freedom; it owes him land, and it owes him education also. It is a debt which will disgrace us before the people if we do not pay it," a debt, he said, that requires "not charity but justice-absolute, immediate, unmixed justice...."

Even the word justice was inadequate to describe an open account unprecedented in world history. "I hate the term justice to the Negro," Phillips said, "There is not wealth enough in all the North to compensate this generation- much less the claim it has as heir to those who have gone before....

There is not (enough) wealth in the nation to give him his rights.... We are not rich enough to give the Negro his rights. For "Two Hundred Years" he has redeemed twenty states from "Savagery and Barbarism." Every house built upon its surface his labor constructed. Every dollar dug from the soil was got by the toil of the Negro.... Agriculture, cities, roads, factories, funded capital- all were made by and belong to the Negro."

That's what Frederick Douglas meant when he said, "The white people of this country can never do to much for us. If they should put a school house at every crossroads of the South, supply each with a teacher... they would not cancel the debt contracted by the long years of slavery and suffering of this people."

Thaddeus Stevens made all this concrete and captured the imagination of the slaves with a notion that was immortalized in the phrase, "Forty acres and a mule." Going back to the Thirty-Seventh Congress and to the act Lincoln underlined and later sabotaged, he introduced resolutions providing for the immediate enforcement of the Confiscation Act of July 1862.

The resolutions provided that the land seized should be distributed among slaves who had been liberated by the war and constitutional amendments and who were living on said land on the 4th of March, 1861, or since; "to each male person who is head of a family, forty acres; to each adult male, whether head of a family or not, forty acres; to each widow who is head of a family, forty acres; to be held by them in fee-simple, but to be inalienable for the next ten years after they become seized thereof...."

The resolutions proposed by the Thirty-seventh Congress and other resolutions of similar depth failed because most Republicans, Lincoln foremost among them, had no intention of transforming American society. They never intended to give blacks any more power than was necessary to check Southern planters. They recoiled instinctively from measures that would have given Blacks a measure of the economic security still denied the white workers of the North. They had never admitted the full logic of the Democratic idea for poor whites; it was unthinkable that they would countenance it for poor Blacks especially since wholesale confiscation of property in the South would have set a bad example for the restless workers of the North and West.

Thaddeus Stevens and his colleagues based their struggle on the Declaration of Independence, which Lincoln reportedly loved but never talked about in concrete struggles. In a great speech, more pertinent and more concrete than the Gettysburg Address, Stevens denounced Lincoln's successor, Andrew Johnson, and other politicians who supported white supremacy; Demagogues of all parties, even some in high authority, gravely shout, "This is the White man's government."

What is implied by this? That one race of men are to have the exclusive right to rule the nation, and to exercise all acts of sovereignty, while all other races and nations and colors are to be their subjects, and have no voice in making the laws and choosing their rulers by whom they are to be governed...." This, Stevens said, was a monstrous proposition; Our fathers repudiated the whole doctoring of the legal superiority of families or races and proclaimed the equality of men before the law. Upon that they created a revolution and built a republic. They were prevented by slavery from perfecting the superstructure whose foundation they had thus broadly laid....

Lincoln said at Gettysburg that the task before the nation was a rededication to what the white fathers had done four score and seven years ago. Stevens, with a larger vision and a bigger heart, said the task before the nation was a rededication to what the white fathers had not done four score and seven years ago. Now was the time, he said, "to complete their work." 'If this republic is not now made to stand on their great principles, it has no honest foundation, an the father of all men will still shake it to its center. If we have not yet been sufficiently scourged for our national sin to teach us to do justice to all God's creatures, without distinction of race or color, we must expect the still more heavy vengeance of an offended father.... Thus, in conclusion; This is not 'a White man's Government," in the exclusive sense in which it is used. To say so is political blasphemy, for it violates the fundamental principles of our gospel of liberty. This is man's Government, the Government of all men alike; not that all men will have equal power and sway within it. Accidental circumstances, natural and acquired endowment and ability, will vary their fortunes. But equal rights to all the privileges of the Government is innate in every immortal being, no matter what the shape or color of the tabernacle which it inhabits...."[80]

"South Carolina had always been pointed to as the typical Slave state. It had, in 1860, 412,320 Negroes and 291,300 Whites. Even at the beginning of the Nineteenth Century, the 200,000 whites were matched by 450,000 Negroes, and the influx from the border and the direct African Slave Trade brought a mass of Black Slaves to support the new cotton kingdom. There had always been small numbers of free Negroes, a little over 3,000 at the beginning of the century, and nearly 10,000 in 1860. Slavery was the driving force of the states industrial and social life; it was this institution that made South Carolina different from the states of the north; it was the principal reason why the white manhood of the state had fought so desperately."[81]

"During the period of Reconstruction (1865-1877), following Slavery and the Civil War, many promises were made to the newly freed Slaves.

8a

Sojourner Truth
1797-1883

Abolitionist and Advocate of women's rights.

These included commitments to racial equality and economic opportunity. But within a short time these promises were compromised, ignored or abandoned. And the years shortly following reconstruction Black people were essentially returned to Slavery in every respect but name. In A few years of Reconstruction in the South the former Slaves made significant progress in Education, Politics, and Economics, but in the short period of approximately one decade it was back to business as usual. Meaning a return to hard-core white supremacy."[82]

"As long as Lincoln and Johnson permitted some Southern whites to participate in Reconstruction, the white believed they could handle Blacks and resurrect the Democratic Party. Even when the presence of Negro troops outraged them, they could protest vigorously to the president. These white Southerners were determined to guide their own destiny and control Negroes. When radical Reconstruction made this impossible, in 1867, they struck with fury and rage. Secret societies grew and spread when it became apparent to Southerners that their control was to be broken by Radical Reconstruction. For ten years after 1867 there flourished the Knights of the white Camelia, The Constitutional Union Guards, The Pale Faces, The white Brotherhood, The Council of Safety, The '76 Association, and The Knights of the Ku Klux Klan. Among the numerous local organizations were the White League of Louisiana, The white Line of Mississippi, and the Rifle Club of South Carolina. White Southerners expected to do by extralegal or blatantly illegal means what had not been allowed by law; To exercise absolute control over Negroes, drive them and their fellows from power, and re-establish "White Supremacy". Radical Reconstruction was to be ended at all costs and the tactics of terrorist groups were the first steps of Southern white leaders toward achieving this goal.

The Camelias and the Klan were the most powerful of the secret orders. Armed with guns, swords, or other weapons, their members patrolled some parts of the South day and night. Scattered union troops proved wholly ineffectual in coping with them, for the members were sworn to secrecy, disguised themselves and their deeds in many ways, and had the support of the white community. The violence, which culminated in the Ku Klux Klan Movement, did not arise solely, however, from the establishment of Radical Reconstruction and the consequent elimination of the Southern white men from public life. As early as 1866, when Southern whites had almost complete charge of reconstruction, a kind of guerrilla warfare was carried on against both Blacks and whites who represented the Washington government in the South. The head of the Freedman's Bureau in Georgia, for example, complained that bands of men calling themselves Regulators, Jayhawkers, and the Black Horse Cavalry, were committing the "most fiendish and diabolical outrages on the freedmen", with the sympathy not only of the populace but the reconstructed governments too.

There were scores of these coercive organizations all over the South. They were formed as white protective societies, and while Southerner leaders enacted the new Black Codes, they were engaged in "keeping the Negro in his place".

They used intimidation, force, ostracism in business and society, bribery at the polls, arson, and even murder to accomplish their deeds. Depriving the Negro of political equality became, to them, a Holy crusade in which a noble end justified any means.

Negroes were run out of communities if they disobeyed orders to desist from voting; and the more resolute and therefore insubordinate Blacks were whipped, maimed, and hanged. In 1871, several Negro officials in South Carolina were given fifteen days to resign and they were warned that if they failed to do so, "then retributive justice will be used as surely as night follows day."[83]

"It was provided in some states, like South Carolina, that any White man whether an officer or not, could arrest a Negro. Upon view of a misdemeanor committed by a person of color, any person present may arrest the offender and take him before the magistrate to be dealt with as the case may require. In case of a misdemeanor committed by a white person toward a person of color, any person may complain to a magistrate, who shall cause the offender to be arrested, and according to the nature of the case to be brought before himself or be taken for trial in the district court."[84]

"Especially in the matter of work was the Negro narrowly restricted. In South Carolina, he must be especially licensed if he was to follow on his own account any employments except that of farmer or servant. The right to sell farm products without written permission or evidence from the employer was forbidden in South Carolina. A person of color who is in the employment of a master, engaged in husbandry, shall not have the right to sell any corn, rice, peas, wheat, or other grain, any flower, cotton, fodder, hay, bacon, fresh meat of any kind, animals of any kind, or any other product on a farm, without having written permission from such master or from the Judge or magistrate."[85]

"The evolution of the Sharecropping and crop-lien systems began during the Civil War itself. In 1861-62, the Union Armies entrenched themselves on the South Carolina sea island. The government was confronted with the problem of providing for the physical needs of the Blacks. There was also the problem of cultivating and harvesting the cotton wanted by the Northern textile mills and a potential source of the revenue for the treasury. In the ensuing years the freedmen suffered from the lack of forethought on the part of government officials and from power rivalries between the treasury and army departments, who were given control over the affairs of the freedmen and plantations.

They suffered also from the differences of opinions among missionaries and philanthropist who were sincerely trying to assist Blacks. Not until the creation of the Freedmen's Bureau in March 1865 was it definitely settled that the war department would have the responsibility of protecting and providing for the welfare of the freedmen.

8b

A sharecropper tries to argue with the landlord.

The results was confusion in freedmen's affairs, gross exploitation of the Negroes by unscrupulous entrepreneurs and, in some cases, by dishonest missionaries and army officers, and frustration for the freedmen who had anticipation, with good reason, of receiving land of their own. The Treasury Department, however, decided to sell most of the plantations for unpaid taxes. After the Civil War when president Andrew Johnson restored most of the plantations to their former owners, Blacks who had bought some land were able to attain titles, but thousands of others who had purchased directly from the government lost their holdings. Practically no effort was made to encourage Black land ownership and regulations were issued by white officials requiring the freedmen to return to the plantations and work for extremely low wages. Under the banks orders, the Negroes were forbidden to leave the plantation without a pass, and "insolence or the absence of perfect "subordination" could result in the freedmen losing pay altogether or food rations.

Frederick Douglas said that the failures of these bank orders re-enslaved the freedmen and made mockery of the Emancipation proclamation of 1863. In 1865 Southern lawmakers enacted Black Codes as a system of social control that would be a substitute for Slavery, fix the Negro in a subordinate place in the social order, and provide a manageable and inexpensive labor force, and blacks who were unemployed or without a permanent residence were declared vagrants. They could be arrested and fined and, if unable to pay, be bound out for terms of labor. In several states the words "master" and "servant" were freely used- and particularly in South Carolina the terms of the contracts were minutely defined. South Carolina went so far as to exclude Negroes from skilled trades.

More uncertainty surrounding the process by which the system of farm tenancy known as sharecropping emerged from the labor contract system that prevailed during the early years of Reconstruction. Under a sharecropping arrangement the freedmen, instead of working for a wage, rented a plot of land and paid to the plantation owner a certain proportion of the cotton crop. The origins of this system are extremely obscure. There is at least occasional evidence that some wartime, Army-supervised contracts provided for sharecropping as an alternative to the wage system. Planters generally would have preferred a system whereby Negroes contracted by the year to work for specified wages, but the shortage of available cash right after the war encouraged them to adopt a plan whereby they shared the crop with the Black workers. Freedmen themselves were largely responsible for the development of sharecropping, because they regarded the contract labor system, under which they worked in labor gangs, as too reminiscent of slavery times. Where they were unable to purchase their own land, as was usually the case, the Negroes preferred to be renters rather than hired laborers.

Renting was desirable, even under sharecropping rather than a cash arrangement, because tenants could organize their own time and be more independent than a hired laborer. More importantly, they could raise their own food. Planters, however, also found advantages in the sharecropping system.

WILLIAM EDWARD BURGHARDT DUBOIS

organizer of the
Niagara Movement and NAACP

10

161

Hired laborers would work no harder than forced too and, despite the law might break their contracts. But sharecroppers had a vested interest in the crops, which they could not afford to leave standing in the fields. Originally the arrangement was one that probably motivated the ex-slaves to work hard for their own advancement.

Moreover, the evolution of the system was complicated by the fact that it was not uncommon at first for hired laborers to be paid in whole or in part with a share of the crop at the end of the year. For some years, in fact, until the courts straightened out the matter, the two types of sharecropping were not clearly distinguishable.

Typically the croppers kept one quarter to one half of the crop, depending on what they supplied in the way of mules, tools, and seed. It was the planter who weighted the cotton and kept the accounts. This system reached its' depths in the Crop-lien. The croppers paid heavily for the purchases they were compelled to make at the plantation store. Buying food and clothing on credit with the crop as lien, they were charged high prices, outrageous interest rates, and were forced to depend upon the planter, particularly in a poor year. Out of this arose the system of debt peonage, whereby insolvent croppers, unable to pay debts from one year to the another, were required by law to work indefinitely for the same unscrupulous planter."[86]

William Edward Burghardt Dubois, was born in Great Barrington, Massachusetts, in 1868 and was the dominant African-American intellectual of his time. Dubois was to study at Harvard University and in Europe. He helped to organize the Niagra Movement and the (NAACP) National Association for the Advancement of Colored People), and served as the editor of its' journal, the "CRISIS." In later life he was active in Pacifist and African Independence Movements and became a citizen of Ghana, West Africa, where he lived until his death in 1963. Dubois was born of African, French and Dutch ancestry, the year of the enfranchisement of the freedmen by the Fifteenth Amendment."[87]

"In January 1906, the Civil Rights organization (Niagra Movement) would be incorporated and the "DECLARATION OF PRINCIPLES" were formed, which declared "We refuse to allow the impression to remain that the Negro American assents to inferiority," Dubois said. "He is submissive under oppression and apologetic before insults. Though helpless we may submit, but the voice of the protest of ten million Americans must never cease to assail the ears of the fellows, so long as America is unjust."[88]

Dr. Dubois went on in his protest by asserting that, "The Negro race in America, "Stolen, Ravished and Degraded," struggling up through difficulties and oppression, needs sympathy and receives criticism; needs help and is given hindrance, needs protection and is given mob violence, needs justice and is given charity, needs leadership and is given cowardice and apology, needs bread and is given stone. This nation will never stand justified before God until these things are changed."[89]

162

"Race relations grew dire in South Carolina after a relatively calm period in the 1880's, when white supremacy had been reestablished by the end of Reconstruction, things deteriorated dramatically in the 1990's. Benjamin J. Brawler, a pioneering South Carolina Black intellectual, wrote that" the nineties were in some ways the darkest that the race has ever experienced since Emancipation...It seemed to the rural Southern Negro that the conditions of Slavery had all but come again." Suddenly, White Southerners moved to disenfranchise the few remaining Black voters; they erected a new system of "Jim Crow" laws to segregate the races; and they lynched thousands of Africans."[90]

Although class is an important variable in all aspects of American life, including the status of Black people, race becomes the main issue in Black-White relations. One is often reminded of the prophecy of W.E.B. Dubois at the turn of the century, "The problem of the twentieth century is the problem of the colour-line, the question is to how far differences of race... are going to be made, hereafter, the basis of denying to over half the world the right of sharing to their utmost ability the opportunities and privileges of modern civilization. To be sure, the darker races are today the least advanced in culture according to European standards. This has not, however, always been the case in the past, and certainly the world's History, both ancient and modern, has given many instances of no despicable ability and capacity among the blackest races of men. In any case, the modern world must remember that in this age...The millions of Black men in Africa, America, and the Islands of the Sea, not to speak of the brown and yellow myriads elsewhere, are bound to have great influence upon the world in the future, by reason of sheer numbers and physical contact.... If, by reason of carelessness, prejudice, greed and injustice, the Black world is to be exploited and ravished and degraded, the results must be deplorable, if not fatal, not simply to them, but to the high ideals of justice, freedom, and culture which a thousand years of Christian civilization have held before Europe."[91]

"One Crucial aspect of racism in the United States has been that for centuries the laws were used to uphold and perpetuate the racism of the society. The proliferation of racist laws over many years reflected the determination to maintain white supremacy in every institution. Two of the most significant judgments occurred in the nineteenth century, one during the Antebellum period and the other in the post Reconstruction. In 1857, in the case of Dread Scott vs. Sanford, chief justice of the supreme court Roger Taney, writing for the majority, declared that "Blacks had no rights which the White man was bound to respect," and in 1896, the court ruled in Plessy vs. Ferguson, that " The argument also assumes that social prejudice maybe overcome by legislation, and that equal rights cannot be secured to the Negro except by enforced commingling of the two races. We cannot accept this proposition." The court concluded "If one race be inferior to the other socially, the constitution of the United States cannot put them on the some plane." This decision upheld the doctoring of "Separate But Equal." The two decisions simply informed both Blacks and whites that segregation was a permanent part of the American way of life."[92]

Beneath the rhetoric of '…life, liberty, and the pursuit of happiness' and that …'all men are created equal' lies the fact of the "Greatest Crimes Ever Committed Against Humanity"

20

According to W.E.B. Dubois, "Africans came to look upon courts as instruments of injustice and oppression, and upon those convicted in them as martyrs and victims."[93]

"The Nineteenth Century closed as it had began, just as, indeed, the Eighteenth Century had closed as it had began, as far as race was concerned. The factor of race haunted the relations of Blacks and whites in the Eighteenth Century and dictated not only the relations of master and Slave but the relations of whites and Blacks who were free. This same factor and the actions of proslavery advocates of race in the Nineteenth Century dominated the thoughts as well as abolitionists, and was a major issue in determining the interpretation of the Constitution and setting into public policy virtually to the end of the Twentieth Century.

Throughout the Nineteenth Century, White Americans could not bring themselves to subscribe to the view that free Black Americans were entitled to the same privileges and rights of citizenship that whites enjoyed. The view that free Blacks had no rights prevailed at the time of the Constitution and was in place when all; Blacks became free in 1865. This was the basis for the policy and practices that persisted throughout the Nineteenth Century and for most of the Twentieth Century."[94]

"They all came to the hanging. There were men in their Sunday-best black suits and hats, women in their long dark dresses sweeping to the ground, and boys with their knickers, white shirts and ties. Some came in buggies and carriages, some on horseback, others walked for hours under the pale November sun. They all wanted to secure the best positions around the new brick courthouse. The early arrivals clambered upon sawhorses or wooden crates to peer over the jail yard fence at the twelve-foot high scaffold. Others perched in trees or leaned out the second floor windows of a nearby bank and general store. It was the first official "Hanging" in Saluda County. Saluda had been carved out of the northern part of the state of South Carolina in 1896. The man sentenced to be hanged that day, November 27, 1908, was a poor Black sharecropper named Will Herrin. Herrin had been working in the cotton fields since he was a boy. On Saturday nights' friends of Will Herrin had gotten together with him to drink, sing, and dance. Now they were coming to pay their last respects to a relative and fellow sharecropper.

For the county's white, it was a day of somber celebration and self congratulation-white supremacy was being forcefully affirmed. Now that it is settled that they will hang a man at Saluda, we look for better times" proclaimed the towns' newspaper, the Saluda Standard. "There was never a time when Negroes were more polite in Saluda." Will Herrin aroused deep anxieties in the local white community. They were members of what seemed a frightening new class of troublemakers whites termed the "New Negro." Will had been born after slavery, so they had not been trained as children to obey white masters. They actually believed that Emancipation made them free and equal. "Most of the men who were masters and most who were Slaves are dead," noted the writer Walter Hines Page.

This brought a grave social danger." The newspaper, "Standard", Quoted with approval a speech by a senator from Mississippi, who declared, "There could never possibly be any social equality between the two races. There is a race prejudice in the South, and I thank God there is."

Saluda's white citizens lamented the disappearance of the "old time darkey" and the rise of the "New Negro." "These younger ebonies of Ethiopian lineage are as different from the old time darkey as the moon differs from the sun," The "Standard" commented sadly. "Many of them will hardly recognize you when they pass you, and some rarely give you road, even though you may have a lady with you…Give us the old time darkey everytime."

The crime for which Will Herrin was to be hanged appeared to confirm the whites worse fears: He had killed his landlord Emanuel Carver. Year after year, Herrin had made what he thought was "A good farm", bringing in twelve or thirteen bales of cotton from the forty acres he was sharecropping. Herrin was "working on halves", meaning that he owed half the crop to carver, but got to keep the other half, less any money advanced him for "furnishings", for food, fertilizer, and seeds. Yet, every year at "settling up time" in the fall, Carver insisted Herrin had no money coming to him. "The man", as Will Herrin called the Whiteland owner "just didn't believe in paying", he told his family. Every year Herrin was left destitute.

Finally in the Autumn of 1908, Will was sure he had "made A big farm" He had harvested sixteen bales of cotton, at about five hundred pounds a bale. It was an excellent crop. "Will jest knowed he was going to collect some money" his niece remembered. But when he went to Carver to collects the landowner said, "you come out even." Carver gave him nothings and kept all the money for which the cotton had been sold. A quiet, stolid man, Herrin did not argue. But his honor had been much offended, the same sense of honor for which white Southerners had fought for so long. He went to his croppers cabin behind the landlord's house and got his single barrel shotgun. On his way back he found Carver in the field and shot him, point blank. Then, as Carver lay dying, Mrs. Carver rushed out to see what the shooting was about, Herrin beat him over the head with his gun. Herrin knew it was a suicidal attack.

He walked the ten miles into Saluda with his gun and turned himself in to the sheriff. The trial took less than half an hour, "for there was really nothing to try", the "Standard' reported. The court appointed a young lawyer who had just finished law school, Rodney Etheredge, to defend Herrin. It was his first case. He had not much chance for display of legal acummen", the paper said.

On the day set for execution, the deputy sheriff, Joe Padgett, granted Herrin's last wish; he brought him a bag of apples. As Herrin ate them, a group of white men prepared an elaborate shroud, complete with cuffs, to cover his head, arms, and chest.

They struggled getting this "toggery" on him, the "Standard" reported, but "during all this he never spoke and was perfectly docile." At last the sheriff announced, "Time's up Will." Herrin carefully put the cores of all the apples he had eaten back into the bag, and then marched off ahead of the sheriff into the jail yard. A loud cry went up from the spectators assembled outside. Herrin walked rapidly up the scaffold, "without a moment's hesitation", and again stood by cooly while the hangman fumbled with the noose. Asked if he had something he wished to say, the condemned man replied, "I will meet in the hereafter with the people who hanged me" Exactly on the dot of noon, the sheriff pulled the trigger to open the trap. Another "Great Yell" went up from the crowd. The widow and the son of Carver were "well pleased to see the execution" 'according to the "Standard." The paper said Herrin's own relatives "repudiated him entirely" because of his crime and would not come to the hanging. But they were all there, including his widow. The whole family was angry, "but what could you do about it?" A nephew recalled. The white man had the law the white man was the law."[95]

For the African, the twentieth Century in America can and should be noted as when the "Devil" himself was at the height of his reign. As a cause of Abolitionists anguish and protest, however, even disfranchisement took second place to "lynching." The number of lynching reached an all time record high of 255 in 1892, and 92 percent of all people lynched were Black and 89 percent Black in the next decade. Even worse, lynching was becoming less a matter of midnight hanging and more a public spectacle accompanied by torture and carried out by burning at the stake. A "Lynching Bee" sometimes became the occasion for a holiday, with railroads running special trains to the event and thousands of men, women and children watching the saturnalia of mutilation, screams, and burning flesh. "It is impossible to speak with self restraint on the subject." Lynch mobs cared not whether their victims were guilty of any crime. They wanted the sight of blood.... "They were savages." "Every participant in such "Lawless Orgies"...is a murderer," declared Thomas J. Morgan, an abolitionist from Chicago. "They subvert the foundations of society; degrade the Blacks to the level of brutes and place the white in the category of wild beasts."[96]

"The hanging of Will Herrin was only one small sign of a "crisis" that overtook the South in the 1890's and the first decade of the Twentieth Century. The White man was angry because of a severe economic recession brought on as the South joined the world market economy. Farm prices plummeted, businesses failed. Conditions got so bad that the editor of the local newspaper advertised, "in order that everyone may have a chance to pay up... we'll take any kind of marketable farm products from those who have not got cash."[97]

In South Carolina, the campaign against Blacks was led by Ben Tillman of Edgefield, who became governor in 1890, and then senator in 1894 on mixing Negrophobia with economic populism. He was a man of commanding stature, intellectual brilliance, and magnetic personality; but his very appearance suggested a certain savagery.

During the crucial election of 1876 that ended Reconstruction, he had been a leader in terrorizing African-Americans through murder. He once declared, "Governor as l am, I'd lead a mob to lynch a man who had ravished a White woman... I justify lynching for rape and, before almighty God I'm not ashamed of it."98

Many Blacks felt that they might choose to find in the intensity of White violence and repression as a sign of hope and progress. From his extensive investigations, Walter White, of the NAACP, concluded that "Lynching is much more an expression of Southern fear of Negro progress than of Negro crime." Lynching, in this view, did not necessarily succeed in reinforcing racial repression; on the contrary, it suggested the refusal of black men and women to submit with equanimity to that repression. None other than Frederick Douglas suggested in 1892 that the racial violence and lynching may actually be "a favorable symptom."

"It is proof that the Negro is not standing still. He is not dead, but alive and active. He is not drifting with the current, but manfully resisting it and fighting his way to better conditions than those of the past, and better than those which popular opinion prescribes for him. He is not contented with his surroundings...."

"'A ship rotting at anchor meets with no resistance, but when she sets sail on the sea, she has to buffet opposing billows. The enemies of the Negro see that he is making progress and they naturally wish to stop him and keep him in just what they consider his proper "Place." They who aspire to higher grades than those fixed for them by society are scouted and scorned as upstarts for their presumptions."

The extraordinary amount of attention and energy expended upon black southerners, Henry M. Turner argued in 1904, refuted most compellingly the charge of inferiority. "More laws have been enacted by the different legislatures of the country, and more judicial decisions have been delivered and proclaimed against this person of inferiority called Negro than have been issued against any people since time began." Based on the attempts to suppress the race, Turner concluded, "It would appear that the Negro is the greatest man on earth."99

"In 1895, with white hysteria about Blacks at fever pitch, Ben Tillman convened a convention to re-write South Carolina's constitution. His triumph was to come up with a law that would disenfranchise Blacks without contravening the Fifteenth Amendment and invite federal intervention.

He found the answer in a complex set of residency requirements and a provision that forced Black voters to answer questions from white officials about the Constitution. One white delegate to the convention, exasperated by his colleagues' worries about the niceties of the new law, said "We don't propose to have any fair elections.... I tell you gentlemen, if we have fair elections we can't carry it." When voter registrar's showed up for three days, the Saluda newspaper reported, they issued registration certificates to nobody whatsoever."

"Jim Crow laws also soon appeared, starting with the railroads. The Saluda newspaper felt they were an urgent necessity. "Give the Negro justice, but for decency's sake protect delicately constituted white ladies from contamination by being thrown in company with an inferior race", it said. Keep the air of our palace cars... from being polluted by the odor Africanus-an element inseparable from a Negro's presence."

Benjamin Mays of South Carolina, recounts that "There wasn't much going for the Negro in the world in which I was born. The shades at darkness were falling fast upon and around him... the ballot was being taken away, segregation was being enacted into law... Injustice in the courts was taken for granted... Books and articles were being published, sermons preached, and anti-Negro speeches made, all saying in substance: "The Negro is a different breed. He is inferior to the White man. At any cost he must be kept down."[100]

In 1897, J. William Thurman, the state prosecutor and political boss of the Edgefield, South Carolina region, was in his office near the Edgefield courthouse. Thurmond was also Senator Ben Tillman's lawyer. As he sat near the open door, Thurmond was accosted by a traveling salesman for a drug company, Willie Harris. Harris is reported to have been drinking, and he berated Thurmond for backing Tillman. An argument quickly followed. Harris called Thurmond "A God-Damn-Dog," and a scoundrel. At that affront to his honor, Thurmond pulled his pistol and mortally wounded Harris. Eyewitnesses said Harris had no gun and made no threatening gesture, and no weapon was found on his body. Nevertheless, Thurmond filed an affidavit swearing that Harris had boasted he was armed with "A damn good knife and A colt's pistol." Harris had lunged at him with the knife, Thurmond insisted, and when Thurmond then kicked him backward out the door, Harris reached for his gun. It was a simple case of self defense, Thurmond asserted. A jury took only thirty-five minutes to acquit Thurmond on murder charges. He was also restored to his post as prosecutor-solicitor, as the Job was called in South Carolina. Later, Senator Tillman rewarded his faithful ally by having him appointed United States Attorney for South Carolina. Thurmond's son, Strom Thurmond, would emulate Tillman, being elected to governor and senator.

In 1948, Strom Thurmond would run for president of the United States as a "Dixiecrat" in order to enforce segregation and keep Blacks "in their place."

Thurmond's killing of the salesman, Willie Harris, occasioned only a little gossip. It was merely a sign of a rising tide of violence in South Carolina in the 1890's. The increase in violence on Blacks was another part of the "Crisis" of the period.

Murder rates had always been high in S. C., but in the 1890's and the first decade of the twentieth century they escalated drastically. The number of murders reported by the states prosecutors rose from 79 in 1887 to 151 in 1891, and then to 210 in 1895. The span of violence reached its' apogee in 1907, when 280 murders were reported.

That is an increase of three and half times in twenty years. By comparison, the national homicide rate only doubled between the thirty years of 1960 and 1990, the period when Americans felt they were besieged by what they believed to be the worse crime wave in American History.

In Saluda, many citizens were appalled by the number of murders. During Saluda's first decade, from 1896 to 1905, there were sixty-six reported homicides, giving it a murder rate of 35 per 100,000. That is higher than the 1992 homicide rate in New York City. "Saluda" wrote the editor of the local newspaper, "has made "A Shameful Record" and this propensity for violence made "Saluda " the wild west of South Carolina."[101]

"Despite southerners' claims or farmers because of disputes over land and payments. In South Carolina, "with the greatest number of lynching", almost half of the incidents began when a Black was accused of killing or assaulting a white man, usually a landlord or overseer. Lynching was another tool to ensure "White control," and it grew, as Blacks became increasingly dissatisfied and discontent; most lynching did not involve rape. Much more often, they were directed against Black sharecroppers refusal to accept their subordinate, oppressed status. Negroes lived under constant pressure and tension all the time. They knew they were not free. They knew that if attacked they dare not strike back-if they wanted to live.... Negroes fought among themselves because they were taking out on other Negroes what they really feared to take out on whites.

It was difficult, virtually impossible to combine manhood and Blackness under one skin in those days. To exercise manhood, as white men displayed it, was to invite disaster. What became the philosophy of most black sharecroppers was that "There is no advantage to life, standing behind some animals ass everyday, and nothing to show for it at the end of the year."[102]

W.E.B. Dubois detected the process from the Black perspective. "There can be no doubt that crime among Negroes has sensibly increased in the last thirty years," Dubois said, in 1903. But," Black Criminality" was not the result of Black bestiality and poverty, he insisted. It was the outcome of a history in which whites had made critical errors.

The Southern police system had been developed in slavery times to deal with Blacks alone, and tacitly assumed that every white man was "IPSO FACTO" a member of that police. Thus, grew up "A Double Standard," which erred on the white side by undue leniency... and erred on the Black side by undue severity, and injustices". After the Civil War, whites had tried to use the legal system to re-enslave Blacks, Dubois added. It was not then a question of crime, but rather one of "Color" that settled a man's conviction.... "Thus, Negroes came to look upon courts as instruments of injustice and oppression, and those convicted in them as martyrs and victims."[103]

In response to all of the lynching, and other injustices, Dubois wrote, "If we expect to gain our rights by nerveless acquiescence in wrong, then we expect to do what no other nation ever did. What must we do then? We must complain. Yes, plain blunt complain, "Ceaseless Agitation," unfailing exposure of dishonesty and wrong- this (is) the ancient, unerring way to liberty, and we must follow it."

"Dubois, at age sixteen was graduated from High school and for the first time went into the South as a scholarship student at Fisk University, where he edited the "Fisk Herald" and wrote his first articles. During the first summers he taught in the sharecropping districts. In 1888, Dubois entered Harvard University, where he won the Boylston Oratorical contest. He was one of six commencement speakers, his subject being "Jefferson Davis." After two years of study in Germany, Dubois returned to Harvard to receive his doctorate in 1895, the first Ph.D. conferred on a "Negro" by that institution. Dubois then served briefly as an instructor at Wilberforce University and at the University of Pennsylvania, then for thirteen years headed the Dept. of History and Economics at Atlanta University. There he conducted the Annual Atlanta Conference on "Negro Problems," which published thirteen documented studies of Negro life.

Dubois advocated the uplifting of African-Americans through an educated Black elite, which was referred to as the "Talented Tenth," or roughly a tenth of the African-American population. He believed that these African Americans must become proficient in education and culture, which would eventually benefit all.

In 1905, Dubois, along with a group of other Black intellectuals, formed the Niagara Movement. The group drew up a platform, which called for "Full Citizenship Rights for Blacks and Public Recognition of Their Contributions."

It was partly due to Booker T. Washington's stress on Industrial rather than Liberal Arts education that controversy developed between his followers and those of W.E.B. Dubois. "Education," said Washington at Tuskegee," is meant to make us give satisfaction, and to get satisfaction out of giving it. It is meant to make us get happiness out of service for our fellows.... No man who has the privilege of rendering service to his fellows ever makes a sacrifice....

Booker T. Washington

11

Booker T. Washington's Tuskegee Normal and Industrial Institute was founded in 1881 and based on a program at Hampton Institute that provided training and preparation for students to survive economically in a segregated society. In Washington's view education for African Americans was for them to become economically self-supporting. In a speech at the Cotton States International Exposition in Atlanta in 1895, Washington said:

> To those of my race who depend on bettering their condition in a foreign
> land, or who underestimate the importance of cultivating friendly relations
> with the Southern white man, who is their next door neighbor, I would say:
> Cast down your bucket where you are - cast it down in making friends in
> every manly way of the people of all races by whom we are surrounded.

There is as much dignity in tilling a field as in writing a poem," said Washington. Dubois, on the other hand, felt, "we shall hardly induce Black men to believe that if their stomach be full, it matters little about their brains." Without disputing the values of industrial education, he continued, "So far as Mr. Washington preaches thrift, patience and industrial training for the masses, we must hold up his hands and strive with him.... But so far as Mr. Washington apologizes for injustice, North or South, does not rightly value the privileges and the duty of voting, belittles the emasculating effects of caste distinctions and opposes the higher training and the ambition of our brighter minds--So far as he, the South, or the nation, does this--we must unceasingly and firmly oppose them. By every civilized and peaceful method we must strive for the rights which the world accords man."[105]

William E. B. DuBois, a young historian and Harvard graduate challenged Washington's passive policies in a series of stirring essays and speeches

"In 1905, Dubois launched the Niagara Movement, advocating the immediate ending of racial discrimination and segregation. He was one of the founders of the (NAACP) National Association For The Advancement of Colored People in 1908. In 1919 Dubois initiated the first of several early Pan-African Congresses in Paris with the hope of focusing world opinion on the conditions and status of Black men everywhere. Setting forth his views in books, articles, poem and speeches, Dubois never ceased his fight against racial and economic exploitation."[106]

"We will not be satisfied to take one jot or one tittle less than our full manhood rights," Dubois proclaimed, in an "Address to the Country," A 1906 statement issued at Harper's Ferry, West Virginia, by the Niagara Movement at its' second annual meeting. Although the exclusively African-American organization folded three years later due to powerful enemies (Black as well as White) and to internal tensions, Dubois carried its' uncompromising, confrontational Civil Rights Elan into the new interracial NAACP, as the December 1910 issue of the "CRISIS" editorial "NAACP" makes clear. Dubois lashed out against or lampooned mercilessly in "CRISIS" magazine not only the flagrantly unconstitutional forms of racial segregation, but social inequality as well.

"We will not be satisfied to take one jot or one tittle less than our full manhood rights," Dubois wrote in "The Address To The Country." " Cannot the nation that has absorbed ten million foreigners into its political life without catastrophe absorb ten million Negro Americans into that same political life at less cost than their unjust and illegal exclusion will involve?

We claim for ourselves every single right that belongs to a free born American, political, civil and social; and until we get these rights we will never cease to protest and to assail the ears of America. The battle we wage is not for ourselves alone but for all true Americans. It is A fight for ideals, lest this, our common fatherland, false to its founding, become in truth the land of the thief and the home of the slave- A by-word and A hissing among the nations for its sounding pretentious and pitiful accomplishments."[107]

12

In one of the most passionate and notable descriptions of the Negro's problem in the early Twentieth Century, Dubois wrote, "The Negro is a sort of a Seventh son, born with a veil, and gifted with second-sight in this American world- a world which yields him no true self-consciousness, but only lets him see himself through the revelation of the other world. It is a peculiar sensation, this double-consciousness, this sense of always looking at one's self through the tape of A world that looks on in amuse contempt and pity. One ever feels his twoness- an American, A Negro; two souls, two thoughts two un-reconciled strivings; two warring ideals in one dark body, whose dogged strength alone keeps it from being-torn asunder.

The history of the American Negro is the history of this strife,-this longing to attain self conscious manhood, to emerge his double self into a better and truer self. In this merging he wishes neither of the older selves to be lost. He would not Africanize America, for America has too much to teach the world and Africa. He would not "Bleach" his Negro "Soul" in a flood of white Americanism, for he knows that Negro blood has a message for the world. He simply wishes to make it possible for a man to be both a Negro and an American, without being cursed and spit upon by his fellows, without having the doors of opportunity closed roughly in his face."[108]

"Why did GOD make me an outcast and a stranger in mine own house?"[109]

"Up to the year 1898, South Carolina had resisted the Jim Crow Car Movement, which had swept the western states of the South 'completely by that time. In that year, however, after several attempts, the proponents of the Jim Crow laws were on the eve of victory. The Charleston News and Courier, The oldest newspaper in the South and a consistent spokesman of conservatism, fired a final broadside shot against extremists in behalf of the conservative creed of race policy. "As we have got along fairly well for a third of a century, including a long period of Reconstruction, without such a measure", wrote the editor, "We can probably get on as well without it." He then called attention to what he considered the absurd consequence to which such a law might lead once the principle of the thing were conceded. "If there must be Jim Crow cars on the railroads, there should be Jim Crow cars on the railways. Also on all passenger boats....If there are to be Jim Crow cars, moreover, there should be Jim Crow waiting saloons at all stations, and Jim Crow eating houses.... There should be Jim Crow sections of the jury box, and a separate Jim Crow clock and witness stand in every court and a Jim Crow Bible for Colored witnesses to kiss. It would be advisable also to have a Jim Crow section in the county auditors' and treasurers' office for the accommodation of colored taxpayers.

The two races are dreadfully mixed in these offices for weeks every year, especially about Christmas.... There should be a Jim Crow department for making returns and paying for the privileges and blessings of citizenship. Perhaps, the best plan would be, after all, to take the short cut to the general end... by establishing two or three Jim Crow counties at once, and turning them over to our Colored citizens for their special and exclusive accommodation"

In resorting to the tactics of "Reductio Ad Absurd" the editor doubtlessly believed that he had dealt the Jim Crow principle a telling blow with his heavy irony. But there is now apparent to us an irony in his argument of which the author was unconscious. For what he intended as a Reductio Ad Absurdum and obviously regarded as an absurdity became in a very short time a reality, and not only that but a reality that was regarded as the only sensible solution to a vexing problem, a solution having the sanction of tradition and long usage.

Apart from the Jim Crow counties and Jim Crow witness stand, all the impossible applications of the principle suggested by the editor in derision had been put into practice-down to and including the Jim Crow Bible."[110]

Dr. Dubois spoke out harshly against the ways of the south, and he criticized the entire existence of the Americas standards towards the freedmen altogether. He said, "merely a concrete test of the underlying principles of the great republic is the Negro problem, and the spiritual striving of the freedmen's sons is the striving of souls whose burden is almost beyond the measure of their strength, but who bare it in the land of their fathers' father, and in the name of human opportunity."[111]

Professor Dubois further believed that the mere presence of a Negro brought about a sense of fear to the whites of the South, particularity when the Black presented themselves to have any kind of reason about them or being a self thinker. Moreover, the South believed an educated Negro to be a dangerous Negro. And the South was not wholly wrong; for education among all kinds of men always has had, and always will have, an element of danger and revolution, of dissatisfaction and discontent," More importantly, "there wasn't a White man in the South who did not honestly regard Emancipation as a crime, and its' practical nullification as a duty."[112]

"As they had in every conflict since the American Revolutionary war, African Americans saw the military as a place to better themselves while serving their country. Black psychiatrist Alvin F. Poussaint, quoted in an article of Ebony magazine in August 23, 1968, "Why Negroes Re-enlist," Explained the Black soldiers voluntary association with the military. "Black men in general, particularity from the South, suffer from low self-esteem because of racism in American society. The Black male has always been castrated by this society and has struggled for a sense of manhood and identity in a white world. Because of the limited opportunities that a racist society allows the Black man for achieving manhood, I think many young Black men gravitate to the armed forces to prove they are men by risking their lives in combat. Superior prowess in combat is one of the most primitive ways of achieving a sense of manhood. The Black man in combat is ready to trade his life for psychological manhood, status, and self-esteem."[113]

From the outset of World War 1, Dr. Dubois urged Black men to assist in the war efforts against the foes of the world in combat. It was presumed that if Black men was willing to fight wars abroad, that this would give him a better chance for equality in America. Therefore, it was the opinion of leaders that we should register for selective service and show our allegiance in this country. Dubois urged "We of the Colored Race have no ordinary interest in the war."

That which the German power represents today spells death to the aspirations of Negroes and all the darker races for equality, freedom and democracy. Let us not hesitate. Let us, while this war last, forget our special grievances and close our ranks shoulder to shoulder with our white fellow citizens and the allied nations that are fighting for democracy. We make no ordinary sacrifice, but we make it gladly and willingly with our eyes lifted to the hills."[114]

"Thus, we lived in the 20th century in the theatre of the absurd. Black men and women pledged for an opportunity to serve their country during World War 1. Although the United States military admitted them, they would not have them in its' own Armed Forces. Instead, they were shunted into the French Army, where they performed with great valor. Hundreds received France's highest military honor, The Croix DE Guerre, but, in the judgment of the United States, not one of them had been brave enough or intrepid enough to receive their own country's highest recognition for valor, The Medal of Honor."[115]

The 369th and 371st Infantry Regiments, which received its training at Camp Jackson, South Carolina, served as part of the 157th French Division under General Gobet, remaining on the front lines for more than three months. Montfauxelles, a strategically vital point German's had held for almost a year, was captured by this regiment. It also took numbers of prisoners, captured a munitions depot and several railroad cars full of supplies. It lost almost half of its' 2,384 men. It was praised by General Gobet as having "A most complete contempt for danger." Other Negro units to serve with distinction in World War 1 were the 370th and the 372nd Infantry, many of whose men were decorated for bravery.

The first American soldier in World War 1 to receive the French Croix De Guerre with star and palm was Sergeant Henry Johnson. The battle in which he fought became known as "The Battle of Henry Johnson." With a fellow soldier of the 369th infantry, Neeham Roberts Johnson was on outpost guard duty before dawn on May 14, 1918, when a raiding party of twenty Germans swooped down upon them and wounded them both with surprise grenades. After Johnson had fired his last bullet the Germans began to drag Roberts away as a prisoner. Using the butt end of his rifle and a bolo knife, Johnson freed Roberts. Both Negroes then killed the four Germans, wounded several others and held their post as the rest fled. Johnson and Roberts were decorated by the French Government and their exploit was headlined in the newspapers back home.

12a

Black southern families were largely confined to laboring in the cotton fields.

During the war, stories of race riots and lynching filled the front pages of newspapers all across the country, rivaling only the war news in death and violence. In July 1917, a massacre occurred in East St. Louis, Illinois, in which many Negroes were burned alive in their homes.

Altogether, there were fifty-eight bombings of Negro homes in that city alone over the next four years. Pamphlets were circulated by Dr. Dubois and the NAACP depicting the "SHAME OF AMERICA" asking the question" Do you know that the United States is the only land on the Earth where human beings are being "BURNED AT THE STAKE."

It indicated that between 1889-1921 that 3,436 people had been lynched and of that number 83 of these were Black women. Moreover it asked the question, "Is rape the cause of these women being lynched?"

On July 28, 1917, thousands marched in New York in protest of the lack of Democracy that was being afforded to Negroes all across the country. Dubois added, "We return, we return from fighting. We return fighting. Make way for Democracy! We saved it in France, and by the Great Jehovah, we will save it in the U.S.A., or know the reason why!" In the name of returning Negro soldiers, so spoke Dubois in the "CRISIS" in the spring of 1919. That summer race riots became race wars; Negroes fought back. After having fought "to make the world safe for Democracy," some were at least determined to protect their own lives on home soil.

Upon returning to the United States from the Paris Peace Conference on April 1, 1919, Dubois wrote in the "CRISIS" in redeeming the "Close Ranks" editorial which he had written in 1917, he addressed "RETURNING SOLDIERS":

"We are returning from war! The "CRISIS" and tens of thousands of Black men were drafted into a great struggle. For bleeding France and what she means and has meant and all mean to us and humanity and against the threat of German race arrogance...."

"This is the country to which we soldiers of Democracy returned. This is the fatherland for which we fought! But it is our fatherland. It was right for us to fight again. The faults of our country are our faults. Under similar circumstances, we would fight again. But by the God of Heaven, we are cowards and jackasses if now that the war is over, we do not marshal every ounce of our brain and brawn to fight a sterner, longer, more unbending battle against the forces of hell in our own land."

The Silent Protest Parade of July 28, 1917 in which thousand of New Yorkers marched bearing banners asking Mr President, Why Not Make America Safe For Democracy? Give Me a Chance to Live Thou Shalt Not Kill.

Under the guidance of the N.A.A.C.P., 10,000 Negroes silently marched down Fifth Ave in New York City. bearing banners protesting such violence, and radical Negro magazines like "Messenger", edited by A. Phillip Randolph and Chandler Owen, published such strong editorials that the Department of Justice felt a Government investigation into their sponsors was required.

In Washington mobs roamed the city for three days. A number of Negroes and whites were killed and scores were injured. That same month in Chicago, with a population of 100,000 Black People, fifteen whites and twenty-three Negroes were killed, almost 600 wounded and 1,000 families burned out. Similar riots occurred in Knoxville, Tennessee, and Omaha, Nebraska, where a Negro was dragged through the streets, shot more than a thousand times and hanged on the main street."[116]

"Lunching represented an ultimate sociological method or racial control and repression, a way of using fear and terror to check "dangerous" tendencies in a black community considered to be ineffectively regimented or supervised.

As such it constituted a confession that the regular institutions of a segregated society provided an inadequate measure of day-to-day control. Ideally speaking, racists admitted, lynching should not have been necessary; and the more educated and sophisticated Southern Negrophobes of the period generally condemned the practice in the abstract, on the conservative grounds that lynching destroyed respect for law and order and predicated Southern society toward anarchy. But since they themselves had no real substitute to offer as a way of achieving objectives they shared with the impassioned mobs, these spokesmen often ended up apologizing for the practice as virtually unavoidable under existing circumstances.

They were compelled, in fact, to devote a great deal of time and energy to the "explanation" of these extralegal executions, because lynching tended to be shocking to the kind of "civilized" sensibilities that were willing to condone milder manifestations of racism. After 1890, lynching constituted the single Southern racial practice calculated to horrify a substantial segment of Northern opinion. Northern opposition to lynching was actually a limited and ineffectual phenomenon during this period, but it was vocal enough to arouse Southern fears of renewed Federal intervention or "interference" with the South's effort to deal with its black population.

15a

In 1925, 40,000 Klansmen parade before the Capitol.

The Negro question presented "Problems" for the theoreticians of segregation and even greater difficulties were encountered by those who attempted to evaluate the practice of lynching. This vicious custom of taking accused Negro offenders out of the hands of the authorities and hanging, shooting, or burning them alive, reached a high point in the 1890's and persisted on a some what diminished scale into the Twentieth Century. More importantly, some Northern Republicans urged that the Federal Government be empowered to protect Southern blacks from mob action."[117]

"There were, in 1919, eighty-three lynching, several were Negro veterans in uniforms, some of whom were burned alive. The Ku Klux Klan held more than 200 public meetings from Indiana to New England to Florida. There were twenty-five major race riots within seven months. Throughout the latter part of the Nineteenth Century and well into the Twentieth Century, lynching had always been used as a method of keeping Blacks in their place, down. For fear of the noose was a constant reminder of whites control for the Negro.

"In 1918, President Woodrow Wilson issued a public statement in which he described lynching as "This Disgraceful Evil" and stated that "Lynching cannot live where the community does not countenance it."

It was Wilson's way of both denouncing lynching and making it clear he would not initiate Federal action to stop it. The NAACP noted that the president's works had merely the effect of keeping news of lynching out of the press."[118]

"Some lynching took place for no other apparent reason than to bring down a black person who had managed to achieve a measure of economic success. Anthony Crawford, born of slave parents, had become a substantial land owner and farmer in Abbeville, South Carolina.

He had twelve sons and four daughters, most of them living nearby. As secretary of the local African Methodist Episcopal Church, he was a pivotal figure in the black community. Few blacks or whites had done more to embrace the gospel of self help. "Anthony Crawford's life and character," one observer noted, "embodied everything that Booker T. Washington held to be virtuous in a Negro. On October 21, 1916, Crawford came to town to sell his cotton. He exchanged harsh words with a local white businessman over the offering price. When a store clerk wielding an ax handle went after Crawford, he backed away only to be arrested and placed in jail, securing him initially from a white mob angry over his reported insolence."

Returning soldiers of the 369th Infantry Regiment wearing the Croix de Guerre, aboard
the S.S. Stockholm, February, 1919. This regiment was the first of the returning American
troops to march under the Arch on Fifth Avenue at Wahington Square.

13

"When a nigger gets impudent we stretch him out and paddle him a bit," the store manager boasted. The president of the National Bank of Abbeville concurred, "Crawford was insolent to a white man and he deserved a thrashing."

Released on bail, Crawford headed toward the gin, where his cotton was waiting. The white mob quickly regrouped and attacked him. Crawford resisted, injuring one of the whites, but the men finally overpowered him and kicked him until he had lost consciousness. The sheriff persuaded the mob to permits him to regain custody of Crawford. From his cell Crawford was heard to say, while spitting blood where they had kicked out his teeth, "I thought I was a good citizen." By not displaying "the humility becoming a "nigger," however, he had become vulnerable. When a false rumor circulated that Crawford might be moved to another jail, the mob mobilized again and easily entered the jail. After shoving Crawford's broken body down three flights of stairs, they mutilated him, dug their heels into his upturned, quivering face, tied a rope around his neck, and dragged him through the streets of the Negro quarters as a warning. Finally, they hung him to a pine tree and emptied their guns into his body.

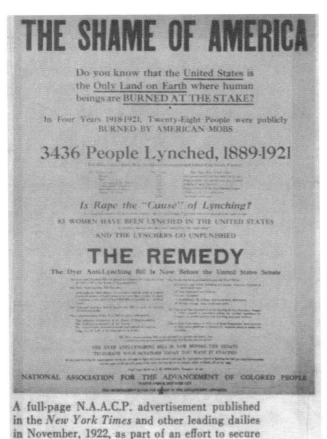

17b

Dr. W. E. B. Du Bois.

A full-page N.A.A.C.P. advertisement published in the *New York Times* and other leading dailies in November, 1922, as part of an effort to secure passage of the Dyer Anti-Lynching Bill and to call attention to America's racial plight.

17

The coroner convened a jury, which quickly reached the verdict that Anthony P. Crawford had come to his death at the hands of parties unknown to the jury. A subsequent citizens meeting ordered the remainder of the Crawford family to leave town within three weeks. A leading South Carolina newspaper had little difficulty in ascertaining the principal reason for Crawford's murder. Crawford was worth around $20,000 and that's more than most white farmers are worth down here.

Property ownership always makes the Negro more assertive, more independent, and the crackers can't stand it." The citizens of Abbeville, regardless of class, demonstrated by their action and inaction, not only extraordinary cowardice, but also their own complicity in the crime.

Pointing to the tree where Crawford was hanged, a resident remarked, "I reckon the crowd wouldn't have been so bloodthirsty, only it's been three years since they had any fun with the niggers, and it seems though they jest have to have a lynching every so often."

If lynchings were calculated to send a forceful message to the Black community and underscore its vulnerability, whites succeeded. But at the same time, it exposed Black men and Women in ways they would never forget, to the moral character of the white man and his community. The impression conveyed was not so much the racial superiority of whites of as their enormous capacity for savagery and cowardice, the way they inflicted their terror as crowds and mobs, rarely as individuals."[119]

"In 1926, in Aiken, South Carolina, three Blacks were lynched in that small resort town. The sheriff in Aiken and three of his deputies had gone to the Lowman family farm to arrest Sam Lowman on charges of selling whiskey. Lowman was gone from the place but following an incident in which his wife Annie was shot to death and his daughter Bertha struck in the mouth, two other family members rushed to the house, further shooting ensued, and the sheriff was killed. Three of the Lowman's were arrested, charged with murder, and convicted in perfunctory trials. Two of the defendants, Demon and Clarence Lowman were sentenced to death, and Bertha Lowman was given life imprisonment.

According to Walter White, spokesman for the National Association for the Advancement of Colored people, the sheriff and his deputies were all members of the Ku Klux Klan. The allegations of whiskey selling against Sam Lowman was without foundation, and the entire incident stemmed from a desire to embarrass William Hartley, the owner of the land Sam Lowman rented. In April 1925, a mob of hooded Klansmen had come to the Lowman home, taken Demon Lowman outside, and severely whipped him, for no reason other than the feud between clansmen and the Lowman's landlord. The Lowman family had good reason to fear the approach of strange whites. In any event, the Supreme Court of South Carolina overturned the convictions, and ordered a new trial, and at that trial the judge ordered a verdict of acquittal for one of the defendants. At this point on October 8, 1926, a lynch mob entered the scene, overpowering the jailor and the sheriff, seizing three Blacks, and taking them to a nearby tourists camp, where some 2,000 whites had assembled. The prisoners were then shot to death.

An NAACP inquiry revealed that the sheriff and the jailor had assisted the lynchers, as had members of the state legislature, governors relatives, and other farmers, lawyers, politicians, and businessmen. In short, a considerable segment of "respectable" Aiken, South Carolina was involved in the lynching.

Early in 1927, the NAACP reacted sharply to what had occurred in Aiken, South Carolina. The association urged President Coolidge not to appoint Thomas G. McLeod, South Carolina's governor at the time of the Aiken's lynching, to the Federal Trade Commission. During 1926, according to the NAACP, thirty-three person's were lynching victims as compared to eighteen in 1925. James W. Johnson linked the Aiken incident and other 1926 lynching to what had taken place in congress regarding anti-lynching legislation. While there was a threat of a Federal Law, with consequent jurisdiction of federal courts over this crime, the lynchers hesitated," Johnson stated. But when the senate refused to act on the Dyer Bill, it was equivalent to serving notice on the lynchers that they could pursue their pastime virtually unmolested."[120]

At the height of the reign of terror towards the freedmen by lynchers and white politicians alike, Dr. Dubois went on to lash out at the power structure of America. He said time and time again, "this, the Black man knows, His is a fight to the finish. Either he dies or he wins.

17a

Ku Klux Klan members. They struck at night, killing or driving off black leaders and the whites who stood by them.

RECORD KEPT BY TUSKEGEE OF LYNCHINGS IN THE FIRST QUARTER OF THE TWENTIETH CENTURY	
1900 — 115	1913 — 52
1901 — 130	1914 — 55
1902 — 92	1915 — 69
1903 — 99	1916 — 54
1904 — 83	1917 — 38
1905 — 62	1918 — 64
1906 — 65	1919 — 83
1907 — 60	1920 — 61
1908 — 97	1921 — 64
1909 — 82	1922 — 57
1910 — 76	1923 — 33
1911 — 67	1924 — 16
1912 — 63	1925 — 17

LYNCHINGS BY NAME AND PLACE FOR
THE FIRST PART OF THE YEAR 1900

Jan.   9 — Henry Giveney, Ripley, Tenn.
Jan.   9 — Roger Giveney, Ripley, Tenn.
Jan. 11 — Rufus Salter, West Springs, S. C.
Jan. 16 — Anderson Gause, Henning, Tenn.
Feb. 17 — William Burts, Basket Mills, S. C.
Mar.   4 — James Crosby, Selo Hatchel, Ala.
Mar.   4 — George Ratcliffe, Clyde, N. C.
Mar. 10 — Thomas Clayton, Hernando, Miss.
Mar. 11 — Unknown Negro, Jannings, Neb.
Mar. 18 — Charles Humphries, Lee County, Ala.
Mar. 18 — John Bailey, Manetta, Ga.
Mar. 22 — George Ritter, Canhaft, N. C.
Mar. 24 — Walter Cotton, Emporia, Va.
Mar. 26 — Lewis Harris, Belair, Md.
Mar. 27 — William Edward, Deer Creek, Miss.
Apr.   3 — Allen Brooks, Berryville, Ga.
Apr.   5 — Unknown Negro, Southampton Co., Va.
Apr. 16 — Moses York, Tunica, Miss.
Apr. 19 — Henry McAfee, Brownsville, Miss.
Apr. 20 — John Peters, Tazewell, W. Va.
Apr. 22 — John Hughley, Allentown, Fla.
Apr. 28 — Mindee Chowgee, Marshall, Mo.

17c

Billie Holiday
1915-1959

Vocalist

16

These four human remains symbolizes, four African-Americans that I knew while growing up in South Carolina. They are reminders of the genocide that African-American people have faced while struggling for survival in America. They Are (From left to right): William James Franklin (chick), Anthony Lee Crosby, Floyd Evans, and Alexander Boyd.

All were victims of an evil epidemic in America called *lynching*, which was the strange fruit that southern trees would bare.

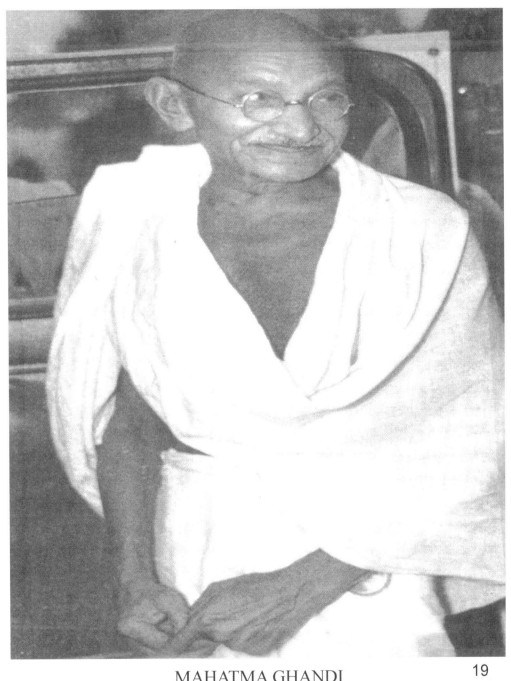

MAHATMA GHANDI

19

He will enter modern civilization in America as a Black Man in terms of perfect and unlimited equality with any white man, or he will enter not at all. Either extermination root and branch, or absolute equality, there can be no compromise."[121]

In 1929, the year started all right. In Atlanta, on January 15, a boy was born on Auburn Avenue and the proud parents named him Martin Luther King, Jr. In July of 1929, the "CRISIS" printed a message to American Negroes from Mahatma Ghandi. That said: "Let not the 12 million Negroes be ashamed of the fact that they are the grandchildren of slaves. There is no dishonor in being slaves. There is dishonor in being slave-owners.

But let us not think of honor or dishonor in connection with the past. Let us realize that the future is with those who would be truthful, pure and loving. For, as the old wise men have said, truth ever is, untruth never was. Love alone binds and truth and love accrue only the humble."[122]

"For the Negro, the Great Depression would bring about near extinction. In the words of many, It was a long cold winter. The sun did not shine again for the Negro until it came up in the wake of defense contract spawned by the rising sun of Nippon. During the Great Depression, Negro America almost fell apart. There was a bitter bite of poverty: "The Negro: Last Hired and First Fired." Businesses tightened their belts and bade Negro employees goodbye. Martons cut their budgets and domestics went home and looked at empty larders.

By 1935, about one out of every four Negroes in America was on relief. The need in urban areas was appalling. In Atlanta Georgia, 65 percent of the Negroes were on public relief; in Norfolk, Virginia, the figure was 81 percent.

In some areas, grown men stood on street corners and offered to sell their services for ten cents an hour. In some areas, like rural South Carolina, slavery returned.

Faded newspapers and cold statistics tell a tale of appalling suffering and privation, of grown men crying and women wringing their hands in empty kitchens; of battered furniture standing on concrete curbs; of crowds protesting and Communists organizing the discontenting White men coming with eviction notices and Republican mothers saying: "Run, boy; and get the Reds"; of big government trucks cruising through Negro neighborhoods and dropping off navy beans and powder milk; of the worldwide indignation over the rape conviction of the Scottsboro Boys on the testimony of two white women of uncertain reputation; and "For White people Only" signs in Birmingham, Alabama.

In Northern cities during the depression, Negroes picketed and boycotted White-staffed businesses in Negro neighborhoods, demanding Jobs. "Don't buy where you can't work," the slogans said. A number of businesses, including the Woolworth chain on the South Side of Chicago, capitulated and did hire Negro clerks. Along New York's 125th Street there were many flourishing white establishments in the heart of Harlem which depended upon Negro patronage but had no Negro employees."123

14

ANTI-NEGRO RIOTERS AGAIN PLY THE TORCH

Three More Bodies Found To-Day Making Total 27—

TORCH LAW SANCTIONED

Prisoners Given to Bloodthirsty Whites by Sheriff, Who Sees Them Lynched

In the April of 1933 edition of the "Crisis", Dr. Dubois continued to demand equal rights for freedmen and stressed unity and addressed criticism from outside sources. The Editor asked the question "Where in heaven's name do we Negroes stand? If we organize separately for anything-Jim Crow"! Scream all the disconsolate; if we organize with white people- Traitors! Pressure! They're betraying us"! Yell all the suspicious. If unable to get the whole loaf, we seize half to ward off starvation. "Compromise"! Yell the scared. If we let half the loaf go and starve, "Why don't you do something?" Yell those same critics, dancing about on their toes."[124]

"When World War II broke out in Europe and the nations shifted to a war footing, many plants with governments contracts refused to employ colored workers. The N.A.A.C.P., Urban League, and others protested to no avail. A. Phillip Randolph, who in 1925 had organized the Brotherhood of Sleeping Car Porters, then proposed a march-on-Washington of some 50,000 to 100,000 Negroes. As large delegations from all across the country left for the capital on June 1, 1941, the president called a conference of Negro leaders. On June 25, President Roosevelt issued Exec.Order 8802 banning discrimination in industries holding government contracts and set up a committee on fair employment practices.

During World War 11, Dorie Miller, a Navy Messman on board the U.S. Battleship Arizona, shot down four Japanese planes over his ship at Pearl Harbor, and became one of the first heroes of World War II.

He was later killed in battle in the Pacific. Colonel Benjamin 0. Davis, Jr., after taking the 99th Pursuit Squadron to Tunisia, returned to organize the 332nd Fighter group, who with more than 3,000 missions in Europe destroyed almost 300 enemy planes. Eighty-eight of the group's pilots, including Colonel Davis, received the Distinguished Flying Cross. And according to Tuskegee Airman Hal Young "there were other all African-American unitsthat made great contributions during WWII who never received any recognition. These units included the 473rd Tank Division and the Communication Line Division in 1943."

On the "Home Front," during World War II, race relations were like a seesaw, rising nobly in some respects while sinking deplorably on others. Southern Negro workers poured into Northern and Western cities. More than 50,000 Negroes went to Detroit to work in many defense industries centered there. Everywhere housing presented a problem, since white workers often resented colored families moving anywhere near them and violently opposed their integration into residential communities. Bombings and forced evictions occurred and serious race riots broke out in Detroit, New York, Mobile, Beaumont, and other communities. There were riots at southern training centers, too, where local racial customs clashed with military attempts to provide decent treatment for black soldiers.

14a

Dorie Miller receives the Navy Cross from Admiral Chester Nimitz.

German prisoners in transit could dine in railway station restaurants, while their Negro guards could not. The facilities for Colored Soldiers were often lacking and USO centers were segregated. The canteens were open to all. For civilians, most CIO unions welcomed Negro members and even in the South some locals were mixed. But limited transportation facilities created grave problems. It was hard for some Negroes to get to their jobs. Trains carrying one overcrowded Jim Crow coach to a Dozen cars for whites would leave Negroes standing on the railway platform

Buses packed with whites would not stop for colored passengers. Black soldiers on furlough sometimes could not get home or, if they did get there, were not able to return to camp on time. Many taxicabs at Washington's Union Station would not carry Colored fares. Negroes were heartened when at war's end the United Nations convened at San Francisco and adopted with U.S. Approval, a charter which proposed to guarantee full "Observance of Human Rights and Fundamental Freedoms for all, without distinction as to race, sex, language or " religion. South of Washington, D.C.; the Jim Crow signs which separated Negroes from whites varied from those on laundries which "will wash whites clothes only" to exclusive whistle-stop privies.

There are "White" and "Colored" water fountains in department stores, separate entrances and separate pay windows in industrial plants. There were some theatres in the south, which Negro patrons could not enter at all, and others where they may gain admittance only via the "Colored" entrance and where they must sit in the top gallery.

Some roadside cafe's have holes cut at the side for "Colored" patrons who may not come in. The "Colored" booths in the rear of record shops where Negroes may play records often put up no restricted signs but post a photograph of Marian Anderson or Duke Ellington."[125]

In a stirring speech on October 20, 1946, at Benedict College in Columbia, S. C., Dr. William E.B. Dubois, stated that "The future of the American Negroes is in the South. Here they have made their greatest contribution to American culture; and here they have suffered the Damnation of Slavery, the Frustration of Reconstruction and the Lynching of Emancipation...." Here is the magnificent climate; here is the fruitful earth under the beauty of the southern sun; and here, if anywhere on earth, is the need of the thinker, the worker, and the dreamer. This is the firing line."[126]

18

Marcus Garvey, organizer of the Universal Negro Improvement Association being led to prison. He advocated the betterment of his people, and a free and united Africa.

Over the years many writers have tried to adequately analyze the struggle that people of color have faced in this American society. There, also have many who have given up on the American system and looked toward other country's for liberty, and equality. The late author James Baldwin, in my opinion, summed up the Blackman's situation in America in the 1950's and 1960's adequately when he stated: "Negroes want to be treated like Men: A perfectly straightforward statement, containing only seven words. People who have mastered Kant, Hegel, Shakespeare, Marx, Freud, and the Bible, find this statement utterly impenetrable. The idea seems to threaten profound barely conscious assumptions. A Kind of panic paralyzes their features, as though they found themselves trapped on the steep place. I once tried to describe to a well-known American intellectual the condition among Negroes in the South. My recital disturbed him and made him indignant and he asked me in perfect innocence, "Why don't all Negroes in the South move North?" I tried to explain what has happened, unfailingly, whenever a significant number of Negroes move north. They do not escape "Jim Crow", they merely encounter another, not-less-deadly variety. They do not move to Chicago, they move to the North; they do not move to New York, they move to Harlem. The pressure within the ghetto causes the ghetto walls to expand, and this expansion is always violent.

18a

The Fighting Men of the
761ˢᵗ Tank Battalion
1894-1962
5th Tank Group-World War II

21

Mr. James Baldwin

Author, Activist, Social Pioneer

White people hold the line as long as they can, and in as many ways as they can, from verbal intimidation to physical violence. But inevitably the border which has divided the ghetto from the rest of the world falls into the hands of the ghetto. The white people fall back bitterly before the Black horde; the landlords make a tidy profit by raising the rents, chopping up the rooms, and all but dispensing with the upkeep; and what has once been a neighborhood turns into a "turf."

This is precisely what happened when the Puerto Ricans arrived in the thousands and the bitterness thus caused is, as I write, being fought out all up and down those streets.

Northerners indulge in an extremely dangerous luxury. They seem to feel that because they fought on the right side during the Civil War, and won, they have earned the right to deplore what is going on in the South, without taking responsibility for it; and that they can ignore what is happening in the Northern cities because what is going on in Little Rock or Birmingham is worse. Well, in the first place, it is not possible for anyone who has not endured both to know which is "worse." I Know Negroes who prefer the South and White Southerners because "at least there, you haven't got to play any guessing games!"

The guessing games referred to have driven more than one Negro into the narcotics ward, the madhouse, or the river. I know another Negro, a man very dear to me, who says, with conviction and truth, "The spirit of the South is the spirit of America" He was born in the North and did his military training in the South. He did not, as far as I can gather, find the South "worse"; he found it, if anything, all too familiar.

In the second place, though, even if Birmingham is worse, no doubt Johannesburg, South Africa, beats it by several miles, and Buchenwald was one of the worse things ever happened in the entire history of the world. The world has never lacked for horrifying examples; but I do not believe that these examples are meant to be used as Justification for our own crimes. This perpetual justification empties the heart of all human feeling. The emptier our hearts become; the greater will be our crimes. Thirdly, the South is not merely an embarrassingly backward region, but a part of this country, and what happens there concerns every one of us.

As far as the "Race Problem" is concerned, there is but one great difference between the Southern white and the Northern. The Southern white remember, historically and in his psyche, a kind of Eden in which he loved Black people and they loved him. Historically, the flaming sword laid across this Eden is the Civil War. Personally, it is Southerners sexual coming of age, when without any warning, unbreakable taboos are set up between himself and the past.

Neither Southerner nor the Northerner is able to look on the Negro simply as a man. It seems to be indispensable to the national self-esteem that the Negro be considered either as a kind of ward (in which case we are told how many Negroes, comparatively, bought Cadillacs last year, and how few comparatively were lynched) or as a victim (in which case we are promised that he will never vote in our assemblies or go to school with our kids). They are two sides of the same coin and the South will not change-cannot change- until the North changes. The country will not change until it re-examines itself and discovers what it really means by freedom.

In the meantime, generations keep being born, bitterness is increased by incompetence, pride, and folly, and the world shrinks around us. It is a terrible, and inexorable law that one cannot deny the humanity of another without diminishing one's own; in the face of one's victim, one see's oneself. Just walk through these city streets in America and see what we, this nation have become."[127]

Mr. James Baldwin was also disillusioned by the "Race Problem" in America and lived out the remainder of his life and died in France. Nevertheless, he like many other Black men and Women see the "Problem" in the South as being only a reflection of the greater "Problem in America" as a whole.

As he neared the middle of the century, W.E.B. Dubois saw no reason to change his prediction that "The problem of the Twentieth Century would be the problem of the color line." Indeed, what he saw merely reaffirmed what he said. He had worked hard to make his prediction inaccurate. Writing, speaking, marching, fighting against injustice and inequality from the beginning of his long and distinguished career, he began to wonder if it had all been in vain. In a poem, he said "The veil of color; drops as drops of night on the Southern seas- vast, sudden, uninspiring. There is hate behind it, and cruelty and tears. As one peers through its intricate, unfathomable pattern of ancient, old, old design, one sees blood and guilt and misunderstanding. And yet it hangs there, this veil, between then and now; between pale and colored and Black and White- between you and me. Surely, it is but a thought- thing, tenuous, intangible; yet just as surely is it true and terrible and not in our little day may you and I lift it."

In the final decade of the life of Dr. William Edward Burghhardt Dubois and in the decade that followed, many Americans insisted that we were at long last creating a society that was color blind. Tragically, Dr. Dubois sank deeper in his pessimism and depression. Disillusioned because the problem was as alive and as intractable in his ninetieth year as it had been sixty years earlier, he gave up on it, became an expatriate, and spent his remaining years in Ghana, West Africa. Dr. Dubois left not only a rich legacy of doing battle to destroy, the "Color line," but the legacy of the "Problem" that he could not solve and that, to him, by the early 1960's, seemed insolvable, he died in 1963."[128]

26

To be honest, I didn't experience as much of "JIM CROW" as my older brothers and sisters and mother and father did while growing up in South Carolina. In the year that Mrs. Rosa Parks refused to give up her seat on that Montgomery, Alabama bus that was the year that I was born, 1955. Although 1955 was when Black people really began to resist the "Hypocrisy" of the Emancipation Proclamation, apartheid was very prevalent and I can remember it very well. For example at the doctor's office they had a separated seating arrangement for Blacks in the "rear" of this long hallway where we waited to be called to see the doctor. I can remember that the area was very cold. Whites were able to go right on in to the office where it was quite warm as I remember. I think the year was about 1959 or 1960. Moreover, I can remember the Trailways bus station in our town when they had separate sections for eating. A window was at the rear of the station where Blacks could receive their food. And of course we had to go to separate swimming pools, and I don't think Blacks were allowed at the golf course except as caddies.

I know that all of this may seem too far fetched for some of our young brothers and sisters to fathom but these are the facts of the matter and its bitter truths. "JIM CROW" was not merely about the physical separation of blacks and whites. Nor was segregation strictly about laws, despite historians' tendency to fix upon such legal landmarks as Plessy v. Ferguson (1896), Brown v. The Board of Education at Topeka, Kansas (1954), and The Civil Rights Act of 1964. In order to maintain dominance, whites needed more than the statutes and signs that specified ""Whites" and "Blacks" only; they had to assert and reiterate "Black Inferiority" with every word and gesture, in every aspect of both public and private life. The noted Theologian Howard Thurman dissected the "anatomy" of segregation with chilling precision in his classic 1965 book, The Luminous Darkness. A white supremacist society must not only "array all the forces of legislation and law enforcement," he wrote; "it must falsify the facts of history, tamper with the insights of religion and religious doctrine, editorialize and slant news and the printed word. On top of that it must keep separate schools, separate churches, separate graveyards, and separate public accommodations-all this in order to freeze the "place" of the Negro in society and guarantee his basic immobility." Yet this was "but a partial indication of the high estimate" that the white south placed upon African-Americans. Once again, to state it categorically," Thurman concludes, "the measure of a man's estimate of your strength is the kind of weapons he feels that he must use in order to hold you fast in a prescribed place."[129]

THE CIVIL RIGHTS MOVEMENT

The mid 1950's and early 1960's brought protests and demonstrations in the form of bus boycotts, sit-ins, and freedom rides throughout the South. On December 5, 1955, Rosa Parks, on an impulse decided suddenly that she wasn't going to obey an ancient custom which required Negroes to yield seats to white customers. Mrs. Parks, a seamstress, was arrested and the Negro community staged a one-day boycott. The one-day boycott grew into a movement that swept across the South. For thirteen months, Negro Montgomery, Alabama, walked. Finally, on December 21, 1956, after a federal court order the busses were integrated."[1]

"In Montgomery, Alabama, where the Negro had one of his finest hours, Martin Luther King, Jr., had moved the struggle from the courtroom to the streets, from law libraries to the pews of the churches, from the mind to the soul. In 1955, Martin Luther King, Jr., fused the elements and added the missing link, that which has sustained and buttoned the Negro community since slavery-the Negro church. By superimposing the image of the Negro preacher on the image of Gandhi, by adding songs and symbols with a palpable significance in the Negro community, Martin Luther King, Jr. transformed a spontaneous racial protest into an awesome passive resistance movement with a method and an ideology. "Love Your Enemies," he commanded, and servants straightened their backs, and sustained a year-long bus boycott, which, as King pointed out, "was one of the greatest (movements) in the history of [any] nation."[2]

"A third generation Baptist preacher, well read in philosophy, Martin Luther King, Jr., was of medium size and girth, brown skinned, with a mustache and interesting eyes that slant upward slightly. Just twenty-seven years old when he burst upon the consciousness of Southerners, King has been likened-to his embarrassment-to Gandhi and Jesus Christ. Like Frederick Douglass, like Gandhi, like Jesus, he had an instinct for symbolic action-he knew how to dramatize truth."[3]

"On February 1, 1960, four North Carolina A & T. University freshman students sat down at a lunch counter in a Woolworth store in Greensboro, North Carolina, they started an unprecedented student protest movement which shook the south to its foundations and set off social tremors that would affect race relations for years to come. Within three months, thousands of Negro-and some White-students were taking seats at "White" lunch counters and requesting service. If arrested, they submitted quietly, if attacked, they refused to fight."[4]

The first outbreak of violence was reported as the demonstrations against lunch counters segregation spread in the South.

Two weeks after the first demonstrations, protesting segregated facilities began at nearby Greensboro, North Carolina; High Point, North Carolina reported a fistfight Monday between whites and Negroes in front of F.W. Woolworth Company store.

In Durham, North Carolina, hundreds of Negro adults, Tuesday night signaled their willingness to boycott chain stores operating segregated eating facilities. They offered to support a growing student sit-down protest as 'the Reverend Martin Luther King, Jr. urged a united front; both whites and Negroes against segregation."[5]

"Martin Luther King, Jr., who led Montgomery Alabama, blacks in a boycott against segregated city buses, repeated this phase time and time again. "We just want to be free." "Let us not fear going to jails" King urged. "We must say that we are willing and prepared to fill up the jail houses in the South." But he cautioned, "Our ultimate aim is not to humiliate the White man but to win his understanding." King termed the current sit-down movement by the students as one of the most significant developments in the Civil Rights struggle. Segregated eating facilities, he said, "are the Black Mans burden and America's shame." He urged repeatedly that the struggle for equality be one of non-violence. He said that "Blacks had made it clear that they would not be satisfied with token integration or segregation in any form."[6]

The movement that first began as a protest against segregated counter facilities, had in a year and a half, embraced parks, swimming pools, theaters, restaurants churches, interstate transportation, voter registration, libraries, museums, art galleries, laundromats, employment, beaches, and courtrooms."[7]

Not allowing anything to be in their way, Blacks were attempting to break the color barriers that had followed us from the times we had been supposedly freed from Slavery. The masses would agree that the 1960's marked one of the most transitional periods in American History. We would not only witness the Vietnam War, poverty in America, energy shortages, governmental assassinations and inflation. Most importantly, the 1960's would also wittiness the revitalization of an oppressed race of people.

With the organizing of the Student Nonviolent Coordinating Committee on April 15,1960, the sit-in movement increased its' effectiveness. SNCC (pronounced SNICK) was heavily involved in the Jail-in movement, which started in Rock Hill, South Carolina, on February 6, 1961, when students refused to pay fines, and requested Jail sentences. The "JAIL NO Bail" movement spread to Atlanta Ga. and other Southern cities.

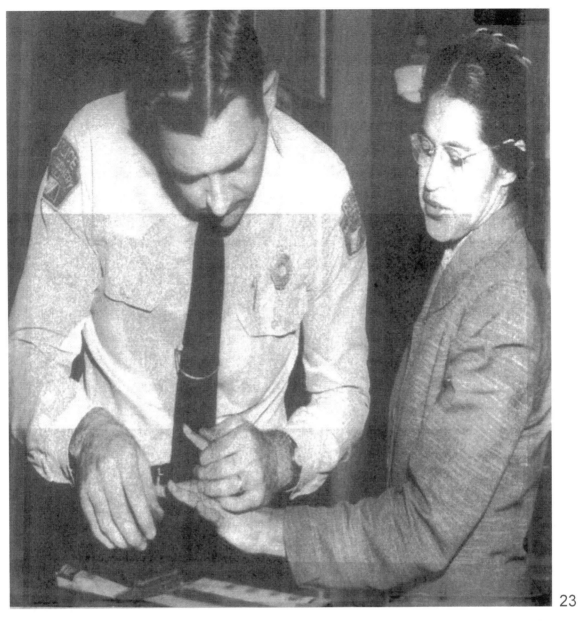

23

Mrs. Rosa Parks, 1913-2005, being fingerprinted in 1955 after her arrest in Montgomery, AL, for violating racial segregation laws on city buses.

SNCC also played an important role in the "FREEDOM RIDE" campaign, which was initiated by thirteen CORE (congress of racial equality) members who set out from Washington, D.C., on May 4, 1961, for an integrated bus ride through the South. Testing compliance with integrated orders of the Interstate Commerce commission and Federal courts, the "FREEDOM RIDERS" crisscrossed the South. At several stops, they were beaten and manhandled."[8]

The first "FREEDOM RIDERs" bus pulled into the Greyhound terminal at Rock Hill, South Carolina. This being the sight of the "JAIL-IN" that was already legendary among SNCC students, John Lewis made an effort to rotate into the position of first tester. As he made his way from the bus toward the white waiting room, the usual tension seemed to coil rather than abate. The Rock Hill terminal was more of a " hangout " than most, filled with pinball machines played by white youths of the type that had become the scourge of the Sit-in movement. One of them was leaning on either side of the door, with about twenty more behind. The first two stepped in front of Lewis to block the entrance. One of them said, "Other side", jerking his thumb toward the Colored entrance. Lewis drew himself up for the standard speech. "I have a right to go in here on the grounds of the Supreme Court Decision in the Boynton case," he said.

There was a pause, followed by a reply of "Shit on that" and a shoving of Lewis back and forth in the doorway. One of the attackers threw a punch that caught Lewis in the mouth, making the first loud pop of fist against flesh on the Freedom Rider. Lewis sank to the ground. More Whites surged toward the primitive sounds of violence. Albert Bigelow, next in line behind Lewis, stepped forward to put his body between Lewis and those kicking him. Bigelow's erect posture and determined passivity- such an alien sight in a fistfight- did not keep the attackers from darting in to strike him on the head and body. Three or four blows dropped Bigelow to one knee, and as one of the attackers lunged toward Bigelow he knocked Genevieve Hughes, the third Freedom Rider in line, sprawling to the floor. Several Rock Hill policemen shouted the fracas down to a sullen lull, and the police captain waded in to extricate Lewis and Bigelow, who were bruised and bleeding but fully conscious. Pointing around disgustedly at the attackers, as though knowing them well from previous juvenile cases, the captain asked Lewis and Bigelow whether they wanted to press assault charges. Both said no. This was not in the spirit of non-violent resistance. Their refusal displeased the captain, who seemed upset that his politically risky offer to arrest local white boys was going to waste. He waved all the suspects away, and the Freedom Riders filed into the waiting room to place their food orders unmolested.

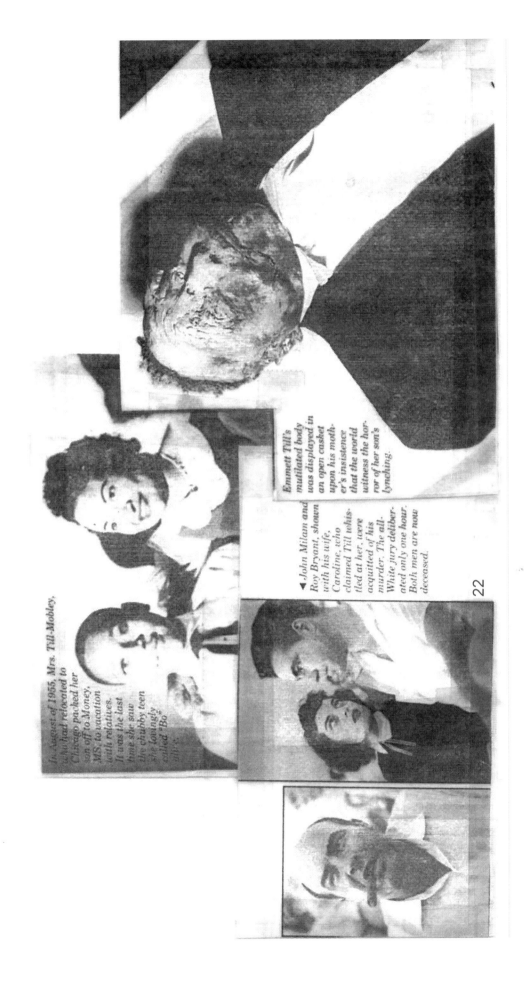

In August of 1955, Mrs. Till-Mobley, who had relocated to Chicago packed her son off to Money, MS, to vacation with relatives. It was the last time she saw the chubby teen she lovingly called "Bo."

Emmett Till's mutilated body was displayed in an open casket upon his mother's insistence that the world witness the horror of her son's lynching.

▼ John Milam and Roy Bryant, shown with his wife, Caroline, who claimed Till whistled at her, were acquitted of his murder. The all-White jury deliberated only one hour. Both men are now deceased.

22

197

Till had been shot above his right ear and the left side of his face had been crushed to the bone.

"Open it up. Let the people see what they did to my boy," Mrs. Till-Mobley screamed when Emmett's body arrived at the A.A. Rayner Funeral Home in Chicago.

What she saw shocked the nation to the horrors of lynching in the South.

"Mr. (A.A.) Rayner did a fantastic job of getting the face back together because when I saw it, the right eye was lying on his cheek. His tongue had been choked out by the weight of the fan and the barbed wire that was around his neck was still attached to the fan, parts of both ears were missing.

"The back of the head was practically separated from the face area. The mouth was wide open. You could only see two of the three remaining teeth..."

Pictures of Till's bloated and mutilated face, published across the country in JET Magazine and newspapers worldwide galvanized the despair and anger of Blacks throughout the nation. The political and social reaction to the gruesome murder is widely considered the spark which ignited America's Civil Rights Movement.

"The movement to end Jim Crow didn't start in Montgomery," said Jackson. "The 1954 Supreme Court decision made Jim Crow illegal. It meant a lot, but it did not translate to mass action. But when Emmett Till was lynched, there was no struggle for definition. His lynching touched our bone marrow."

Public pressure forced Mississippi officials to hold a murder trial in Sumner, MS. It lasted only five days and the all-White jury took only one hour and seven minutes to acquit Bryant and Milam, who later publicly admitted to the murder. Both men are now dead.

"The struggle for our emancipation is a history of strong, magnificent women," said the Rev. Jesse L. Jackson.

He ranked Mrs. Till-Mobley among an honor roll of great women in the history of Black America: "Harriet Tubman, Sojourner Truth, Ida B. Wells, Constance Baker Motley, Madame C.J. Walker, Fannie Lou Hamer, Rosa Parks and Gertrude Johnson Williams, mother of JET Publisher John H. Johnson."

And he compared her maternal devotion to that of Biblical heroines the Virgin Mary and Jochebed, whose son Moses led the Jews from bondage in Egypt.

Comedian/human rights activist Dick Gregory said, "It was not Emmett Till's death, but Mrs. Till-Mobley's ability to say to JET Magazine, 'I will share this tragedy with you in order to share it with the world. And it was that picture in the magazine that brought lynchings to a standstill.

The next Trailways bus arrived two hours late to find the terminal closed, locked up tight. Local contacts informed the second group of the attack as they drove them to an evening mass meeting at Friendship Junior College, where the students of the Rock Hill "Jail-ins" were enrolled. The Freedom Riders were saluted that night for maintaining their composure and goodwill through their first "CRISIS."[9]

Similar occurrences took place at Orangeburg, S.C. with the Freedom Riders. Students at South Carolina State College and Claflin College also performed "Sit-ins" at lunch counters to protest segregation."[10]

After a group of riders were attacked in Montgomery, Alabama, on May 20, 1961, Attorney General Robert Kennedy dispatched some six hundred marshals to the spot. Governor Patterson later declared martial law and called out the National Guard.

The whole campaign converged on Jackson, Mississippi, where scores of riders were arrested.

On December 12, 1961, the "Freedom Ride" movement merged into a massive city-by-city assault that may prove to be the pattern of the future. The arrest of twelve "Freedom Riders" in Georgia precipitated the militant Albany Movement- the general name for a coordinated, city-wide campaign by Martin Luther King, Jr., SNCC, and some elements of CORE, and the NAACP."[11]

After the arrest of over 500 Freedom riders in Jackson, Mississippi, earlier in the fall of that same year, King became more committed toward the Freedom Riders. King plunged into a fund raising campaign to help cover the Freedom Riders legal expenses, soliciting contributions from various Jewish and Christian organizations and addressing rallies for the riders at St. Louis and other places. He also helped the Freedom Ride Coordinating committee line up scholarships for student riders in need of financial assistance for the fall term. In an article published that fall in the New York Times Magazine, King tried to interpret the mission of the Freedom Rider for white liberals. "He is carrying forward a revolutionary destiny of a whole people consciously and deliberately," King wrote. "Hence, the extraordinary willingness to fill the jails as if they were honors classes." King pointed out that Negro Collegians use to ape white students, dressing and acting like them and aspiring to a professional life cast in the image of their white middle-class counterparts. But this was no longer the case.

Through the Sit-ins and Freedom Rides, Negro students were initiating change and liberating themselves from social and psychological servitude. And consider their achievements. To date, lunch counters had been desegregated in 150 Southern cities. And Negro students were determined to stand-in, sit-in, kneel-in and ride-in until every facility in the United States supposedly open to the public admitted Negroes, Latinos, Indians, Jews, or "what-have-you." It was time for all America, King asserted, to join the students in a campaign to "End Jim Crow Now."

As it turns out, the "Freedom Riders" dealt a death blow to Jim Crow bus facilities. At Robert Kennedy's request the Interstate Commerce Commission that September issued regulations ending segregated facilities in interstate bus stations; the regulations were to take effect on November 1. King pronounced this "A remarkable victory" and attributed it to "the way in which the "Freedom Riders" dramatized the travel conditions in our nation for persons of color."

But it would take two years of moping-up activities before Kennedy could announc that Systematic segregation of Negroes in the interstate transportation has disappeared." As he reflected on the "Freedom Rides", King found another reason for their spectacular success. "Without the presence of the press, there might have been untold massacres in the South. The world seldom believes the horror stories of history until they are documented via the mass media.

Certainly, there would not have been sufficient pressure to warrant a ruling by the ICC had not this situation been so well publicized." The lesson seemed unmistakable; to attain real success in Civil rights, do something dramatic enough to command national media attention. As events were to prove, King learned that lesson better than any Negro leader of his generation.

The sit-in movement, patterned on the passive resistance techniques of Mahatma Ghandi, raced across the South. Chain stores, department stores, libraries, supermarkets, and movie theatres, were hit by demonstrations picket lines and boycotts. By February 10, the movement had spread to fifteen Southern cities in five states. By September, 1961, more than 100 cities in twenty states had been affect by sit-ins."[12]

"At Orangeburg, South Carolina,... some four hundred student from South Carolina State and Claflin Colleges marched downtown to sit at the segregated lunch counters.

Forewarned, local police and units of special state agents intercepted them with massed force, firing tear gas and water hoses before they arrested 388 of the student marchers. Doused, choking students, herded into an enclosed park, found themselves as stunned by their own calm by the ferocity of the police rebuff. Charles Drew leader of the Orangeburg March would always recall looking back at the melee from a police car after his arrest, to see one of the hulking local football stars, David "Deacon" Jones, holding in his arms a crippled female student who had been knocked down by the firehoses. The expression on Jones' face was one of peaceful sadness instead of rage. The sight of it haunted Drew. Although he had little use for nonviolence or even Christianity, he became convinced that an inescapable power could be buried in doctrines of meekness and humanity. Orangeburg was the first of some forty new cities that experienced student demonstrations, as the sit-in movement spreader into Georgia, West Virginia, Texas, and Arkansas."[13]

As the Freedom Rides and Sit-ins continued to spread throughout the South, Blacks inevitably had to protect themselves from the attacks of some [Caucasian] terrorists, the Ku Klux Klan. "Holding a meeting in Alabama, the Klan burned crosses outside Tuscaloosa, the sight of the University of Alabama. There Blacks were expected to enroll in the predominantly white University's summer school during that week."[14]

Having established the fact that they did not want anything to do with integration, the incident at the University of Alabama marked only the continuing "CRISIS" of racial haters and bigotry in the struggle for equality for Negroes.

"Most Caucasian Southerners and probably a portion of Southern conditioned Negroes, tended to see the white violence to non-violent demonstrators as a natural response, a cause and effect. As the movement would continue, more white racist violence would occurs. In the South, many white people would speak of the most beautiful, most peaceful demonstrations, as "Riots" and this was translated into public policy and opinion --unconstitutional arrests and police harassment."[15]

The presence of Caucasian racist violence remained a very significant phenomena for Blacks. "Memphis Norman, a young Black man, was severely beaten and kicked to the ground by angry Whites in Jackson, Mississippi, because he had ordered a cup of coffee and a sandwich at a "White Only" lunch counter. However, he called his experience "worthwhile."[16]

Lunch counters were not the only places that Blacks were not welcomed. Moreover, it seems that the Caucasian man was extremely desperate in his efforts to keep the two races apart, even in the house of the Lord. "Church officials turned away seventeen Negroes from four white Protestant churches in downtown Jackson, Mississippi. The minister and the assistant pastor of the capitals largest church said he would ask for new assignment because they did not want to serve with Negroes."[17]

The Black church has always played a very meaningful role throughout the campaign for racial equality in America. The church became a meeting place for Black leaders of the Civil Rights Movement to discuss their strategies and also a target that the Ku Klux Klan would assault. "On Sunday September 23, 1963, a bomb exploded in the Sixteenth Avenue Baptist Church just across the street from the Human Rights Headquarters in Montgomery, Alabama. When the explosion occurred Sunday school was in session. Four young girls: Cynthia Wesley, Denise Mcnair, Carol Robertson, and Addie MacCollins, were killed. Two other young blacks, Johnny Robinson and Virgil Wade, were fatally shot during the disturbances that followed the bombing. The death of these six young Blacks were a bitter end to the high hopes of Blacks that summer. The death of President John F. Kennedy would be only a month away as the need for a strong Civil Rights Bill was desperately needed to be passed by Congress. Nine months after the assassination of President Kennedy, President Lyndon B. Johnson signed the Civil Rights Bill of 1964 as a result of the massive march on the nation's capitol. In spite of the fact that an interracial council had been set up as promised, no Caucasians in Birmingham thought much of submitting to the testing that day. Caucasians and Blacks in Birmingham still did not know one another."[18]

For Blacks, the opportunity to be equal means not only the right to an equal chance for available Jobs, but social equality as well. " In 1963, the unemployment rates for Black men had consistently ran more than twice as high as for Caucasian men since 1951. Black women's rate of unemployment had been between 66 percent and 100 percent higher than the rate of unemployment between Caucasian women.

24

25

27

28

29

30

31

32

33

Today our unemployment rate is TWO times that of Caucasians. Every recession demonstrates the old adage that Blacks are the 'Last Hired and First Fired." More importantly, they are generally concentrated in the lower and unskilled jobs. Moreover, Blacks in 1963 were suffering discrimination in federally financed training for defense jobs, applying to employment by the federal government, and to training programs administered by the federal agencies.

"Deeply divided on the idea of suffrage qualifications, America's founding fathers left the matter to the state. "Plainly, there was to be no unqualified federal right to vote. Freedom at the polls is important, not only to insure that government shall have the strength of popular support, but also to insure citizens that their interests will be respected by those in Power."[19]

In 1963, the United States had been over the decades plagued with recessions and severe poverty. More importantly, Negroes have had to suffer more than their equal share of this despair. The years of the fifties and sixties brought the plight of Negro hunger and poverty in America to the forefront of governmental statistics.

According to author Michael Harrington, author of "The Other America", "The main concentration of rural poverty has been Southern. In South Carolina, for example, over half of the farm units are in the bottom-income categories of the Department of Agriculture. One statistic should illuminate this problem dramatically. Poor farmers and sharecroppers live in a society with an incredibly productive agricultural system. Yet, according to governmental figures, in the mid-fifties some fifty-six percent of low-income farm families were deficient in one or more basic nutrients in the diet. The rural poor who did not live on farming were even worse off; seventy percent suffered from this deficiency. Thus, there is "hunger" in the midst of abundance."

By saying that rural poverty is most heavily concentrated in the South, one is also indicating that it has a racial aspect. In a state like South Carolina, the Negro poor farmer is not simply impoverished; he is terrorized as well. The Southern Negroes who had been making news by boycotts and sit-ins are city people, concentrated in larger numbers forming communities, they have a cohesion and social strength that is able to stand up to the forces of racism. But the rural Negro is isolated, living in a place of backwardness and ignorance. As such, he is the perfect target for the traditional methods of terrorism. Two means are employed in making this Southern Negro sharecropping poverty a special horror. The Klan or the Citizen's Council can use physical violence or intimidation.

The car that approaches a shack in the middle of the night is a threat, or the racist can call in the bills at the local store, or even eliminate sharecropping units. Hundreds of thousands of them have disappeared in the last two decades."[20]

Living with the harsh severity and reality of hunger, Negroes were literally in misery by every conceivable fact and statistic. Negro leaders knew that there had to be something done.

Therefore, more demonstrations and protests were held to demonstrate governmental failures toward Negroes. The most notable protest occurred in 1963 where thousands of Negroes converged on Washington D.C., to bring the message to the attention of the nation and the world, that Negroes would not settle for inequality in America. This is where Martin L. King, Jr., delivered his famous "I Have A Dream" speech. Delivered on the steps at the Lincoln Memorial in Washington, D. C., On August 28, 1963. Dr. King said:

"Five score years ago, a great American, in whose symbolic shadow we stand, signed the Emancipation Proclamation. This momentous decree came as a great beacon light of hope to millions of Negro slaves, who had been seared in the flames of withering injustice. It comes as a joyous daybreak to end the long night of captivity. But one hundred years later, we must face the tragic fact that the Negro is still not free. One hundred years later, the life of the Negro is still sadly crippled by the manacles of segregation and the chains of discrimination. One hundred years later, the Negro lives on a lonely island of poverty, in the midst of a vast ocean of prosperity. One hundred years later, the Negro is still languishing in the corners of American society, and finds himself an exile in his own land. So we have come here today to dramatize an appalling condition.

In a sense we have come to our nation's capital to cash a check. When the architects of our republic wrote the magnificent words of the Constitution and the Declaration of Independence, they were signing a "Promissory Note",to which every American was to fall heir. This note was a promise that all men would be guaranteed "The Inalienable Rights of Life, Liberty, and the Pursuit of Happiness." It is obvious today that America has defaulted on this "Promissory Note" insofar as her citizens of color are concerned. Instead of honoring this sacred obligation, America has given the Negro people a "Bad Check", which has come back marked "Insufficient Funds." But we refuse to believe that the bank of "Justice" is bankrupt. We refuse to believe that there are "Insufficient Funds" in the great vaults of opportunity of this nation. So we have come to cash a "check", that will give us upon demand the riches of "Freedom" ,and the security of "Justice." We have also come to this "Hallowed" spot to remind America of the fierce urgency of now. This is no time to engage in the luxury of cooling off, or to take the tranquilizing drug of gradualism. Now is the time to rise from the dark and desolate valley of segregation to the sunlit path of racial "Justice." Now is the time to open the doors of opportunity to all of GOD'S children. Now is the time to lift our nation from the quicksands of racial injustice to the solid rock of "Brotherhood."

It would be fatal for the nation to overlook the urgency of the moment, and to underestimate the determination of the Negro. This sweltering summer of the Negro's legitimate discontent will not pass until there is an invigorating autumn of freedom and equality. Nineteen sixty-three is not an end, but a beginning. Those who hope that the Negro needed to blow off steam, and will now be content, will have a rude awakening if the nation returns to business as usual.

38

Assassinated at the height of the fury, NAACP leader Medgar Evers lay in state mourned by millions including his widow, Myrlie

There will be neither rest nor tranquility in America, until the Negro is granted his full citizenship rights. The whirlwinds of revolt will continue to shake the foundations of our nation, until the bright day of justice emerges. But there is something that I must say to my people who stand on the warm threshold that leads into the palace of justice. In the process of gaining our rightful place, we must not be guilty of wrongful deeds. Let us not seek to satisfy our thirst for freedom by drinking from the cup of bitterness and hatred.

We must forever conduct our struggle on the high plane of dignity and discipline. We must not allow our creative protest to generate into physical violence. Again and again, we must rise to the majestic heights of meeting physical force with soul force. The marvelous new militancy which has engulfed the Negro community must not lead us to distrust of all white people, for many of our white brothers, as evident by their presence here today, have come to realize that their destiny is tied up with our destiny and their freedom is inextricably bound to our freedom. We cannot walk alone.

And as we walk, we must make the pledge that we shall march ahead. We cannot turn back. There are those who are asking the devotees of the civil rights, "When will you be satisfied?" We can never be satisfied as long as our bodies, heavy with the fatigue of travel, cannot gain lodging in the motels of the highways and the hotels of the cities. We cannot be satisfied as long as the Negro's basic mobility is from a smaller ghetto to a larger one. We can never be satisfied as long as a Negro in Mississippi cannot vote, and a Negro in New York believes he has nothing for which to vote. No, no, we are not satisfied, and we will not be satisfied, until justice roll down like waters, and righteousness like a mighty stream.

I am not unmindful that some of you have come here out of great trials and tribulations. Some of you have come fresh from narrow cells. Some of you have come from areas where your quest for freedom left you battered by the storms of persecution, and staggered by the winds of police brutality. You have been the veterans of creative suffering. Continue to work with the faith, "that unearned suffering is redemptive."

Go back to Mississippi, go back to Alabama, go back to Georgia, go back to Louisiana, go back to the slums and ghettos of our northern cities, knowing that somehow this situation can and will be changed. Let us not wallow in the valley of despair. I say to you today, my friends, that in spite of the difficulties and frustrations of the moment, I still have a dream.

It is deeply rooted in the American dream. I have a dream that one day this nation will rise up and live out the true meaning of its creed: "We hold these truths to be self evident that "All Men Are Created Equal." I have a dream that one day on the red hills of Georgia, the sons of former slaves and the sons of former slave owners, will be able to sit down together at a table of brotherhood.

34

35

PRESIDENT JOHN F. KENNEDY (right) and advisor, ponder solutions to the social unrest in Birmingham, Ala., and throughout the South in 1963.

I have a dream that one day, even the state of Mississippi, a desert state, sweltering with the heat of injustice and oppression, will be transformed into an oasis of freedom and justice.

I have a dream that my four little children, will one day live in a nation where they will not be judged by the color of their skin, but by the content of their character. I have a dream today.

I have a dream that one day, every valley shall be exalted, every hill and mountain shall be made low, the rough places will be made plain, and the crooked places will be made straight, and the glory of the Lord shall be revealed, and all flesh shall see it together.

This is our hope. This is the faith with which I return to the South. With this faith we will be able to hew out of the mountain of despair a stone of hope. With this faith we will be able to transform the jangling discords of our nation into a beautiful symphony of brotherhood. With this faith we will be able to work together, to pray together, to struggle together, to go to jail together, to stand up for freedom together, knowing that we will be free one day. This will be the day when all of God's Children will be able to sing with a new meaning, "My country, Tis of thee, sweet land of "Liberty," of thee I sing. Land where my fathers died, land of the pilgrim's pride, from every mountainside, let freedom ring."

And if America is to be a great nation this must become true. So let freedom ring from the prodigious hilltops of New Hampshire. Let freedom ring from the mighty mountains of New York. Let freedom ring from the heightening Alleghenies of Pennsylvania! Let freedom ring from the snowcapped Rockies of Colorado! Let freedom ring from the curvaceous peaks of California! But not only that; let freedom ring from Stone Mountain of Georgia! Let freedom ring from Lookout Mountain of Tennessee! Let freedom ring from every hill and every molehill of Mississippi. From every mountainside, let freedom ring.

When we let freedom ring, when we let it ring from every village and every hamlet, from every state and every city, we will be able to speed up that day when "All of God's Children," Black men and white men, Jews and Gentiles, Protestants and Catholics, will be able to join hands and sing in the words of the old Negro spiritual, "Free At Last! Free At Last! Thank God, Almighty, We are Free At Last!"[21]

On August 28, 1963, newspapers at home and abroad carried reports of the Washington march and excerpts from King's speech and editorial notices outside the South were almost all favorable. Journalist David Halberstam caught the art in King's performance and later said that the affair reminded him of "A great televised morality play."

But along with the accounts of the march came news that W.E.B. Dubois, the celebrated "Negro Intellectual," cofounder of the NAACP and longtime editor of the "CRISIS", Historian and author among many other books of the inimitable: "The Souls of Black Folk", and "Black Reconstruction", was dead in Ghana, West Africa, at the age of ninety-five. King had exchanged correspondence with him during the Montgomery Bus boycott, and Dubois had praised King as "honest, straight-forward, well-trained, and knowing the limits."

44

Dr. William Edward Burghardt DuBois. Historian, author, poet and social pioneer. 1868-1963

But Dubois had given up on America so embittered in his later years that he had become a communist, and an expatriate, brooding on the tragedy of the age; "not that men are wicked- who is good? Not that men are ignorant-what is truth? Nay, but that men know so little of men."[22]

Dr. King concurred with professor Dubois insofar as the "Racial Crisis" was concerned. King asserted that, "The rumblings of discontent in Asia and Africa are expressions of a quest for freedom and human dignity by people who have long been the victims of colonialism and imperialism. So in a real sense the "Racial Crisis" in America is a part of the larger "World Crisis."

"In the present "Crisis" America can achieve either racial justice or the ultimate social psychosis that can only lead to domestic suicide. The democratic ideal of freedom and equality will be fulfilled for all- or all human beings will share in the resulting social and spiritual doom. In short, this "Crisis" has the potential for democracy's fulfillment or fascism's triumph; for social progress or retrogression. We can choose either to walk the high road of human "Brotherhood", or to tread the low road of Man's inhumanity to Man."[23]

Moreover, Dr. King researched and concluded that: "The idea of an "Inferior" or "Superior Race" has been refuted by the best evidence of the science of anthropology. Great anthropologists, like Ruth Benedict, Margaret Mead, and Melville J. Herskovits, agree that, although there may be inferior and superior individuals within all races, there is no superior or inferior race. In the final analysis the "Problem of Race" is not a political but a "Moral Issue."[24]

Dr. King also believed that "The Negro cannot win the respect of his oppressor by acquiescing; he merely increases the oppressor's arrogance and contempt.

Acquiescence is interpreted as proof of the Negro's inferiority. The Negro cannot win the respect of the white people of the South or the people of the world if he is willing to sell the future of his children for his personal and immediate comfort and safety."

Dr. King further believed that, "Any real change in the status quo depends on the continued creative action to sharpen the conscience of the nation and establish a climate in which even the most recalcitrant elements are forced to admit that change is necessary."[25]

"Mississippi was the state with the worst record of repression of Black's right to vote. A man had been shot down on the highway in the small Mississippi town of McComb; a town filled with wretchedly housed sharecroppers in the poorest part of the state, where the cotton fields were. He was reportedly killed because he attempted to register to vote."[26]

Voting in Mississippi was without a doubt the most vital weapon that Blacks had to express their interests in the governing of that state or any state in the union. Blacks who tried to assist other Blacks in voter registration usually met the same kind of misfortune, brutality.

41

On August 28, 1963, hundreds of thousands gathered in the nations capital, protesting poverty and hunger in America.

42 The March on Washington will be remembered for King's "I Have a Dream" speech , and the crowd's hopeful jubilation , . On a Sunday morning, less than three weeks later, a bomb struck Birmingham's Sixteenth Street Baptist Church. Bayonet-bearing Alabama troopers guarded the scene of the bombing which critically injured ten-year-old Sarah Collins and killed four young girls, including her sister. Mourners at the funeral were overcome by grief (82), a mood echoed by the nation itself just a few weeks later at the funeral of President John F. Kennedy .

43

"In Greenwood, Mississippi, Black leaders charged that four voter registration workers, three women, had been beaten when they entered a "White Only" rest room in a bus stop."[27]

In a country who's doctoring states "Life, Liberty, and the Pursuit of Happiness," it was evident that Blacks would be the recipient of neither.

In most Southern states, Civil Rights workers organized campaigns to try to get Blacks to overcome their fear and register to vote, However, as workers had since the movement began, they ran the risk of losing their lives for assisting Blacks in their attempt to gain access to the polls. On the very first day of the campaign, three young Civil Rights workers disappeared. One was a Mississippi black man James Chaney, twenty-one years old, and the others were two Caucasian workers from New York. They had been arrested the night before near Philadelphia, Mississippi, and released after a few hours. Before they could get back to their headquarters they vanished. The search took up half the summer. A witness told the FBI where to look. On August 4, 1964, the bulldozer rambled through the piney woods near Jackson, Mississippi, where the three bodies were found. Later, three Klan members were arrested, including one deputy sheriff."[28]

At the time Johnson signed the Voting-Rights Bill, King was increasingly apprehensive about administration policies in Vietnam. For more than twenty years war had racked that distant Asian land, as communist forces under Ho Chi Minh battled to liberate their country, first from the French, then from the United States. After France withdrew in 1955, the U.S. moved in, ignored an international agreement in Geneva that called for free elections, and installed a repressive, anti-communist regime in South Vietnam, supplying it with money, weapons, and military advisers.

From the outset, American policy makers viewed Ho Chi Minh's government in North Vietnam as part of a world Communist conspiracy directed by Moscow and Peking. If Communism were not halted in Vietnam, they feared, then all Asia would succumb. American intervention, of course, aroused Ho Chi Minh, who rushed help to nationalist guerillas in South Vietnam and set out to unite all of Vietnam under his leadership. With civil war raging across South Vietnam, the United States stepped up its' flow of military aid to Saigon. Under Kennedy, the number of American Advisers rose to 23,000, but Kennedy became disillusioned with American involvement in Vietnam and actually devised a disengagement plan before he was assassinated in 1963. Johnson, however, nullified the plan and continued American assistance to South Vietnam."[29]

"South Vietnam represented an oasis of democracy in an area of the world that was steadily being taken over by Communism, and Johnson felt it was the duty of the United States to preserve that oasis. Under the Kennedy Administration, military advisers and equipment had been supplied to South Vietnam, but over the years North Vietnam, aided by weapons and weapons from the Soviet Union and Communist China, had made territorial gains and in response American fighting men had also been committed to the war.

The majority of these soldiers were draftees, and the majority of those were Blacks. College students could get student deferments, but most Blacks did not go to college and could not escape the draft.

King began to criticize publicly the fact that while Blacks constituted only 10 percent of the population, they made up 40 percent of the fighting forces in Vietnam, and to ask why they should fight for a country in which they were unable to attend school with Whites. He spoke at anti-war rallies in various parts of the country warning that a confrontation between the United States and China in Vietnam could lead to world war III, and urging a negotiated settlement. He also questioned the moral right of the United States to intervene in what was essentially another country's civil war."[30]

"Negroes" and poor people generally are bearing the heaviest burden of this (Vietnam) war. If America's soul becomes totally poisoned, part of the autopsy must read "Vietnam," Dr. King declared."[31]

The events in Vietnam were troubling to Dr. King. He could not bear to see this country muscling its way into the internal affairs of another nation, bombing and shooting people-and brown-skinned people at that- under the auspicious quest of stopping Communism. He wondered when would America understand the Nationalistic attitude engulfing people of color in the entire world, Vietnam not excluded. Dr. King wondered if America would ever be on the right side of the revolutionary spirit of the age. Martin Luther King, Jr. hated war and denounced "the madness of militarism," since Montgomery days, and had long hoped that once he and the Southern Christian Leadership Conference had broken down Dixie's racial barriers, they could apply the creative non-violence to the world theatre.

Dr. King said that he was not going to sit by and see the war escalate without saying something about it. He also felt that it was worthless to talk about integrating if there is no world to integrate in. Therefore, he felt that the war in Vietnam must be stopped!

"He was roundly criticized for his statements. Other Black leaders felt he was wrong to try to involve the Civil Rights Movement with the Anti-war movement. Southern and conservative whites called him a communist, and plenty of other whites resented his public criticism of the United States Government. One day in Atlanta he found an envelope on his desk containing photographs of himself and tape recordings of his conversations in situations, which if made public, would seriously damage his reputation. There was no note with the material, but the message was clear. If he did not stop his campaign against U.S. involvement in the war, the material would be made public. In the past, his advisers had warned King that his telephones and motel rooms might be bugged, but he had not heeded the warning. Now he realized he'd been spied on for years, probably by the F.B.I.."[32]

45

Dr. and Mrs. King accepting the Nobel Peace Prize in Oslo, Norway, in 1964.

45a

Ralph Bunche
1904-1971
Diplomat and First African-American
to Win a Nobel Peace Prize

52

Dr. King speaks at an anti-war demonstration outside the United Nations in April 1967. He was criticized for his anti-war crusade by both whites and blacks who felt he was weakening the civil rights crusade. (UNITED PRESS INTERNATIONAL)

53

"While white America, especially those from the upper classes, avoided the inconveniences, dangers, and hardships of military life, young Black men eagerly volunteered or readily accepted the draft. However, not all African Americans shared this view of the military in Southeast Asia.

From the beginning of the war, some Black leaders recognized Vietnam as a drain on the energy and budgetary funds needed to advance Civil Rights. As the war progressed, Blacks as a whole realized, too, that they were paying a higher price in casualties than were whites. As one Black soldier remarked about the military in Vietnam "It's the kind of integration that could kill you."[33]

Most whites who were in Vietnam served in administrative units in the rear at headquarters? Blacks made up the majority of the fighting forces, serving disproportionately in combat units, called infantry and in reconnaissance units, on the frontlines. The burden of the war fell on the shoulders of my cousins like: Bobby Robinson, Charlie Mobley, Ernest Shivers, Larry Hill, and other close friends like Howard Chambers, Walter Chambers, Carlton Carter, and Leslie Bell. Some units on the frontlines were all African-American, and like the "Brothers" have said, "The "white boys" were at the rear in fear." Sadly enough, all of my brothers came back to America to nothing but more racism and discrimination just like I did.

According to Bobby Murphy of Sumpter, South Carolina, he recalls returning home from Vietnam in 1967 to nothing but racism in the form of segregated eating facilities and bathrooms. He further stated "that African-American soldiers could not leave the post often times for fear of being lynched by the local Ku Klux Klansmen who were very strong in the area of Shaw Air Force Base, in South Carolina. Moreover, African-American soldiers weren't only experiencing racism on the home front.

According to yet another Vietnam Veteran, R.W. Williams, the superior officers in Vietnam, who were often whites, would wait until near the end of the tour of duty for the African-American soldiers in Vietnam then find some little senseless offense against the particular soldier in order to justify the soldier's receiving a Bad Conduct discharge or a dishonorable discharge, lessening his chances for success when he does return to the United States.

According to John Hatcher, President of the N.A.A.C.P. for the Ventura County Chapter in Ventura, California, this was not uncommon. Moreover, Mr. Hatcher, who also served as the EEOC officer, was very appalled by the disproportionate number of African-Americans who was receiving dishonorable discharges or other than honorable discharges at the time we talked in 1991.

Black leaders advocating self-defensive measures to achieve equality were the first to oppose the Vietnam War. One of the initial spokesmen was Malcolm X. In a talk with Black teenagers in McComb, Mississippi, on December 31, 1964, Malcolm declared that, "The United States was the most "Hypocritical Government" since the world began."

He explained that the United States was "suppose to be a democracy, Suppose to be for freedom, and all of that kind of stuff when they want to draft you and put you in the Army and send you to Saigon to fight for them-and then you've got to turn around and all night long discuss how you're going to get a right to register and vote without being murdered".

He told reporters, "I don't believe that we're going to overcome (by) singing. If you're going to get yourself a .45 and start singing, "we shall overcome," well I'm with you." Although Malcolm X was pessimistic about the value of peaceful protests marches, pressure from Civil Rights groups eventually persuaded congress to pass a number of major bills outlawing a wide range of racially discriminatory practices. Among them were the Civil Rights Act of 1964 and the Economic Opportunity Act. Yet he continued to insist that the new laws were only showpieces and would not lead to any substantial improvement for Blacks. "You don't stick a knife in a man's back nine inches and pull it out six inches and say you're making progress," he argued. Black America was still seething, according to him, and he pointed to recent outbreaks of racial violence in Northern cities as signs that the ghettos were about to erupt. At a series of rallies in June of 1964, Malcolm X issued a call to Blacks of all nations to unite behind a "Revolutionary Movement" that would sweep aside all vestiges of racial oppression. "Revolution is like a forest fire, "he said, "It burns everything in its path."

Malcolm X also envisioned the OAAU (Organization of African-American Unity) as a Black Nationalist Organization. Its agenda called for workers throughout the world to unite for the purpose of dismantling the capitalist economic system of private and corporate ownership of goods and property, on which most Western nations rested. He, thus, hoped to merge the Black Power Movement with Socialism, an economic system in which goods and property are owned and controlled by the state.

So grand a mission required large funds-something Malcolm X sorely lacked- and he quickly set about raising money. In June of 1964, he embarked on a busy schedule of speaking engagements and fundraising rallies. He also launched a lobbying campaign at the United Nations, which he urged to pass a resolution condemning American racial policies.

In July of 1964, Malcolm X flew to Cairo, Egypt, where he addressed a group of representatives of African nations at a conference sponsored by the OAU (Organization of African Unity). The delegates treated their guest as if he were an official American Ambassador and listened intently to his words. Our "Problems" are your "Problems," he told them. He then went on to argue, "that the struggle of (African-Americans) paralleled the efforts of the emerging Third World Nations." After he gave his address, Malcolm X consulted with Islamic Clergymen for ideas about expanding his ministry in America. He then took an extended tour of Africa. He was feted at several receptions given by heads of state, including his longtime hero Jomo Kenyatta, President of Kenya, as he outlined his program for an international Black Liberation Movement.

48

Malcolm X in Harlem, New York

Malcolm X had been taught by the Honorable Elijah Muhammad and the Nation of Islam, who"cited the portrayal of Jesus Christ and the other Biblical Prophets as whites as a typical example of the desire of whites to make Blacks feel racially inferior. According to Elijah Muhnmmad," All the Prophets and Jesus Christ, (including Moses), were Blacks whose teachings had been corrupted by whites."[34]

As it was stated earlier in the study, Malcolm X had been inspired by the Honorable Elijah Muhammads' teachings while in prison. "The Black Prisoner", said Mr. Muhammad, "symbolized white society's "Crime" of keeping Black men oppressed and deprived, and ignorant, and unable to get decent jobs, turning them into criminals."[35]

"According to Malcolm, many who had heard him somewhere in person, or on television, or those who read something I've said, will think I went to school far beyond the eighth grade. This impression is due entirely to my prison studies.

It had really begun back in the Charleston prison. Every book I picked up had few sentences which didn't contain anywhere from one to nearly all of the words that might as well have been in Chinese. When I just skipped those words, of course, I really ended up with little idea of what the book said. So I had come to the Norfolk Prison Colony still going through only book-reading motions. Pretty soon, I would have quit even these motions, unless I had received the motivation that I did.

I saw that the best thing I could do was get hold of a dictionary to study, to learn some words. I was lucky enough to reason also that I should try to improve my penmanship. It was sad. I couldn't even write in a straight line. It was both ideas together that moved me to request a dictionary along with some tablets and pencils from the Norfolk Prison Colony school.

I spent two days just riffling uncertainly through the dictionary's pages. I'd never realized that so many words existed! I didn't know which words I needed to learn. Finally, just to start some kind of action, I began copying. In my slow, painstaking, ragged handwriting, I copied into my tablet everything printed on that first page, down to the punctuation marks. I believe it took me a day. Then, aloud, I read back, to myself, everything I'd written on the tablet. Over and over, aloud, to myself I read my own handwriting. I woke up the next morning, thinking about those words immensely proud to realize that not only had I written so much at one time, but I'd written words that I never knew were in the world. Moreover, with a little effort, I also could remember what many of these words meant. I reviewed the words whose meanings I didn't remember. Funny thing, from the dictionary first page right now, that "aardvark" springs to mind. The dictionary had a picture of it, a long-tailed, low-eared, burrowing African mammal, which lives off termites caught by sticking out its tongue as an anteater does for ants.

I was so fascinated that I went on - I copied the dictionary's next page. And the same experience came when I studied that. With every succeeding page, I also learned of people and places and events from history. Actually the dictionary is like a miniature encyclopedia.

Finally the dictionary's A section had filled a whole tablet - and I went on into the B's. That was the way I started copying what eventually became the entire dictionary. It went a lot faster after so much practice helped me to pick up handwriting speed.

Between what I wrote in my tablet, and writing letters, during the rest of my time in prison I would guess I wrote a million words. I suppose it was inevitable that as my word-base broadened, I could for the first time pick up a book and read and now began to understand what the book was saying. Anyone who has read a great deal can imagine the new world that opens. Let me tell you something, from then until I left that prison, in every free moment I had, if I was not reading in the library, I was reading on my bunk. You couldn't have gotten me out of books with a wedge. Between Mr. Muhammad's teachings...and my readings of books, months passed without my even thinking about being imprisoned. In fact, up to then, I never had been so truly free in my life.

The teachings of Mr. Muhammad stressed how history had been "Whitened" when white men had written history books, the black man simply had been left out. Mr. Muhammed couldn't have said anything that would have struck me much harder. I had never forgotten how when my class, me and all of those whites, had studied seventh-grade United States History back in Mason, the history of the Negro had been covered in one paragraph, and the teacher had gotten a big laugh with his joke, "Negroes" feet are so big that when they walk, they leave a hole in the ground."

This is one reason why Mr. Muhammad's teachings spread so swiftly all over the United States, among all Negroes, whether or not they became followers of Mr. Muhammad. The teachings ring true-to every Negro. You can hardly show me a black adult in America-or a white one, for that matter-who knows from the history books anything like the truth about the black man's role. In my own case, once I heard of the "Glorious history of the black man," I took special pains to hunt in the library for books that would inform me on details about "Black History." I found books like: Will Durant's Story of Civilization. I read H. G. Wells Outline of History. The "Souls of Black Folk" by W. E. B. Dubois gave me a glimpse into Black peoples history before they came to (America). Carter G. Woodson's Negro History opened my eyes about Black Empires before the Black slave was brought to the United States, and the early Negro struggles for freedom.

J. A. Rogers' three volumes of Sex and Race told about race mixing before Christ's time; about Aesop being a Black man who told fables; about Egypt's Pharaohs; about the great Coptic Christian Empires; about Ethiopia, the earth's oldest continuous Black Civilization, as China is the oldest continuous civilization. Mr. Muhammad's teachings about how the white man had been created led me to Findings in Genetics by Gregor Mendel. (The dictionary's G section was where I had learned what "Genetics" meant.) I really studied this book by the Austrian monk. Reading it over and over, especially certain sections, helped me to understand that if you started with a Black man, a white man could be produced; but starting with a white man, you never could produce a Black man- because the white gene is recessive. And since no one disputes that there was but one original man, the conclusion is clear.

During the last year or so, in the New York Times, Arnold Toynbee used the word "Bleached" in describing the white man. (His words were: "whites (i.e. bleached) human beings of North European origin...".) Toynbee also referred to the European geographic area as only a peninsula of Asia. He said there is no such thing as Europe. And if you look at the globe, you will see for yourself that America is only an extension of Asia. (But at the same time Toynbee is among those who have helped to "Bleach History." He has written that Africa was the only continent that produced no history. He won't write that again. Every day now the truth is coming to light). I never will forget how shocked I was when I began reading about slavery's total horror. It made such an impact upon me that it later became one of my favorite subjects when I became a minister of Mr. Muhammad's. "The World's Most Monstrous "Crime," the "Sin", and the "Blood", on the white man's hands, are almost impossible to believe.

Books like the one by Frederick Olmstead opened my eyes to the horrors suffered when the slave was landed in the United States. The European woman, Fannie Kimball, who had married a Southern white slave owner, described how human beings were degraded. Of course I read Uncle Tom's Cabin. In fact, I believe that's the only novel I have ever read since I started serious reading.

Parkhurst's collection also contained some bound pamphlets of the Abolitionist Anti-slavery Society of New England. I read descriptions of atrocities, I saw those illustrations of Black Slave Women tied up and flogged with whips; of Black mothers watching their babies being dragged off, never to be seen by their mothers again; of dogs chasing after slaves, and of the fugitive slave-catchers, evil white men with whips and clubs and chains and guns. I read about the slave preacher, Rev. Nat Turner, who put the fear of God into the white slave-master. Nat Turner wasn't going around preaching pie-in-the-sky and "Non-violent" freedom for the black man. There in Virginia one night in 1831, Nat and seven other slaves started out at his master's home and through the night they went from one plantation "big house" to the next, killing, until by the next morning 57 white people were dead and Nat had about seventy slaves following him. White people, terrified for their lives, fled from their homes, locked themselves up in public buildings, hid in the woods, and some even left the state. A small army of soldiers took two months to catch and hang Nat Turner. Somewhere I have read that Nat Turner's example is said to have inspired John Brown to invade Virginia and attack Harper's Ferry nearly thirty years later, with thirteen white men and five Negroes.

I read Herodotus, "the father of History," or, rather, I read about him. And I read the histories of various nations, which opened my eyes gradually, then wider and wider, to how the whole world's white men had indeed acted like "Devils", pillaging and raping and bleeding and draining the whole world's nonwhite people. I remember, for instance, books such as Will Durant's story of Oriental Civilization, and Mahatma Ghandhi's "Accounts Of The Struggle," to drive the British out of India.

Book after book showed me how the white man had brought upon the world's black, brown, and yellow peoples every variety of the sufferings of exploitation. I saw how since the Sixteenth Century, the so-called "Christian Trader" white man began to ply the seas in his lust for Asian and African empires, and plunder, and overpower. I read, I saw, how the white man never has gone among the non-white people bearing the cross in the true manner and spirit of Christ's teachings-"Meek, Humble, and Christ-like."

I perceived, as I read, how the collective white man had been actually nothing but a "Piratical Opportunist" who used Faustian Machinations to make his own Christianity his initial wedge in criminal conquests. First, always "Religiously," he branded "Heathen" and "Pagan" labels upon ancient non-white cultures and civilizations. The stage thus set, he then turned upon his non-white victims his weapons of war.

I read how, entering India-half a billion deeply religious brown people- the British white man, by 1759, through promises, trickery and manipulation, controlled much of India through Great Britain's East India Company. The parasitical British Administration kept tentacle out to half of the subcontinent.

In 1857, some of the desperate people of India finally mutinied-and, excepting the African Slave Trade, nowhere has history recorded any more unnecessary bestial and ruthless human carnage than the British suppression of the non-white Indian people.

Over 115 million African people (close to the 1930's population of the United Sates) were murdered or enslaved during the slave trade. And I read how when the slave market was glutted, the cannibalistic white powers of Europe next carved up, as their colonies, the richest areas of the continent. And Europe's chancelleries for the next century played a chess game of naked exploitation and power from Cape Horn to Cairo.

Those books were providing indisputable proof that the "Collective White Man" had acted like a "Devil", in virtually every contact he had with the world's collective non-white man. When the white man professes ignorance about why the Chinese hate him so, my mind can't help flashing back to what I read, there in prison, about how the blood forebears of this same white man raped China at a time when China was trusting and helpless. Those original white "Christian traders" sent into China millions of pounds of opium. By 1839, so many of the Chinese were addicted that China's desperate government destroyed twenty thousand chests of opium.

The white man promptly declared the first opium war. Imagine! Declaring war upon someone who objects to being narcotized! The Chinese were severely beaten, with Chinese-invented gunpowder. The Treaty of Nanking made China pay the British white man for the destroyed opium, maiming China's industrial development. After a second opium war, Peking was looted and burned. "Kill the foreign white devils!" was the 1901 Chinese war cry in the "Boxer Rebellion." Losing again, this time the Chinese were driven from Peking's choicest areas. The vicious, arrogant white man put up the famous signs, "Chinese and dogs not allowed."

After World War II, Red China closed its doors to the Western white world. Some observers inside Red China have reported that the world has never known such a "Hate-White Campaign" as is now going on in this non-white country where, present birth-rates continuing, in fifty more years Chinese will be half the earth's population. Moreover, it seems that more Chinese chickens will soon come home to roost, with China's recent nuclear tests.

Let us face reality. We can see in the United Nations a new world order being shaped, along the color lines- an alliance among the non-white nations. America's U.N. Ambassador Adlai Stevenson complained not long ago that in the United Nations "a skin game" was being played.

He was right. He was facing reality. A "skin game" is being played. But Ambassador Stevenson sounded like Jesse James accusing the marshals of carrying a gun. Because who in the world's history ever played a worse "skin game" than the white man?

The American Black Man is the world's most "Shameful Case of Minority Oppression." What makes the Black man think of himself as only an internal United States issue is just a catch-phrase, two words, "Civil Rights." How is the Black man going to get "Civil Rights" before first he wins "Human Rights?" If the American Black man will start thinking about his "Human Rights," and then start thinking of himself as part of the world's "Great Peoples," he will see he has a case for the United Nations. I can't think of a better case! "Four Hundred Years" of Black Blood and sweat invested here in America, and the white man still has the Black man begging for what every white immigrant fresh off the ship can take for granted the minute he walks down the gangplank.

I don't think anybody ever got more out of going to prison than I did. In fact, prison enabled me to study far more intensively than I would have if my life had gone differently and I had attended some college. I imagine that of the biggest troubles with colleges is there are too many distractions, too much panty-raiding, fraternities, and boola-boola and all of that. Where else but in a prison could I have attacked my ignorance by being able to study intensely sometimes as much as fifteen hours a day?

I'll tell you something. The whole stream of Western philosophy has now wound up in a cul-de-sac. The white man has perpetuated upon himself, as well as upon the Black man, so gigantic a fraud that he has put himself into a crack. He did it through his elaborate, neurotic necessity to hide the Black man's true role in history.

Today the white man is faced head on with what is happening on the Black continent, Africa. Look at the artifacts being discovered there, that are proving over and over again, how the Black man had great, fine, sensitive civilizations before the white man was out of the cave.

History has been so "whitened" by the white man that even the Black professors have known little more than the most ignorant Black man about the talents and rich civilizations and cultures of the Black man of millenniums ago.

I have lectured in Negro colleges and some of these brainwashed Black Ph.D.'s, with their suspenders dragging the ground with degrees, have to run to the white man's newspapers calling me a "Black fanatic."

Why, a lot of them are fifty years behind the times. If I were president of one of these Black colleges, I'd hock the campus if I had to, to send a bunch of Black students off digging in Africa for more, more and more proof of the Black race's historical greatness.

The white man now is in Africa digging and searching. Practically every week, we read about some great new find from Africa's lost civilizations. All that's new is white sciences attitude. The ancient civilizations of the Black man have been buried in the Black Continent all the time. Here is an example: A British Anthropologist named Dr. Louis S. B. Leakey is displaying some fossil bones-a foot, part of a hand, some jaws, and skull fragments.

On the basis of these, Dr. Leakey has said "it's time to rewrite completely the history of man's origin. This species of man lived 1,818,036 years before Christ. And these bones were found in Tanganyika, in the black continent.

It's a crime, the lie that has been told to generations of Black men and white men both. Little innocent Black children, born of parents who believed that their race had no history. Little Black children seeing, before they could talk, that their parents considered themselves inferior. Innocent Black children growing up, living out their lives, dying of old age -and all of their lives ashamed of being Black. But the truth is pouring out of the bag now.

The white man has completely erased the slaves past, a Negro in America can never know his true family name, or even what group he was descended from: the Mandingos, the Wolof, the Serer, the Fula, the Fanti, the Ashanti, or others. I told some of my co-convicts that some slaves brought from Africa spoke Arabic, and were Islamic in their religion. A lot of these convicts still would not believe it unless they could see that a white man had said it. I would read to these brothers selected passages from white men's books. I'd explain to them that the real truth was known to some white men, the scholars; but there had been a conspiracy down through the generations to keep the truth from Black men. I would keep a close watch on how each one of the convicts reacted. I always had to be careful. I never knew when some brainwashed Black (person), some dyed-in-the-wool Uncle Tom, would nod at me and then go running to tell the white man. When one was ripe-and I could tell- then away from the rest, I'd drop it on him, what Mr. Muhammad taught: "The white man is the devil." That would shock many of them-until they started thinking about it.

This is probably as big a single worry as the American prison system has today-the way the Muslim teachings circulated among all Negroes in the country, are converting new Muslims among black men in prison, and black men are in prison in far greater numbers than their proportion in the population.

The reason is that among all Negroes the Black convict is the most perfectly preconditioned to hear the words, "The white man is the devil." You tell that to any Negro, except for those relatively few "integration-mad" so-called "intellectual," and those Black men who are otherwise fat, happy, and deaf, dumb, and blind, with their crumbs from the white man's rich table, you have struck a nerve center in the American Black man.

He may take a day to react, a month, a year; he may never respond, openly; but of one thing you can be sure-when he thinks about his own life, he is going to see where, to him, personally, the white man sure has acted like a devil. And, as I say, above all Negroes, the Black prisoner, here is a Black man caged behind bars, probably for years, put there by the white man.

Usually the convict comes from among those bottom-of-the-pile Negroes, the Negroes who through their entire lives have been kicked about, treated like children-Negroes who never have met one white man who didn't either take something from them or do something to them. You let this caged-up Black man start thinking, the same way I did when I first heard Mr. Elijah Muhammad's teachings. Let him start thinking how, with better breaks when he was young and ambitious he might have been a lawyer, a doctor, a scientist, anything. You let this caged up Black man start realizing, as I did, how from the first landing of the first slave ship, the millions of Black men in America have been like "Sheep in a den of wolves." That's why Black prisoners become Muslims so fast when Elijah Muhammad's teachings filter into their cages by way of other Muslim convicts. "The white man is the "Devil" is a perfect echo of that Black convict's lifelong experience."[36]

During the spring of nineteen fifty-two, I joyously wrote Elijah Muhammad and my family that the Massachusetts State Parole Board had voted that I should be released. But still a few months were taken up with the red tape delay of paper work that went back and forth, arranging for my parole release in the custody of my older brother, Wilford, in Detroit, who now managed a furniture store. Wilford got the Jew who owned the store to sign a promise that upon release I would be given immediate employment. My going to Detroit instead of back to Harlem or Boston was influenced by my family's feeling expressed in their letters. It was in August when they gave me a lecture, a cheap L'il Abner suit and a small amount of money, and I walked out of the gate. I never looked back, but that doesn't make me any different from a million inmates who have left a prison behind them."[37]

The address of Temple Number One was 1470 Frederick Street, I think. The first Temple to be formed, back in 1931, by Master W. D. Fard, was formed in Detroit, Michigan. I never had seen any Christian-believing Negroes conduct themselves like the Muslims, the individuals and the families alike. The men were quietly, tastefully dressed. The women wore ankle-length gowns, no makeup, scarves covered their heads, and the neat children were mannerly not only to adults but to other children as well.

I had never dreamed of anything like that atmosphere among Black people who had learned to be proud they were black, who had learned to love other Black people instead of being jealous and suspicious. I thrilled to how the Muslim men used both hands to grasp a Black brother's both hands, voicing and smiling our happiness to meet him again.

The Muslim sisters, both married and single, were given an honor and respect that I'd never seen Black men give to their women, and it felt wonderful to me. The salutations which we all exchanged were warm, filled with mutual respect and dignity; "Brother"... "Sister"... "Ma'am", "Sir." Even children speaking to other children used these terms, Beautiful!

The blackboard had fixed upon it in permanent paint, on one side, the United States flag and under it the words "Slavery, Suffering and Death", then the word "Christianity" alongside the cross. Beneath the cross was a painting of a black man hanging from a tree. I thought it was outrageous that our small temple still had some empty seats. I complained to my brother Wilfred that there should be no empty seats, with the surrounding streets full of our brainwashed Black brothers and sisters, drinking, cursing, fighting, dancing, carousing, and using dope-the very things that Mr. Muhammad taught were helping the Black man to stay under the heel of the white man here in America."[38]

"During a convention lull, I asked Mr. Muhammad how many Muslims were supposed to be in our Temple Number One in Detroit. He said, there are supposed to be thousands." "Yes, sir," I said. "Sir, What is your opinion of the best way of getting thousands there?" "Go after the young people, he said. "Once you get them, the older ones will follow through shame."

I made up my mind that we were going to follow that advice. Back in Detroit, I talked to my brother Wilfred. I offered my services to our temple's minister, Lemuel Hassan. He shared my determination that we should apply Mr. Muhammad's formula in a recruitment drive. Beginning that day, every evening, straight from work at the furniture store, I went doing what we Muslim's later came to call "Fishing." I knew the thinking and the language of ghetto streets; "My man, let me pull your coat to something".

My application had, of course, been made and during this time I received from Chicago my "X." The Muslim's "X" symbolized the true African family name that he never could know. For me, my "X" replaced the white slavemaster name of "Little" which some blue-eyed "Devil" named little had imposed upon my paternal forebears. The receipt of my "X" meant that forever after in the Nation of Islam, I would be known as Malcolm X. Mr. Muhammad taught that we would keep this "X" until God Himself returned and gave us a Holy Name from His own mouth.

Recruit as I would in the Detroit ghetto bars, in the poolrooms, and on the corners, I found my poor, ignorant, brainwashed black brothers mostly too deaf dumb, and blind, mentally, morally, and spiritually, to respond. It angered me that only now and then would one display even a little curiosity about the teachings that would resurrect the Black man. These few I would almost beg to visit Temple Number One at our next meeting. But then not half of those who agreed to come would actually show up.

Malcolm X speaking to the Nation of Islam.

46

Gradually, enough were made interested, though, that each month, a few more automobiles lengthened our caravans to Temple Two in Chicago. But even after seeing and hearing Elijah Muhammad in person, only a few of the interested visitors would apply by formal letter to Mr. Muhammad to be accepted for Nation of Islam membership.

With a few months of plugging away, however, our storefront Temple One about tripled its membership. And that so deeply pleased Mr. Muhammad that he paid us the honor of a personal visit.

Mr. Muhammad gave me warm praise when Minister Lemuel Hassan told how hard I had labored in the cause of Islam. Our caravans grew. I remember with what pride we led twenty-five automobiles to Chicago. And each time we went we were honored with dinner at the home of Elijah Muhammad. He was interested in my potential, I could tell from things he would say. And I worshiped him.

In early 1953, I left the furniture store. I earned a little better weekly paycheck working at the Gar Wood Factory in Detroit, Where big garage truck bodies were made. I cleaned up behind the welders each time they finished another truck body.

Mr. Muhammad was saying by this time at his dinner table that one of his worst needs was more young men willing to work as hard as they could have to in order to bear the responsibilities of his ministers. He was saying that the teachings should be spreading further than they had, and temples needed to be established in other cities.

It simply had never occurred to me that I might be a minister. I had never felt remotely qualified to directly represent Mr. Muhammad. If someone had asked me about becoming a minister, I would have been astonished, and told them I was happy and willing to serve Mr. Muhammad in the lowliest capacity.

I don't know if Mr. Muhammad suggested it or if our Temple One Minister Lemuel Hassan on his own decision encouraged me to address our assembled brothers and sisters. I know that I testified to what Mr. Muhammad's teachings had done for me: "If I told you the life I have lived, you would find it hard to believe me.... When I say something about the white man, I am not talking about someone I don't know...."

Soon after that, Minister Lemuel Hassan urged me to address the brothers and sisters with an extemporaneous lecture. I was uncertain, and hesitant-but at least I had debated in prison, and I tried my best. (Of course, I can't remember exactly what I said, but I do know that in my beginning efforts my favorite subject was Christianity and the horrors of slavery, where I felt well equipped from so much reading in prison.)

"My brothers and sisters, our white slave-master's Christian religion has taught us Black people in the wilderness of North America that we will sprout wings when we die and fly up into the sky where God will have for us a special place called Heaven. This is the white man's Christian religion used to brainwash us Black people! We have accepted it! we have embraced it!

We have believed it! We have practiced it! And while we are doing all of that, for himself this "Blue-Eyed Devil" has twisted his Christianity, to keep his foot on our backs... to keep our eyes fixed on the "pie in the sky" and "heaven in the hereafter..."while he enjoys his heaven right here...on this earth...in this life."

In the summer of 1953-all praise is due to Allah-I was named Detroit Temple Number One's Assistant Minister. Everyday after work, I walked, "fishing" for potential convert's in the Detroit Black ghetto. I saw the African features of my Black brothers and sisters whom the devilish white man had brainwashed. I saw the hair as mine had been for years, conked by cooking it with lye until it lay limp, looking straight like the white man's hair. Time and again Mr. Muhammad's teachings were rebuked and even ridiculed.... "Aw, man, get out of my face, you Niggers are Crazy!" My head would reel sometimes, with mingled anger and pity for my poor blind Black brothers. I couldn't wait for the next time our Minister Lemuel Hassan would let me speak: "We didn't land on Plymouth Rock, My Brothers and Sisters-Plymouth Rock landed on us!"... "Give all you can to help Messenger Elijah Muhammad's independence program for the Black Man!... This white man always has "Controlled" us Black people by keeping us running to him begging, 'Please lawdy, please Mr. white man, boss, would you push me off another crumb down from your table that's sagging with riches...." ..my beautiful, Black brothers and sisters! And when we say 'Black,' we mean everything not white, brothers and sisters! Because look at your skins! We're all Black to the white man, but we're a thousand and one different colors. Turn around, look at each other! what shade of Black African polluted by the devil white man are you? You see me- well, in the streets they used to call me "Detroit Red." Yes! Yes, "that Raping," "Red-Headed Devil" was my grandfather! That close, yes! My mother's father! She didn't like to speak of it, can you blame her? She said she never laid eyes on him! She was glad for that! I'm glad for her! If I could drain away his blood that pollutes my body, and pollute my complexion, I'd do it! "Because I hate every drop of that "Rapist's" blood that's in me!

"And it's not just me, it's all of us! During slavery, think of it, it was a rare case when one of our Black grandmothers, our great grandmothers, and our great-great-grandmothers who escaped the white "Rapist" slavemaster. That rapist slavemaster who emasculated the Black man... with threats, with fear,...until even today the Black man lives with fear of the white man in his heart! Lives even today still under the heel of the white man. "Think of it-think of that Black slave man filled with fear and dread, hearing the screams of his wife, his mother, his daughter being taken-in the barn, the kitchen, in the bushes! Think of it, my dear brothers and sisters! Think of hearing wives, mothers, daughters, being "Raped!"

And you were too filled with fear of the rapist to do anything about it! And his vicious, animal attacks' offspring, this white man named things like "Mulatto" and 'Quadroom' and 'Octoroon' and all those other things that he has called us-you and me-when he is not calling us 'Nigger'!

"Turn around and look at each other, brothers and sisters, and think of this! You and me, polluted all these colors-and this "Devil" has the arrogance and the gall to think we, "His Victims," should love him!"

I would become so choked up that sometimes I would walk in the streets until late into the night. Sometimes I would speak to no one for hours, thinking to myself about what the white man has done to our poor people here in America."[39]

"Every time I spoke at our Temple One, my voice would still be hoarse from the last time. My throat took a long time to get into condition. "Do you know why the white man really hates you? It's because every time he see's your face, he sees a mirror of his "Crime"- and his guilty conscience can't bear to face it! "Every white man in America, when he looks into a Black man's eyes, should fall to his knees and say "I'm sorry," I'm sorry-my kind has committed "History's Greatest Crime" against your kind; will you give me a chance to atone? But do you brothers and sisters expect any white man to do that? No, you know better. And why won't he do it? Because he can't do it. The white man was created a "Devil," to bring chaos upon this earth...."[40]

"Malcolm X was the prophet of Black rage primarily because of his great love for Black people. His love was neither abstract nor ephemeral. Rather, it was a concrete connection with a degraded and devalued people in need of "Psychic Conversion." This is why Malcolm X's articulation of Black rage was not directed first and foremost at white America. Rather, Malcolm believed that if Black people felt the love that motivated that rage, the love would produce a "Psychic Conversion" in black people; they would affirm themselves as "Human Beings," no longer viewing their "Bodies," "Minds," and "Souls" through white lenses, and believing themselves capable of taking control of their own destinies.

In American society-especially during Malcolm X's life in the 1950's and early 1960's-such a "Psychic Conversion" could easily result in death. A proud, self affirming Black person who truly believed in the capacity of Black people to throw off the yokes of white racist oppression and control their own destiny usually ended up as one of those "Strange Fruits That Southern Trees Bore," about which the great Billie Holliday poignantly sang. So when Malcolm X articulated Black rage, he knew he also had to exemplify in his own life the courage and sacrifice that any truly self-loving Black person needs in order to confront the frightening consequences of being self-loving in American society. In other words, Malcolm X sharply crystallized the relation of Black affirmation of self, Black desire for freedom, Black rage against the American society, and the likelihood of early Black death.

Malcolm X's notion of "Psychic Conversion" holds that Black people must no longer view themselves through white lenses. He claims Black people will never value themselves as long as they subscribe to a standard of evaluation that devalues them."[41]

"Malcolm X was the first real Black spokesperson who looked ferocious white racism in the eye didn't blink, and lived long enough to tell America the truth about this glaring "Hypocrisy" in a bold and defiant manner. Unlike Elijah Muhammad and Martin Luther King, Jr., he did not live long enough to forge his own distinctive ideas and ways of channeling Black rage in constructive channels to change American society. Only if we are as willing as Malcolm X to grow and confront the new challenges posed by the Black rage of our day will we take the Black freedom struggle to a new and higher level. The future of this country may well depend on it."[42]

47   **Malcolm X** in Cairo, Egypt in 1964 meeting with Muslim scholars and clergy before speaking to the Organization of African Unity on the parallels of the African American struggle, and the struggle of emerging African nations.

With Black churches being burned to the ground, voter registration volunteers beaten and arrested, the need for social justice was needed more than ever before. Early in 1965, Martin Luther King, Jr. started a series of demonstrations in Selma and Montgomery, Alabama, to show the need for a new law because the old Civil Rights laws were not working. Caucasians had always been at the root of all of the violence that had occurred throughout Blacks' plight for Civil Rights. It was more visible to Blacks that they were up against a people who were not willing to accept him as a man, not to mention an opportunity to be considered equal; even in a country in which his labor had laid the foundation for. As the marchers got underway, members of Dr. King's group met a determined opposition.

"One day, King and his followers tried to march from Selma to Montgomery, Alabama, the site of the state capital. State police and members of the sheriffs department broke up the march with tear gas and clubs. Three more people were killed, eighty-seven of the marchers were injured." President Johnson sent federal troops into the state to protect the marchers from more brutality. President Johnson then began work on a new and stricter proposal than the 1964 Civil Rights Act that would insure that all blacks would have the right to vote. President Lyndon B. Johnson also advocated that the Black man's cause must be one of all Americans."[43]

"Although fighting was occurring in the Southern states more frequently, the worst violence occurred outside of the south in the Watts section of Los Angeles, California, in 1965. It was reported that in six days and nights of fighting, thirty-five persons, mostly blacks, were killed, two thousand were injured, and a dozen more stores were burned down. Worst riots hit Detroit, Michigan, in 1967, where whole blocks went up in flames. Again, Blacks suffered most from the violence. One Black youth is quoted as saying, "I don't care about dying, because right now I'm barely living."[44]

At this critical juncture, Dr. King felt that all he had taught was being put to test. He would come to believe that the only way for the movement to gain support was to organize another non-violent march on Washington. This would be a summer long camp-out campaign, not only for Blacks, but also for all the poor. Blacks, Whites, Indians, Puerto-Ricans, and Latino-Americans, all would be urged to join in the protest.

During the worst of the fighting and rioting, President Lyndon B. Johnson named a commission of White and Black leaders to study the violence and to recommend ways to bring the fighting to an end. It was not until the Spring of 1968 that the commission would report on its' findings.

The commission said, "Our nation is moving toward two societies, one Black and one White, "Separate but Unequal." The report called for an end to the rioting, and it found that much of the fighting was due to "White Racism." It is time now to turn with all the purpose at our command to the major "unfinished business" of the nation. It is time to make good the "Promise" of American Democracy to all citizens."[45]

As long as the regular Army and draftees assumed most of the burden of fighting in Vietnam, white America remained mostly detached. The sons of the upper and middle class easily attained school deferments from the draft to attend college and stay on for post graduate study until reaching age twenty-six, then no longer eligible for the draft. The sons of the influential secured slots in local reserve and national guard units, where they endured a few hours of monthly drill at a local armory instead of daily fighting in the rice paddies and jungles of Vietnam. Some who could not remain in school or gain a coveted slot in the local national guard unit found doctors anxious to meet the perceived needs of their communities, to write histories for "football Knees", asthma", or other disabilities that qualified them for medical deferment."[46]

"Blacks also were aware that they were suffering more than their fare share of death and carnage in Southeast Asia. During the first years of U.S. combat units' involved in Vietnam, African-Americans, 13.5 percent of the military-age population, made up 10.6 percent of the total force in the war zone. Blacks in general, however, initially served in disproportionate numbers in infantry units that sustained the vast majority of casualties. As a result, in 1965-67, 20 percent of U.S. battlefield casualties in Vietnam were African-Americans."[47]

"On April 24, 1967, General William C. Westmoreland, commander of U.S. Forces in Vietnam, addressed the legislation in his native state of South Carolina, which he noted later in his auto-biography. "I saw not a Black face except those of the janitors standing in the rear...." Nevertheless, Westmoreland told the gathering that the Black Soldiers was serving in Vietnam "With distinction equal to his whitecomrade in arms."[48]

"During the last full year of the draft in 1972, African-Americans made up 12.6 percent of the armed forces' enlisted ranks-17% of the Army, 12.6 % of the Air Force, 6.4% of the Navy, and 13.7 % of the Marine Corps. These numbers experienced a steady upward growth in the all-volunteer force, with African-Americans reaching 22.1% of the enlisted total force in 1981 to 33.2 % of the Army, 16.5% of the Air Force, 12.0 percent of the Navy, and 22 % of the Marine Corps.

The number of African-American officers also increased after the first decade of the all-volunteer force, but not at the same accelerated rate as the enlisted percentage. In 1972, 2.3 % of the armed forces' officers were African-American; 3.9 % of the Army, 1.7% of the Air Force, 0.9% of the Navy and 1.5 % of the Marine Corps. By 1981 the number of African-American officers had increased to 5.3% of the armed forces' total: 7.8% Army, 4.8% Air Force, 2.7% Navy, and 4.0% Marine Corps.

Many whites were extremely happy with an all-volunteer concept of the military and cared little about who filled the ranks as long as it was not them or their sons."[49]

Personally, I don't view myself as a true patriot as to why I served in the military. To be honest, I was looking to better myself in life with some skills when I enlisted and to get a better chance at having an opportunity to own my own business. Historically, I know, too, that we African-Americans viewed the opportunity to serve in the military as our commitment to becoming a part of the American society as well or as our loyalty to America. However, it's hard to totally commits to a society that still "Lynches" me, and still "Hates" me, and still treats me like a second class citizens or three-fifths of a man. African-Americans have lived virtually in "A State Of Emergency" psychologically in America, from fear of being either "Strung up", "Burned UP" or either "Eaten up," by the oppressor, literally for more than Three Hundred Years. Moreover, the oppressor, in an attempt to further demean and yet de-humanize African-Americans, give names to their "DOGS" and their other animal pets that they keep locked up in their zoos, the traditional slave names that they once labeled upon African-Americans in order to make themselves feel superior to at least something that they can own. I guess that's just the way "SATAN" works.

Poverty is nothing new to most African-Americans. It seems that economic strife, poverty, and oppression met my ancestors here in America as soon as the slave ships were unloaded and essentially never went away.

It is extremely difficult to pull oneself up out of poverty when you're constantly under the lash of racism and discrimination which has been the case here in America for its' citizens of African ancestry. I don't believe that whites could have endured what my people have had to endure here in this society.

In his final address to the Southern Christian Leadership Conference in 1967, Martin Luther King, Jr., gave what is considered to be his most "Radical" speech. In it he made note of the tragic legacy that we as African-Americans have faced and just where we stood in relation to this society at that time. In a speech entitled: "Where Do We Go From Here?" He said, "Now in order to answer that question "Where Do We Go From Here?" Which is our theme, we must first honestly recognize where we are now.

When the Constitution was written, a "Strange" formula to determine taxes and representation, declared that the (Negro) was sixty percent of a person. Today, another curious formula seems to declare that the (Negro) is fifty percent of a person. Of the good things in life, the (Negro) has approximately one half those of whites. Of the bad things of life he has twice those of whites. Thus, half all (Negroes) live in sub-standard housing. And (Negroes) have half the incomes of whites. When we view the negative experiences of life, the (Negro) has a double share. There are twice as many (Negroes) unemployed in comparison to whites The rate of infant mortality among (Negroes) is double that of whites, and there are twice as many (Negroes) dying in Vietnam as whites in proportion to their size in the population. In other spheres, the figures are equally as alarming.

37

The
charred
remains
of a
house
of
worship.

In elementary schools, (Negroes) lag one to three years behind whites, and their segregated schools receive substantially less money per student than the white schools. One twentieth as many (Negroes) as whites attends college. Of all employed (Negroes) seventy five percent hold menial jobs. This is where we are!

Where do we go from here? First, we must massively assert our dignity and worth. We must stand up amidst a system that still oppresses us and develop an unassailable and majestic sense of values. "We must no longer be ashamed of being Black." The job of arousing manhood within a people that have been taught for so many centuries that they are nobody is not easy.

Even semantics have conspired to make that which is Black seem ugly and degrading. In Roget's Thesaurus there are 120 synonymy for blackness and at least sixty of them are offensive, as for example; blot, soot, grim, devil and foul. And there are some 134 synonyms for whiteness and all are favorable, expressed in such words as purity, cleanliness, chastity and innocence. A white lie is better than a Black lie. The most degenerate member of a family is a "Black sheep."

Ossie Davis has suggested that maybe the English language should be reconstructed so that teachers will not be forced to teach the (Negro) child sixty ways to despise himself. And thereby perpetuate his false sense of inferiority, and the white child 134 ways to adore himself, and thereby perpetuate his false sense of superiority.

The tendency to ignore the (Negro's) contribution to American life and to strip him of his personhood is as old as the earliest history books and as contemporary as the morning newspaper. To upset this "Cultural Homicide," the (Negro) must rise up with an Affirmation of his own Olympian manhood. Any movement for the (Negro's) freedom that overlooks this necessity is only waiting to be buried. As long as the mind is enslaved, the body can never be free. Psychological Freedom, "a firm sense of Self-Esteem," is the most powerful weapon against the long night of physical slavery. No Lincoln Emancipation Proclamation or Johnson Civil Rights Bill can totally bring this kind of freedom. The (Negro) will only be free when he reaches down to the inner depths of his own being and signs with pen and ink of assertive manhood his own Emancipation Proclamation.

And, with a spirit straining toward true self-esteem, the (Negro) must boldly throw off the manacles of self-abeg-nation and say to himself and to the world," I Am somebody." I am a person. I am a man with dignity and honor. I have a rich and noble history. How painful and exploited that history has been. Yes, I was a slave through my foreparents and I am not ashamed of that. I'm more ashamed of the people who were so "Sinful" to make me a slave." Yes, we must stand up and say, I'm Black and I'm Beautiful," and this self affirmation is the Black man's need, made compelling by the white man's "Crimes" against him.

39

40

Confined to an Alabama jail cell
for eight days in April 1963,
King composed one of his most
passionate arguments for nonviolent resistance, "Letter from Birmingham Jail." "Any law that
degrades human personality is unjust," he wrote in the essay. "All
segregation statutes are unjust because segregation distorts the soul
and damages the personality."

King speaks at a Mississippi voter registration drive in June 1966. At left is Stokely Carmichael, who replaced John Lewis as chairman of the Student Nonviolent Coordinating Committee (SNCC) and lobbied for blacks to take a more militant approach to gaining their rights.

50

51

King is stoned by white homeowners in a Chicago suburb during an August 1966 protest march for desegregated housing. He said afterward that he had "never seen anything so hostile and so hateful as I've seen here today."

From the old plantations of the South to the newer ghettos of the North, the Negro has been confined to a life of "Voicelessness and Powerlessness." Stripped of the right to make decisions concerning his life and destiny he has been subjected to the authoritarian and sometimes-whimsical decisions of this white power structure. The plantations and ghettos were created by those who had power, but to confine those who had no power and to perpetuate their powerlessness. Their problem of transforming the ghetto, therefore, is a problem of power confrontation of the voices of power demanding change and the forces of power dedicated to the preserving of the status quo. Now power properly understood is nothing but the ability to achieve purpose. It is the strength required to bring about social, political, and economic change. Walter Reuther defined power one day. He said, 'Power is the ability of a labor union, like the UAW, to make the most powerful corporation in the world, like General Motors, say, 'Yes' when it wants to say 'No.' That's power."

Now a lot of us are preachers, and all of us have our moral convictions and concerns, and so often have problems with power. There is nothing wrong with power if power is used correctly. You see, what happened is that some of our philosophers got off base. And one of the great "Problems" of history is that the concept of love and power have usually been contrasted as opposites-polar opposites- so that love is identified with a resignation of power, and power with a denial of love.

It was this misinterpretation that caused Nietzschean, who was a philosopher of the will to power, to reject the Nietzschean philosophy of the will to power in the name of the Christian idea of love. Now, we've got to get this thing right. What is needed is a realization that power without love is reckless and abusive, and love without power is sentimental and anemic. Power at best is love implementing the demands of justice, and justice at its best is power correcting everything that stands against love. And this is what we must see as we move on. What has happened is that we have had it wrong and confused in our own country, and this has led African-Americans in the past to seek their goals through power devoid of love and conscience.

This is leading a few extremists today to advocate for (Negroes) the same destructive and consciousless power that they have justly abhorred in whites. It is precisely this collision of immoral power with powerless morality, which constitutes the major "CRISIS" of our times.

We must develop a program that will drive the nation to a "Guaranteed Annual Income." Now, early in this century this proposal would have been greeted with ridicule and denunciation, as destructive of initiative and responsibility. At that time, economic status was considered the measure of the individual's ability and talents. And, in the thinking of that day, the absence of worldly goods indicated a want of industrious habits and moral fiber. We've come a long way in our understanding of human motivation and of the blind operation of our economic system.

Now we realize that dislocations in the market operations of our economy, and the prevalence of discrimination, thrust people into idleness and bind them in constant or frequent unemployment against their will.

Today the poor are less often dismissed, I hope, from our consciences by being branded as inferior or incompetent. We also know that no matter how dynamically the economy develops and expands, it does not eliminate poverty. The problem indicates that our emphasis must be two-fold. We must create full employment or we must create incomes. People must be made consumers by one method or the other. Once they are placed in this position we need to be concerned that the potential of the individual is not wasted. New forms of work that enhances the social good will have to be devised for those for whom traditional jobs are not available.

In 1879, Henry George anticipated this state of affairs when he wrote in Progress and poverty, The fact is that the work which improves the condition of mankind, the work which extends knowledge and increases power and enriches literature and elevates thought, is not done to secure a living. It is not the work of slaves driven to their tasks either by the taskmaster, or by animal necessity. It is the work of men who somehow find a form of work that brings a security for its own sake and a state of society where want is abolished. Work of this sort could be enormously increased, and we are likely to find that the problems of housing and education, instead of preceding the elimination of poverty, will themselves be affected if poverty is first abolished.

The poor transformed into purchasers will do a great deal on their own to alter housing decay. (Negros) who have a double disability will have a greater effect on discrimination when they have the additional weapon of cash to use in their struggle.

Beyond these advantages, a host of positive psychological changes inevitably will result from widespread economic security. This dignity of the individual will flourish when the decisions concerning his life are in his own hands, when he has the means to seek the self-improvement. Personal conflicts among husbands, wives, and children will diminish when the unjust measurement of human worth on the scale of dollars is eliminated.

Now our country can do this. John Galbraith said that a "Guaranteed Annual income" could be done for about twenty billion dollars a year. And I say to you today, that if our nation can spend thirty-five billion dollars per year to fight an unjust, evil war in Vietnam, and twenty billion dollars to put a man on the moon, it ought to be able to spend a billion dollars to put God's children on their own two feet right here on earth.

Now, let me say briefly that we must reaffirm our commitment to nonviolence. I want to stress this. The futility of violence in the struggle for racial justice has been tragically etched in all of the recent (Negro) riots. Yesterday, I tried to analyze the riots and deal with their causes. Today I want to give the other side.

There is certainly something painfully sad about a riot. One sees screaming youngsters and angry adults fighting hopelessly and aimlessly against impossible odds. And deep down within them you can see a desire for self-destruction, a kind of "suicidal" longing.

Occasionally (African-Americans) contend that the 1965 Watts riots and the other riots in various cities represented effective Civil Rights action. But those who express this view always end up with the stumbling words when asked what concrete gains have been won as a result. At best, the riots have produced little additional anti-poverty money allotted by frightened government officials, and a few water-sprinklers to cool the children of the ghettos. It is something like improving the food in the prison while the people remain securely incarcerated behind bars. Nowhere have the riots won any concrete improvement such as have the organized protests demonstrations. When one tries to pin down advocates of violence as to what acts would be effective, the answers are blatantly illogical. Sometimes they talk of overthrowing racist state and local governments and they talk about guerilla warfare. They fail to see that no internal revolution has ever succeeded in overthrowing a government by violence unless the government had already lost the allegiance and effective control of its' armed forces. Anyone in his right mind knows that this will not happen in the United States. In a violent racial situation, the power structure has The local police, The State Troopers, The National Guard, and finally, the Army to call on- all of which are predominantly white. Furthermore, few if any violent revolutions have been successful unless the violent minority had the sympathy and support of the non-resistant majority.

Castro may have had only a few Cubans actually fighting with him up in the hills, but he could have never overthrown the Batista Regime unless he had the sympathy of the vast majority of the Cuban people.

It is perfectly clear that a violent revolution on the part of the American Blacks would find no sympathy and support from the white population and very little from the majority of the (Negroes) themselves. This is no time for romantic illusion and empty philosophical debate about freedom. This is a time for action.

What is needed is a strategy for change, a tactical program that will bring the (Negro) into the mainstream of American life as quickly as possible. So far, this has only been offered by the non-violent movement. Without recognizing this we will end up with resolutions that don't solve, answers that don't answer, and explanations that don't explain.

And so I say to you today, that I still stand by non-violence. And I am still convinced that it is the most potent weapon available to the (Negro) in his struggle for justice in this country. And the other thing is that I am concerned about a better world. I'm concerned about justice.

I'm concerned about brotherhood. I'm concerned about the truth. And when one is concerned about these, he can never advocate violence. For through violence you may murder a murderer, but you can't murder a murder. Through violence you may murder a liar, but you can't establish the truth. Through violence you may murder a hater, but you can't murder hate. Darkness cannot put out darkness. Only light can do that.

And I say to you, I have also decided to stick to love. For I know that love is ultimately the only answer to mankind's problems. And I'm going to talk it everywhere I go. I know it isn't popular to talk about it in some circles today. I'm not talking about "Emotional Bosh" when I talk about love. I'm talking about a strong, demanding love. And I've seen too much hate. I've seen too much hate on the faces of sheriffs in the South. I've seen hate on the faces of too many Klansmen and too many white citizens Councilmen in the South to want to hate myself, because everytime I see it, I know that it does something to their faces and their personalities and I say to myself that "Hate is too great a burden to bare." I have decided to love. If you are seeking the higher good, I think you can find it through love. And the beautiful thing is that we are moving against wrong when we do it, because John was right, God is love. He who hates does not know God, but he who has love has the key that unlocks the door to the meaning of ultimate reality.

I want to say to you as I move toward my conclusion, as we talk about "Where do we go from here," that we honestly face the fact that the movement must address itself to the question of "Restructuring The Whole of American Society." There are forty-million poor people here. And one day we must ask the question, "Why are there forty-million poor people in America?" And when you begin to ask that question, you are raising questions about the economic system, about a broader "Distribution of Wealth."

When you ask questions, you begin to question the capitalistic economy. And I'm simply saying that more and more, we've got to begin to ask questions about the whole society. We are called upon to help the discouraged beggars in life's marketplace. But one day we must come to see that an edifice which produces beggars needs restructuring.

It means that questions must be raised. You see, my friends, when you deal with this, you begin to ask the question, "Who Own's The Oil?" You begin to ask the question, "Who owns the iron ore?" You begin to ask the question, "Why is it that people have to pay water bills in a world that is two-thirds water?" These questions must be asked. Now don't think that you have me in a "bind" today. I'm not talking about communism. What I'm saying to you this morning is that communism forgets that life is individual. Capitalism forgets that life is social, and the kingdom of brotherhood is found neither in the thesis of communism nor the antithesis of capitalism but in a higher synthesis. It is found in a higher synthesis that combines the truths of both. Now, when I 'say question the whole society, it means ultimately coming to see that "The problem of "Racism," The Problem Of "Economic Exploitation," and "The Problem Of War," are all tied together. These are the triple evils that are interrelated.

lf you let me be a preacher just a little bit. One night a juror came to Jesus and he wanted to be saved. Jesus didn't get bogged down in the kind of isolated approach of what he shouldn't do to be saved. Jesus didn't say, "Now Nicodemus, you must stop lying." He didn't say, "Nicodemus you must stop cheating if you are doing that." He didn't say, Nicodemus, you must not commit adultery." He didn't say, "Nicodemus, now you must stop drinking liquor if you are doing that excessively."

He said something altogether different, because Jesus realized something basic-that if a man will lie, he will steal. And if a man will steal, he will kill. So instead of just getting bogged down in one thing, Jesus looked at him and said, "Nicodemus , you must be born again."

He said , in other words, "Your whole structure must be changed." A nation that will keep a people in slavery for "244 years" will "Thingify" them, make them things. Therefore, they will exploit them, and poor people generally, "Economically." And a nation that will exploit economically will have to have foreign investments and everything else, and will have to use its military might to protect them. All of these problems are tied together. What I am saying today is that we must go from this convention and say, "America, You must be born again!"

So, I conclude by saying again today that we have a difficult task and let's go out with a "divine dissatisfaction." Let us be dissatisfied until America will no longer have a high blood of creeds and an anemia of deeds. Let us be dissatisfied until the tragic walls that separate the outer city of wealth and comfort and the inner city of poverty and despair shall be crushed by the battering rams of the forces of justice. Let us be dissatisfied until those that live on the outskirts of hope are brought into the metropolis of daily security. Let us be dissatisfied until slums are cast into the junk heaps of history, and every family is living in a decent and sanitary home.

Let us be dissatisfied until the dark yesterdays of segregated schools be transformed into bright tomorrows of quality, integrated education. Let us be dissatisfied until integration is not seen as a "Problem" but as an opportunity to participate in the beauty of diversity.

Let us be dissatisfied until men and women, "However Black they maybe," will be judged on the basis of the content of their character and not on the basis of the color of their skin. Let us be dissatisfied. Let us be dissatisfied, until every state capitol houses a governor who will do justly, who will love mercy, and who will walk humbly with his God.

Let us be dissatisfied until from every city hall, justice will roll down like waters from a mighty stream. Let us be dissatisfied until that day when the lion and the lamb will lie down together, and every man will sit under his own vine and fig tree and none shall be afraid.

Let us be dissatisfied. And men will recognize that out of one blood God made all men to dwell upon the face of the earth. Let us be dissatisfied until that day when nobody will shout "WHITEPOWER!" - when nobody will shout "BLACK POWER!" - But everybody will talk about "GOD'S POWER!" and " HUMAN POWER!"

I must confess, my friends, that the road ahead will not always be smooth. There will still be rocky places of frustration and meandering points of bewilderment. There will be inevitable setbacks here and there. There will be those moments when the buoyancy of hope will be transformed into the fatigue of despair. Our dreams will sometimes be shattered and our ethical hopes blasted.

"We may again with tear-drenched eyes have to stand before the bier of some courageous Civil Rights worker whose life will be snuffed out by the dastardly acts of bloodthirsty mobs." Difficult and painful as it is, we must walk on in the days ahead with an audacious faith in the future. And as we continue our chartered course, we may gain consolation in the words so nobly left by that black bard who was a great freedom fighter of yesterday, James Weldon Johnson: "Stony the road we trod, Bitter the chastening rod, Felt in the days when hope unborn had died.

Yet with a steady beat, Have not our weary feet, come to the place for which our fathers sighed? We have come over the way, That with tears hath been watered, we have come treading our path, through the blood of the slaughtered. Out from the gloomy past, til now we stand at last, where the bright gleam of our bright star is cast."

Let this affirmation be our ringing cry. It will give us the courage to face the uncertainties of the future. It will give our tired feet new strength as we continue our forward stride toward the city of freedom. When our days become dreary with low-hovering clouds of despair, and when our nights become darker than a thousand midnights, let us remember that there is a creative force in the universe, working to pull down the gigantic mountain of evil, a power that is able to make a way out of no way and transform dark yesterdays into bright tomorrows.

Let us realize the arc of the moral universe is long but it bends toward justice. Let us realize that William Cullen Bryant is right: That truth crushed to earth will rise again."

Let us go out realizing that "The Bible Is Right:" "Be not deceived, God is not mocked. Whatsoever a man soweth, that shall he also reap." This is for hope for the future, and with this faith we will be able to sing in some not too distant tomorrow with a cosmic past tense, we have overcome, We have overcome, deep in my heart, I did believe, We Would Overcome."[50]

I can not give the appropriate appraisal to the men and women, both black and white, who gave their lives in yet another of America's Revolutions. Their numbers are countless and their contributions enormous and they will live on in the minds of the people who are the survivors of those hard fought battles, and who are the products of that era. The role of Dr. Martin Luther King, Jr. goes above all in the avocation of "A Peaceful Means" to achieve Civil Rights for all Americans.

It was in Memphis, Tennessee, after answering the call of sanitation workers that he delivered a sermon that will long be remembered in the minds of men, perhaps until eternity. Recalling that his life had been threatened, he said "It didn't really matter anymore because I have been to the mountain top, and I've looked over and I've seen the promised land. I may not get there with you, but mine eyes have seen the glory of the coming of the lord." The next day, Dr. King was shot to death in Memphis as he stood on the balcony of the Lorraine Motel. Dr. Kings philosophy was to campaign non-violently for social change in America.

 For decades after his death and even until today there have been allegations of a vast government conspiracy, James Earl Ray, including the U. S. Army, for the death of Dr. Martin Luther King, Jr."51

"As for Malcolm X, King met him once in Washington, D.C., and thought of him to be "Very Articulate," and with a great concern for the "Problems" Negroes faced as a race. But as he told Playboy Magazine later, he wished that Malcolm would talk less about violence, "because violence is not going to solve our problem. And in his litany of articulating the despair of the Negro without offering any positive, creative alternative, I feel that Malcolm has done himself and our people a great disservice. Fiery, demagogic oratory in the Black ghettos, urging Negroes to arm themselves and prepare to engage in violence, as he has done, can reap nothing but grief."52

While living in Atlanta, Ga., in 1994, I had the opportunity to visit the Martin Luther King, Jr. Memorial on King Memorial Drive. I can honestly say that it was the greatest experience in my life. Although I have traveled quite extensively while serving in the U. S. Navy and visiting over 30 foreign countries, that visit was unparalleled. I felt a great sadness to come over me as I recall. I also felt that we had indeed suffered a great loss. And to be sure, I am resentful, still. He was indeed our "Ghandi" and our "Crusader without violence." He was also an idealist in this realistic world of hatred, racism, and injustice.

But in one period of time, he led the greatest revolt on oppression in the known history of man. To me he was a "Great Man" who stood for something, his people. I've heard him say that "If a man does not have something that he is willing to die for, than he does not have a reason to live." He died standing up for his people, me.

*On February 6, 1968, **King** and other clergymen joined forces with 2,500 supporters at the Tomb of the Unknown Soldier in Arlington National Cemetery for a demonstration against the Vietnam War. King said on his decision to take a public stand on the war, " I could no longer remain silent about an issue that was destroying the soul of our nation."*

54

55

56

*On March 28, 1968, **King** joined forces with co- worker Ralph Jackson (second from left), the Reverned Ralph Abernathy (right), and hundreds of others in Memphis for a demonstration in support of striking laborers.*

"The era of the sixties was a watershed period in American history because for the first time we decided as a people to overcome the racial divide and declare war on poverty. Within two years, legal barriers against Black access to civil and voting rights were erased. Within eight years, half of America's poor people were lifted out of poverty. And within a decade, the number of poor old people was more than cut in half.

Contrary to the popular myths about the sixties, this was a brief moment in which we confronted our most explosive issues as a people: racial hierarchy, and the mal distribution of wealth and power. But it did not last long. As the economy slumped, black rage escalated and white backlash set in. And, for nearly two decades, we witnessed a decline in the real wages of most Americans, a new racial divide in the minds and streets of fellow citizens, an massive transfer of wealth from working people to the well-to-do, and an increase in drugs and guns (along with fear and violence) of American life. Many conservative Republicans played the old racial card to remain in office and most liberal democrats lacked the courage to tell the truth about the new levels of decline and decay engulfing us.

Instead, we as a people tolerated levels of suffering and misery among the disadvantaged (especially among poor children of all colors, caught in a vicious natural lottery!), lost faith in our money-driven political system, and lived lives of hedonistic evasion and narcissistic avoidance as the racial divide expanded and the gaps between rich, poor, and working people increased.

49

Martin Luther King, Jr. and Malcolm X, two diametrically opposed
wings of the Black activist movement who waged an often bitter
contest for the loyalties of the African American community.
Malcolm X sharply criticized King's nonviolent protest tactics and
his support of integration.

58

April 4, 1968, 6:00 P.M.: A mortally wounded King lies on the balcony of the Lorrraine Motel in Memphis, Tennessee, while his colleagues point to the rooming house from which James Earl Ray fired the fatal shot.

We now find ourselves hungry for quick solutions and thirsty for overnight cures for deep economic, cultural, and political problems that were allowed to fester for decades. And, most sadly, we seem to lack the patience, courage, and hope necessary to reconstruct our public life-the very lifeblood of any democracy."53

Having been born in the South, in Chester, South Carolina, on November 17, 1955, 1 know racism all too well. Located in the rural South, Chester was one of those southern towns that epitomized all the wrongdoings that had been inflicted upon Blacks by Caucasians. My parents, grandparents, great grandparents, and great-great grandparents were all sharecroppers and tenant farmers; evolving right out of the evil system of slavery. My folks had lived on Oliphants quarters for many generations, where I was born. I've learned that it was referred to as "Oliphants quarters" because this was where the slaves was housed. My fathers' name is John and my mothers' name is Margaret.

59

60

Coretta Scott King comforts her youngest daughter, Bernice, during funeral services for the slain civil rights leader at the Ebenezer Baptist Church in Atlanta.

61

Thousand of mourners follow the farm wagon that carried King's coffin through the streets of his hometown, Atlanta, on April 9, 1968. The wagon and mules were symbols of the Poor People's Campaign, the civil rights leader's attempt to call attention to the plight of the nation's poor.

62

The Rev. Dr Martin Luther King, Jr.: Civil Rights Leader, Philosopher and Social Pioneer.

They had seven children to survive and currently there are six of us still living. There would have been eight of us but one other of my brothers died shortly after birth in 1953, he had already been named Nathaniel. I was the sixth born out of the birth of eight. Born in rural South Carolina in the mid nineteen fifties, I feel that it's a miracle that I survived given the poverty, racism, and other social and economic conditions in which we were confronted with.

I am the sixth generation of the people from the Bantu Group from the Cameroon, Western Africa in my family to be born in America. I guess you could say that we were poor when I look back on it. But at the time I would say that everything seemed normal. Well to be honest, who can tell what is normal or not at the age of three or four. Looking at it now all I know is that I was here. Now I know why I have such a great love for my Grandmother, it's because she is the first person that I saw when I was first able to be aware of the world around me.

The earliest memory of my life is when I was playing on the floor with chairs with my younger brother Charles; it must have been around 1958 because he was born in 1957. We had been left in the care of my grandmother, Henryetta, to take care of us while my mother had gone to work in the nearby town of Chester. Chester was about twelve miles from the Oliphants farm. All of my grandmother's sisters and brothers, fathers and mothers, uncles and aunts, cousins, nieces, nephews, friends, and extended families, had labored from as far back as the 1850's for these people, the Oliphants, and some other white people whom they had bought the farm from. My grandmother's grandmother Ellen and great aunt Mary had been born slaves in South Carolina in the 1850's. They died in the 1950's at the age 101 years old and 104 years old respectively. My grandmother's stepmother, Rosa, died in 1974, she was born in the 1880's. She was my great grandfathers second wife who's name was Henry. Henry ironically had a previous wife who's name was Rosa as well. God only knows where we are all scattered. We are the result of the "Inhumanity" brought on by the great cotton curtains evil. Perhaps due to the lack of adequate records kept by plantation owners and my family too, it has been impossible to trace the origin of my family back to the date when we first laid our feet on this American soil.

The courthouse in Chester doesn't have accurate records nor documentation past the births of my great-great Aunt Mary or my great great-grandmother Ellen. For all I know they could have very well been bought and sold from one of the "Nigger Pens" located in Charleston, S.C., where the slaves were kept after they were unloaded from the slave ships and waiting for a buyer. Moreover, the breeding process that took place on the plantations did not allow or warrant adequate records to be kept for another potential field hand.

63

HENRYETTA STRADFORD-BOYD, 1909-2005

My father's families' birth records are even more obscure; we get lost trying to find evidence of their births even one generation back. Another point to be made is that often times new members to the families would be delivered by "Mid-Wives", other slave women who delivered babies, and they would not keep records. At any rate, the search is still incomplete.

The only source of knowing where exactly we came from comes through our family's oral history as told by my grandmother Henryetta and her side of the family. As my grandmother Henrietta who was born in 1909, in Chester, South Carolina, re-collects , her grandfather Gayton Stradford had said that his grandfather, Joseph Singletons, who she referred to as (Papa Sang), had said that he had came from across the Ocean on a slave ship from Cameroon, West Africa. I am the sixth generation in my family to be born in America.

In the late 1950's my grandmother, Henryetta, would still go to cotton fields to help her brother, Eleazar, to pick the cotton on the stretch of land in which he had been allocated to sharecrop by the Oliphant's. Actually it was all the work that they had ever known. She, Henryetta, wouldn't leave us at the house alone, so sometimes she would leave us at grand ma Rosa's house while she went to the fields to pick cotton. On not so hot days she would carry us to the fields with her. My great grand ma Rosa had labored in those cotton fields all of her life, and now being too old to work anymore would watch over us for my grandmother Henryetta. I was about five or six years old when I got my first exposure to picking cotton. My older brothers and sisters had more exposure to working the fields than I did. My brothers and sisters names in the order of their births are: James, Rosetta, Isaiah, Helen, Nathaniel, Willie (me), Charles, and Omar. All except Omar was born in the rural area in the county of Chester, or "in the country" as we described the rural areas in those days where the sharecropping houses were located.

The house we lived in was a two-room wooden one with no paint on the wood. These two rooms included the kitchen. Whenever it would rain there would be a lot of noise caused by the rain splashing against our tin-top roofed house. Mr. Oliphant was not concerned about how our house looked; I believe he was more concerned about how many bails of his cotton we could pick each year. We had a toilet located about 50 yards in the back of the house that really smelled bad. Momma never let us go back there by ourselves. Across the way were acres and acres of cotton in rows for as far as the eye could see. I knew that there was a railroad track up there somewhere because I could sometimes hear a train. I later came to know that there was a train track there; and it would always come at twelve o'clock noon to let us know that it was time to eat our mid-day meals when we were in the fields.

My mother and father, Margaret and John Robert, went into Chester to work because they would make more money there than picking cotton for the elephants. My father got a job at an elementary school called College Street Elementary School in Chester. I've come to know that this was one of perhaps many jobs that he held. He also mentioned driving a lumber truck for a lumber company at one point or another. Whether he was a janitor at an elementary school or a truck driver for a lumber company, either one was better for him than picking cotton on Oliphants farm.

Moreover, we always had enough food to eat as far as I can recall. I honestly believe that the reason that he is still alive today is the fact that he got us, and himself away from those cotton fields and that sharecropping regime employed in the South for decades and centuries.

As I look back I see that every one of my uncles that stayed on and worked for the Oliphants in those quarters have long been dead and gone. I believe that since John Robert refused to work for the Oliphants and put the various poisons and other pesticides down on the crops in order to fight off the insects, such as the Boll weevil, that he is still alive today. The poisons and other pesticides that they used in those measures were very strong and I believe that as a result of many, many years of exposure to it eventually killed them off as well as the insects that they were trying to kill off.

My mother, Margaret, got a job with a laundry and dry cleaners in Chester on Saluda Street. I can recall hearing her say that she made some where between twelve to fifteen dollars a week when she first began in the early fifties. I realize now that they were only looking for a better way of life for us. Black people in those days were usually limited to the cotton fields. I believe that's why we had to move away from Oliphants Quarters due to the fact that John Robert and Margaret wouldn't pick Oliphants cotton. Therefore, the Oliphants asked all of us to move on because he wanted to sell the house that we lived in because it wasn't doing him any good just having it sit there and we wasn't working for him in his cotton fields. We all moved about five miles up the way to a house owned by another white man named Mr. Lawson, including my grandmother Henrietta. It was a little closer to Chester. However, we still went back down to the Oliphants to help our uncle Eleazar, uncle Marion, and uncle Quit to pick cotton for the Oliphants, along with my grand mother, Henryetta, who were their sister. Margaret was my grandmother Henryetta's only child, and Margaret wasn't about to leave her mother down on Oliphants quarters to pick cotton for the Oliphants day in and day out. I can remember that those were some pretty hot days in the fields around two O'clock in the afternoon. Momma, Henrietta, would always keep some cool ice water for us to drink while we worked with her in the fields.

In those cotton fields, the air was very thick and hot. The heat from the South Carolina sun and humidity made it normal to work in a constant state of exhaustion. We worked from dew until almost dust dark. The bottom of my feet seemed to sometimes have edges on them, and often there were no feeling at all in my toes. Momma always said that she felt "Light-Headed" from having to bend over for so long and so much in order to pick the cotton.

At the end of the day, after we had weighted the days pickings up, we would walk back to the cotton house where all of the cotton was stored. As we would walk, sometimes I would take my shoes off because my shoes would feel so heavy on my feet that they made that dirt road walk from the cotton fields seem to last for hours. I would walk on the side of the road in the grass in my bare feet because it was cooler there.

The middle of the dirt road was too hot from the heat of the all day sun shining down on it. I would try to avoid stepping on rocks because they were the hottest and they would burn the bottom of my feet if I did. More importantly, I had to watch out for snakes along the side of the road in the grass, because if you would get bit by one you could die before the ambulance could get to you or you could get to the hospital. I can never forget the words of my grandmother telling me too watch for snakes as we would pick cotton in the hot sun.

She said that all she intended too do was to take the best of care of us and that she didn't want any thing too happen to us that was bad for us. At any rate, this was the most important warning that she could have given to us at that time.

If one of us had been bitten by one of these snakes, we would have died before we could have gotten to the hospital, due to the fact that it was so hot and the hospital was so far away. The nearest medical facility at that time was in Chester at twelve miles away.

For me, this is only a part of the curse that God put on the children of the Israelites for the disobedience of their fore parents. For it is prophesized in the Holy Bible in the Twenty-eighth chapter and Fifteenth Verse of Deuteronomy which states: "But it shall come to pass, if thou wilt not harken unto the voice of the Lord thy God, to observe and do all his laws, statutes, and commandments which I command thee this day, that all these curse shall come upon thee and overtake thee." Moses goes on to tell the Israelites in Verse Sixty-eight: "And the Lord shall bring thee into Egypt again with ships, by the way whereof I spake unto thee, thou shalt see it no more again; and there Ye shall be sold unto your enemies for bond men and bond women, and no man shall buy you." Apparently, this is the misery and torture that my family had to endure for generations and generations. I would often wonder why it is that the white man in the long white station wagon (Oliphant), would drive up to where we were picking cotton and tell my uncle where he wanted us to pick the cotton at; and get in his car and drive away and not help us to work in the fields. Later my father would explain to me that Oliphant was only the "DEVIL," which means- an evil demon or a mischievous person, a daring and clever person, and a wicked or malevant person, and a foe of God. At the end of the harvest time I would hear my uncle tell my grandmother that " Well, Mr. Oliphant said that we didn't clear very much money this year but maybe next year things will be better." However the nickles and dimes that we did clear went towards shoes, shirts, and overalls that we wore to school for the years that we worked in Oliphants fields.

The house at Lawson's was a little larger, maybe it had three rooms compared to the two rooms that we had at Oliphants Quarters. More importantly, I don't recall seeing any snakes crawling up beside the house as I had seen at the house down beside the road at Oliphant Quarters. We didn't stay at Lawson's very long because he wanted us to move on because he wanted to have the house torn down, what left of it, in order for him to build a new one for himself to live in. I think we must have stayed there for two or three years, maybe.

We moved on again and into the inner city of Chester after we left Lawson's house. I believe that Chester must have had a total population of about 25,000 or so in 1960. Although it was only a small textile mill town it was better than living on Oliphants Quarters. I think we all agreed to that over the years. It also had a very bad reputation for having a large population of (KKK) Ku Klux Klan. In fact John Robert told me that over the years he had lost a lot of friends to lynching, beatings, and dragging with trucks, cars or what have you, at the hands of the Klan.

Moreover, he said that when they use to come into town that whenever they would meet a white person on the side walk, that they would have to get off of the side walk and let the white people pass and then get back up on the side walk when they had passed. Also, if the person was a white woman they had to take off their hats or else they would be subject to being beaten by a mob of whites for being an "Uppity Nigger" who had forgotten his place. I also remember that when we would come into town that all of the (Colored People) would all park their cars in the same place, on the outside of town along Number 9 Highway from where we had come into the town. The bus station had a hole cut in the back window from which food was passed to the (Negro) customers because we weren't allowed to come inside and order and sit down and eat it.

We moved to an area called Railroad Avenue (and yes, it was across the tracks), we had to cross over some railroad tracks and down a dirt road to get to the house. But at least John Robert and Margaret would be closer to their work. The year was 1959 or 1960 because I started school shortly after we moved there in 1960. Although Mr. Thurgood Marshall had won a land mark Supreme Court decision in Brown vs. The Board of Education at Topeka, Kansas, in 1954, to overturn the Plessy vs. Ferguerson decision of 1896, saying that "Segregation was constitutionals" The integration decision of 1954 didn't seem to have any affect on school segregation in South Carolina or at least in Chester. I entered a totally segregated York Road Elementary School in 1960 to begin my first year of formal schooling. We had gone from having a three-room house at Lawson's to having a two-room house once again at Railroad Avenue. But I guess at the age of six years old who knew the difference between good and bad times; everything seemed so normal at the time. The house on Railroad Avenue was falling down, so John Robert found us somewhere else to stay that wasn't very far from where we already were. The house was on McClure Street still in the inner city of Chester off Saluda street. I was really glad that we moved too because I didn't like York Road School. Perhaps I didn't like it because I wasn't there but half of the school year before we moved to McClure Street.

Uncle Eleazar would still come by and pick us up to go out to the cotton fields along with our grandmother, Henryetta, to help him pick Oliphant's cotton. I guess my first real friend outside of my brother Charles was Tom Wiley. Tom was a little Black boy who I had met while we lived at Railroad Avenue. Tom Wiley's house was as run down as ours was and we played together.

Since we didn't move very far from Railroad Avenue to McClure Street, I would still see Tom Wiley sometimes but we didn't play together as much as we use to. Since we had moved to McClure Street in East Chester this also meant that I would be going to a new school after Christmas. The new school was called South Side Elementary School, I suppose it was called that because it was located on the south side of town. This was in 1961 and Uncle Eleazar would still come by and pick up my grandmother to help him to pick Oliphant's cotton.

In the fall of each year we would go to the field with our grandmother Henryetta, to help pick cotton in order to help buy our school clothes and shoes to wear to school.

I met some more friends on McClure Street; Ernest, Greg, David, and Melvin. Later I would meet Claude, Hiawatha, Timmy, and Terry. My new schoolteacher name was Ms. Rainey, and I liked being in her class a lot. I guess you could say that she had a very good approach and a very positive demeanor with me and the other children also. I had also met some good friends at school; Johnny, Joe, Floyd, Andrew, Johnnie Mae, and Nevada. These friendships lasted throughout elementary school and into high school as well as adulthood.

Southside Elementary was segregated as well but everything seemed normal and all of the other children seemed to be very happy there though it seems when we would be out for recess or at lunchtime while we played all over the school grounds. Sure our school didn't have heat sometimes in the winter, and sometimes in the summer we didn't have cool air, and it would get so hot in the rooms that it was hard to stay awake. But we kids didn't have a choice; we had to go to school. Our books were the one's that had already been used by the white kids at the white schools and they didn't want them anymore so they gave them to the Black schools. Moreover, our school buses were old with no heat and broke down very often along side the roads as we traveled to and from school. Southside Elementary School was a wonderful place for me. I met other children who were the same as me who I felt liked me very much and we had very few bullies. More importantly, my sister Helen was only three grades ahead of me and she looked out for me. My two older brothers, James and Isaiah, must not have liked school very much because for whatever reason they quit school early on before finishing. My two older sisters, Rosetta and Helen, wouldn't let me quit and they would whip me and make me go if I didn't want to go. I remember my older sister Rosetta would take me to the bus stop with a belt and put me on the bus and if I got off of the bus, she would tare me up and put me back on the bus again.

To say that it was hard for blacks to maintain a stable household in the fifties and sixties is a drastic understatement. Just keeping a roof over our head was an added constant threat to maintain.

One night as I was laying in the bed on a Saturday evening I heard John Robert arguing with the owners of the red house at 111 McClure St., over what I don't know.

This, however, subsequently led to us having to move again and at the time when all seemed to be going pretty good with new friends and all. My grandmother Henryetta walked up the street and talked to an old man named Mr. Gist, an older black man, who told her he was going to be leaving South Carolina to go up North and live with his children. Mr. Gist apparently told my grandmother that we could move into his house at 122 Mclure St. temporarily until he could sell the property because shortly thereafter we moved up the street. This was another three room house and although there was about nine of us we all seemed to be getting along fine there for a couple of years.

Over the years, I've come to learn that, in his quest for wealth and power the Caucasian man has demonstrated himself as being the "DEVIL." This is what my ancestors the "SLAVES" said of him and I'm not going to undermine their "Horrific Sufferings" by saying that he's not or that they were wrong about him.

I don't have any bitter feelings towards my father, then or now for our upbringing because now I know how tough it must have been for him being an African-American in predominantly white America, especially with eight other people to look out for. He has stuck by us all the way through, and is in my opinion, a true American hero. He told me about times when they couldn't come into town or be found in town after dark. He said that they had to get off the sidewalk to allow whites to pass by or they would be whipped or attacked and probably beaten to death for disobeying the white man's laws in the 1930's and 1940's. I still get very angry with him when I hear him say yes sir to a white man or yes ma'am to a white woman.

My grandmother would still go to the cotton field to help out uncle Eleazar. Sometimes after school we would ride the school bus down there to help out until nightfall. But my grandmother didn't want us to pick cotton, she wanted us to go to school and get an education so we wouldn't have to work hard all of our lives like she had too. She said, " It's hard on a-body to have to bend over all day long in the hot sun and pick cotton." She didn't want her daughter Margaret to have to do that either. So I know that she didn't want her grand children (us) to have to do it either. My grandmother Henryetta picked cotton for her brother Eleazar on Oliphants Quarters until about 1967 or 1968, until she couldn't do it any more, because her legs were too swollen. She complained about her back and her head was bothering her too badly to continue. She decided to quit picking cotton and stay home and look after us and take care of the house that she had found for us just up the street on McClure St. and still in East Chester.

East Chester was a relatively large community of black people who were bonded together who had similar interests, just trying to live. It was the closest community of black people located in the inner city of Chester to Qliphants Quarters on the number 9 highway in the city limits.

My mother Margaret found another job at another laundry in Charlotte, North Carolina, because the $12 per week job in Chester wasn't paying her enough to support seven of us children.

My father John Robert also found a job in Charlotte as a handy man at a realty company, who rebuilt and cleaned up apartments after people had moved out of them. I think the jobs in Charlotte paid them both more than the twelve dollars and fifty dollars a week that they had been making in Chester. So they drove there every day, sometimes six days a week fifty miles one way and back for the next thirty-eight years. Sometimes they would look very worn out and tired but they kept on going.

I finished up at Southside Elementary School in 1966 and luckily for me my junior high school was on McClure Street just a few houses down the street. Therefore, when I began junior high school, I didn't have to ride a school bus I could walk to school in about ten minutes. In 1967, I began junior high school at Finley Jr. High in east Chester. I was about twelve years old or so at that time. I suppose I was beginning to take a look around me to see what I could see in my community and environment. To be sure, I felt that I was a little different from some of the other kids. I soon began to listen to what they were saying and I figured out that it most definitely had something to do with the color of my skin. I was darker than most them. I was bordering on the color of a blueish black with big red eyes and white teeth, and most of them were mulatto or mixed races.

I've come to know that during slavery, the white slave owners had raped a lot of our women, causing a large population of mulattos through miscegenation creating a hybrid or mixed race of people. In South Carolina, in 1967, it was not yet fashionable, or not yet looked upon as being the popular thing to be if you were very dark-skinned as I was. Apparently society had told the lighter skinned blacks, although still considered to be (Negroes) by the white establishment, that they were better or occupied a higher social status, than (Negroes) who was of pure African blood as I was. Moreover, white society had labeled "everything light to be right, and if you were black, to get back."

I felt a terrible badge of degradation if someone called me black, because society had told me and my peers that "white was right." I tended to stay away from people who were of lighter skinned than I was because I couldn't stand the shame and limitations that went along with my skin color. The lighter skinned boys and girls tended to hang around each other and the darker skinned boys and girls tended to hang around closer to each other as well. Now I can see how the William Lynch Plan was still in effect in my adolescent years, and in some respects has significant influence on some of our people today. More importantly, we fought among ourselves if someone called you black. You fought the person because you had to protect yourself from that grave put down. I fought back because I wanted that person to know that I was just as good as he was.

Although I might not have felt as good about myself as he did inside, because society had told me that I was not as good as the lighter- skinned person. Because of the shame or the lack of wholeness or even the lack of being considered human, the affects of which would make me strike back. Whatever erroneous results produced by the negative connotation, "Black", we were still at any rate, divided on the issue of "The Color Line." It implied that somehow God's creation was imperfect. I have since learned that most American Blacks are mulatto, 70%.

I met some more of the kids after we moved up the street to the Gist house at 122 McClure street in East Chester. Most of the kids that I noticed were close to my age.

I met Eric, Johnathan, John, Fay, Bug Bailey, Rabbit, Roosevelt and Ronald. We all would get together and throw rocks at the white boys that lived in the mill village behind Finley Jr. High School, which was a segregated all black school where I was currently enrolled. To this day, I still don't know what differences there were to cause us, whites and blacks, to be at odds with each other. Too have to resort to such drastic measures, as having to bombard each other with rocks, stones, bricks, and bottles; rather than reach some agreed upon mutual bilateral arrangement, that would prohibit such warlike outbreaks between the two rivals, was unconscionable. It seemed that we just hated each other for no apparent reason.

Hence, this was the first time I had ever come in contact with Caucasian people. I liked Finley Junior High a great deal. Not only because it was right there on my same street but because I had kept the same friends that I had spent six years with at Southside Elementary School. Although I did feel the peer pressure of being sometimes made ashamed of being different, darker completion than most of the other students, I kind of stuck with the darker-skinned kids who were just like me (not mixed). I liked Mr. Moore's Geography class most of all in Jr. High I suppose. He taught World Geography and he also had maps and charts to prove what he was saying. He went over the land and oceans of the entire world; Longitudinal and Latitudinal; Equatorial, Hemispherical, and Continentally, and climatically as well. This seemed to be quite a bit to grasp for the grandson of a sharecropper from Oliphants Quarters. However, some of the students did grasp the material that was put forth and some did not. But at Finley Jr. High in 1967, it was what was going on at night at the baseball park that was what counted the most with us. The East Chester Dodgers was playing the Brooklyn Giants for first place in the Negro Baseball Little League and to be the best in town. Although I had made the team as an outfielder, our coach, Mr. Mobley, had trained me carefully to be his ace pitcher for the Dodgers in the all Negro Little League Baseball in Chester. My opponent and the starting pitcher for the Brooklyn Giants was a guy who I had known from all the way back to the fourth grade at Southside Elementary School, William Henry Jackson (WEECHIE).

Honestly speaking, I thought Weechie was a much better than me because he had a real nasty curve ball and he could control it real well. He wasn't an overpowering pitcher but he could fool our hitters with that breaking curve ball and he often did. Also the Giants had good depth at pitching because besides Weechie there was James Henry Johnson (Beaver) and Bernard Foster (Nard).

Now for us to beat the Giants with all their pitching and great hitting, excellent coaching, and their intimidating and dominating background, we would need to play an excellent game and not get frustrated with each other. We'd have to make very few mistakes if any. I'd have to pitch my best game and keep my balls down low as John Robert told me too, as he was standing behind the fence at home plate.

Our guys would have to hit the ball well too, get on base and score some runs. Moreover, we'd have to have had meditated all day long at school, and pray that we would win the game.

Hence, on this night in east Chester we beat the mighty Brooklyn Giants because we accomplished what we set out to do. All the girls from the East side really loved me too from that point on. And some of them even started calling me Willie Mays because I could not only pitch, I could hit good too, run real fast, and catch also. Actually I must have played every position on the team at one time or another during my five year career. There was a lot of tradition and pride in the east Chester Dodgers because I had seen a lot of great players like Michael Goode, Bonnie Williams, Toot Davis, and Fats Caldwell, all wore Dodger Blue and were from the East side. Although we never won the first place trophy during my career with the team, the reputation of the east Chester Dodgers will never be forgotten. I can remember hitting only five or six homeruns in my career, but the triples, doubles, and singles, and competitive defensive plays gave me a spot on the all star team for three of the five years that I played. Moreover, the once little shy dark skinned boy from Oliphants Quarters had become somebody in the eyes of his peers.

More importantly, some of the young girls respected me too. They said more to me than just go on with your "Black" self. They made me feel like a human being too. All of the people would be real friendly to me after we won a game and were not too hard on me if we lost. After the games sometimes me and some of the other fellows from the Dodgers would stop off on the way home and get some beer at the Leghorn Cafe, The Dew Drop Inn, or the Birdllane Cafe on our East side. Our team controlled everything from the Cemetary Street to Saluda Street, And from Loomis Street to Lancaster Street including Oak Street, Caldwell Street. From McClure Street down Patrick Street to the Mill Village to where the white boys lived. From Carr Street to over across the railroad tracks onto Mobley Street, all of which came under the souvernity of East Chester. The Ku Klux Klan was not allowed in East Chester because they knew that our people in East Chester had plenty guns and would use them. Yes, Negroes in East Chester was real bad in the 1960's. We had to be bad, or they, the Klan, would have rode right in and killed us all.

In the summer months I would sell newspapers on Mondays and Wednesdays since the papers came out on those days. Another friend of mine, Rabbit McClurkin, and me would sell our papers at the mill on Saluda St. and fight for the best spots to get customers as they left the mill from working. On other days in the summers I would look for yards to cut with the lawn mower that we owned in order to make a little money or so to maybe go swimming at the East Chester pool on Cemetary Street.

Those sure were some hot days in the summertime in South Carolina. I can see why so many slaves are said to have died in the fields from heat exhaustion or sun stroke during slavery in South Carolina. I often wonder where "Rabbit" is now. I have heard that he had amassed quite an extensive "rap sheet" with the state and living up north now, at any rate, I hope he's OK!

I think it must have been April of 1968 that one morning I woke up and saw Finley Jr. High School on fire from our front yard. I later learned that the burning of our Jr. high school was a further insult on Black People that co-ensided with the murdering of the Rev. Dr. Martin Luther King, Jr., in Memphis, Tennessee, by the White People of Chester. John Robert said that it was the "DEVIL" in a people that would make someone do something like this.

Since our jr. high school had been burned down, and it was suspected that some of the white people from the mill village, who lived right behind it had did it, we had to go down town to finish the eighth grade with the white kids in 1968. In 1968 the closest that I had come to a white boy was throwing rocks at them that lived on the mill village. Me, Rabbit, Eric, Ronald, Claude, Joe B., David, Bug, Tyrone, and Fay, would all gather and bombard the white boys with rocks and whatever else we could and throw at them. But now I'd have to go to school with them because they had burned our school down. Therefore, I went to Brockman Jr. High School in downtown Chester for one year, 1968. There were so many fights that I can't count them. We just didn't get along. Many of my friends that I had known all the way from Southside Elementary School quit school. I think that it was because some of the white teachers didn't want us there, and they tried to make it real hard for us. More importantly, they did not encourage us to do well and they essentially looked over us and preferred their own white students to succeed rather than us. Looking back on school integration, in my opinion it was like leading the sheep to the wolves.

By having the Black students at the mercy of the white teachers, it was kind of like we were invisible in those classrooms. It was as if we did not even exist in history except as slaves. To be sure, I really can't recall a dam thing that I learned in the time that I spent at Brockman Jr. High except that the white man does hate me and for no particular reason except that I'm different. After I had completed my eighth grade year at Brockman Jr. High, we had a choice whether to continue on in the white school system or go back across town to our own school. I chose to go back across town to Finley Senior High in East Chester.

I chose to go there because my sisters Rosetta and Helen had and was going there. Rosetta had graduated from there in 1966 and Helen was a senior in 1969-70.

Moreover, Finley Sr. High was close to home in East Chester on Caldwell St. and I could walk to school and I wouldn't have to ride a bus. I can remember having some good times at Finley Sr. High during my ninth grade year. A lot of the upper class people there already knew me because they knew James, Isaiah, Rosetta and Helen, my sisters and brothers.

Also, they knew me because I pitched for the East Chester Dodgers and Finley Sr. High was located in East Chester so I felt right at home. However, this was to be a very short homecoming because in 1970 and 1971 forced integration in South Carolina made it a law that we all go to Chester Senior High with the white students.

I began my Tenth Grade school year at Chester Sr. High. Well it was just as everyone had expected. There was lots of fighting between students and teachers, teachers and teachers, parents and teachers, and students and policemen. There were riots at school with the policemen who had dogs, firehouses, and tear gases, etc; and nobody was learning a damn thing. I had tried out for the high school baseball team but was not chosen because they wanted an equal amount of black and white players on the team and if I had been chosen it would have made an unequal number of black and white players and they said they wanted to keep the team at an equal balance. At any rate, this was the lie that the coach had told me anyway. So when the fighting began I was already angry over the fact that I had not been selected for the baseball team.

Therefore, I didn't play any sports in high school except for pickup games against classes in intramural competition at school. I was just content with going to class because many of my friends had quit school anyway. They had quit because of expulsion that resulted from the fighting and riots and since they had closed down Finley High they felt that they would not be treated fairly by the white teachers anyway, so many of the Black kids just lost interest and quit school. I remember one teacher that I had at Chester High whose name was Mr. Massey. Mr. Massey had taught at Finley Sr. High so he knew some of our families, sisters and brothers. Mr. Massey knew Rosetta and Helen because he had taught both of them at Finley Sr. High.

He was a Black man who taught History. Mr. Massey taught me the blind map of the United States, and he taught us the capitals of each state in the union including Hawaii and Alaska. He taught us the United States Constitution and it's preamble. He taught us the Bill of Rights to the Constitution and the importance of the 13th, 14th, and 15th Amendments as they relate to slavery. Somehow he incorporated United States History and Black American History together, although in my opinion they are totally different. He incorporated the two leaving neither the Black Students nor the white students feeling left out.

Although his counterpart Mrs. Hendricks, a white history teacher, had said of us, why don't all those Negro students go back across town to their own school because we don't want them over here? As for Mr. Massey, his intellect was his most positive characteristic. Always very well attired, I could tell he had fought diligently and earned his reputation as a well educated man and well respected throughout the area.

The white teachers, in my opinion, tried to discourage us from educating ourselves by giving us bad grades in their schools. Therefore, we would not be able to compete with the whites in gaining employment. Moreover, the white teachers just didn't seem to be enthusiastic about us being there at their school. Perhaps they wanted black students to remain ignorant about who they were by making it appear that we had no positive history, except slavery.

This discrimination was a white attempt to keep blacks as social and economic "outcasts" in the American system, especially in the south. The mulattos were expected to blend in better with the whites and become a part of the society.

However, the non-mulattos were expected to remain in a subordinate position and die out as planned. I've even heard of what was referred to as the "paper bag test," meaning that if your skin was lighter than a brown paper bag, that you'd be accepted by the society better than if your skin was of original African origin.

In retrospect, I can see now why the white teachers were reluctant to teach us the truth about what had happened there in South Carolina. How could they stomach to tell us that our grandmothers and grandfathers had been the victims of the "Greatest Crime Ever Committed Against Humanity," when they were the beneficiaries of their ancestors gross "Crimes?"

Later at our High School graduation, Mr. Massey played the piano at the ceremony to receive our high school diplomas in 1973. I was the only guy from the East Side to receive their high school diploma because all of the other guys from the East side had quit school for whatever reasons. Perhaps it was due to the fact that in 1969 we had moved again from the East side to Frazier Park, closer to Chester High, and I had left all of my old friends and made some new one's. But my heart was still in East Chester. I really had a chance to mix with some good people in East Chester and I'll remember them for the rest of my life.

After I finished high school in 1973, I moved to Charlotte, North Carolina, to look for a good job because I wasn't able to find a good one in Chester. A lot of the guys on the East side wasn't doing anything but going to jail and I didn't want to fall into that cycle. Therefore, I went to Charlotte where my grandmother's brother and my uncle Henry lived to look for a good job. I packed one suitcase and set out on the most memorable journey beginning in 1973. This was the first time that I had left home on my own and to be honest I was scared as hell at the age of seventeen.

When I got of the Trailways bus in Charlotte, I took the city bus over to uncle Henry's house. He told me that he too didn't like Chester because it didn't have much too offer him. So he had left Chester in 1948 and moved to Charlotte. He had found a better life for him there instead of Chester. My Aunt Ozzie, Uncle Henry's wife, put me in touch with their son Johnny Lee (Butch), who was a couple of years older than I was a few days later.

I found a job at one of the local hospitals as a custodian and I must have worked there for a couple of months. However, I did not find the work to be very challenging and the pay was not good at all. To be certain there is not much excitement in picking up paper and mopping floors in a hospital. More importantly, all of the older Black people who worked there as janitors were encouraging me not to get stuck in that type of work for the rest of my life, because I was young and had my whole future ahead of me. I remember walking in downtown Charlotte one day after I had picked up my check from the hospital and passing by the Armed Forces building on Tryon Street.

I went in and talked first with the Air Force recruiter. He gave me a test and told me to keep in touch with him because he would have to get back with me in order to let me know the results of the test. At any rate, I did not keep in touch with him. I also talked to the Navy Recruiter and took a test and he called me in a couple of days and asked me when would I like to leave for basic training. I told him that I was still seventeen and that after my eighteenth birthday on the seventeenth of November, that anytime after that would be all right with me. He said that he could not promise me where I would be sent after basic training and that there was still a war going on in Vietnam. I decided to go back to Chester for Thanksgiving and Christmas that year 1973, since we had decided that I would leave for basic training on the 26 of December of '73 the day after Christmas. So I left from Chester to go to Fort Jackson, S. C., for boot camp. On the day after Christmas John Robert dropped me of at the bus station. He told me that "If you just believe in the Lord you'll be safe." He also gave me a Bible and told me to read it in my spare time. He told me to take care and to keep in touch with them. Then I got on the Trailways bus and left.

When I got to Fort Jackson, S.C., they swore me in after taking a few physicals and then I was "In the Navy." The next day I flew to Orlando, Florida, for boot camp. When I got to Florida, it was as hot as hell in the mid-wintertime. I was assigned to Company 321 and we had been chosen as the drill team company to perform at various ceremonies and graduations with our rifles and bayonets. We had to practice for long periods of time plus have the usual locker inspections and personal uniform inspections. There were lots of exercise and obstacle course training for physical fitness, swimming qualifications and life saving techniques, etc. Sometimes things got very hard and very difficult for me, but I always remembered that things were even harder and even more difficult for me in Chester.

Sometimes tensions among the recruits rose and fights started. On one occasion a white boy named Suggs told me that "You are the Blackest Nigger Bastard" that he had ever Seem" We fought for almost thirty minutes until the CC (company commander) Chief Jones came in and stopped the fight. I don't recall having any blood on me. However, I did see some coming from the bottom part of his mouth on the left side. We both got extra duty for two weeks and restricted to the barracks for about two weeks also.

I still had drill team practice and physical fitness training (PT). Some of the other brothers from South Carolina said that they were watching my back to make sure that it would be a one on one fight and that no one else would help him out.

There were four of us from South Carolina in my company (321). Delton Canzater was from Columbia, South Carolina, Timothy Marshall was from Batesburg, South Carolina, Gerald Broughton was from Charleston, South Carolina, and me, Willie Boyd was from Chester, South Carolina. After we finished boot camp we four got assigned to the U. S. S. Patterson DE-1061.

Since none of us had been assigned (AIT) Advanced Intensive Training, or given an "A" School to prepare for a specific rating (job), like the white boys were, we left boot camp and went straight to the ship after a two week period of leave.

We four met back up in Trenton, New Jersey, at Mcguires Air Force Base to fly on board a TWA night flight to Napoles, Italy, where our ship was docked. It was a terrible fight to Italy with so much turbulence that I often felt that the plane was going to crash. It seemed that the plane was taking 200 to 300 feet drops in altitude as we were crossing the Atlantic Ocean. It took us about 13 1/2 hours but it was exciting to get there. We also made stops in Madrid, Spain, and Athens, Greece, before going on to Napoles, Italy. I went aboard ship on April 13, 1974, and it was cold and raining in Napoles that night at about 4 o'clock in the morning. I wondered what in the hell had I gotten myself into now. Command histories noted that in May 1974 the Patterson participated in an unspecified "Special Operation". The Boatswain's Mate 2nd Class Petty Officer Bob Watson, a black man, showed us to our berthing area in the forward part of the ship. That's where first Division slept in which we had been assigned. Someone asked Watson what time was breakfast? He said not to worry that some one will be in to see that you don't miss it." And sure enough at 6 am the lights came on and someone was pulling the covers off me and screaming at me to "Get out of that Rack" Reveilles, Reveilles, Reveille! All hands heave out and trice up, breakfast is now being served on the mess decks. All I could think of after a thirteen hour flight and two hours of sleep was "What did he say?"

The ship was getting underway the next morning and I heard that we were going out to sea for about twenty-eight days doing maneuvers off the coast of Cypress in the waters of the Eastern Mediterranean Sea.

The division in which I had been assigned was in charge of being underway lookouts, helmsmen, and lee helmsmen to steer the ship and order to the engine room certain speeds that we would be traveling. After we had been out for some days I heard that we were traveling through the Straits of Messina and the Straits of Bonafacio in the Mediterranean Sea. We took on fuel and stores while the ship was underway from another ship. We finally met up with other ships, the U.S.S. Forrestal, the U.S.S. Santa Barbara, the U.S.S. Detroit, and performed operations for what seemed to be for weeks.

64

Tangier, Moracco in North Africa, 1974.

All this time I was standing lookout watches while we were underway. The chief Boatswain's Mate was a Black man named Chief Smith from somewhere in Louisiana, and he kept a close eye on us four from South Carolina, maybe because he was from the South too. He never had much to say to us, but he sure did talk to Watson a lot. I soon learned that our ship was to act as a picket ship or screen ship for the task force. And since our ship had sonar we had the abilities to detect underwater targets and pass the information on to (SOPA) the senior officer presently afloat. Generally this meant an aircraft carrier whomever we were operating with; the Kennedy, the Roosevelt, Forrestal, Saratoga, Independence, America, or the Nimitz.

We operated once for about ninety-four days at sea in the Eastern Mediterranean Sea in 1974. On Christmas in 1974, I spent in Marseilles, Frances and New Years as well. By this time I had made E-3 Seaman.

I didn't want to stay in first division and stand lookout watches all the time. Because all we did while we were in port was clean the ship and paint all the time. I asked the chief if it would be all right for me to strike for something or apply for another job on the ship. He said that he thought that I would make a good boatswain's Mate but whatever I wanted to do was alright with him because we had just got some new guys in the division.

As a lookout watch I use to talk to some guy on the phone circuit in a place called (combat) or CIC, Combat Information Center. This guy seemed to have all the answers about the ships, planes, and submarines that we lookouts couldn't even see, and this fascinated me. One day I had gone in the room where he was to see how he could be right on top of everything like that. The guy on the Radar was a Black man named Levon Frazer. I remember I use to see him in the galley with clean clothes on all the time, unlike all of us deck apes in first division. I told him that I had ordered the Radarman 3&2 Course from the ships personnel office and that I wanted to be a Radarman. He said that this was great and that if I had any questions just ask him and he'll help me. When the course arrived in the personnel once I began to read it over right away. I remember sometimes I would fall asleep at night reading my RD 3&2 manual because this was something that I really wanted. The striker board met and Chief Smith told the XO (Executive Officer) and the division officer that I was a hard working and reliable man and he thought that I deserved a chance in CIC. The first class or LPO (leading Petty Officer) was a man named Kay Vest, RD-1, who soon made chief radar man before leaving the ship. He said that he'd give me a chance to make petty officer and that he had two other seamen who had not passed the exam for Radar man third Class. But he took me in the division and started me out behind the status boards as a plotter.

He also told me to stick with Levon Frazer because Frazer was pretty sharp and that if I had any questions to ask him or Frazer. I continued to study my RD 3&2 manual at night or whenever I wasn't on watch.

Whenever we were steaming independently I was on the surface search radar console in CIC. Sometimes when Vest or Frazer wasn't in the same watch section as me and some of my other peers were in CIC, like Mike Veda, John Naglee, and Barry Weinzimmer, all white men in our division, they tried to intimidate me by saying things like "smile nigger, show us your teeth so we can see you; you're so black that we can't tell if you are still over there. So smile and show us your teeth; Ni, Ni, Ni, Ni, NIGGER!" I knew that they only wanted me to blow up and fight them and that way I'd be put out of the division and have to go back to chipping paint and standing lookout watches.

Therefore, I just ignored them and kept on doing my job. More importantly, I was very upset a lot of the time because my sister Helen had written me and told me that the Ku Klux Klan had been lynching and burning crosses in Chester some more.

CERTIFICATE OF APPOINTMENT

To all who shall see these presents, greeting:

Know Ye, that by authority vested in me and reposing special trust
and confidence in the patriotism, valor, fidelity and abilities of

Willie Bernard BOYD

I do hereby appoint you to the rate of

Operations Specialist Third Class

in the

UNITED STATES NAVY

to rank as such from the 16th day of June , nineteen hundred and *seventy-
six*

TO THE APPOINTEE

Your appointment as a petty officer in the United States Navy makes you heir to a long and
proud tradition of Naval leadership. By accepting this appointment, you are charged with
demonstrating those standards of performance, moral courage, and dedication to the Navy and
the Nation which may serve as an enviable example to your fellow Navy men and women.

Your desire to excel and to guide others must be boundless; your appearance must be a model
for others and your performance must be a continual reflection of your sincerity, attention to
duty, and moral responsibility. By exhibiting unfailing trust and obedience toward superiors,
cooperation and loyalty to your peers, and understanding and strength to your subordinates,
you will contribute greatly to the effectiveness and good name of the United States Navy.

Given under my hand at *sea enroute Port Mahon, Spain*
this 16th day of June in the year of our Lord nineteen hundred and *seventy-
six.*

B. R. COX
Commander, U.S. Navy
Commanding Officer

NAVPERS 1430/7 (USN) (5-67)
S/N 0106.071.0700

GPO:1967-O-270-130

276

In fact they had lynched a friend of mine whom I had played baseball against when I was with the East Chester Dodgers in the Little League. Moreover, I was already under a great deal of stress because I was studying for the RD 3&2 exam that was coming up soon so I didn't need any bullshit from these crackers. So one morning they called all of us to the mess decks who were up for the next higher rate. I went down there to take the exam because I had been studying for it and I felt that I was ready. At any rate, we were already at sea and I had been already doing the job as a radar man very well, so I believed. Two other guys' from my division came and took the exam along with me. One of the guy's had even been to the Radar man "A" school who's name was Michael Creel. He had come to the division after I did and had the benefit of (AIT) advanced intensive training and I had not. Also there was another guy named Mercier, but everybody called him mouse, which had already been in the division (OI) when I got there from 1st division.

So we three got our rulers, dividers, pencils, and paper and went down to the mess decks for the test. It seemed that pretty much of what was on the test was what we had been doing out at sea. I had to simulate tracking a surface contact; course, speed, CPA (closest point of approach of another ship to our ship), time of CPA, distance of the target, target angle, intercept course, charts, maps, navigation, search procedures; time in and time out on search path, man overboard procedures, publications for tactical maneuvers, communications publications, Naval Warfare Publications, plotting, internal and external communications. After I had finished the exam, I told Vest and Frazer that I felt pretty good about how I had did on the test. More importantly, when the test results came back from Washington, DC, in about six weeks my name had been posted outside of the personnel office as having passed the RD 3&2 exam and had been promoted to the next highest pay grade. I was later assigned the duties of "CHART" PO for our division's navigational duties in CIC. On the other hand, Creel and Mercier had not passed the RD 3&2 exam for promotion.

Now I was going to be over these two white boys who had failed the exam. I could have rubbed it in their face but I did not, because I did not want to embarrass them and anyway I still had to work with them. One morning the Captain called all of us who had passed the exams up to the flying bridge and gave us all of our certificates; which read in part: Given under my hand at "SEA" to Port Mahon, Spain, in the year of our lord 1976." Spain would be our last stop in the Mediterranean Sea before coming back across the Atlantic home to Philadelphia, Pa., and to the shipyards. We had completed the Anti-submarine Warfare Operations in the Black Sea near Istanbul, Turkey. Two of my fellow South Carolinians had not completed the tour of duty aboard the U.S.S. Patterson with me. Gerald Broughton and Delton Canzater were relieved of their duty because they were sick all of the time.

Broughton would get seasick every time the ship would leave the pier and Canzater had come down with some other mental problems that were probably stress related. However, Timothy Marshall from Batesburg, South Carolina, had traveled the seas and oceans with me all the way.

I remember that I wrote to a university about enrollment, if I decided to get out of the Navy and they had responded favorably. So when I got back to the United States and to Philadelphia, I looked forward to leaving the Patterson, because she was going into the shipyards. I knew that I would be very bored just sitting up beside the pier all the time. I stayed in Philadelphia for a few months awaiting the end of my active duty obligation in the Navy. Philadelphia was a great city to me with lots of sights to see; the liberty bell of course, and a great historic city in all respects.

Moreover, the media and other sports attractions were very enthusiastic. The first person that I heard on the radio after returning to the States was Stevie Wonder, performing his "Songs in the key Of Life" album. It made me very proud to hear his song "Blackman", and "Isn't She Lovely."

Down just a few blocks from the shipyard was the Spectrum sports arena where the Philadelphia 76ers played basketball. They had just acquired a doctor by the name of "Julius Erving" to help them to perform surgery on the rest of the National Basketball Association. More importantly, it was the country's Bi-Centennial year so there were lots of festivities in the air in the "City of Brotherly Love."

However, the winters are very cold and being a southerner as I was, I could feel the winter coming on abruptly. I was very glad when November came and I was Honorably Discharged. The Captain and Executive Officer had talked to me personally and asked me if I wanted to stay in the Navy.

However, I told them that I had already been accepted and ready to enter the university that I had chosen to enter. I thought that I was making the right decision to accept the Honorable Discharge and get out of the Navy. They had offered me an opportunity to become a candidate for (OCS) Officers Candidacy School at Annapolis Naval Academy at Annapolis, Maryland; I thought I would prefer to attend University much closer to home in Charlotte, North Carolina. Therefore, I came back to Chester from Philadelphia in December of 1976 and began University in January of 1977 at Johnson C. Smith University in Charlotte, North Carolina. I was glad to be back in the United States after traveling to all those other countries, maybe over twenty-five in all. I went to Spain, France, Italy, Greece, Turkey, Cypress, Morocco, Algiers, Kenya, Lebanon, Yugoslavia, the Caribbean Islands, Cuba, and some other Middle Eastern countries.

I was very glad to be near my family in South Carolina. I was also enjoying being out of the Navy and going to school. I felt that I was making the transition very well.

This was an opportunity for me to get reacquainted with my "Roots" so to speak since I had just left a predominately all white Navy. I guess what I was after most of all was a good education from an institution that I could afford to attend. I also wanted to know more about myself. I never thought that I'd have an opportunity to go to college since my folks could not afford to send me, they just didn't have the money.

COMMANDING OFFICER
USS PATTERSON (DE 1061)
FPO, NEW YORK 09501

16 November 1976

While assigned to the USS PATTERSON, Mr. Boyd was
an energetic, conscientious, and enthusiastic worker.
Through a program of self-study he acquired the professional knowledge and expertise required to switch
from a position as a non-rated deck hand to the demanding field of Operations Specialist. This was a difficult transition and a significant accomplishment to
attain without the benefit of formal training. Mr.
Boyd performed all tasks assigned in an excellent
manner.

I feel confident that through the continued
diligence and conscientious effort he demonstrated in
his service at this command he will succeed in any
civilian endeavors he might undertake.

D. R. COX
COMMANDING OFFICER

279

My intentions were to continue to study communications as I was in while I was serving in the Navy. However, I could not help but to enjoy studying History because it had been explained to me I thought very thoroughly in high school by Mr. Massey. I really enjoyed Dr. Thomas's History classes and another Blackman Mr. Hines had spent twenty-seven years in the military before he had gone back and earned his degree in History. They were very interesting to me and I learned quite a bit while studying with them, I was also fulfilling the requirements for a degree in Communications and in History. As I was entering the second half of my third year of studies at Johnson C. Smith University I seemed to notice a pattern that had developed between one of my History professors and I. Dr. Hermitt and I had difficulties agreeing upon the fact of whether or not the people who were the victims of the European-African Slave Trade were merely "bodies" as he would like to refer to them or whether they were indeed human beings who had "SOULS" as well.

I tended to believe that they were human beings who were the victims of the most horrific and evil deeds that had ever been casted upon any human beings. However, not to the agreement of Dr. Hermitt. I felt and still feel that since these were my people and ancestors who were chained down to the bottom of those Slave ships like animals; goats, dogs, horses, pigs; that I should at least be given an opportunity to express how I felt about the horrible "CRISIS." Moreover, I felt that if the African chiefs would have killed off the European traders initially, that Blacks in America would not be on the lower spectrum of the socio-economic table that we presently occupy in America.

Hence, Dr. Hermitt being a Northern carpet bagging Caucasian that he was, didn't think that I was deserving of a passing mark in his African History course-231.

This resulted in my having to select another course under another professor in order to fulfill the requirements towards a Bachelors Degree in History and Communications. I elected to take Dr. Thomas' class, a well-mannered black man from Virginia. Dr. Thomas and I reached a mutual understanding about the plight of African Americans promptly. Since he too was a man of color we discussed the Civil Rights Movement from 1968 and all of its ramifications. I completed the course in Historiography and the research. Hence, there too lied the presence of Dr. Dubois' prognosis into the twentieth century of the "colorline."

I want to re-emphasize the point that my academic advisor at Smith University got all fired up at the fact of my leaving the military after my first enlistment. He made the suggestion one day that "so many of us Blacks get out of the military after our first enlistment."

He had some preconceived notion that we should not leave after our first enlistment. Therefore, in retaliation to me for leaving the military, he gave me three below average marks in his classes that I took under him. At any rate, I took the classes over under the Black professors and made passing grades.

Dr. Hermitt and I disagreed on the matter of the European-African TransAtlantic Slave Trade because he felt that the trade was good because the people that were involved were merely "Bodies." I, on the other hand, felt that each of the people onboard the slave ships had a "SOUL" and was as human as he and I. I felt that they should not have been treated as animals; beaten, raped, castrated, or thrown over the side to be eaten alive by sharks, or simply drown to death. Therefore, here in too lied the problem of the Twentieth Century, the Colorline. Dr. Hermitt was of Dutch ancestry and I am of African ancestry. The Dutch were very much so involved in the Slave Trade. Therefore, Dr. Hermitt was merely reflecting the points of view of his forefathers and his fellow Dutchmen. However, I saw that it was my people, my forefathers, and grandmothers, and I, we are all the "Victims" of this "Murderous Holocaust." Moreover, I told Dr. Hermitte that it was my belief that if the African chiefs and kings had killed of the European traders instead of dealing with them, that our people in America today would not be at the bottom of the social and economic ladder today in America. Furthermore, we would not have had to endure the "Ridicule" of the white society and have to digest being made a mockery of by a people who don't have the moral standards of the people who's being oppressed by the dominate culture here in America."

Dr. Hermitt became very furious with me from that point on and failed me in every class that I took with him. The university was not willing to support me in my protest of Dr. Hermitt; therefore, I finished up my Historiography class with Dr. Thomas and decided that I had had enough of them, and they, perhaps of me too.

They were not willing to stand behind me so I left about 12-semester hrs. short of my Bachelors Degree in History. I'm glad to report that I left Dr. Hermitt still alive. I felt like killing him. But I didn't because I didn't want that blood on my hands!

I took some transferable classes at the local community college but the registrar was reluctant to admit them even though the grades were all "A." Even more provocative was the fact that I felt that "JIM CROW" had made his way into a predominantly African-American institution of higher learning. Dr. Hermitt was proof enough for me that whites were very naive about the point of view of blacks even though it was my ancestors that had gone through the terrible nightmare of slavery. There were times when I wanted to take more violent measures against him but I figured that would only further give the university a negative image of my family and me. My uncle Henry lived just a few blocks down the boulevard on Beatties Ford Road and I didn't want to give them a bad name by kicking Dr. Hermitts ass or causing trouble or anything so I just let it go.

I had continued to stay on in the U.S. Navy Reserve after I had gotten off of active duty. I would go to the reserve center in Charlotte one weekend per month and two weeks in the summer. I would go up to Brooklyn, New York for two weeks of active duty in the summer and spend the time aboard ship working on their navigation charts. While at the reserve center in Charlotte I was assigned to instructing new recruits in various procedures used aboard ship because some of them had never been aboard one.

I could tell that some of the people there were very stunned to see a black man who could do more than sweep floors or clean bathrooms. I told them exactly what we had been doing aboard ship in regard to plotting and how to track a contact on a maneuvering board, how to operate the surface search radar, how to plot on the DRT-dead reckoning tracer. I went over ASW (anti-submarine warfare) operations, AA (anti-air warfare) operations, and the entire duties of the Radar man rating. I also knew that these were some of the people who elected not to go aboard ship during the country's war in Vietnam, but rather they chose to keep their jobs at home and go to work everyday, and watch the war on television each night on the CBS Evening News.

Every time I looked at one of them I would think about my cousins Charlie Mobley, Bobby Robinson, Vernell Gray, Ernest Shivers and Larry Hill, and some of the other brothers who had been drafted into the army. They had gotten blown up over there and shot up on the front lines in Vietnam. I thought that these son's of bitches wouldn't even go sail their own country's ships in a country where they had all of the privileges of being first class citizens. Moreover, I always had thoughts of whether some of these guys that I was instructing at the center were some of the people who had lynched my friend William James Franklin (Chickie-Boo), who I had played baseball against when I was with the Dodgers in East Chester as a kid. I also wondered if some of these guys were the one's who tied up the Crosby man behind a truck and drove him for about ten or twelve miles down Orr's Road, a dirt road, to his death in 1975 while I was overseas.

I continued to go to the reserve center until I got my Honorable Discharge from the U.S. Navy in 1979. In fact, I drilled with them until about 1981 instructing plotting and operating procedures. People often asked me why I didn't make a career of the Navy?

Well in my heart and in my mind I didn't think that it would be right for me to stay in the Navy and represent a country who was lynching up my friends and tying them up behind trucks and dragging them down dirt roads to their deaths. I just didn't see the correlation between that and saying that this is a free country. In fact, I can remember coming back from overseas after tracking Soviet submarines in the Black sea region, to have to march down the streets with my friends and family in Chester to protest lynching and church burnings in 1975.

In the Navy, and in the military in general, there are always the possibilities of death. There is of course war. Then, too, there are always the possibilities of equipment malfunctioning. In the case of ships there's always the possibilities of collisions. Then too there is internal fighting among sailors aboard ship that has resulted in the loss of life.

I've always felt that I did not want to die for this country' because we blacks have not received full economic, political, and social justice or equality in America. More importantly, I've always felt that my main fight is here in America trying to obtain this desired end. Nevertheless, I tried to be conscientious while serving in the U.S. Navy. I've always felt that the biggest warfare would be waged for me here in America. I have never considered myself to be a hero and I have never wanted to be.

However, there has been some people who I looked up to while I was in the Navy and who I'll never forget. One of those people was Vernon Foster who I worked with aboard the U.S.S. Patterson FF-1061 from 1974-1977. When I got to the ship Foster was a Quartermaster Seaman E-3.

When I got promoted to Radar man 3rd Class, Foster was promoted to Quartermaster 2nd Class E-5. We would always work on the navigation charts together because while he was doing visual navigation on the bridge we Radar men would be doing Radar navigation down below in CIC. We would have to correlate our charts to make sure that we had laid the same proposed course in order to navigate the ship accurately. I was the chart petty officer for 0I Division (operations intelligence) and Foster was the chart petty officer for ON Division (operations Navigation). Some nights when we were underway and I was the CIC watch supervisor, I would go up on the bridge and compare his Omega-Loran navigational fixes to my DRT- Latitude and Longitude fixes to see if we were navigating along the same proposed course. When the ship would hit port somewhere, we would all go out on liberty together just to let our feet touch the ground. Sometimes we would have been at sea for sixty or seventy days without seeing land, even on the radar. It was a great honor to have served with Senior Chief Vernon Foster; I learned how to be a sailor through people like him. It was a great shock to me to learn of his death even at ten years after it occurred. I'll never forget him.

It was while reading through a "JET Magazine" one day that I learned of his tragic death and I was extremely overtaken with his mothers pain, humility and the faith that she demonstrated in her lost. Responding to the Jet Magazine Interview she said, "I resent him having died for something as senseless as this," lamented Mrs. Mim Gaines, Whose son, Senior Chief Petty Officer Vernon Foster, was one of the Blacks killed when an Exocet Sea-skimming Missile exploded into the port hull of the U. S. S. Stark, the Guided-Missile Frigate on which he was serving. At least seven Blacks sailors were among the 37 killed aboard the stark in the Persian Gulf when the ship was attacked by an Iraqi warplane. The Iraqi Government called the attack an "accident." Only twenty-four of the dead seamen had been identified at "JET" press time. Twenty-one sailors were injured.

In addition to Foster, 33, of Jacksonville, FL, other Black sailors identified were: Dexter Dwayne Grissett, 19 Macon, Ga.; Ronnie George Lockett, 30, Bessemer, Ala.; Vincent Lenard Ulmer, 21, Bay Minette, Ala. (Missing, presumed dead) and Lloyd Anthony Wilson, 24, Summerville, S. C.; Braddy Otis Brown 28, Bessemer, Ala.; Antonio Armando Daniels, 21, Greeleyville, S. C.

The Stark, a guided-missile frigate with a crew of 200, was part of the Middle East Task Force fleet assigned to protect oil-shipping lanes in the Persian Gulf. Iraqi government officials maintained the pilot who fired the missile at the Stark believed it was an Iranian vessel. Iraq and Iran have been warring for seven years.

65

*Damaged by missile, Stark is escort-
ed to port by patrol boat.*

Blacks Among 37 Sailors Killed In Attack On Stark

"Who am I to say they should not have been there," said Deborah Kirkland, of Tallahassee, Fla., whose son, petty officer Christopher Jones, survived, "I don't think the U. S. Should retaliate. You don t take a life for a life."54 Nevertheless, It hurts me to see such a good man die; I'll remember QMSC Foster for the rest of my life, (aka-Sea Dragons).

I have had several jobs over the years that I have enjoyed. However, it seems to appear that I have been expendable to a majority of my former employers. One example is when I was a (temporary) employee with IBM (International Business Machine). In 1982 I was working with IBM in Charlotte, North Carolina, in their operations center and data processing operations. I had really been working my ass off for that company. I had gone to work in the snow and sleet as I was supposed to during the winter months, although the other employees had called in sick saying that they couldn't make it because of the bad weather. I didn't call in sick, I went to work. I operated about sixty-five tape drives and two CRT'S (cathode ray tubes) consoles using TCS (time constant systems) and TSO (time sharing options) with JES-2 & JES-3 (Job entry systems languages). I also used MVS (multiple virtual storage), OS (operating systems), VS (virtual storage) languages, etc.

I had been there for about seven months including a one-month extension that I had asked for and received. At the end of my seven months I remember saying to the third line manager, who's name was Deke Kenniston, that I really liked the job and was very hopeful of staying on. He angrily replied "Hey Boy! Didn't I tell you that we have some other people coming here from up state New York and that you'd have to leave in order to make room for them "I replied to him, "Sir I have traveled around the world and back, Do you still consider me to be a BOY." After sailing ships and fighting wars that you people made and ran from, do you still consider me to be not yet a man?

He didn't have anything else to say to me and just walked away. At the end of the week my supervisor, Kevin Schroder came to me and said to me, "I'm sorry Willie, I guess this is it." The ironic thing about it is that there was a white guy there named Karl who was a Navy Veteran too. They kept him and let me go. He told me that in his opinion that they were wrong." I did not challenge their decision. More importantly, I had a very hard time explaining that to my mother Margaret in Chester when I went back down there.

There was just a lot of racism in the corporate world and still is, and I hope that she can understand this fact.

Moreover, to further illustrate the extent of the problem of the Color line, sometimes when me and some of the others in my department would go to lunch together while working for IBM, certain restaurants that we would go to were very racist towards us. At one restaurant that was close to our facility, the waitresses, a white woman, would serve us hamburgers, and I know I remember that it looked as if it had a bug in it and that something was crawling out of it.

On one occasion this happened and our department coordinator, who was a Black woman, saw the roach crawl from under my sandwich. She said, "put it down Willie and let's get out of here." To say that they did not need or want our business or money is an understatement. Therefore, we never went back to that restaurant again.

To be sure, well to place the matter in its' proper perspective, there has been a number of occasions that I'm sure that I have been discriminated against and I can document them well. For example, the last hired and the first fired on jobs that I was well qualified for. Moreover, there have been times that I have not been selected for certain positions because I was a Blackman and I was very qualified for. I have been victimized by having had racial slurs made towards me in levels of the professional structure where you might think that racism didn't exist. Even when I worked as an EEG technician, there were incidences where I was treated very unprofessional from people at a higher level. Such as that to be of such low moral character. One of my coworkers in the laboratory even refused to work with me because I was black. She felt that the white race was being taken over economically by members of other races and that I was taking up a slot on the payroll that should have been given to a white person. Moreover, she felt that since whites made up only ten percent of the world population that whites were slowly becoming extinct.

It later occurred to me that here is a racist bigot who has been reading too much of that racist Neo-Nazi and Ku Klux Klan material, who is using that propaganda of the white race extinction to be the underline basis for her negative actions towards me. Even some of the Physicians were racist and wanted to provide better care for some of the patients than they provided for others. One of the doctors who was doing research at the University never had a patient in her research project that was not a white person. This seemed to puzzle me because I knew that there were a number of people who were suffering from the illnesses that was in her area of care. However, in my entire two years of affiliation with the EEG laboratory I can't recall ever seeing her have a person of color in her care. This goes on to illustrate to me that the color-line is very much so prevalent in all walks of life in America as we close out the Twentieth Century. Racism really bothers me especially when it affects my well-being.

There have been timed when I've wanted to take some action against racial prejudice that was of a violent nature and take out my anger on the perpetrators who created it. But I know that if I had resorted to such drastic measures as having gone and get a gun or an AK-47 automatic weapon, like some of those little immature white boys who have been in the news as of late, that I would only be undermining my people and just as much of the hypocracy that I abhor so much in some Whites.

They would not just lock me up and feed me like some gorilla or some other animal in a cage, they would no doubt be putting my ass in the gas chamber for a lethal injection of poison after waiting on death row for God knows how long.

On another occasion, I was working at another Company in Charlotte, North Carolina, in 1979. I was working as a Computer Aided Draftsman and Engineering Draftsman in the Design Engineering section of the company.

What we did was generate electrical, technical, and civil schematics using a CRT (cathode ray tube) and a drafting table to draw these schematics on the screen. Later these designs would be printed out on a plotter and onto a legend with borders at various sizes. These drawings could be later used for reference or stored and used at a later time. I had been working there for about 2 years when they hired this white boy named Drew. He was some country looking hick who reminded me of a scarecrow with one tooth missing in the front. One day this low life looking back woods man pulled what looked to be a pillowcase out of his pocket and put it on his head and said to me, "Hey look Willie I'm the Klan, see me!" Hey, I took this fool serious and went and told the department manager Bill. I told him, "Hey Bill, this fool is in here advocating racism and murder, violence, and oppression on the job and right down the road in Chester about forty miles they're burning down our houses, churches, and lynching up my friends. Now I don't think it's right for that Klansman to be in here making fun of the situation while all of that is going on." I told him that, "What I need to do is go home and get my shot gun and come back and blow his head off, but I know that I'll wind up in the penitentiary for the rest of my life for killing him.

Therefore, I think I'd better just get the hell out of here." I went back to Chester for a while and stayed with my family until I felt better. Yet again, I had a real hard time explaining this one again to my mother and to my two sisters. But when I told John Robert what had happened, he was glad that I had not tried to do something crazy like kill the cracker- Klansman.

I had stayed at my mother and fathers house in Chester, South Carolina, for about three or four months after leaving IBM in 1982 when I started receiving letters from the United States Coast Guard. They had gotten my name from the Navy Reserve station where I use to attend on weekends for the meetings but were no longer attending the drills.

I had decided to call up the recruiter on one occasion to see what they had to offer me for my services. The guy that I spoke to told me that if I decided to become a part of the Coast Guard that he could guarantee me that I could keep my same rank that I had as a Petty Officer in the Navy, and that since I had completed over ninety semester hours in an accredited university that I could be considered for a commission as an Officer.

Of course all of this sounded good to me so I asked the recruiter when would I be able to leave and where would I be stationed.

He told me that he had done some further looking into my prospects as working as a Radar man in the Coast Guard and found that they did not have the billet readily available as a radar man for me but he wondered if I would be interested in becoming a Radioman instead. I told him that I did not know much about that area of operations but I would be willing to give it a shot. He told me that he wanted me to go to a school that was located in Petaluma, CA. for the Radioman rating. I left for the school in November of 1982 for Petaluma, CA. When I arrived on the station in Petaluma I was very tired from the fight across the United States. It was yet another scary night with lots of turbulence particularly as we were landing in San Francisco.

The town of Petaluma was located north of San Francisco across the Golden Gate Bridge. At first everything seemed to be going well for me I thought I was doing well in my duties and classes.

However, on one particular Friday I remember checking the watch bill that had been posted and saw that my name was not on it for the weekend duty so I decided to go into San Francisco for the weekend. When I returned from being on pass I learned that I had been written up for missing duty and had been placed on restriction. This was very unusual for me I thought because I thought because I knew that I had checked the watch bill before I left on pass. Two weeks later the same thing happened to me and when I went before the captain he told me that I had two violations of article 92, which is, unauthorized absences and that I would remain on restriction and would be given another assignment besides the Radioman school. I was assigned to the facilities crew that was in charge of cleaning up the entire Base.

While I was in the facilities department I met another Black man from Alabama who was also a former Radioman who told me that the same thing had happened to him. When we talked further we figured out that we must have been intentionally led to believe that we did not have the duty on the given days and that a new watch bill had been posted after we had gone on pass to make it appear that we had intentionally neglected our duties and gone ahead with out proper authorization.

I believe there were two watch bills made up, one with my name on it and one without my name on it. After I had left on pass the one with my name on it was then posted making me AWOL. I had gone into this organization with the best of intentions but at this point it did not seem to be working out at all. Moreover, there weren't very many black people around and certainly none who were in any position of authority. Then also I had began to hear rumors of how many blacks who had been there before me and who had failed amidst racial allegations.

I recall having kept some of the manuals that I used in the Navy aboard ship as reference materials. When the security was going through my room at the Coast Guard Station in Petaluma, they confiscated all of my books that I had brought there with me.

They had me thinking that I would also be going to court martial for having classified material in my possession.

There was no way that they could have made a charge like that stick because I was not trying to sell the manuals or pass them on to any unauthorized person I was using them strictly for reference. To illustrate just how racist these people were against blacks in the Coast Guard, I remember being in the Enlisted Men's Club one day after work and I just happened to see the Master Chief Radioman in there. He was not in his uniform and it appeared that he was having a few drinks so I went over and spoke to him. He did not appear to be drunk and it really startled me when the first thing that came out of his mouth was derogatory towards me. I said, "how are you Master Chief?"

His reply was "Well Boy they haven't locked your Black-Ass up yet!" From that point on I knew that these people were not the kind of people that I wanted to be associated with in any way. Altogether I must have stayed in Petaluma, Ca. For about seven or eight months before I was asked by the personnel department if there was anywhere in particular that I would like to be permanently stationed in order to serve out my enlistment. I told them that I would like to be somewhere close to home and preferably in South Carolina.

The personnel department told me that they could transfer me to the Coast Guard base in Charleston, South Carolina and that sounded to be the ideal place for me. When I arrived in Charleston the weather was hot and very humid to me and I was not use to it because I had been on the west coast where the weather was much cooler all the time. I was assigned to the boat crew, which was similar to the deck force aboard the ship that I was on in the Navy.

The people that I worked with were all white and I could tell that they had their little circle of friends that all stuck together. I did not want to become a part of any circle of people all I wanted to do was to do the job that had been assigned to me. I could tell that they had made me an outcast by the way that they spoke to me and to be sure I did not feel very welcomed there. I was always assigned remedial duties such as sweeping and mopping hallways and painting on the boat docks. I can recall that one day I was told to go to the paint locker and get some paint and return to the boat dock.

When I returned to the Docks I learned that I had been written up by the second-class petty officer because he said that I had taken too long to return to my assigned work area to work. I could tell that this person had a real deep resentment and a cultural bias towards people who were not the same as he was and blacks in particular. The lieutenant over the department in which I had been assigned was probably the worst of all. His name was Lt. Sawyer and a real redneck if ever I had seen one. For being late back to the boat docks I was placed on restriction and given extra duty as my punishment. It was said to me by the one who wrote me up "well in the old days we would take you out back and whip you with a whip or something." I replied, "Well you might as well go on and kill me because I would definitely be back to kill you."

Well a couple of weeks passed and I was very depressed about being there with all of those rednecks and listening to all of those supposed funny racial jokes so one night after dark on a Friday night I packed all of my civilian clothes and left.

I remember that I had met this little Mexican girl on the Greyhound Bus when I was traveling from San Francisco to Charleston and we had spent the night in a hotel in Fort Worth, Texas, because she was from that area. I had called her a couple of times when I had got to Charleston, S.C. and she had told me to come back that way some time and see her if I was in the area again. When I left that night the weather was good in Charleston. But by the time I got to Dallas, Texas, on that following Saturday afternoon it was pouring down rain. It was raining so hard that I had to pull my Ford Granada over and into a rest area for a while because I could not see the road very well.

When I finally made it to Virginia Garcia's house it was late on that Saturday night and she was very glad to see me again. She had asked me to bring some reliable transportation for us to get around in so my car came in very handy for her to get to work in. I guess I had been there for a week or so when I met this Black man who worked for Piccadilly Restaurant as a cook and I asked if he had any work at the restaurant that I could do because I was looking for a job. He told me to come by on that Monday and fill out an application and so I did. I believe that I must have been there for about a month or more and the work area was very hot all the time because I was working in the kitchen where all of the ovens were.

I had almost forgot about the Coast Guard until one day when I called home to Chester and my mother told me that they had been calling her house asking her where I was and that if she knew that she should tell them. At any rate, they apparently had traced my telephone call to where I was living with Virginia in Arlington, Texas, and came to the apartment and asked Virginia about me while I was at work.

She told them that I was at the restaurant and they came over and arrested me on the job. I stayed in jail in the city of Arlington, Texas, for about two days before I was flown back to Charleston, S.C., where I was taken to the brig on the Naval Base to await court martial. I was in the brig for at least one week before I went to court martial. During the trial I felt like I was the main attraction at a lynching and I never stood a chance. I didn't even get the opportunity to tell my side of the story or exactly why I had gone AWOL. The military defender that they assigned to represent me didn't put up any kind of defense for me; actually he gave me right to the government's prosecutor to lynch. These were all Southern white men and I somehow knew that their decision would not be a just one. When the Judge rendered the decision he didn't even call me by my correct name. He said "Willie B. Boar", referring to the Boar War's in South Africa; I sentence you to be confined in the brig for a period of ninety days at hard labor. I was then taken back to the brig to commence my sentence.

I stayed in solitary confinement for another week until I convinced the guards that I was not going to commit suicide but rather serve out my sentence. I was then released out into the general prison population where I was given a daily work assignment. I was assigned to the grounds crew who would go out every day and cut the grass on the Navy Base.

This may sound easy but it was hard work because I had to push this big mower that was designed and normally operated by itself by having a belt going to one of the wheels from the motor. However, the belt had been taken off the wheel and I had to push the heavy machine all day long in the hot South Carolina sun. Some of the men would pass out from heat exhaustion due to the prolonged exposure to the hot sun. My clothes would be ringing wet with sweat. After a while the body would not yields any more water and sometimes I wished that I would pass out in order to stop the torture. At the end of the day my body would be so stiff that it would take all night for the feelings to come back into my arms and legs. I pushed that big mower for five days a week and exercised all day on Saturday in the compound under a chained locked fence with armed guards looking on.

On Sunday they let us play softball on the compound for recreation. Some of the guards would try to provoke fights between the inmates and sometimes they would just straight out harass me by calling me names. One of the white guards called me a "SEAL" one day and he began to make the sounds like a seal and started to flap his hands like a seal at me. At first it made me very angry and humiliated but I later came to realize just how stupid he was. I thought to myself that this guy must not have very much going for himself if all he could do in life was just sit there and watch me all day and make faces at me. There were an assortment of prisoners in there with me; thieves, attempted murderers, and other crooks and con artists. One guy was in there for stabbing his white chief he said that he was being harnassed to much by him.

This was a Mexican fellow. Another guy, who was a Blackman, was in there because he had stolen some money and cashed checks from the disbursing office aboard his ship. I think altogether there were about sixty of us in there for various reasons. To be sure, it seemed that my time there would never end.

After serving eighty-eight days of hard labor I was finally set free. The executive officer of the Coast Guard base had come over to see me on one occasion and asked me if I wanted to continue my enlistment at the base. I promptly told him no and requested an immediate discharge upon release from the brig. I felt there was no need for me to give them ole' Southern boys any more chances for me to get in serious trouble by killing some of them and then be given some serious prison time. So upon release from the brig this concluded my military career, gladly. I feel that my life have been spared by God as far as the military is concerned. Moreover, I think that I had an opportunity to experience the good and the worse of it. Most importantly, I traveled around the world and spent time incarcerated I remained alive through it all.

Looking back on South Carolina the only love that I could ever have for that place is the love that I feel for my family who still live there. For me it has never done anything for me to love it. They burned down our churches and schools, lynch and murder my friends, so what kind of love is that they have shown to me?

As we close out the Twentieth Century there's yet massive incidents of hate and bigotry that still exists there more so than any where else in this country. For example, while reading the Los Angeles Times newspaper a couple of summers ago I ran across the most interesting and disturbing article entitled, "A Clan and the Klan in South Carolina." It began by saying that, "for three generations the Haley Family have had a reputation for trouble," authorities say. Now, members of the family are linked to the Ku Klux Klan and some are accused of conspiring to burn Black churches.

Manning, South Carolina-The way Lester Haley tells it, the Ku Klux Klan in these parts was nothing but a social club-a few good ol' boys who got together now and then for meetings, turkey shoots and the like. As a social leader, he said he doused down hotheads who tried to cause trouble.

But sitting in his trailer, his rebel flag propped up in one corner, a shrine of Elvis Presley in another, Haley had to admit that he did not do a very good job. During his two-year reign as exalted Cyclops, authorities say, Klansmen tried to start a race war. Haley denies that. But, there's no denying that church arsons, knifings, and beatings all occurred during his watch. Of the almost 300 church fires that Federal authorities have investigated since the start of 1995, the only charges of conspiracy involving an organized hate group are aimed at the local Klansmen.

Now Haley's brother and former brother-in-law are in prison on arson charges. Another brother is living large, having allegedly traded information on his kin for his own freedom. And Lester Haley, at 58 the oldest brother, is waiting to see if he, too, will be charged with burning churches as the federal investigation continues. That trouble trailed the Haley family comes as no surprise to folk who live in this heavily forested part of the Carolina lowlands. For three generations, the Haley name has been legend. "They have a reputation for stealing; they have a reputation for burning, they have a reputation for everything under the sun," said Horace Swilley, who was sheriff of Clarendon County for 12 years until 1992. To understand what really happened here, local authorities say, you must first understand the Haleys.

A burley man with a steely countenance, Lester Haley says the large family came by its bad name honorably- its members stand up for themselves. That often means getting into scraps. But others here say that doesn't begin to explain the Haley aura.

Sue Nell Hinkle, one of Lester's five sisters, says the family reputation started with their late father, Lamont Pleasant Haley. Some folks called him the "swamp man," she said, because he lived by himself out in the woods and was said to be eccentric.

"My daddy's the one who started the arson in the family," she said. "My daddy burned my momma's house down." That rumor has never been proved, but three of his children have since served time for starting fires, including Hinkle herself before she says she found the Lord.

In addition, two members of the younger generation-Lester's son and stepson-have faced charges of murder. The stepson, acquitted of murder in 1980, was himself shot to death by an acquaintance in 1993. With all of the problems they have endured, some family members say the Haleys are cursed. But Kenneth Gardner, for one, has little sympathy.

"There is fear and awe about the Haley name down there," said Gardner, who lives in nearby Sumpter. His 29 year-old son was killed in a bar room brawl in 1993 by Lester, Jr. The bar was filled with people, but most everyone said they were looking the other way. Before the case could go to trial, one "very valuable witness" died in an apartment fire, said sheriff Hoyt Collins, who called the fire "suspicious." Unable to prove murder, prosecutors agreed to a plea bargain. The judge could have sent Lester Jr. to prison for three years, but suspended his sentence." I liked to fainted," said Collins. "I will feel to my dying day that there was a very serious injustice done to my son," said Gardner.

KLAN: Black-Church Arson Trial

ERIC GLENN / For The Times

Lester Haley, a former leader of his local KKK chapter, denies his group took part in black-church burnings.

KLAN: Ex-Members Face Arson Charges

66

A Clan and the Klan in S. Carolina

■ For three generations, the Haleys have had a reputation for trouble, authorities say. Now, members of the family are linked to the KKK and some are accused of conspiring to burn black churches.

A Pattern of Racial Abuse

Alleging that the Haley's have been protected by what he calls Clarendon County's "criminal injustice system," Gardner has tried unsuccessfully to get federal and state authorities to investigate.

The most notorious member of the Haley family is Romeo, Lester's charismatic 49-year- old brother. He has a long string of convictions ranging from arson and assault with intent to kill to drug distribution. He has avoided long stays in prison, apparently by becoming a snitch for police, which has not endeared him to his kin. Romeo Haley declined to speak with a reporter. "He stated to me one day that he had been working (for previous sheriffs as an informant) for 20 years," Collins said. I told him I couldn't operate that way." Swilley, the former sheriff, says Romeo Haley "acted as an informant," but he denies ever having cut any deals with him. "I didn't trust him any further than I could throw him,"Swilley said.

But Collins says Romeo Haley has a pattern of cutting deals, and is now providing information on his family members to federal authorities in the church-burning investigation in return for leniency on charges of pre arms violation against him. When the Mt. Zion AME Church in Greeleyville burned down one night in June of last year, authorities first chalked it up as an electrical fire. Macedonia Baptist Church in nearby Bloomville burned down two nights later. An accident of nature, the fire chief said. Never mind that the pastor at Mt. Zion maintains the breaker box had been turned off and members at Macedonia say that there had been no lightning the night of their fire. And never mind that the pastor at Macedonia had already complained to the sheriff about finding Klan posters nailed to the church door and about the Klan holding disruptive rallies nearby during services. No serious probes were conducted.

Authorities arrested two of the arsonists within days of the fires; but-as it happened-that was just a coincidence. Timothy Welch, 23, and Christopher Cox, 22, members of Lester Haley's Klan chapter were brought in for questioning about the beating and stabbing of a black man who'd recently been attacked at random as he waited for a bus. Once in custody, Welch and Cox voluntarily confessed to the other crimes, officials said. In part because of potential civil rights violations but also because of the Haley connection, the sheriff immediately requested federal assistance, said Joe Floyd, who then was Collins' deputy chief and isn't now the Manning police chief. He said federal help was needed because he and Collins' didn't know who in their department might have had past relationships with the Haleys that could taint the investigation.

Floyd complained, however, that federal authorities did not take the case seriously until early this year, when the staggering number of church fires nationally prompted president Clinton to declare the arson investigations a top priority.

Cox and Welch told federal agents they had been ordered to set the fires by superiors in the Klan. They told authorities that Arthur Haley, Lester's 51-year old brother, had provided them with fuel and that Hubert Howell, Arthur's former brother-in-law showed them how to mix it. The two older men now are charged with participating in a conspiracy to burn black churches, among other crimes, and are being held without bail. Their trial had been scheduled for the next year.

Lester Haley, who says he dropped out of the Klan last year when all the trouble started, strenuously denies that his family members were involved. "Those boys done that on their own" he insists of the fires. He maintains the whole thing is a government frame up. The arrest of Ku Klux Klansmen for burning churches "lit up the whole county," Lester Haley said. "When they said one of those boys had a Klan card on him it got everybody's attention." In an unusual lawsuit filed last week, the Klan is accusing the sheriff's department of using illegal measures to drive the group out of the county. State level leaders of the Christian Knights of the Ku Klux Klan say sheriff's deputies violated the groups rights by aiming rifles at Klansmen during rallies, tearing down legally posted fliers and searching Klan members without cause. North Carolina Imperial Wizard Virgil Griffin and Grand Dragon Horace King of South Carolina are seeking $200,000 for emotional distress, injury to reputation and court costs. Collins denies the charges. Lester Haley says, however, that local authorities had a much more personal goal in mind than damaging the Klan. "When it comes down to it," he said, "they're targeting the Haley Family."

For the Rev. Terrance G. Macker, pastor of Mt Zion AME Church, the problems are far larger than one trouble-prone family. According to him and other local African Americans, racial inequity and intimidation are the norm in this part of South Carolina. This week, Gov. David Beasley even cited the animosities here as one of the reasons he believes the Confederate battle flag should no longer fly atop the state capitol, the last statehouse to still haul it up each day.

Noting that members of the same statewide Klan organization to which the Haleys belong were charged last month with shooting into a crowd of black people on a street in Pelion, S.C. Mackey said, "These types of things go on and no one in the past has been stepping up to say this cannot go on any longer." Mackey is helping to organize a march, now for April, that he hopes will bring people from around the country to Clarendon It's time to stand up and say in America that were not going to take it anymore," "I'm calling for the government and law enforcement of South Carolina to do their job Mackey said, he thinks his church was burned because of his outspokenness on racial and social issues. His only personal encounter with a member of the Haley family occurred last year, before the fires. He said that when he passed Arthur Haley on a sidewalk in downtown Greeleyville, Haley insulted him with a racial slur. "If that preacher said it he's a liar," Lester Haley said. He depicts Arthur as a kind-hearted Klansman who treated black people fairly.

But Manual Leroy Thompson, a 35 year-old African American whose car and workplace were torched in 1994 and 1995, said Arthur Haley threatened him during a sidewalk confrontation two years ago. Thompson said he approached Haley because he suspected him of putting up Ku Klux Klan posters at the recycling center where he worked.

The posters depicted a hooded Klansman and the caption: We're watching you." When Arthur Haley defiantly insisted he would put his posters up anywhere he wanted, Thompson said he told him, "You're not going to put them up on my job. If you do I'm going to pull them down" He said Haley responded by saying, "Boy, you don't know whom you're messing with." Then one morning Thompson arrived at work and found someone had burned the building down. Not long after that, someone set his car on fire.

After someone shot and killed his dog, he said, "I had to keep my children in the house. I couldn't let them go out in the yard to play at all." The federal indictment accuses Rowell of burning the building and Rowell and Haley of setting the car on fire. It also charges the men with other crimes, including burning down a migrant camp that was populated by Mexican farm workers and co-owned by Everett Haley, a wealthy farmer who is a distant cousin to Lester and part of the so-called "good Haley" family branch. Collins said the" bad Haley" brothers had a dispute with Everett Haley.

The brothers wanted to hunt deer with their dogs, but Everett wouldn't let them cross his land. A Judge denied bail because of supposed threats Arthur Haley made to a witness and because authorities found an arsenal of 13 rifles and shotguns in his possession. The Haleys insist that Arthur, who suffers from a number of ailments, including a nervous disorder runs in the family, chronic ear infections and kidney stones, is not receiving the proper medications in prison. When a reporter visited recently, one of Arthur's sisters and his wife were sitting around the telephone in tears because an expected call from Arthur in prison did not come.

"He's going to die," said Sue Nell Hinkle. "They're killing him." Lester insists that it is an injustice to keep his brother locked up, comparing it to the government siege on Waco and Ruby Ridge in which innocent people were killed. "They're doing the same thing here to my brother," he said. Across the street from Lester Haley lives a cousin who flies an upside-down U. S. Flag from a pole in his yard-a sign of his contempt for the government. Lester Haley said he shares that contempt for excessive government control. The people in power "do not give a damn about a poor white man or a poor black man," he said. "If they got the little office or money then the hell with you." "The little guy has a hard time," he said. A poor white man catches hell in this country. Poor Black people do, too. But a Black man will stick up for another Black man a lot quicker than a white person will." Such social inequities provide his rational for joining the Klan in 1994 and for agreeing to become its local leader.

67

Absalm Jones

Richard Allen

Founding Fathers of Black America included Absalom Jones, the first Black priest in the U.S., and Richard Allen, founder of AME (African Methodist Episcopal) church and the first Black Bishop. Allen and Jones were in the forefront of the movement that led to the founding of major African -Amreican institutions.

They also are his explanation for the troubles that seem to follow the family like a hungry hound. Lester Haley an ex-welder, who makes a living building patios and waterfront docks, said he went to his first Klan rally in 1994 "to see what it was all about.

"They were talking about the government... one thing and another," he said. He went back the next day. Then he attended another rally a month later. This time he got an application and joined. "It was kinda stupid in a way," he said of joining. "I thought I could make changes." When the local leader quit, Lester said he was one of the four or five members who kept the organization going.

Active membership grew to perhaps a dozen, he said. "It really didn't amount to anything. More or less just a get together." Haley insisted that he and his brother Arthur are not racists. "I look at a man as an individual. I don't look at a man for his color," he said. "The Klan wasn't just against Black people. It was against homosexuality, abortion, against a lot of government crap you have to put with."

During local rallies the speakers were high-level Klan leaders from Columbia, the state capital, and farther away. He said he asked the grand dragon to tone down the racist language and asked that the members not display guns. Then, to avoid offending the sensitivities of African Americans, he said he asked the sheriff not to bring Black deputies to monitor the rallies. "At the Klan meetings they used the N---- word a lot," he said. I told him they don't need to listen to that if they don't have to." Despite all of his supposed attempts to keep the peace, he acknowledges that his membership included troublemakers. When some members caught a black man tearing down directional signs pointing the way to one of their rallies, Haley said he had to restrain Christopher Cox to keep him from beating the man. Another time, Cox and another Klansman tried to pick a fight with a different black man on the street, he said. "I wouldn't let them do that." The black church is attacked frequently in Klan speeches, he said. "It's always the same. They go on and on about the blacks going to church to get information about how to vote and to get benefits and to get government cheese- that sort of thing." An impressionable young person might be influenced by the speeches, he acknowledged, but he insisted that no one was ever directed to destroy churches.

And no Haley family member, he insisted, ever played a part. "There wasn't any campaign to burn those churches," he said. "It looks like it became some kind of fad."55

It is very humiliating and depressing to have to endure the same demonic and devil-ish behavior from the same perpetrator for centuries. However, this is what people of African descent have had to endure while striving to exist here in America. It seems that the harassment on the part of the oppressor will never end. It is extremely disgusting that time after time we people who are the children of a group of people who were once slaves in this society would be continuously harassed and provoked to reach to the vile nature of the oppressors and resort to violence in retaliation to some gross violation, of our civil and human rights.

Due to the lack of the fear of GOD, the oppressor will go to any lengths to intimidate people of color. The oppressor will even destroy the house of prayer in an attempt to harass and put fear in the hearts of my people. The occurrences of church burnings in South Carolina has reached such proportions that it has struck in my hometown again. It has struck in the sanctuary where my niece was married in 1998, but this was in 2002, the twenty-first century.

THE CHESTER

News & Reporter

CHESTER COUNTY'S HOMETOWN NEWSPAPER FOR 133 YEARS

Wednesday, March 6, 2002

THREE SECTION

Issue. No. 19
Chester, South Carolina

Church fire was arson

Damage estimate to building more than $500,000

BY JAMEY O. SHEPHERD
Staff Writer

BLACKSTOCK — Arson has been ruled the cause of the fire that destroyed Antioch Baptist Church in Blackstock and a reward of at least $6,000 for information in the case is being offered.

The early Sunday morning fire destroyed the church sanctuary, built in 1934, and two additions, a social hall and Sunday school rooms. Estimated damage to the church is more than $500,000, according to Calvin Dukes, claims manager of Southern Mutual Church Insurance Co.

The Chester- County Sheriff's Department, the State Law Enforcement Division, the FBI and the ATF are investigating the case. Agents from the various agencies have been at the site, 2452 Boyd Road, at various times through Tuesday.

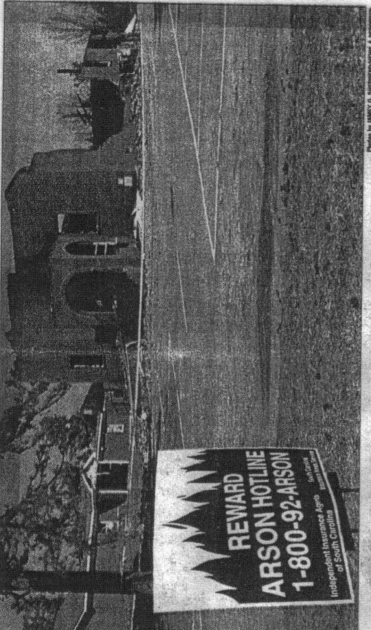

Photo by JAMEY O. SHEPHERD/A writer

Though the buildings were destroyed by fire, the pastor of Antioch Baptist Church says the church is alive and the congregation will have services this Sunday at another church. The Antioch congregation plans to rebuild at the site.

REWARD
ARSON HOTLINE
1-800-92-ARSON
Independent Insurance Agents of South Carolina

69

301

Though the buildings were destroyed by fire, the pastor of Antioch Baptist Church says the church is alive and the congregation will have services this Sunday at another church. The Antioch congregation plans to rebuild at the site.

Above, investigators search the fire rubble at Antioch Tuesday morning. At left is what's left of the entrance of the sanctuary, which was built in 1934 and was the oldest part of the church. This church was first organized in 1906; some current members have ancestors who were founders.

State Law Enforcement Division, the FBI and the ATF are investigating the case. Agents from the various agencies have been at the site, 2452 Boyd Road, at various times through Tuesday.

Sheriff Robby Benson released a statement Monday saying that SLED laboratory tests revealed that arson is the cause of the fire. The sheriff, however, declined to say anything specific about the investigation.

He wouldn't say what evidence led investigators to conclude arson was the cause and whether there are any suspects in the case. "I can't get into details," he said Tuesday.

Benson did say, however, that his deputies have stepped up patrols around area churches. One alarming thing he says his deputies have found is that many of the churches they have checked on have not had locked doors.

70

Antioch congregation 'devastated but not remorseful'

BY JAMEY O. SHEPHERD
Staff Writer

The man who has been pastor of Antioch Baptist Church for the past 14 years says some good has already come from the intentionally-set fire that destroyed his congregation's church buildings.

"This has helped us to realize that we have strength that we didn't know we had," explained the Rev. Paul F. Long.

When he first received the call of the fire Sunday morning, Long said he hoped it was a prank or an exaggeration. But when he first spotted the flames as he drove to the fire, Long said he knew how serious the fire was.

What wasn't damaged by fire was so damaged by water that it can't be repaired, Long said in an interview Tuesday. Gone are the sanctuary that was built in 1934, the fellowship hall that was added in 1986 and the $175,000 educational wing that was just completed last year.

"I'm devastated about it, but, believe it or not, I'm not remorseful," Long said, adding a bit later that his parishioners feel the same way.

"They have the same attitude — they are devastated but not remorseful."

That attitude, Long said, is a Christian attitude. Citing the Romans 12:19 passage in the Bible, Long said it is neither his place nor his congregation's place to seek vengeance against the one who caused the fire. That would be God's place, he said.

Long, however, said he would like to talk with whomever set the fire to serve as witness to the individual and to ask the individual to repent and seek forgiveness for his or her sins.

Antioch is not destroyed by the fire, Long stressed. "The building is gone but not the church, because the church is within us," he explained.

This Sunday, he said, the church will continue on with its services at the old Brown's Chapel AME Zion Church in Lowrys. Members there agreed to let Antioch members use their old facility until they can rebuild.

Long said offers to start a community fund-raiser for Antioch have been made, but he said his church wishes to spearhead its own fund-raisers. "We don't want to make it a community effort when it's something we can do ourselves," he said.

He declined to say how much insurance would help, but he described the church's insurance coverage as adequate.

Donations to help the church, he said, would certainly be appreciated, though.

They can be sent to Antioch Baptist Church, 103 Hope St., Chester, 29796.

71

303

Well, the only thing that I can say to the recent church burning incidents is that Frederick Douglas was right in that "A ship rotting at anchor meets no resistance, but when she sets sail on the sea, she has to buffet opposing billows. The enemies of the (African-American) see that he is making progress and they naturally wish to stop him and keep him in just what they consider to be his proper place. They who aspire to higher grades than those fixed for them by this society are scouted and scorned as upstarts for their presumptions."

Just as South Carolina has the history of being the state with the most stringent slave code laws, it is very appearant that it has the record of being the state with the most racist attacks on Black churches by whites in an a attempt to further promote social inequality, oppression and intimidate black people.

The denial of those who were obviously involved in the burning of those churches is proportional to the denial of hundreds of years of the same chagrins perpetrated by these same elements. Hence, as we close out the Twentieth Century the division of the races on the basis of color is very much apparent.

The saga of the burning of black churches is only yet another of the wrongs that people of color have had to endure in this American society, and in Africa, and Europe, as well. The plight of "Evil" that has been inflicted upon black people at the hands of whites have far reaching connotations that have affected the social and economic fabric not only of this American way of life but the relationship between the three principal countries involved.

"In 1998, at Goree Island, Senegal, West Africa, Standing at the transit point for millions of manacled Africans en route to slavery in the new world, President Clinton on Thursday, April 2, declared this picturesque isle's horrible past to be as much a part of American as African History. The visit to Goree Island was the crowning gesture of Clinton's 12-day African tour, which was as much about affirming Black Americans as it was about building new ties with Africa. "I am proud to be a president of a nation of many colors," Clinton said, addressing a group of residents of the small island and mainlanders from Dakar, the capital of Senegal, which is two miles away. Clinton paid special tribute to African Americans in his delegation and the rest of the 30 million Americans who are the descended from the people uprooted from Africa. "The long journey of African Americans proves that the spirit can never be enslaved," he said. The speech came after Clinton and First Lady Hillary Rodham Clinton toured the rouge-colored Slave house where millions of Africans ended their lives as free people and became captives of white men sending them across the ocean to an unknown future.

When they reached the "Door of no return," through which the millions of Africans were marched onto ships, the first couple paused, holding hands and staring somberly and silently out across the Atlantic Ocean. Above the door is written in French: "Door Of No Return."

72   The " Door Of No Return " Goree Island Near Senegal, West Africa

Through this door for a voyage without return they would go, their eyes fixed on the infinity of their suffering." As the pulsating sound of African drums filled the air, the President crouched down and went into the punishment cell for slaves who had balked at their fate. The ceiling was too low for an adult to stand. The curator showed the president a manacle and the 22-pound ball that was attached to it. "Some of the people weighted only 60-kilos (l32-pounds), and they were carrying this around," Clinton remarked.

Stopping to talk to several dozen American children touring the site, Clinton said: "When you get home, tell everybody else what you saw." After walking around, Clinton joined several islanders and Dakar residents who had been listening to bongo drums and enjoying a cool sea breeze as they waited for him in the dusty square near the docks. "In 1776, when our nation was founded on the promise of freedom as God's right to all human beings, a new building was dedicated here on Goree Island to the selling of human beings in bondage to America," Clinton said, referring to a slave house.

"Goree Island is, therefore, as much a part of our history as a part of African history." Untold numbers of men, women and children from what are now Nigeria, Cameroon, Ghana, Senegal, Benin and Congo passed through Goree on the way to the U. S., the West Indies and Latin America. Over the centuries, the island's ownership was disputed by the Dutch, Portuguese, French and British-all traded in human beings. "We cannot push time backward through the door of no return. We have lived our history," Clinton added gravely. But what can be done, he stressed, is to continue to address the legacy of slavery that haunts America and move forward to a new partnership between the United States and Africa after decades of neglect.

"I pledge to the partnership based on people of Africa that we will reach over this ocean to build a new friendship and respect."

Throughout his six-nation odyssey, Clinton focused on the positive stories of an Africa that he says is undergoing a renaissance. His goal, he said, was to replace America's dismal, stereotypical view of Africa with a picture of a thriving, diverse continent full of opportunity." I have seen the faces of Africa's future," he said, praising those whom he had met on his African travels. Clinton, who arrived in Washington late Thursday, said earlier in the day that he would never forget the strength he saw in South African President Nelson Mandela when visiting his old prison cell on Robben Island; the promise in the children of Uganda who are now offered education because of the Democratic progress in their country; the courage of genocide survivors he met in Rwanda; or the warmth extended to him by hundreds of thousands of Ghanaians who greeted him almost two weeks ago in Accra.

The President was not the only one moved by the Goree trip. The delegation that traveled with him, members of congress and his administrations many of them African Americans stopped to pray, holding hands in a circle, after leaving the slave house.

The Rev. Jesse Jackson, who led the prayer, broke into tears. "I found myself feeling a combination of pain and anger and wondering about man's inhumanity to man. I know it was way back then, but how could it have happened?" Asked Rep. Maxine Waters (D - Los Angeles) after touring the slave house. When the Rev. Jackson asked us to pray, I prayed to God to take away my anger and give me a "Forgiving spirit." Waters, who journeyed throughout Africa with the president, said she thought Clinton's trip to Goree Island was vital for the message it would send to African-Americans who suffered from racism and feel a "Lack of Wholeness" and to those Americans who deny that slavery's legacy still plagues U. S. Society. "'It's important to come to Goree Island so people can see this as real and not just a figment of our imagination," Waters added. Clinton's visit also was significant to the Senegalese, who saw it as an acknowledgment of wrong. "Goree reminds us of the humiliation which man inflicted on his neighbor," President Abdou Diouf said in French before introducing Clinton to the crowd. "We will never forget," he said, and then added in English: "Forgive, not forget."

Demba Diene, 37, a waiter, said he would never forget this day. "It's very important because it will remind the world of the horror of slavery" Diene said. Thursday was not the first time on this trip that Clinton had talked about slavery. In Uganda, he said European Americans were wrong to profit from slavery and included it in a list of America's sins against Africa. That declaration and his speech Thursday stopped short of the formal apology that some African-Americans have sought."56

I feel that an apology to black Americans for the hundreds of years of slavery and injustices against our fore parents would be an insult and would only be like pouring salt on an open wound. Moreover, an apology could not make up for the murdering and genocide of our people. I will try to forgive, and live, but I will never forget!
To be sure, America does owe the African American people a debt that cannot be paid and any kind of monetary reparations would only be a prerequisite for an immeasurable debt owed for the atrocious sins committed against our people. I, too, believe that based on the precedent established in the so-called "Jewish Holocaust," of "unjust Enrichment", that this procedure should be applied here too in regard to reparations for people who are the descendants of the "World's Greatest Holocaust," The "African-American Holocaust."

1). Lerone Bennett, Jr., <u>Before The Mayflower, A History Of Black America</u>, Penguin Books and Johnson Publishing Co., New York, 1961, 1969, 1988, pp. 315

2). Bennett, <u>Before The Mayflower, Ibid.</u> pp. 313

3). Bennett, <u>Before The Mayflower, Ibid.</u> pp. 314

4). Bennett, <u>Before The Mayflower, Ibid.</u> pp. 319

5). Pat Waters, <u>Down To Now</u>, Pantheon Books, New York, 1971, pp. 83

6). Bennett, <u>Before The Mayflower, Ibid.</u> pp. 322

7). Taylor Branch, <u>Parting The Waters-America In The King Years (1954 -1963</u>, Touchstone Books, Simon and Schuster, Inc., New York, London, Toronto, Sydney, Tokyo, 1988, pp. 415-416

8). Branch, <u>Ibid.</u> pp. 283

9). Bennett, <u>Before The Mayflower, Ibid.</u> pp. 322-323

10). Stephen B. Oats, <u>Let The Trumpets Sound-The Life of Martin Luther King, Jr.,</u> Mentone Books, New American Library, New York, 1982, Pp. 171-172

11). Branch, <u>Ibid.</u> pp. 283

12). <u>The New York Times</u>, June 10, 1963, pp.20-c

13). Waters, <u>Ibid.</u> pp. 110

14). <u>The New York Times, Ibid.</u> pp. 29-c

15). <u>The New York Times, Ibid.</u> pp. 19-c

16). Emma Gelders Stern, "<u>I Have A Dream</u>", Alfred A. Knopf, Inc., New York, 1965, pp. 191

17). Stern, <u>Ibid.</u> pp. 193

18). Whitney M. Young, Jr., "<u>To Be Equal</u>," McGraw-Hill Publishing co., New York, 1964, pp. 55

19). Wallace Mendelson, "<u>Discrimination</u>", Princeton Hall Publishing co., New York, 1962, pp. 6

20). Michael Harrington, "<u>The Other America,</u>" Penguin Books, Baltimore, MD. 1962, pp. 48-49

21). Oats, <u>Ibid.</u> pp. 252-255

22). Oats, <u>Ibid.</u> pp. 256-257

23). Lotte Hoskins, "<u>I Have A Dream</u>"-<u>The Quotations Of Martin Luther King, Jr.,</u> Grosset, Dunlap and Droke House Publishers, Inc., New York, 1968, pp. 115-116

24). Hoskins, <u>Ibid.</u> pp. 115

25). Hoskins, <u>Ibid.</u> pp. 1

26). Stern, <u>Ibid.</u> pp. 198

27). <u>The New York Times, Ibid.</u> pp. 19-c

28). Peter Goldman, <u>Civil Rights: The Challenge Of The Fourteenth Amendment</u>, Coward-McCann, Inc., New York, 1970, pp. 13

29). Oats, <u>Ibid.</u> pp. 363

30). James Haskins, <u>The Life And Death Of Martin Luther King, Jr.,</u> Lothrop, Lee, and Sheppard Co., New York, 1977, pp. 98

31). Hoskins, <u>Ibid.</u> pp. 146

32). Haskins, <u>Ibid.</u> pp. 98-99

33). Michael Lee Lanning (Lt. Col.-Ret.), <u>The African-American Soldier-From Crypus Attucks To Colin Powell</u>, Birch Lane Press Books, Carol Publishing Group, Secaucus, New Jersey, 1977, pp. 255

34). Jack Rummel, <u>Malcolm X- Black Americans Of Achievement</u>, Chelsea House Publishers, New York, Philadelphia, 1989, pp. 256

35). Alex Haley, <u>The Autobiography Of Malcolm X</u>, Ballantine Books, New York, 1964, 1965, 1999, pp. 172

36). Haley, <u>Ibid.</u> pp. 174-187

37). Haley, <u>Ibid.</u> pp. 195

38). Haley, <u>Ibid.</u> pp. 198-199

39). Haley, <u>Ibid.</u> pp. 202-206

40). Haley, <u>Ibid.</u> pp. 208

41). Cornell West, <u>RACE MATTERS</u>, Vintage Books, Random House, Inc., New York, 1993, pp. 136-137

42). West, <u>Ibid.</u> pp. 151

43). Goldman, <u>Ibid.</u> pp. 96

44). Goldman, <u>Ibid.</u> pp. 109

45). Goldman, <u>Ibid.</u> pp. 113

46). Lanning, <u>Ibid.</u> pp. 255

47). Lanning, <u>Ibid.</u> pp. 257

48). Lanning, <u>Ibid.</u> pp. 252

49). Lanning, <u>Ibid.</u> pp. 278-279

50). James M. Washington, <u>A Testament Of Hope-The Essential Writings And Speeches Of Martin Luther King, Jr.,</u> Harper-Collins Publishing

Co., New York, 1986, pp. 245-252

51). Robert Jakoubek, <u>Martin Luther King, Jr.-Civil Rights Leader</u>, Chelsea House Publishers and Grolier Incorporated, Danbury, Connecticut, 1989, pp. 134-137

52). Oats, <u>Ibid</u>. pp. 246

53). West, <u>Ibid</u>. pp. 157-158

54). "<u>JET MAGAZINE,</u>" A Johnson Publication, June 8, 1987, pp. 14

55). <u>The Los Angeles Times</u>, November 30, 1996, pp. A-18, A-20

56). <u>The Los Angeles Times</u>, April 3, 1998, pp.1 & pp. A-16

CONFLICTING RELIGIOUS BELIEFS AND PRACTICES

In researching the background of the various people who would promote such exploitations of others for centuries, it is almost inconceivable to cite the urgency and dire base nature of such proponents. More importantly, when one looks for the manner of a people who would indulge in such "Crimes" as cruel as the slave trade, it is extremely necessary to find the exact motives and cite the desperation of such a people. To fully understand the nature of such a people one must first identify the origin of his existence. Professor Arthur Koestler traces the origins of such a people to the Caucasus Mountains.

"About the time when Charlemagne was crowned Emperor of the West, the eastern confines of Europe between the Caucasus and the Volga were ruled by a Jewish state, Known as the Khazar Empire. At the peak of its power, from the Seventh to the Tenth Centuries AD, it played a significant part in shaping the destinies of mediaeval, and consequently of modern Europe.

The country of the Khazars, a people of Turkisk stock, occupied a strategic key position at the vital gateway between the Black Sea and the Caspian Sea, where the great Eastern powers of the period confronted each other. It acted as a buffer protecting Byzantium against invasions by the lusty barbarian men of the northern Steppes- Bulgars, Magyars, Pechenegs, etc.- and later, the Vikings and the Russians.

The Khazar country... lay across the natural line of advance of the Arabs. Within a few years of the death of Muhammad (632 AD) the armies of the Caliphate, sweeping northward through the wreckage of two empires and carrying all before them, reached the great mountain barrier of the Caucasus. This barrier once passed, the road lay open to the lands of Eastern Europe. As it was, on the line of the Caucasus the Arabs met the forces of an organized military power, which effectively prevented them from extending their conquests in this direction. The wars of the Arabs and the Khazars, which lasted more than a hundred years, though little is known of them, thus have considerable historical importance. The victorious Muslims were met and held by the forces of the Khazar Kingdom. It can scarcely be doubted that but for the existence of the Khazars in the region north of the Caucasus, Byzantium, the bulwark of European civilization in the east, would have found itself outflanked by the Arabs, and the history of Christendom and Islam might well have been very different from what we know. It is perhaps not surprising, given these circumstances that in 732 AD - after a resounding Khazar victory over the Arabs - the future Emperor Constantine V married a Khazar princess.

73

The Caucasus Mountains

In due time their son became the Emperor Leo IV, known as Leo the Khazar. Ironically, the last battle in the war, 737 AD, ended in a Khazar defeat. But by that time the impetus of the Muslim Holy War was spent, the Caliphate was rocked by internal dissensions, and the Arab invaders retraced their steps across the Caucasus without having gained a permanent foothold in the north, whereas the Khazars became more powerful then they had previously been.

A few yeas later, probably 740 AD, the king, his court and the military ruling class embraced the Jewish faith, and Judaism became the state religion of the Khazars. This investigation cannot go into the problems, but we shall, however, look to the remarks it has of an ethnically "Non-Jewish" people. Moreover, that this official conversion - in defiance of Christianity by Byzantium, the Muslim influence from the east, and in spite of the political pressure of these two powers - to a religion which had no support from any political power, has come as a surprise to all concerned with the Khazars, and cannot be considered as accidental, but must be regarded as a sign of the independent policy pursued by that kingdom. Thus, the general picture that emerges from this investigation is that of a migration of the Khazars into those regions of Eastern Europe- Russia and Poland- where at the dawn of the modern age, the greatest concentrations of Jews were found. This provides evidence that the Eastern European Jews, and, hence, world Jewry - must be of Khazar, and not of Schemitic origin. The apprehension of the release of this information is quite notable and obviously to avoid upsetting the believers in the dogma of the "Chosen Race."

The Turkish-speaking Karaites (a fundamentalist Jewish sect) have affirmed a connection with the Khazars. There seems to be a considerable amount of evidence attesting to the continued presence in Europe of descendants of the Khazars. Thus, in quantitative terms, these ramifications have very significant implications. The descendants of these settlements of Khazars-those who stayed where they were, those who emigrated to the United States and to other countries, and those who went to Israel-now constitute the large majority of world Jewry. The fact that the large majority of surviving Jews in the world today is of Eastern European descent, and thus of Khazar origin. Therefore, this being established means that their ancestors came not from the Jordan but from the Volga, not from Canaan but from the Caucasus, once believed to be the cradle of the Aryan race; and that genetically they are more closely related to the Hun, Uigur and the Magyar than to the seed of Abraham, Isaac, and Jacob. Therefore, in this case the term "Anti-Semitism" becomes void of meaning and the perpetrators of "History's Greatest Fraud" and lie is disclosed.

As to the Khazars, an Eye-witness Arab chronicler writes, "they are to the north of the inhibited earth towards the 7th clime, having over their heads the constellation of the plough. Their land is cold and wet. Accordingly, their complexions are white, their eyes blue, their hair flowing and predominantly reddish, their bodies large and their nature's cold. Their general aspect is wild."

In the Book of Job in the Holy Bible the Prophet describes these detestable creatures in detail. He says that their father who was Japhete, Noah's third son who was younger than his forefather, Shem, was the most detestable creatures of the Lord. (JOB: 30) But now they that are younger then I have me in derision, whose fathers I would have disdained to set with the dogs of my flock.

Yea, whereto might the strength of their hands profit me, in whom old age was perished?

For want and famine they were solitary; fleeing into the wilderness in former time desolate and waste.

Who cut up mallows by the bushes, and juniper roots for their meat.

They were driven forth from among men, (they cried after them as after a thief;)

To dwell in the cliffs of the valleys, in caves of the earth, and in the rocks.

Among the bushes they brayed; under the nettles they were gathered together.

They were children of fools, Yea, children of base men: they were viler than the earth.

And now am I their song, Yea, I am their byword.

They abhor me, they flee far from me, and spare not to spit in my face.

A Georgian chronicler, echoing an ancient tradition, identifies them with the hosts of "Gog and Magog"- wild men with hideous faces, and the manners of wild beasts, eaters of blood." An Armenian writer refers to the horrible multitude of Khazars With insolent, broad lashless faces and long falling hair, like women. Yakubi, A Ninth Century Arab historian, traces the origin of the Khazars back to Japheteth, the third son of Noah. It is also the origins of the Huns, Alans, Avars, Bulgars, Magyars, Bashkirs, Burtas, Sabirs, Uigurs, Saragurs, Onogurs, Utigurs, Kutrigurs, Tarniaks, Kotragars, Khabars, Zabenders, Pechenegs, Ghuzz, Kumans, Kipchaks, and dozens of other people who at one time or another in the lifetime of the Khazar Kingdom passed through the turnstiles of these migratory playgrounds. All that can be said is that the Khazars were a group who erupted from the Asian Steppes, probably in the 5th Century of our era. Most likely the word is derived from the Turkish root "Gaz" or" to wander, "meaning "nomadic."[1]

They had no religion, which would link them to God, nor are they guided by reason; they do not worship anything. The traveler could not get over their dirtiness.

They do not wash themselves after defecating or urinating? Nor do they bathe after seminal pollution or on other occasions. They refuse to have anything to do with water, particularly in winter...." When their leader took off his luxurious coat to don a new coat the mission had brought him, they saw his under clothes were fraying apart from dirt, for it is their custom never to take off the garment they wear close to their bodied until it disintegrates. Another group shaves their beards and eat their lice.

They search the folds of their under garments and crack the lice with their teeth. It is the custom of the king of the Khazars to have twenty-five wives. Thus, Khazaria was by no means isolated from the civilized world; compared to its tribal neighbors in the north it was a cosmopolitan country. Some are of the opinion that "Gog and Magog" are the Khazars. (Gen: 10), (1Chr.1: 1-7).

The religion of the Hebrews had exercised a profound influence on the creed of Islam, and it had been a basis for Christianity; as at the beginning of the Eighth Century the world had been polarized by Christianity and Islam. The Khazar Empire represented a third force, which had proved equal to either of them, both as an adversary and an ally. But it could only maintain its independence by accepting neither Christianity nor Islam - for either choice would have automatically subordinated it to the authority of the Roman emperor or the Caliph of Baghdad. Thus, the Khazar leaders were motivated by Judaism because it was a reputable religion with "sacred books" which both Christians and Mohammedans respected; it elevated him above the "Heathen Barbarians," and secured him against the interference of the Caliph or Emperor. But he did not adopt along with circumcision, the intolerance of the Jewish cult. He allowed the mass of his people to abide in their "Heathendom" and worship their idols.

The people under Khazar suzerainty included the Bulgars (Bulgarians), Bursas, Ghuzz (French), Magyars (Hungarians), the Gothics (Germans), and the Greek Colonies of the Crimea, and the Slavonic in the Northwestern woodlands. They were, in respect to their language and constitution, the most repulsive of men. Their language sounded entirely like the croaking of frogs. They were dirty in appearance, contemptible in manners, base in nature. The general characteristics of the Ghuzz, and other peoples, were a remarkable mixture of (Heathenism) and savagery. Their women wear no veils in the presence of their men or strangers. Nor, do the women cover any parts of their bodies in the presence of people. One day our traveler stayed at the place of the Ghuzz, and were sitting around; his wife was also present. As we conversed the woman uncovered her private parts and scratched them, as we all saw it. We covered our faces and said, "May GOD forgive me!"

The husband laughed and said "we uncover it in your presence so that you may see and restrain yourselves; but it cannot be attained. This is better than when it is covered up and yet attainable." Adultry is alien to them; yet when they discover that someone is an adulterer, they split him in two halves.

This they do by bringing together two branches of trees, tie him to the branches and then let both trees go so that the man tied to them is torn in two. All in all, it is not an engaging picture. The travelers' contempt for the "Barbarians" was profound. Aroused by their uncleanliness, and indecent exposure, and the savagery of their punishment without indignation. Among the Volga Bulgars, Iln Fadlan found a strange custom. When they observe a man who excels through quick-wittedness and knowledge, they say, "for this one is more befitting to serve our lord." They seize him, put a rope around his neck, and hang him on a tree, where he is left until he rots away.

It is difficult to form a mental picture of these bizarre people whose savagery sticks out even in that savage age. The Arab chroniclers were so baffled by them ... and utterly disgusted by the filth and obscene habits that the following passage on the accounts of the "RUS" occurs just before his earlier quotes on the Khazars: "In the morning a servant girl brings a basin full of water to the master of the household; he rinses his face and hair in it, spits and blows his nose into the basin, which the girl then hands on to the next person, who does likewise, until all who are in the house have used the basin to blow their noses, spit and wash their face and hair in it."

About the pagan religion the traveler asked through his interpreter one of the natives the reason for his worshipping a wooden penis, and notes down his reply: 'Because I issued from something similar and know of no other creator who made me.' He then adds that 'some of them believe in twelve deities, a God for winter, another for summer, one for the rain, one for the wind, one for the trees, one for men, one for the horse, one for water, one for the night, one for the day, a God of death and one for the earth; while that God who dwells in the sky is the greatest among them, but takes counsel with the others and thus all are contented with each other's doings. We have seen a group among them which worships snakes, and a group which worships fish, and a group which worships cranes."[2]

"It is the custom of the King of the Khazars to have twenty-five wives, each of the wives is the daughter of a king who owes him allegiance. He takes them by consent or by force. He has sixty girls for concubines. Ibn Fadlan's travel report, as far as it is preserved, contained the words: "The Khazars and their King are all Jews. The Bulgars and all their neighbors are subject to him. They treat him with worshipful obedience. Some are of the opinion that "Gog and Magog" are the Khazars."[3]

The Asian armies- Mongolians, Chinese, and Persians- were unquestionably the masters of the art of war during the medival ages and evil in the world as such. Hence, it was not just ignorance that sustained ideas of a land populated with monsters and fanatic beings; they were also given credence by the writings of early Christian scholars. St. Augustine had written about the existence of monsters, declaring their creation to have been an important part of Gods great plan, so that man would not be perplexed by the birth of the malformed or insane.

Under the authority of Christian teachings the regions to the east also became associated with certain Biblical localities, like terrestrial paradise, the land inhabited by "Gog and Magog" - the latter being the land beyond Alexander's Gate (The Derbent Pass in the Caucasus Mountains) where Alexander IV is said to have imprisoned two foul giants, "Gog and Magog." According to the Book of Revelations, they would be released by "Satan" to destroy Jerusalem and bring destruction upon the world."[4]

"Our traveler was also utterly disgusted by the filthy and obscene habits of the "Russ", whom he met at the Volga in the land of the Bulgars. "They are the filthiest creatures of the Lord." Not one of them goes to satisfy a natural need alone. Each one of them has a sword because of lack of security and treachery among them, for if a man has even a little wealth, his own brother and friend who is with him, covet it, and seek to kill and despoil him."[5]

Thus, in a comparative analysis of the customs of the people who inhibit the African continent to the people who inhibit the region of Eastern Europe during the same period, the contrasting levels of "Barbarianism" is unparallel.

"In the first century; AD. the Chinese had drove these disagreeable Hun neighbors Westward, and thus, started one of those periodic avalanches which swept for many centuries from Asia toward the West. From the Fifth Century onward, many of these Westward bound people were called by their "Generic" name of "TURKS."[6]

Though the Khazar courts conversion was no doubt politically motivated, it would still be absurd to imagine that they embraced overnight, blindly; a religion whose tenants were unknown to them. In fact, however, they had been well acquainted with Jews and their religions for at least a century before the conversion, through the continued influx of refugees from religious persecution in Byzantium, and to a lesser extent, from countries in Asia Minor conquered by the Arabs."[7]

"Khazaria became a relatively civilized country among the "Barbarians" of the north, yet, not committed to either of the militant creeds, and so it became a natural haven for the periodic exodus of Jews under Byzantine rule, threatened by forced conversion and other pressures. Persecution in varied forms had started with Justinian 1 (527-565), and assumed particularly vicious forms under Heraclius in the Seventh Century, Leo III in the Eighth, Basil and Leo IV in the Ninth, Romans in the Tenth. Thus, Leo III, who ruled during two decades immediately preceding the Khazar conversion to Judaism attempted to end anomaly (of the tolerated status of Jews), at one blow by ordering all of his Jewish subjects to be baptized. Although the implementation of the order seemed to have been rather ineffective, it led to the flight of a considerable number of Jews from Byzantium. Anyone refusing to accept his or her erroneous belief was placed in an olive mill under a wooden press, and squeezed in a way olives is squeezed in the mill."[8]

"The reason for the conversion to Judaism of the King of the Khazars, who had previously been a "Pagan," is as follows: He had "adopted" Christianity. Then he recognized its' falsehood and discussed this matter which greatly worried him, with one of his high officials. The latter said to him: O'King, those in possession of "Sacred Scriptures" fall into three groups. Summond them and ask them to state their case, then follow the one who is in possession of the truth. So he sent to the Christians for a Bishop. Now there was with the King a Jew, skilled in argument, who engaged him in disputation. He asked the Bishop: "What do you say of "Moses," the son of Amram, and the "Torah," which was revealed to him? The Bishop replied: "Moses is a prophet and the "Torah" speaks the truth." Then the Jew said to the King: "He has already admitted the truth of my creed. Ask him now what he believes in. So the King asked him and he replied: "I say that "Jesus," the Messiah is the son of Mary, he is the word, and he has revealed the mysteries in the name of God." Then said the Jew to the King of the Khazars: "He preaches a doctoring of which I know not, while he accepts my propositions."

But the Bishop was not strong enough in producing evidence. Then the king asked for a Muslim, and they sent him a scholarly, clever man, who was good at arguments. But the Jew hired someone who poisoned him on the journey, and he died. And the Jew succeeded in winning the King for his faith, so that he embraced Judaism. The actual conversion of the Khazars took place through an "exchange of letters" in Hebrew between Hasdai lbn Shaprut, the Jewish Chief Minister of the Caliph of Cordoba, and [Joseph], King of the Khazars around (954-961), AD. Joseph, "not being of Jewish descent," belonged, of course, to none of the "Twelve Tribes," provides a genealogy of a different kind. King Josephs' lineage is through his ancestor "King Bulan," a conqueror who drove out idolaters and sorcerers from his land.

Subsequently, an Angel appeared to King Bulan in his dreams, exhorting him to worship the only true God, and promising him that in exchange he would bless and multiply King Bulan's offspring, and deliver his enemies into his hand, and make his kingdom last to the end of the worlds. This, of course, is implied by the story of the "Covenant" in Genesis; and it implies that the Khazars, too, claimed the status of "The Chosen Race," who made their own covenant with the Lord, even though "They were "not" descended from Abraham's seed." Joseph also relates how the Angel appeared once more to the dreaming King, and bade him to build a place of worship in which the Lord may dwell, for: 'the sky and the skies above are not large enough to hold me." As a result of a series of letters, King Bulan's fame spread to other countries, the Kingdom of "Edom" and the King of the Ishmaelim. Joseph then proceeds to provide a genealogy of his people. Though a fierce "Jew-ish" Nationalist, and proud of wielding the Sceptre of Judah; he cannot, and does not, claim for them Schemitic descent; he traces their ancestry not to Shem, but to Noah's third son, Japheth; or more precisely to Japheth's grandson, Togarma, the ancestor of all Turkish people.

We have found in the family registry's of our fathers, that Torgarma had ten sons, and the names of their offspring are as follows: Vigur, Dursu, Avars, Huns, Basilii, Tamiakh, Khazars, Zagora, Bulgars, Sabir. We are the sons of Khazar, the Seventh...."

After the genealogy, [Joseph] mentions briefly some military conquests by his ancestors, which carried them as far as the Danube. From this day onward, [Joseph] continues, "The Lord gave him strength and aided him; he had himself and his followers "circumcised" and sent for the "Jewish Sages" who taught him the "Law'" and explained to him the "Commandments." There followed more boasts about military victories, conquered nations, etc."9

"Thus, Khazaria was very much "on the map." A warrior nation, of "Turkish Jews" seemed as strange as a "Circumcised Unicorn." By 864 AD, there appeared an expose' that stated "There exist people under the sky in regions where no Christian can be found, whose name is 'Gog and Magog', and who are Huns; among them is one called "Gazari" who are circumcised, and observe Judaism in its' entirety."10

"Toward the end of the first millennium, the most important settlements of Western European Jews were in France and the Rhineland. Some of these communities had probably been founded in Roman days, between "The Destruction of Jerusalem" and the decline of the Roman Empire. [Jews] had settled in many of the greater cities under its rule, and were later on reinforced by immigrants from Italy, France, and the Mediterranean. One group even crossed the English Channel, invited by "William the Conqueror" because he needed capital and enterprise. This tiny [Jew-ish] community in England played a leading part in the country's economic establishment- much more so than its opposite number in Poland; Yet, in contrast to Poland, it could not rely on a network of [Jew-ish] small towns to provide it with a mass - basis of humble craftsmen, of lower middle-class artisans and workmen, caterers and innkeepers; it had no roots in the people. The Jews of France and Germany faced the same obstacles. The dreary tale always starts with a honeymoon and ends with bloodshed.

In the beginning the Jews are pampered with special charters, privileges, and favors. They are "Personae Gratae" "because they alone have the secret of how to keep the wheels of the economy turning." The entire economic commerce of Western Europe was largely in [Jew-ish] hands, not excluding "The Slave Trade."11

"Due to the mass expulsion of these "CONVERTED JEWS" from England, Portugal, and Spain, Charles Town, (South Carolina), became a sanctuary from the late 1600s for Sephardim and other Jewish refugees from Europe. The city eventually contained the largest community of [Jews] of any urban settlement in colonial North America."12 "Today, most of those who claim [Jew-ish] descent now make up the modern world Jewry in the United States, and Israel."13

The greatest present day conflict from an international perspective is the one that persists between the modem day Jews and the Palestinians in the Middle East.

This "Crisis" between the two factions is largely viewed by African-Americans as not really having any bearing on their well being.

However, for the purpose of argument and perhaps some clarity and validity on the true "Indigenous" people of and what has become such an unclear situation in that region, here is another view.

"Originally all Hamites and Schemites (or Semites) were Black people. Abraham was a Black Shemite and a descendant of Schem. The name of Abraham was Abram before he was referred to as Abraham. The three Hebrew patriarchs were Abraham, Isaac, and Jacob. This Jacob begot twelve sons, who later fathered the twelve tribes of Israel. Abraham was the father not only of the Hebrew-Israelite nation, but also of the Arab nation. Abraham, Isaac, Jacob, and the Twelve Tribes of "Israel" were all black people.

After Joseph was sold down into Egypt as a slave, we find in the forty-second chapter of Genesis that he has become the Viceroy of Egypt. Joseph's ten brothers came into Egypt (Egypt is in Africa) to buy corn because a famine was in the land. All newcomers who came into Egypt had to buy corn from Joseph; but when Joseph's ten brothers came to Africa they did not recognize him. They did not recognize him because Joseph had grown up and the Egyptians were a black people like the sons of Jacob. Jacobs's ten sons considered Joseph to be another Black Egyptian. This is true because the ten brothers returned and reported to their father: "The man who is the Lord of the land spoke roughly to us...."' Moreover, if Joseph had been Caucasian he would have aroused the curiosity of his brothers very rapidly. Furthermore, in many places in the Bible we find the sons of Jacob and the later Israelites taking Black Canaanite women for wives. If the ancient Israelites were not originally Black, they would be after the intermingling with Black Canaanite men and women.

When the king (Pharaoh) of Egypt promulgated an edict to cast all the Hebrew male babies into the Nile River, Miriam and her mother hid the baby "Moses" in a basket alongside the river. Meanwhile, Pharaoh's daughter came down to the Nile to wash herself, and she saw the basket and the baby, Moses. Pharaoh's daughter knew that the baby was a Hebrew and she adopted him. If Moses had been a Caucasian baby, it would have been difficult to conceal him from her father's anger. In the period of Moses, the Black Egyptians enslaved Black Jews. Finally, to further prove that the Jews were a Black skin people is the Leprosy laws, written in the thirteenth Chapter of Leviticus. The strangest and most amazing phenomena concerning Biblical leprosy were that the skin turned white. These laws of Leprosy were given to the nation of Israel and they could not apply to a white nation."[14]

"In the year 331, BC. Alexander the Great defeated the Persian Emperor, Darius, at the Battle of Gaugamela and a new master emerged on the World stage and transformed the history and culture of three continents.

However, Alexander died in the prime of his life at the age of thirty-two because of debauchery and intoxication. Before the death of Alexander, his desire was to establish a Eurasia. His scheme was to amalgamate the Greeks with the Asians. This was implemented by the widespread marriage of his troops with [colored] women of the east.

After the death of Alexander the Great, his vast empire was divided among his generals. Ptolemy received Egypt and Seleucus received Asia. As time elapsed, there was constant war between these two dynasties. By the year 198 B. C., the descendants of General Seleucus had their capital in Syria, just north of Palestine. In the same year the Seleucid Dynasty in Syria compelled Egypt to give up Palestine, the land of the Jews. The king of Syria at this time was Antiochus III. When Antiochus IV usurped the throne in Syria (175-163 B. C.), he entertained the thought of uniting Alexander's empire. This meant the conquest of Egypt. However, the province that bordered on Egypt was Palestine, which stood in his way. At this time, the Jews would not accept Greek culture; nevertheless, Antiochus was determined to Helenize the Jews.

The army of Antiochus marched into Palestine to support Menelaus, the leader of the pro-Syrian party, as a result, many Jews were killed; others escaped to the hills and to Egypt. Only those Jews that supported Antiochus' policies remained in Jerusalem. An edict was promulgated interdicting the observance of the holidays, the Sabbath, and circumcision. A statue of Jupiter was erected in the Holy Temple above the altar. To this statue the people brought the sacrifices of pig meat, the animal that is an abomination to the Jews. Because of this religious persecution, many other Jews fled into African countries such as Egypt, Ethiopia, and Cyrenaica (Libya). Throughout the last twenty-five hundred years, the main factors that have contributed to the social migration of the Jews were wars, religious persecution, and commerce. All these factors mere operating and gave rise to the African-Jewish population.

In the year 65 B. C. the Roman armies under General Pompey captured Jerusalem. In 70 A.D. General Vespasian and his son, Titus put an end to the Jewish state with great slaughter. During the period of the military governors of Palestine, many outrages and atrocities were committed against the residue of the people. During the period from Pompey to Julius, it has been estimated that over 1,000,000 Jews fled into Africa, fleeing from Roman persecution and slavery. The slave markets were full of black Jewish slaves. "And the Lord shall scatter thee among all people, from the one end of the earth even onto the other. And there thou shall serve other gods, which neither thou nor thy fathers have known, even wood and stone" (Deut. 28:64). This prophecy and all the residue of the prophecies contained in Deuteronomy 28: 15-68 befell the Black Jews after they disobeyed the laws of God. Many nations transported the Jews into slavery, and the sons of Israel transmigrated to every continent. It is certain that the Jews had migrated all across North Africa by the second century. Some scholars fix the date earlier than this.

The pagans and the Romans attacked the Jews indiscriminately, both the Jewish soldiers and the uninvolved peaceful population, without mercy. As a result of the merciless attack, many Jews fled to those parts of northwest Africa known as Tunisia, Algeria, Morocco, and Mauritania. Many other Jews fled to the areas where Rome did not have any jurisdiction. This was to the region of the South, the Sahara Desert and the Sudan.

Such is the explanation of how the Sahara Desert first acquired Jewish people toughened by a fighting tradition and possessed of physical characteristics (Blacks), which, it is said, still make them approximate very closely the original Jewish population of Palestine.

At the beginning of the 6th century these Jews are found in Spain before the Mohammedan conquest. Spain is known to the Jews as the classical land of crypto-Judaism, because they feigned Christianity but practiced Jewish ritual in secret. As early as the Roman period, the Jews of Spain had been large in number and influential. Many of them claimed to be the descendants of noble Jews in Jerusalem who had been carried into exile by General Titus.

In 616 A. D. the big shock came; the King ordered the "Baptism" of all Jews in his domain, under the penalty of expulsion and the loss of all their property. According to Catholic authorities, ninety thousand embraced Christianity at this time. This was forced Baptism. In the seventh century the Jews were threatened with the penalty of slavery if they were found practicing Judaism. This cruel policy caused many Jews to flee to the Mediterranean and western coast of Africa. The southern most point of Spain after you cross the Straits of Gibraltar leads you to the Northern or western coast of Africa. Throughout the middle Ages many European governments expelled their Jews; these "Black Jews" migrated to neighboring countries in Africa. "The Lord shall cause thee to be smitten before thine enemies; thou shalt go out one way against them, and flee seven ways before them, and shalt be removed into all the kingdoms of the earth. (Deut. 28:25).15

It was January 2, 1492 A. D., when the Moorish stronghold of Granada surrendered to the armies of King Ferdinand and Queen Isabella. For the first time since the year 711, all of Spain was in Christian hands. The decree to expel the Jews from Spain was signed on March 31. The reason given for the expulsion of the Jews was that it was thought they corrupted the converted Jews by privately encouraging them in disloyalty to Christianity. The ultimatum given to the Jews expired August 1, 1492. But the last group of Jews did not leave until August 2, 1492.

In order to satisfy Queen Isabella of Spain, King Manoel of Portugal promulgated a royal decree expelling the "Black Jews" and Moors from his country in 1496. These "Black Jews" who were expelled from Spain and Portugal were scattered throughout the Mediterranean coasts.

An estimated 100,000 Jews departed from Spain and Portugal during the persecution and the expulsion. Some of these Jews went to Northern Europe, Italy and Turkey; but most of them went to Moslem countries of northern and western Africa. These "Black Jews" would naturally go to African countries most of all, because of less persecution and they could disguise themselves easily among other blacks.

R. H. M. Elwes gives a graphic description of the Portuguese Jew, Baruch Spinoza: "Middle-sized, good features, skin somewhat Black, Black curly hair, long eyebrows of the same color, so that one might know by his looks that he was a descendant from Portuguese Jews.

When these "Black Jews" were expelled from Spain, about 100,000 entered Portugal. They were permitted to enter under the condition that they pay the poll tax, with the understanding that they would leave the country within eight months. Also at this time the king obligated himself to take the Jews wherever they desired at the termination of the eight months.

When the time expired, many Jews were stranded because the king did not provide enough ships in time. All the "Black Jews" who were left behind were deprived of their freedom and sold into slavery.

During the reign of King Joao II (or John II), seven hundred Black Hebrew children were ruthlessly taken away from their parents in Portugal and transported to the Islands of San Thome, off the west coast of Africa. This island is located near Nigeria, Cameroon, and Gabon and was founded by the Portuguese in 1471. In the year 1484, King John of Portugal, who reigned from 1441-1495, offered the "Black Jews" of his kingdom the choice of baptism or settling at San Thome. Multitudes of Jews were sent to this island during the reign of King John II. These "Black Jews," or "Judeos" as the Portuguese called them, are serious, reserved and wealthy, holding most of all the trade in their hands."[16]

"The "Black Jews" who migrated to the Sudan from the north converged with the Jews migrating from the eastern Sudan to the countries of the Niger River. It is a known "Fact" that the Jews and Judaism were in Africa fifteen hundred years before Islam and that every where the Arabs went the Jews were already there."[17] The "Black African Hebrews" had settlements not only in the interior of Africa; but they also had communities on the west coast of Africa from Morocco to Angola. It was observed that the composite religious culture of some of the inhabitants of Senegambia (or Senegal) and Guinea; in Senegal, there "is a complete medley of Judaism and Mohammadism, and is difficult to say which occupies the most prominent place, or exerts the greatest influence upon the character of the people."

In northern Guinea, or Portuguese Guinea, Judaism is more highly practiced; some of the more outstanding rites are purifications, the observance of the new moons, a designated period of the weeping for the dead, during which time they wear sack cloths and ashes; bloody animal sacrifices, with the careful sprinkling of blood upon the door posts and the altars; the division of the group into different families, frequently into twelve parts (the twelve tribes of Israel); formal processions, circumcision, and various other practices, probably of Hebrew derivation.

Like the "Black Jews" in America, some of the Jews of Guinea didn't remember their original nationality. This deplorable ignorance is attributed to various causes: (1) The fall of the Hebrew Kingdom, (2) The lack of communication with Jewish education centers, (3) Intense persecution, and the deliberate blotting out of the mind their true nationality. In most cases these Hebrews, by race and by faith, sought to hide their origin, which had become a burden to them. Moreover, the persecution of the "Black Jews" in Portugal was so ruthless and frequent that the Jews did not divulge to their children the secret of their religion until they had attained the age of reason. The Hebrew Religion is such that if you deny your religion, you will eventually deny your nationality. Sociologists and psychologists know and history has proven that if you deny your culture and nationality over a long period of time you will totally forget it through a process of assimilation.

The Black Jews came to Africa not only by land but also by sea. In the year 1484 King John of Portugal deported great numbers of Black Jews to the African Island of San Thome. The Island of San Thome, near Nigeria and the Cameroon, was discovered by the Portuguese in 1471, and it was established as a penal colony; to this island Jews were sent who would not accept baptism. However, the Kings ulterior motive was to establish a commercial base for his growing empire in Africa. Soon the Black Jews in Portugal and Portuguese colonial possessions became known as "Black Portuguese" because they were born in Portugal and they knew Portugal's history, culture, and language.

King John of Portugal furnished ships in order to deport the Jews to any country they desired; however, unscrupulous Portuguese sea captains exacted as much money as they could from the Jews and dumped their human cargo at various places along the West African coast. The Portuguese were the first Europeans to establish colonies on the West African coast. They came first as merchants, and secondly as conquerors and slavers. Senegal was discovered by the Portuguese in the Fifteenth century, and the first settlements are believed to have been Black Portuguese; the Gambia River mouth was discovered by the Portuguese in the fifteenth century; Sierra Leone was visited by the Portuguese in 1462; Guinea was discovered by the Portuguese in 1446; the Island of San Thome discovered by the Portuguese in 1471, the new inhabitants were "Black Jews" deported there in 1484; "Black Jews" migrated to the Angola coast from San Thome between 1484 and 1499."[18]

Rachel, a young Ethiopian Jew now living in Israel, displays a photograph of her family left behind in Ethiopia. She discovered the photo among ones brought to her school by visitors who had been to her hometown in Ethiopia and had photographed members of the village. Rachel says she likes living in Israel with her sister, but that she is sad much of the time due to the separation from the rest of her family. Currently, some 16,000 Ethiopian Jews live in Israel, but between 7,000 and 10,000 remain in Ethiopia, waiting to be rescued.

74

It is certain that many "Black Jews" of Portugal, San Thome, and Angola who became victims of the Portuguese Inquisition and persecution were "sold in The Slave Trade." This Atlantic Slave Trade lasted more than Four Hundred Years, from 1444 to 1880 in some parts of South America.

Some scholars have located Black Jews within the entire Niger River bend; the countries in this territory that have contained Black African Jews include the following: Upper Volta, Ivory Coast, Ghana, Togo, Dahomey, and Nigeria. Dr. J. Kreppel reported in 1926 that there existed a large Hebrew community of "Black Jews" in the interior of Dahomey, West Africa. These Hebrews have their own central temple where they sacrifice animals. In their temple are found many laws engraved on tablets, which are attached to the temple walls. They have a high priest with a large number of priestly families, whose members walk from house to house rendering educational and religious instructions to each family of the community. Moreover, these "Black Jews" have their own Chumash (The five books of Moses) written on old parchment in Hebrew letters but they have no other books. What little Judaism they possess was transmitted to them from their ancestors. Dr. Kreppel says they observe the Sabbath and other Hebrew customs, despite the pressure from their pagan environment."[19]

"Dr. Allen H. Goodbey postulates the position that "Black Jews" were on the West African coast from Senegal to Angola and they, the Jews, were driven to this area from Central Sudan by Moslem propagandist. Having a knowledge of the "Black Jews" in the United States, Dr. Goodbey arrived at this conclusion: "These facts have peculiar significance when the presence of Judaism among American (Blacks) is to be considered.

Hundreds of thousands of slaves were brought to America from Western Africa during the days of the Slave Traffic, beginning nearly four hundred years ago. As persecuted communities, they were rather more in danger than other (Africans) of being raided by war parties and sold as slaves. It may be concluded certain that many Black Hebrews were among the slaves brought to America. Dr. Allen H. Goodbey and Rabbi Mathew organized a Hebrew congregation in 1918 and proclaimed that: "The Black People of the United States and the West Indies "Are" The Original Black Hebrews."

There are hundreds of thousands of Black African Hebrews scattered throughout the United States, not only in the urban areas, but also in the rural communities of this nation. With the revelation of ample historical evidence, the authenticity of these Black Hebrews can no longer be questioned. Hence, according to Biblical Prophecy, the Black Hebrews were supposed to have gone into slavery and captivity. Thus we read of the prophet Jeremiah saying: "Judah is gone into captivity because of affliction, and because of great servitude: she dwelleths among the "Heathen," she findeth no rest: all her persecutors overtook her between the straits." As the historical evidence indicates, the Black Hebrews were "Snatched" from the west coast of Africa and sold into captivity.

Jeremiah again says: "For, Lo, the days come, saith the Lord, that I will bring again the captivity of my people Israel and Judah, saith the Lord: And I will cause them to return to the land that I gave to their fathers, and they shall possess it."

"For it shall come to pass in that day, saith the Lord of hosts, that I will break his yoke from off thy neck, and will burst thy bonds, and strangers shall no more make him serve. Therefore, fear thou not, O my servant Jacob, saith the Lord; neither be dismayed, O Israel: for, Lo, I will save thee from afar, and thy seed from the land of their captivity; and Jacob shall return, and shall be at rest and tranquil, and none shall make him afraid."

The prophet Ezekiel prophesized about the plight of the Black Hebrews in "The valley of the dry bones," representing slavery and oppression under other nations. "Then he said unto me, son of man, these bones are the whole house of Israel: Behold, they say, our bones are dried, and our hope is lost: we are cut off." "Therefore prophesied and say to unto them, Thus saith the Lord God; Behold I will open your graves, and cause you to come up out of your graves and bring you into the land of Israel. The prophet Ezekiel calls the country wherein the Black Hebrews are oppressed, "GRAVES." "And ye shall know that I am the Lord, when I have opened up your graves, O my people, and brought you up out of your graves." "And shall put my spirit in you, and ye shall know that I the Lord have spoken it, and performed it, saith the Lord."[20]

These facts about the Black Hebrews have been known for decades. Dr. Godbey was professor of the Old Testament at Duke University in Durham, North Carolina. He knew the entire truth about the Black Jews, but he considered it unwise to reveal everything. Dr. Godbey was writing primarily to a "white Southern audience" in 1930.

At this time the Ku Klux Klan was in its' heyday, and he did not want any repercussions. Moreover, if Dr. Godbey had said positively that the "Za Dynasty" and the "Original Jews" were Black, the power structure and the clergy would have come down on him like a storm!"[21]

Personally, I find it to be very appalling that the major universities all across this land still do not teach the truth to the people. Neither was I ever told of this by that "Devil" Dr. Hermitt at J. C. Smith University. I yet feel that they do a "Grave Disservice" in "Mis-Educating" our people about who we really are! I was not made aware of these facts until 1998 when I had the pleasure of meeting with Dr. Windsor, personally.

Its' Heritage, Random House, New York, 1976, pp. 13-22

2). Koestler, Ibid. pp. 38-40

3). Koestler, Ibid. pp. 45-46

4). Robert Marshall, Storm From The East- From Genghis Khan To
Khubilai Kahn, The University of California Press, Berkley,
and Los Angeles, California, 1993, pp. 120-121

5). Koestler, Ibid. pp. 90-91

6). Koestler, Ibid. pp. 21

7). Koestler, Ibid. pp. 59-60

8). Koestler, Ibid., pp. 60-61

9). Koestler, Ibid., pp. 63-73

10). Koestler, Ibid., pp. 80-81

11). Koestler, Ibid., pp. 159-161

12). David Robertson, Denmark Vesey-The Buried History of America's
Largest Slave Rebellion And The Man Who Led It, Alfred A. Knopf,
New York, 1999, pp. 16

13). Koestler, Ibid., pp. 16

14). Rudolph R. Windsor, From Babylon To Timbuktu- A History Of The
Ancient Black Races Including: The Black Hebrews, Windsors Golden
Series, Atlanta, Georgia, 1969, pp. 33-35

15). Windsor, Ibid., pp. 83-87

16). Windsor, Ibid., pp. 115-116

17). Windsor, Ibid., pp. 120

18). Windsor, Ibid., pp. 122-125

19). Windsor, Ibid., pp. 129-131

20). Windsor, Ibid., pp. 132-134

21). Windsor, Ibid., pp. 146

ORIGINS, CULTURES AND CUSTOMS

The Bantu-Speaking Peoples

Late in the year 1482, ten years before Columbus led his three small ships to the New World, a Portuguese captain named Diogo Cao sailed three battered, sea-worn little ships into the estuary of a great river on the western coast of central Africa, and there anchored to seek fresh water and food. The river, which the local peoples called Zaire, soon came to be known to Europe as the Congo. The populous Black peoples whom Diogo Cao met there, and with whom he soon established cordial relations, identified themselves as subjects of the Mani Kango, or "King of the Kingdom of Kongo."

Diogo Cao did not know it, but he was the first know European to visit the lands of the far-flung peoples whom we call today the Bantu-speaking people. After Cao's visits (he made two later voyages to Kongo as well) hundreds of European ships, form England, France, Holland, Denmark, Sweden, Purssia, and other countries joined those of Portugal in calling at points along the Atlantic and Indian Ocean coasts of Africa South of the equator, establishing contact with new groups of Africans, each of which seemed different in many respect from the others. For nearly four hundred years Europeans dealt with the many peoples of Africa South of the equator without recognizing that they were all closely related, one group to another, despite apparent differences in language, dress, way of living, political organization, and race.

Europe was so impressed with the wealth, pageantry, and obvious lordliness of the king of Kongo and his court that they often spoke of his country as the most civilized in Africa. Nor was Kongo the only kingdom that demanded the respect of Europe; as early as 1500, and up until the 1860's Europeans continued to find still other highly civilized states in the interior of central and southern Africa - their kings powerful and commanding, their armies numerous and their exports of gold, ivory, and copper impressive.

Not all the peoples of Southern and Central Africa earned such favorable European reactions, however. Many, both along the coasts and in the interior, spent much of their time herding cattle, producing little wealth and giving no evidence of the kind of complex political organization which was so distinctive in Kongo, Mwene Mutapa, Changamire, Buganda, and some other states. Europeans eventually came to look down on these postural, less materially developed peoples, especially after the first permanent European settlement were founded in South Africa, and the European colonist began to realize that their guns and ammunition gave them power over the Africans whose lands they coveted.

Yet today we know that almost all the African peoples south of the equator, whatever early Europeans may have thought of them, are members of one great language group, sharing a common history and a common civilization.

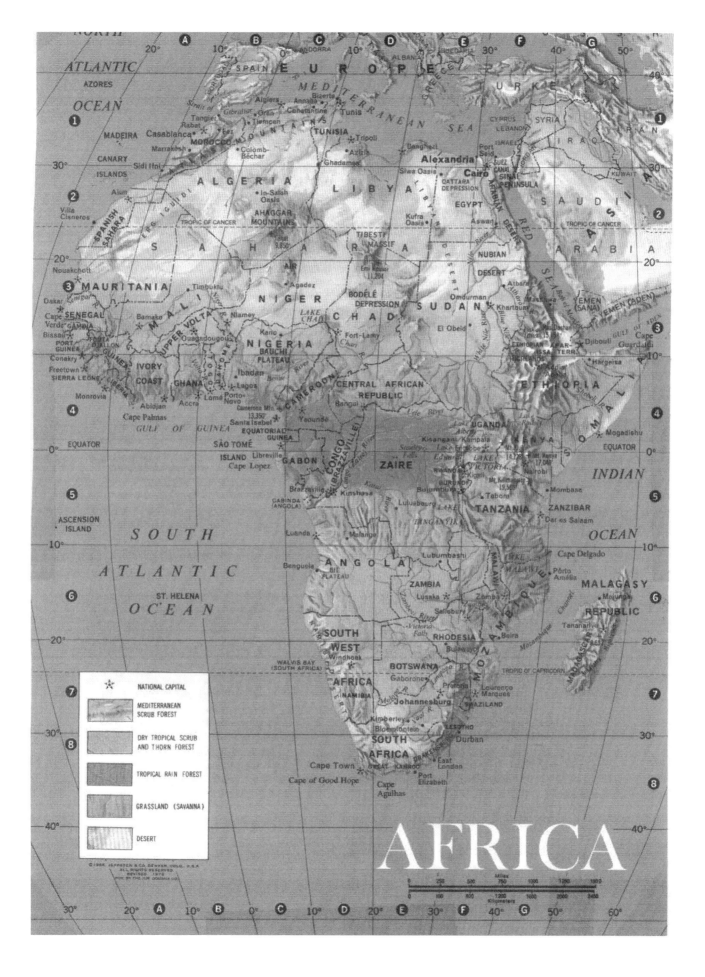

AFRICA

The modern countries of Angola, Botswana, Burundi, Cameroon, Congo (Brazzaville), Gabon, Kenya, Lesotho, Malawi, Mozambique, Namibia (South-West Africa), Republic of South Africa, [Zimbabwe], Rwanda, Swaziland, Tanzania, Uganda, Congo, (with the capital at Brazzaville), and Zambia are all largely populated by Bantu speaking peoples, and there are other Bantu speakers living in a few neighboring countries. All together nearly one-third of the peoples of Africa, or roughly 100 million, speak one or another of the Bantu languages.

These numerous and widely dispersed peoples cover roughly one-third of the African continent; their territory totals more than 4 million square miles, a land mass more than twice as large as Europe, and a little larger than the United States including Alaska.

In many ways the differences among this huge group of peoples seem more impressive than any similarities. They differ widely in racial composition, for example. Some are short and slight of build, with yellowish or light brown skins and facial features which set them apart from the more Negroid peoples of West Africa. Others exhibit evidence of long mixture with Caucasoid peoples, so that they now have brown skin and wavy hair. Still others are closely similar to the Negroid peoples of West Africa, with dark brown skins, tightly curled hair, fleshy lips, and broad, flat noses. Some are unusually tall, with men averaging over six feet, and have tightly curled hair and dark skin but thin lips and sharp noses. Little wonder that Europeans could remain ignorant, for four centuries, of the common origins and underlying unity of civilization of such heterogeneous peoples.

By the mid-nineteenth century missionaries and scholarly travelers had learned a number of African languages and recorded them in dictionaries and grammars. European philologists (students of language) realized, upon comparing these languages, that most of those in central and Southern Africa were remarkably similar in structure and word forms. One of the earliest of these scholars, Wilhelm Bleek of Germany, coined the term Bantu when he found that almost every language spoken in South and Central Africa used the same word, Abantu, to refer to "men" or the "the people." In these same languages Amuntu, the singular form of the same word, was universally used to mean "a man."

Bleek, and other scholars who followed him, found that the Bantu languages showed their common ancestry in many other ways as well. Almost all contained a core of common words (although the words had begun to change form in some, as in European languages the Latin uno has changed to one, ein, un, etc.) All formed the difference between singular and plural by changing the prefix, and prefix changes were also used to indicate the agreement of adjectives, pronouns, and verbs with the nouns to which they referred.

In the decades that followed the work of Bleek and other philologists, most of the Bantu languages have been studied, and each newly studied one reflects the same basic characteristics as the others.

Today between three hundred and four hundred Bantu languages are recognized; it is impossible to be precise as to the number, since scholars often do not agree on whether certain languages are sufficiently different from others to be called separate languages rather than dialects.

These three or four hundred languages differ from each other in varying degrees. Some are as dissimilar as French and Rumanian, while others are closer than Spanish and Portuguese. Although we say that the numerous Bantu languages are "mutually unintelligible," meaning that a person speaking one cannot converse with a person speaking another this tends to overstate their dissimilarity. It has been found that a person from Zulu land, for example, can go to Uganda, more than two thousand miles away, and learn the language sufficiently to carry on a limited conversation within a few weeks. The deep common roots and the basic similarities in structure and vocabulary are as real as the differences, clearly.

Until the essential unity of the Bantu languages was recognized, Europeans were far more impressed by the elements of diversity among the Bantu-speaking peoples. Even today Europeans who are skeptical of African capabilities or who have negative images of Africans prefer to stress their differences. Thus in white South Africa it is a widespread belief among the ruling group that the subordinate African majority is composed of a number of separate groups, each speaking its own language and each far more concerned with its tribal identity than with any sense of unity with other Africans.

As we will see, in later chapters, there is indeed much variety among the multitudinous Bantu-speaking peoples. The more intensively one studies them, however, the more one is struck with the essential uniformity of their religions, world views, ideas about life, and attitudes about political and social organization-and the fact of their common origins. And despite their diversity, they are bound together by a history, which is one of the most exciting and fascinating sagas in the history of all mankind.

The history of the Bantu-speaking peoples is unusual because it is one of constant migrations from several points of origin. In these numerous and complex migrations small groups of Bantu colonists spread themselves, together with their languages and their common civilization, over the vast area that they now occupy, in little more than a thousand years. For the most part they quickly absorbed, usually by intermarriage, the more primitive peoples who inhabited the area before they came. In a few cases the Bantu themselves adopted much of the culture of the indigenous peoples, and in other cases a fusion of cultures resulted. The settlement of this vast region in such a comparatively short space of time represented a population movement of epic proportions.

In fact, the sheer scale it is comparable to the settlement of the Americas by the ancestors of the Indians, the explosions of the Arab peoples following the birth of the Muslim religion, and the worldwide colonization by Europeans after the Age of Discovery in the fifteenth and sixteenth centuries.

Reconstructing the historical process, by which the Bantu speakers spread themselves so widely, establishing their civilization in each new area, is an intellectually demanding task. Yet it is a thrilling one, somewhat like unraveling an intricate puzzle. Had the Bantu-speaking peoples used writing, the task might have been far less difficult, and perhaps less exciting as well. But with a few isolated exceptions they used no writing until the past century or so, and they moved so extensively that they built few of the great stone edifices and monuments that have helped so much to unravel the history of Egypt, Sumeria, and other early civilizations.

In the absence of writing, and with few enduring monuments of stone, how have scholars been able to reconstruct Bantu history? As we shall see, they have used great ingenuity, ferreting out bits and pieces of information from archeology, linguistic analysis, anthropology, botany, zoology, chemistry, and other sciences, combining this information with the "Oral Histories" passed on from one generation to the next in almost all Bantu societies. The result is far from a neat historical picture, with all-important details filled in. Yet it is equally far from being vague guesswork. The major routes of migrations, the reasons for undertaking them, and the methods by which they were carried out, as well as the accomplishments of the Bantu speakers in each of their new homelands have been sketched out well enough so that most scholars are in agreement. Research continues, and each new piece of information is quickly fitted into the overall outline; sometimes new information requires a significant change in the broad outline of Bantu History, but more often it serves to fill in missing detail and to clarify unclear areas.

Before we begin the story of the ancient Bantu-speaking peoples, it will help if we look briefly at the modern Bantu peoples and the lands in which they live.

Moving South from Eastern Nigeria, near the border between Nigeria and Cameroon one very quickly reaches Bantu country. Many of the peoples in the Eastern part of Nigeria speak languages, which are related to the Bantu group, though they are not sufficiently similar to be classed as Bantu languages. In the Northwestern part of Cameroon (and on the offshore island of Fernando Po) live many peoples speaking different Bantu languages, including the Duala, from whom comes the name of Douala, one of Cameroon's leading cities. Farther south live one of the first large groups, the Fang, who spread over a wide territory of Cameroon and adjacent Gabon.

In Gabon and Congo (Brazzaville) live numerous other Bantu speakers, one of the more numerous being the Teke (more properly, the Bateke; many Bantu-speaking peoples use the prefix ba as the plural as the plural for their group, while an individual is indicated by the prefix m, am, or um. For simplicity we will generally not use the prefixes).

Immediately to the south of the lands of the Teke and related groups are the Kongo, whom Diogo Cao visited and from whom both the river and the modern country have taken their name. Inland, due east from the Kongo, live the Chokwe, Lunda, and Luba, each of which has achieved special prominence in African History.

These peoples are among the more numerous and influential in modern Congo [Brazaville], which renamed itself in 1998), as well as in Angola.

In both Angola and Namibia (the official name for South-West Africa) there are numerous Bantu groups, with the Mbunda of Angola and the Ovambo and Herero of Namibia being best known.

In the modern Republic of South Africa, together with neighboring Botswana, Lesotho, and Swaziland, most of the Bantu-speaking peoples belong to societies that speak either Sotho languages (as do the people of Lesotho and Botswana) or Nguni languages (including those of the Zulu, Xhosa, and Swazi).

Much of Rhodesia (Zimbabwe) and parts of Mozambique are dominated by various widely dispersed clans of Shona peoples, but other groups are also important. In [Zimbabwe] live the Matabele (or Ndebele) a group of Ngumi speakers who invaded and conquered part of Shona territory in the nineteenth century. Both in [Zimbabwe] and in southern Mozambique are the numerous Tonga-speaking peoples; they are divided, like the Nguni to their south, into several language groups.

Farther north, in Malawi, Zambia, Tanzania, and northern Mozambique, live large numbers of Bantu-speaking peoples. Most are divided into moderate-sized language groups, of whom a few of the more notable are the Lozi and Bemba of Zambia; the Yao, found in both Malawi and Tanzania; and the Chewa, found in Malawi and Zambia. Still farther north, both Burundi and Rwanda are populated by Bantu-speaking peoples.

Tanzania contains dozens of Bantu-speaking groups, none being nationally prominent; the Sukuma and Nyamwezi are among the most populous. Neighboring Kenya is inhabited by both Bantu-speaking peoples and peoples of a quite different origin, the Niloties. Among the Bantu speakers the most prominent are the Kikuyu and the Wakamba.

Like Kenya, Uganda contains large numbers of both Bantu- and Nilotic- speaking peoples, with the Bantu-speaking Baganda (from whom the modern country took its name) being the most numerous and prominent.

Small groups of Bantu-speaking peoples migrated even farther north, beyond the equator, into modern Somalia. Still others are found in the Central African Republic, in the center of the African continent east of Cameroon.

Finally, located along the Indian Ocean coast between southern Mozambique and Somalia, live dozens of relatively small Bantu-speaking groups who have had close contact with Arab traders and settlers for more than a thousand years.

Out of this long contact grew a distinctive culture and language, the Swahili, which helps to lend uniformity to the peoples over nearly two thousand miles of coastline. Their culture is clearly Bantu, and the Swahili language is Bantu. But Arab customs and words have been blended with Bantu in the Swahili area to produce a unique civilization.

The perceptive reader may have noticed that so far the term "tribe" has not been used to describe any of the Bantu-speaking peoples. The use of the word "tribe" can be so misleading and inaccurate that it is best to avoid it entirely, instead using such terms as "group," "society," "ethnic group," "population," or "language group." Very few of the peoples in any part of Africa live in what we think of as tribal groups. This fact is so important to our understanding of the history and achievements of the Bantu-speaking peoples that we must digress for a moment to clarify it.

The way in which Bantu-speaking Africans govern themselves has varied from region to region. But the great majority has lived in states headed by kings, so that we must recognize the kingdom as being the most typical kind of Bantu political organization.

Bantu social organization has typically been in small families, which are in turn part of lineages; everyone in the lineage traces descent back, through many generations, to a common ancestor. When that descent is traced through the females of the family (from daughter to mother to grand-mother, etc.), it is called "matrilineal," and the common ancestors of the clan are women. If descent is traced through the male line, as it is in most Bantu societies, it is called "patrilineal," and the common ancestor of the lineage is a man.

In Bantu societies these lineages may have tens, or even hundreds, of thousands of members, so that it is impossible for each person to trace his ancestry through every generation to the common ancestor. The members of the lineage simply assume that they have a common ancestor because the traditions of their lineage say so. Each lineage has a story, or myth, of how it came into being; the ancestor has a name, is believed to have been a person of unusual abilities, and is said to have performed many wonderful feats and to have possessed great wisdom.

When a powerful lineage moved into a new area, perhaps conquering the people who were already settled there, its prestige may have been so great that the conquered people eventually accepted the tradition of the ruling lineage's ancestor. Thus many of the lineages include people who are not really descended from the mythical ancestor, but who nevertheless believe that they are.

The social organization of lineages and the political organization of kingdoms are often, in Bantu society, two very different things. Peoples living in a kingdom may be of several different lineages, and the king is usually selected from one of the lineages, which is more powerful and prestigious than the others. It has occasionally happened that peoples of one large lineage are split between two different kingdoms

When we use the term "tribe" we usually think of a people who speak a common language, share a common culture, recognize descent from the same ancestor, and acknowledge the authority of a common leader. This clearly is not the case in many Bantu societies. A number of lineages speak the same language and share a common culture but feel no close kinship to each other, inhabit separate territories, and may acknowledge completely different leaders. They may well recognize a vague connection because of the common language and customs, but often will feel that this is of no importance in their daily lives. The obligations of a person to his or her lineage or king usually are much more important than any obligation to other peoples who happen to speak the same language but are of different lineages or kingdoms.

Another reason it is misleading to use "tribe" is the fact that we associate the word with primitive society and behavior. As we will see in later chapters, the Bantu peoples were far from primitive in social organization, culture, or behavior. They were a civilized people, capable of creating elaborate kingdoms and empires; impressive tools, farms, and cities; great works of art and architecture; powerful poetry and oral literature; and religions with a Supreme Being and deep moral values.

Yet, as we have already noted, the Bantu peoples differed much from each other. In their migrations they came into close contact with many other peoples, and often absorbed customs and techniques from them. As they moved, constantly settling new lands farther and farther from their point of origin, they found many different geographical environments. Each of these environments called for new ways of tilling the soil and tending herds of cattle, sheep, or goats. And each new environment offered different challenges and opportunities. Some, such as present-day Zimbabwe, and Congo, were rich in minerals, so that the Bantu peoples who settled there became proficient miners and workers of copper, tin, iron, and gold. Others were rich in stone that could be used for temples and public buildings, and in those areas the Bantu peoples erected impressive structures. Still others offered good grazing lands that were poorly suited to growing crops, and in these areas the Bantu came to rely heavily on their herds for their livelihood.

The result, after centuries of pioneering migrations, was a fascinating patchwork of cultures and ways of living. Yet at a deeper level, in social and political organization, religion, and philosophy, the underlying base of Bantu civilization could still be recognized. It is this complex blend of difference and uniformity, which lends such excitement to the saga of the Bantu peoples.

Long after it was recognized that the Bantu-speaking peoples were of common origin, despite their variety and the vast territory they inhabit, their place of origin was unknown. Scholars began to suggest theories, usually based more on speculation than on scientific evidence, but there was little agreement among the numerous theories that began to appear as early as 1900.

One theory, based on the fact that most Bantu-speaking peoples in South Africa had legends which told of migrations from the north, held that they originated somewhere near the Great Lakes of East Africa, in the vicinity of Uganda. This theory suggested that the Bantu ancestors had, in very ancient times, been influenced by the Egyptian civilization of the Nile River but had become increasingly primitive as they moved ever farther south from the source of civilization.

Another theory influenced by the racial diversity of the Bantu-speaking peoples along the Indian Ocean coast and in parts of southern Africa, speculated that the Bantu peoples were the descendants of intermarriages between unknown Africans, perhaps African-Hebrews, and immigrants from Egypt, Arabia, or the Far East.

It was not until the early 1950's that a theory of origin based on scientific studies of African languages by Joseph Greenberg, an American linguist and anthropologist. Greenberg assembled information on the vocabularies and grammars of most African languages. In comparing them, he found that the Bantu languages showed certain similarities to a cluster of languages spoken by peoples living between the high plateau of central Nigeria and the area of the Cameroon where the nearest of the true Bantu languages could be found.

Greenberg established clearly that the Bantu languages, numerous though they were, were related to other languages spoken throughout West African and could be classed as a division of the great African language family he named Congo-Kordofanian. Having established the relationship between Bantu and West African languages, a relationship, which was closest in the area where Nigeria and Cameroon adjoin, Greenberg concluded that the ancestors of the Bantu had migrated southward from that area.

At about the same time a British linguist, Malcolm Guthrie, was engaged in painstaking research on the Bantu languages themselves. Using a large number of common word roots, he made statistical comparisons of the appearance of each word root in widely dispersed Bantu languages.

From his analysis an interesting pattern emerged. The languages which had the largest number of basic word roots were Bemba and Luba, in the Katanga region of Zaire and adjacent Zambia; the farther away from this area a language was spoken, the fewer roots it had in common with the other Bantu languages analyzed.

While Guthrie's findings did not invalidate the relationship Greenberg had found between Bantu and West African languages, Guthrie concluded that the origin of Bantu languages (the "cradle land," as he termed it) was in the Katanga region of Central Africa. Using statistical methods, he found evidence that other Bantu speakers had apparently migrated away from this cradle land, first to the east and west, then later to the north and south. And for a few years after the publication of these studies by Greenberg and Guthrie there was a lively controversy in scholarly circles.

Some scholars, more persuaded by Greenberg's research, argued that the Bantu ancestors came from Nigeria and had fanned out southward to cover all of Africa south of the equator. Others, impressed by Guthrie's findings, insisted that the earliest Bantu speakers came from Central Africa and migrated north and south.

In the past few years most scholars have devoted their energies to reconciling these two theories. It is now generally accepted that the ancestors of the Bantu-speaking peoples did come from the Nigeria-Cameroon area, as suggested by Greenberg, but that they established a new home in the Katanga region and from there migrated outward in the pattern suggested by Guthrie.

The Nigeria-Cameroon homeland of the Bantu ancestors is a country of grasses and woodlands with a moderate amount of rain each year. The people now living there grow corn, millet, beans, some rice, and various root crops such as cassava and yams. The Katanga region has a very similar geography and produces many of the same crops. Because of this close similarity in the two environments, it is logical that an agricultural people migrating from the Nigeria-Cameroon region would adapt easily and quickly to a new homeland in Katanga.

The story of the Bantu origins begins between 1000 and 500 B.C., when the population of West Africa was expanding into all arable areas and was beginning to overpopulate its territory. Nigeria was already, at that early date, an emerging center of cultural progress. Nigerian archeologists have uncovered rich evidence of a prosperous agricultural people with an impressive artistic tradition, centered on the Nigerian plateau only a few hundred miles north and west of the Bantu ancestral area.

By 500 B.C. there was considerable pressure to find new lands to support the expanding population of central and eastern Nigeria.

The Atlantic Ocean blocked expansion to the southwest, and the Great Plains to the north and east was already occupied by agricultural peoples. The only possible route of expansion lay to the south. In that direction stretch the vast tropical rain forests of the Congo Basin, a country of heavy rainfall, dense forests of towering trees, and numerous rivers, streams, and swamps. The rain forests were very sparsely populated at the time, because they were inhospitable to farming.

The need to find new lands eventually forced ambitious, adventurous pioneers to move into the Congo rain forests. It is likely that the first pioneers were fishermen, who knew how to build sturdy, large canoes from the giant trees of the forests. They are believed to have known agriculture as well, their women growing garden crops while the men fished. As early as 500 B.C. family groups of these fishermen-farmers were exploring the numerous streams and rivers of Cameroon, most of which flow southward into the great Congo River system. Setting up small villages in clearings along the waterways, they moved slowly but inexorably southward into the heart of the Congo region.

Eventually they moved up other rivers and streams, which flow west and north from their origins in Katanga and East Africa.

By about 100 B.C. parties of these pioneers are believed to have reached the Katanga area, where they found drier grasslands and forests similar to those of their ancestral homeland. Here the cultivation of grains and numerous vegetables was profitable, and fishing became a less important side activity. By about A.D. 100 the ancestral Bantu had established a rapidly growing new population center, based on farming, in the Katanga environment. From this region they continued to expand both eastward and westward, reaching the Atlantic Ocean and the Indian Ocean by about A.D. 400.

These early pioneers, moving restlessly generation after generation to found new settlements, must have been hardy and brave. And they were far from primitive in their knowledge of arts and crafts. Their relatives in Central Nigeria had learned how to mine iron ore and smelt it to produce raw iron as early as 500 B.C., and from the raw iron they forged durable blades for hoes, axes, knives, and spears. If the pioneer ancestors of the Bantu peoples did not take this knowledge of iron working with them on their migrations, they soon added it to their already formidable technology. With iron axes they were able to fell trees and clear new lands easily, and with iron weapons they could defend themselves from wild animals or the few hostile peoples they met in their migrations.

Archeologists have found evidence of iron working in central Nigeria as early as about 500 B.C., and in Central Africa, not far from the new Bantu cradle land, about A.D. 100. The moist earth and dense vegetation of the Congo Basin have thwarted archeological research, however, and most of the relics the Bantu ancestors left in their journeys through that region have decomposed.

Most of the new lands the Bantu ancestors settled were sparsely populated by peoples of the Khoisan language family, who have survived into historical times in Southern Africa as the groups known to Europeans as (Bushmen and Hottentots.) (These are names coined by Europeans, and are never used by Khoisan peoples to refer to themselves.) The ancient Khoisan peoples lived over much of Africa from Nigeria and Ethiopia to the southern tip of the continent, but they were hunters whose way of life was much simpler than that of the Bantu. As the Bantu moved into the territories of the Khoisan peoples, they absorbed most of them by intermarriage, so that gradually these peoples disappeared except in the southernmost areas of Africa. Their yellowish skin color and physical features have survived in some Bantu populations, however, as has their unique use of clicks in speaking. Today certain large Bantu groups, such as the Xhosa and Zulu of South Africa, use Khoisan clicks in their languages; Miriam Makeba, the prominent African singer, has made these exotic click sounds familiar to all Americans who have heard her.

Since the Khoisan peoples were not farmers, there was no basis for conflict over territory between them and the immigrating Bantu. Even today small bands of " Bushman" hunters trade the game they have killed to Bantu farmers for grains and pottery, or work as laborers on Bantu farms.

Over a long period the Khoisan peoples were absorbed into the stronger, more numerous Bantu populations, but it is not likely that the two groups were frequently at war with each other.

There has been too little archeological research yet done to establish with any accuracy the dates when the first ancestral Bantu speakers established settlements in the Katanga area. Most linguists believe that it would have taken roughly two thousand years for the Bantu languages to reach their present state of diversity from each other, assuming they all stem from one ancestor language. This would suggest that the first group settled in Katanga between 100 B.C. and A.D. 100. This is, of course, a very rough estimate, and the correct date could be as much as two or three centuries earlier or later.

One archeological find, however, tends to confirm the estimate. In the Machili Forest Station of Zambia, several hundred miles southeast of the Katanga area, evidence of iron working and pottery in the style of later Bantu peoples has been found, and dated at approximately A.D. 100. Similar finds still farther south, in [Zimbabwe] (especially at the site of the famous stone ruins at Zimbabwe), date at about A.D. 300-400. And even farther south, in the Transvaal province of South Africa, further evidence of iron working and pottery in the Bantu tradition has been dated at about A.D. 800-900.

Guthrie's linguistic analysis is thus supported, in rough outline, by archeology, especially in his conclusion that the people of the Katanga cradle land moved gradually south over a period of centuries.

By about A.D. 500 ancient Bantu-speaking peoples had settled a vast belt of central African lands stretching between the Atlantic and Indian oceans. They covered parts of the modern countries of Angola, Zaire, Zambia, Zimbabwe, Malawi, and Mozambique. As they expanded they carried with them their practices of sowing millet and other grain crops, of fashioning good pottery, and of iron working. In areas that had rich soil and ample rainfall they became densely populate and prosperous.

Soon offshoots of people, moving in small family groups of one or two men with their wives and children, were pressing north and south. They are known to have reached the rich farming country of southern Uganda before A.D. 1000, and had moved up the Indian Ocean coast into Somalia by about the same period. Arabic records from the period show that there were Bantu peoples living near Mogadishu, the ancient city that is the capital of modern Somalia.

Other groups had entered what is today South Africa before A.D. 1000, and continued to move gradually south in that area until about A.D. 1500, when they reached their southern most limit of expansion.

As the Bantu migrants fanned out in every direction from their cradle land, they followed those routes, which were best for farming and avoided areas, which were too dry or too swampy for their grain crops. In several large regions they bypassed inhospitable territories, moving into them only many centuries later when forced to do so by population pressure. One such area was central Tanganyika, a dry country with poor soil and unpredictable rainfall. Another was Southwestern Africa, much of which lies within the great Kalahari Desert. In that area Bantu-speaking peoples moved into the more favorable sectors of land in the highlands of Central Namibia (South-West Africa), but left the arid sections along the coast and in the south to the Khoisan hunters.

Most of the ancient Bantu migrants passed through the Congo rain forests without establishing large settlements. It is believed that those who remained there were few in number, living in small settlements along the rivers and streams, eking out a living by fishing and a little farming. During the late part of the first millennium, however and possibly after A.D. 1000, the continually expanding Bantu population of the Katanga cradle land region began to move into the rain forest in larger numbers, clearing lands away from the waterways and gradually building permanent farming communities.
They were able to undertake this new settlement of the rain forests because they had learned how to grow several tuber plants, notably yams and coco yams (taro), which had been imported into African from Indonesia during the first millennium. These plants, nutritious and high yielding, grew well in areas of heavy rainfall, and are believed to have greater food value than the few native African tubers that the early Bantu knew how to grow.

Using the Asian root crops as a basis for a new kind of agriculture, the Bantu-speaking peoples implanted themselves firmly in what had previously been inhospitable land. By the period A.D. 1300 - 1500 they were settled throughout the Congo Basin rain forests.

This new wave of immigrants, originating in the Katanga cradle land, apparently absorbed most of their distant relatives who had settled along the waterways many centuries before. Today the Bantu peoples of the rain forest speak languages, which are relatively closely related to Luba, Lunda, Bemba, and others in the cradle land region, rather than to the "Bantoid" languages of the Nigeria-Cameroon area.

In their extensive migrations between about A.D. 100 and 1500 the Bantu-speaking peoples adapted themselves, where necessary, to the varied conditions they found in each new environment. By 1500 some, such as those in the Congo rain forest, lived by farming root crops.

Others, such as the Luba, Lunda, Bemba, and many others in the savannas and dry woodlands, depended upon the cultivation of millet, eleusine (an Ethiopian grain somewhat similar to millet), sorghum, and vegetables. Still others, in the rich, well-watered country around Lake Victoria Nyanza, had learned to cultivate bananas and plantains for their main food supply.

In the many dry areas of central and southern Africa where grains do not produce good yields, many of the Bantu settlers switched to animal husbandry as a primary source of food, herding cattle, sheep and goats. A few, forced by population pressure into areas where cattle could not thrive, turned to hunting and gathering wild foods. Still others, who settled around lakes and waterways rich in fish, depended mainly on fishing and farming.

This quality of adaptability resulted in a mosaic of peoples whose life-style was very different from each other. It was not until European students of language realized the close relationship among the languages of these otherwise dissimilar people that it could be recognized that they were of one basic stock. As more information has been accumulated, however, similarities other than language have become apparent: religion, philosophy, social organization, political organization, and many arts and crafts.

Where the Bantu peoples found hospitable new lands on which to settle, they sank deep roots, which produced a proud civilization. Although all the Bantu-speaking peoples share a common origin and a similar potential for civilization, it was those groups who found rich soil and mineral resources that developed the impressive states and empires that are among the proudest Bantu achievements.

The great kingdom that Diogo Cao visited was one of the most illustrious ever created by the Bantu-speaking peoples. And its centuries of close contact with Portugal, launched by Cao's mission, provide one of the most poignant examples of "Destructive" European influence in African history.

The kingdom of Kongo was centered in the northern part of what is today the Portuguese colony of Angola. At its zenith it stretched more than 200 miles from north to south, between the modern Congo (Brazzaville) and the modern Angolan capital of Luanda and roughly the same distance east to west between the Atlantic Ocean and modern [Brazzaville], the capital of Congo. Within this region of 40,000 to 50,000 square miles the Mani Kongo ruled supreme, while numerous lesser kings and chiefs around his borders paid him tribute and respected his considerable military and economic power.

Archeological research in the Kongo region is still too scanty to reveal the history of the peoples who lived there before the founding of the kingdom of Kongo. Yet there must have been a long period of development before this event, which has been dated at somewhere between A.D. 1325 and 1375.

The ancestor of the Bakongo people were almost certainly living in or very near the area by A.D. 1000, speaking the Kongo language and supporting themselves, as their descendants did, by cultivating millet, cassava, beans, and vegetables, as well as by fishing in the Congo River and the other rivers and streams that flow through the area.

The early history of the kingdom itself is known only through the oral history or legend of the people, which weaves religious and mythical features into a generally factual account. According to the oral history, the kingdom was founded by a famous chieftain named Ntinu Wene, from whom most Kongolese claim descent. Historians believe that Ntinu Wene was a real man, and that he was indeed the first king who ruled over the powerful kingdom of Kongo. Oral history, however, endows him with semi divine status and magical powers, and claims for him many exploits, which may be untrue or exaggerated. To understand how the Kongolese blend fact and fiction into the oral history it is necessary to understand something of their religion.

The Kongolese religion, once one understands, its quite logic based on a belief in a Supreme Being, whom the Kongolese call Nzambi Mpungu. He believed to be a remote and omnipotent spirit who created all things, but who is so lordly and great that he created a variety of spirits to watch over the mundane affairs of men and earth. These spirits are of two kinds: The spirits of great ancestors and the spirits of nature. Nzambi Mpungu created nature spirits to govern the weather, crops, fire, rivers, disease, and other phenomena of nature. Man must be careful not to offend these spirits lest they punish him by bringing about famine, epidemics, floods or other misfortunes.

Ancestor spirits are all the members of the family who have died, but only those who were especially good, wise, or powerful during life exercise important power as spirits. Their main function is to watch over the affairs of their descendants, rewarding those who do good and punishing those who do evil. The living must revere these powerful ancestor spirits, observe the family traditions and morals, which they laid down, and sacrifice to them to show that they are remembered and respected.

Because ancestors are powerful spiritual beings, legend tends to portray them as having had supernatural powers even when they were alive. Thus, an important military victory by a revered chief of the ancient past may be attributed to his powers of magic as well as to his superior knowledge of military strategy and his bravery.

Kongolese oral history is based on chronological list of kings and chiefs, in which names and exploits of each become the main content of the nation's history. Although modern scholars have been able to verify that these oral histories are based on real men and events, the powers and adventures of the more ancient rulers are undoubtedly exaggerated because of their having become, after death, important ancestor spirits within the Kongolese religion.

Ntinu Wene, as the founder of the kingdom, is a complex figure in Kongolese oral history. He is believed to have been a man, with all the vices and virtues which real men possess; he was capable of great charity, generosity, mercy, and wisdom, but he also, on occasion, was cunning, treacherous, and vengeful. The command over magical forces attributed to him makes him seem an awesome figure, whose good will men are anxious to attract, but whose ill will they try desperately to avoid.

Kongolese oral history tells nothing of the area and the people before Ntinu Wene. Yet there were certainly many extended families of Bakongo in the area before he arrived, each family headed by a chief whose power depended on the wealth and population of the lineage he headed. By A.D. 1200-1300 the more powerful of these chiefs were much like minor kings, each ruling his own territory of several thousand people. There must have been frequent tensions and convicts between these petty kings and chiefs, as each struggled to expand his power and to secure his territory against encroachments from neighbors.

Throughout the area that the Congo kingdom covers, as well as for hundreds of miles to the north, east, and south, small kingdoms seem to have existed well before the Fourteenth Century. The legends of some peoples attribute the origins of their kingdoms to groups migrating into the country from the east, from the lands around Stanley Pool on the Congo River, where modern Brazzaville is built. In a vast region of several hundred thousand square miles there may have been several dozen small kingdoms and chiefdoms in existence by about 1300, inhabited by Bantu-speaking peoples more or less closely related to the Bakongo.

From one of these small chiefdoms came Ntinu Wene, son of the Chief of Bungu, with a troop of soldiers, onto the plains of Kongo south of the Congo River. He quickly subdued resistance, built a fortified capital at a town called Mbanza, and married a girl whose relatives were prominent spiritual leaders of the area. His wife's kin accepted Ntinu Wene and hailed him as the Mani Kongo, or "King of the kingdom of Kongo."

With this title, the support of the local aristocracy, a strong capital as base, and a seasoned army, Ntinu Wene began a campaign of conquest that within a few years allowed him to incorporate the chiefdoms of Mpemba, Nsundi, Mbamba, Mbata, Mpangu, and Soyo into his kingdom. These six lands became the six central provinces of the kingdom. Each was ruled by a governor, appointed by the Mani Kongo, except for Mbata, whose governor was automatically the hereditary head of the Mbata royal clan, since Mbata had voluntarily accepted Ntinu Wene's kingship.

The date of Ntinu Wene's death is unknown, although it was sometime between about 1375 and 1400. When he died, he left a strong and united kingdom, ruled by a recognized government that was centered at the capital of Mbanza.

The ordinary Kongolese was pleased by these marks of his king's power, wealth, and prestige, although his own life was humble in comparison. Most of the people were farmers and artisans, living in small villages of a few hundred or less, although many traveled to Mbanza, the capital, to marvel at the crowds and the pageantry of the court. Mbanza itself was a city, with a population of more than fifteen thousand, and its markets bustled with activity.

Although other strong kingdoms flanked Kongo to the north, south, and east, none was capable of military threat to it, and several, such as Dembo, Ndongo, and Matamba to the south, sent annual tribute to supported Mbanza and usually Kongo in disputes with other kingdoms.

This was still the case a century later, when Portuguese ships began calling along the coast. Diogo Cao and those who followed him recognized that the Mani Kongo headed a powerful, well-organized, and wealthy state, the largest and most prestigious on the Atlantic coast of central Africa.

From the time of Diogo Cao on, numerous written records have survived to tell of the life of the Kongo people, the affairs of their kingdom, and the ebb and flow of its national career. At the pinnacle of the state was the king, the Mani Kongo, the reigning monarch being Nzinga Kuwu during the early years of Portuguese contact. The king was believed by the people to have powers conferred on him by God that enabled him to safeguard the productivity of the kingdom's farms and the well being of its subjects. Ordinary people were forbidden to observe him eating or drinking, on pain of death. The king was the head of the judicial system of the state, as well as of its political and religious structures. Only he could exact the death penalty for crimes, and other sentences could be appealed to him.

All male descendants of Ntinu Wene were legally entitled to the throne, and numerous factions and parties grew up around the more prominent and powerful heirs. Frequently, when an old king died, to leading heirs and their supporters came to blows with their rivals, although the winner - who was eventually crowned by a small committee consisting of the queen mother and a member of the royal cabinet - was accepted by all once his claims proved superior.

The king administered the country through a cabinet made up of the governors of the six provinces, a retinue of personal aides, and a palace guard that served as the nucleus of the national army. Each of the governors headed an administration of provincial aides, district administrators, and village heads. Taxes were levied by the king, and collected by the provincial governors through their administrative subordinates.

The group around the king and his palace was large, and there was much pomp and pageantry designed to add to the king's majesty and dignity. He wore robes of office decorated with ostrich feathers, leopard skins, shells, and much gold and copper. His retinue included a host of personal aides, servants, and pages, in addition to governors, military commanders, wives, and the queen mother. Europeans, from the time of Diogo Cao on, were deeply impressed by the lordliness of the king and the size and complexity of his entourage.

The ordinary Kongolese was pleased by these marks of his king's power, wealth, and prestige, although his own life was humble in comparison. Most of the people were farmers and artisans, living in small villages of a few hundred or less, although many traveled to Mbanza, the capital, to marvel at the crowds and the pageantry of the court. Mbanza itself was a city, with a population of more than fifteen thousand, and its markets bustled with activity.

Most Kongolese lived by growing millet, sorghum, yams, bananas, beans, peas, watermelons, and many other fruits or vegetables, although a few fished and hunted to provide variety to the diet of their families. The soil was not rich, so the farmers used the typical African farming system of shifting cultivation. In this system the farmer selected a plot of a few acres at the beginning of the dry season, cut down all the trees and underbrush, and then burned them when they were dry. He then turned the earth with a hoe, mixing the ashes with the soil to add to its fertility.

After harvesting one crop, he planted a different crop, until, after two or three years, the plot lost its natural fertility and the farmer moved to a nearby plot that had been similarly prepared. The exhausted plots were left fallow for up to fifteen years, during which time weeds, small trees, and underbrush grew and helped to restore the plot's fertility.

Because of this system villages often moved from one spot to another, so that the farmers would be within easy walking distance of the plots being tilled. As the population of a village increased, small groups often moved farther away in search of less densely inhabited lands; this frequent movement, carried on over a period of centuries, was the basic pattern by which all the Bantu-speaking peoples migrated to populate Southern Africa.

The necessity of shifting from one plot to another, and occasionally moving villages, discouraged the building of elaborate, permanent homes and the acquisition of numerous personal possessions. Most people lived in small houses of dried mud plastered on a wooden framework, with roofs made of woven grass, palm fronds, or reeds. They valued their pots, weapons, tools, clothing, and jewelry, and a few simple items of furniture such as cots, chests, and stools, all of which were easily moved. Many also treasured fine carvings of wood or stone by Kongolese artists, which symbolized revered ancestors.

After the Portuguese came, life changed somewhat, even for the ordinary farmer, because the Portuguese brought new crops from the new World: maize, tomatoes, potatoes, pineapples, tobacco, and manioc. These crops added to the produce of Kongolese farms, and some, such as maize, were so valuable that they became more important than the plants earlier cultivated. The Portuguese and other Europeans who came later also brought a variety of new goods: knives, scissors, needles, nails, guns, fine cloth, shoes, mirrors, and rum.

Even though the Kongolese craftsmen knew how to produce most of these goods themselves, those brought by the Europeans were much less expensive, so after several centuries much of the craftsmanship of Kongo deteriorated.

Although the bulk of work in all of Kongo was carried out by the Kongolese peasants and artisans, the kingdom had long used slaves as workers. Slaves were people from the other kingdoms who had been captured in wars, or occasionally konogolese who had committed serious crimes or rebelled against the authority of the throne. Most slaves were owned by the king, the royal family, or the powerful nobility who governed the provinces and districts. These high-born people used slaves to farm their lands and to maintain their households. Slaves were also frequently used as soldiers, domestic servants, and personal assistants. In traditional Kongo society slaves had a legally recognized status and were protected by law from inhumane treatment or separation from their wives and children, unless they disobeyed their masters.

When the Portuguese first arrived in Kongo, they were exploring the Atlantic Ocean coasts of Western Africa in search of a sea route to the Indies and the legendary lands of Prester John.

Prester John was believed to be a powerful Christian king, whose kingdom was thought to be located somewhere in Africa (or in India), surrounded by hostile Muslim powers. The Portuguese believed that they might form an alliance with Priester John to crush the power of Islam, which had long dominated Northern Africa and the Middle East and which stood between Europe and the rich trade of the Far East. As the Portuguese explored Africa in search of Prester John and a route to the Indies, they were also alert to opportunities for trade in Africa, and it was the wealth and majesty of the Kongo court which led them to hope that lucrative trade might be carried on there.

Portuguese traders quickly recognized potential profits in the ivory, gold, silver, copper, and slaves, which were so abundant in the Kongo capital. The slave trade had already begun farther north, because slaves were needed to work in Spain and Portugal and to serve as farm laborers on the rapidly expanding plantations of the Canary Islands, Madeira, Sao Thome, and other Atlantic islands of the coast of Africa. Within a few decades after the first Portuguese ships began calling at Kongo, that kingdom was selling as many as four thousand slaves a year to eager Portuguese slave traders.

The first few decades of contact between Portugal and Kongo were dominated by the slave trade and the reign of one of the most remarkable kings in African History; Kongo's Affonso I. Affonso's forty-year reign witnessed such dramatic developments that it is still the favorite theme of Kongolese storytellers. When Diogo Cao first visited Kongo, the reigning king was Nzinga Kuwu. He welcomed the visitors, and on Cao's second visit in 1485 willingly sent four of his noblemen back with him to Portugal, in exchange for four missionaries who had been brought to preach Christianity.

Over the next few years several Portuguese expeditions came to Kongo, each time bringing new missionaries, traders, and artisans, and returning to Portugal with Kongolese ambassadors and students. In 1491 Nzinga Kuwu embraced Christianity and was baptized as King Joao I; most of his family and court were baptized along with him.

One of Nzinga's sons who accepted Christianity was Nzinga Mbemba, head of the province of Nsundi, who took the Christian name Affonso when he was baptized. His mother, the queen mother of the kingdom, took the name Eleanor.

A few years after accepting Christianity Nzinga Kuwu and one son renounced the new faith, reverting to the traditional Kongolese religion, but Eleanor and Affonso remained loyal Christians. When the old king died, in 1506, Affonso was forced to battle for the throne against his non-Christian brother, who had a larger army. According to Kongolese legend, Affonso easily vanquished the opposition because God sent angels to fight with his troops, and in late 1506 the devoutly Christian Affonso I, became Kongo's new monarch. Affonso was both a shrewd politician and a visionary leader. He persuaded the chief priest of the traditional faith to accept Christianity, at least in outward appearance, and put him in charge of all Catholic relics and holy objects. He proclaimed that his right to rule was blessed by the God of the Christians, and called on all Kongolese to accept the new faith.

To help with conversions and instruction in Christianity he wrote to the king of Portugal, Manuel I, to ask for large numbers of priests, teachers, doctors, masons, and carpenters, who would set up schools, build churches, spread the gospel, and help care for the sick.

Many documents survive to tell of Affonso's effort to transform Kongo into a modern Christian kingdom; there are even twenty-two letters written by Affonso himself to Portugal's King Manuel and his successor, Joao. These accounts and letters make it clear that Affonso was a deep believer in Christianity, and that he hoped to use Portuguese knowledge to educate his people, improve their health, and expand the wealth and prestige of his kingdom. He sent ambassadors to Rome as well as to Portugal, seeking papal recognition of his throne as Christian. And, wise in the ways of politics, he was also fully aware that many Portuguese traders and men of power were more interested in exploiting his country than in helping it become a great Christian force in Africa. Throughout a reign of forty years he remained steadfast in his faith and his vision of a greater Kongo, despite constant intrigue, internal dissension, and efforts by the Portuguese to subvert his authority and thwart his noble campaign of national development.

One of Affonso's first acts was to change the name of his capital from Mbanza to Sao Salvador. He built a large church of stone and mortar, a school for the children of the nobility, and residences for the priests and teachers he had requested from Portugal.

He continued to send young men to Europe for education-one of whom, his own son Dom Henrique, became a priest and a delegate to Rome and eventually was consecrated as the first Kongolese bishop.

The chief opposition to Affonso's grand design came from an alliance of his own vassals and Portuguese traders in Sao Thome, the nearest and most powerful Portuguese base. The governor of Sao Thome had been granted a Portuguese royal charter to control the trade with Kongo, and was growing wealthy on this trade and the burgeoning sugar production of' his fertile island. His numerous trading agents in Kongo resented Affonso's efforts to maintains close relations with Lisbon and to secure Vatican recognition, and they found ready allies among the many district noblemen of Kongo who preferred to trade directly with the Portuguese without Affonso's supervision.

By 1526 the situation was so bad that Affonso Thome wrote to Lisbon to complain that the Sao Thome traders were conspiring with his vassals to kidnap Kongolese citizens into slavery, including even members of the royal family. He beseeched his brother king in Lisbon to help him rectify this sad state of affairs, indicating that he might ban the entire slave trade if matters did not improve.

Things were made worse by the ineffectiveness of the missionaries, teachers, and artisans sent by Portugal. They were few in number, and many became infected by the avarice for quick profits that motivated the Portuguese traders. Almost all the priests owned slaves and engaged in the buying and selling of slaves. They set a poor example of Christian enlightenment, and were feeble instruments for carrying out Affonso's dream of converting his kingdom to a powerful Christian nation.

History shows that Affonso failed in his great design, not until the past few decades have the Kongo people begun to forge ahead in education and technological development. Yet his accomplishments were impressive. He made Europe aware of the fact that there were kings of vision and power in the heart of Africa. He enlarged his kingdom, maintained internal order and peace, and exercised strong influence over powerful kingdoms beyond his borders. In the face of the constant intrigues between Portuguese slave traders and avaricious Kongolese vassals, restive under Affonso's progressive regime, his long reign alone testifies to his skills as a leader. His dream of a great Christian Kongo was doomed by the forces arrayed against it, the forces that valued profits and exploitation more highly than nobler goals. But his faith, courage, vision, and political genius left their stamp on Kongo's history, serving as a shining example to countless later generations of the greatness that once was.

Affonso died about 1545, but the exact date and cause of his death are unknown. He was succeeded briefly by Pedro I, a relative who enjoyed the strong support of the Portuguese powers in Sao Thome, but the Kongolese people rebelled and installed Affonso's grandson, Dom Diogo I, as the legitimate king.

So great was their respect for Affonso's memory that after his death no man could be crowned unless he could prove that he was a direct descendant of Affonso, through one of his two sons or his one daughter.

Diogo I, was an able king, ruling very much in the same style as his grandfather, but was constantly beset by the same problems of Portuguese intrigue and rebellious vassals. He reigned from 1545 until his death in 1561. One major event during his reign was the successful Declaration of Independence by the kingdom of Ndongo, a strong neighboring state which had previously acknowledged Kongo's overlordship.

Ndongo lay nearly three hundred miles to the south of Kongo, along the Atlantic Ocean coast and to some distance into the interior. It was founded formally in about 1500, and its first kings, called Ngola, sent occasional tribute to Sao Salvador and allowed much of its trade to flow through Kongo, although rather unwillingly. Late in the reign of Affonso I Portuguese traders came in increasing numbers directly to Ndongo and the Ngola attempted to establish relations with both Lisbon and Sao Thome. Officially Lisbon was bound by a treaty with Kongo which prohibited direct Portuguese relations with Ndongo, but Sao Thome encouraged direct trade and contact. In 1556 Diogo raised a Kongolese army to march against Ndongo, hoping to force the Ngola to cease his efforts to bypass Kongo. When the two armies met, Ndongo was successful, dealing a severe defeat to Diogo's troops and forcing them to withdraw back to Kongo. From this time on Ndongo regarded itself as a completely sovereign kingdom, and Kongo was unable to prevent it from trading directly with Portugal and Sao Thome. Diogo's defeat proved to be a blow to the powerful reputation Kongo enjoyed in central Africa, and it also opened the path to the later Portuguese invasion of Ndongo and the conquest of the port of Luanda. In 1575, at a period when Kongo itself was at war with invaders from the interior, Portuguese troops landed at Luanda, seized the port, and began a campaign to conquer Ndongo which lasted for nearly a century.

With the conquest of Luanda, however, Portugal gained a permanent foothold on the coast of central Africa which has lasted until today; Luanda is the bustling modern capital of the Portuguese colony of Angola (whose name comes from the ancient title Ngola).

Diogo died in 1561, and was succeeded by several kings whose reigns were troubled and brief. In 1567 Alvare I became king. Almost as soon as he began to consolidate his power and restore internal order, the kingdom was invaded by fierce contingents of Jaga warriors from deep in the interior. The exact origin of the Jaga is unknown, but they are believed to have been a group of warriors related to the Luba and Lunda of central Zaire and Angola, who migrated from their homeland during a period of internal upheaval in order to seek their fortunes among the prosperous kingdoms to the west.

The Jaga soldiers moved rapidly, recruiting both troops and wives among groups whom they conquered. They are known to have been skillful fighters who employed a variety of tricks and strategies to defeat larger forces.

Between about 1560 and 1580 they ravaged nearly a thousand miles of land between Loango, north of Kongo, and the Cunene River, far to the south of Benguela in modern Angola.

When the Jaga fell upon Kongo, Alvare's troops were quickly defeated, and he was forced to seek refuge on an island in the Zaire (Congo) River. The Jaga roamed the Kongo countryside, razing crops and terrorizing the people. Repeatedly Alvare called upon Portugal for aid, but it was not until 1571 that an army was sent, under the command of the governor of Sao Thome, to assist him. By this time the country was in a state of near-prostration. The Jaga had seized thousands of people, including many members of the nobility, for sale to Portuguese slave traders, and famine gripped the land.

The Sao Thome army, six hundred men armed with arquebuses, marched with Alvare's troops against the Jaga and, after four years of battle, expelled them from Kongo. During this period the Portuguese virtually ruled the country, and Alvare had little power to do anything but work with them in the task of defeating the Jaga.

It was during this period of Portuguese occupation of Kongo that Portugal invaded Ndongo, confident that Alvare could make no protest. When the Portuguese forces withdrew from Kongo in 1576, Alvare began to restore his kingdom to order, while the Portuguese concentrated their attention on the war against Ndongo and the establishment of a permanent base there.

Alvare was able to use the peace brought to Kongo with great profit. He moved rapidly to reestablish his government, and prosperity quickly returned as the farmers planted their crops and internal order prevailed.

There is some evidence that Alvare, in his appeals for aid against the Jaga, had promised to surrender Kongo's sovereignty to Portugal; upon the return of peace, however, he made it clear that he intended to restore Kongo to its earlier glory in every respect, and to guard against too much Portuguese influence in its affairs. In this effort he was successful; when he died, in 1584, the kingdom was as strong and united as it had ever been.

Alvare I's policies were continued by his son and successor, Alvare II, one of the last of Kongo's great kings. Both monarchs sought more priests, teachers, and technicians from Portugal, Spain, and other European countries, and both strove to gain Vatican recognition of Kongo as a Christian power. In this campaign Alvare II was successful. During his reign, between 1584 and 1614, the Pope received permanent ambassadors to Rome from the Mani Kongo. Alvare II also decreed that Portuguese titles of nobility be used officially in Kongo, that Portuguese be the official court language, and that Portuguese dress and etiquette be approved for noble Kongolese.

Despite Alvare's success in gaining Vatican recognition and his encouragement of Portuguese styles at the court in Sao Salvador, he was unable-like his father-to secure enough help from Portugal to make the major economic progress he sought. Few missionaries and teachers were sent; of these, many died each year of tropical diseases, and others succumbed to the opportunities to acquire wealth and power through the slave trade. By the time Alvare II died in 1614, there was little more change outside the court than had been achieved by Affonso I, a century earlier, when the modernization program had been first conceived.

The sad fact is that the modernizing ambitions of Kongo's kings from Affonso I on were inconsistent with the desire of Portugal to reap profits from Kongo and other central African kingdoms through the slave trade. Portuguese kings and high church officials signed generous treaties with Kongo, and made numerous pronouncements about their sincere wish to aid in the development of Kongo as an enlightened, progressive Christian nation. But their words were belied and subverted by the avarice of wealthy men in Lisbon, Madrid, and Sao Thome, and by the corruption and ineffectiveness of most of their emissaries to Kongo.

For more than a century Portugal regarded Kongo as too strong for outright invasion and conquest. But Portugal's wealthy slave traders and plantation owners resented the efforts by Kongo's kings to regulate the slave trade and the behavior of Portuguese traders in the kingdom, and they campaigned constantly to persuade Lisbon to restrain the Kongolese kings. The Portuguese invasion of Ndongo and the establishment of a base at Luanda were the first permanent successes of this anit-Kongolese policy. With Portuguese foothold in central Africa next door to Kong, Portuguese economic interests could operate without the interference of Kongo's kings.

The Portuguese invasion of Ndongo altered the balance of power in central Africa slowly but surely. Before about 1575 the affairs of Kongo had been decided by internal forces and by the ebb and flow of the relationship with Portugal and Sao Thome.

After 1575 relations with Ndongo and the Portuguese governor at Luanda became matters of vital importance as well. For a time Kongo tended to support the Portuguese wars against Ndongo (which lasted for nearly a century before Ndongo was finally conquered and the colony of Angola was securely under Portuguese control), because it had long regarded Ndono as a vassal state. In 1581, for example, Alvare I sent an army to assist the Portuguese against Ndongo, but it was defeated.

During the 1580's Kongo began to realize that strong Portuguese presence in Angola was dangerous, and under Alvare II it began to support the Ndongo cause.

In 1589 Alvare entered into an alliance with Ndongo, and the allied states enlisted the support of Jaga chieftains and the inland state of Matamba. In that year their combined armies met the Portuguese army and severely defeated it, driving it back to the sea, where it took refuge in the fort at Luanda.

For some reason which no record clarifies, the African allies did not follow up their victory, but instead allowed the Portuguese to remain in Luanda unmolested. For many years afterward there were temporary alliances between Kongo and Ndongö, which allowed both kingdoms to resist Portuguese conquest, although they were never powerful enough to dislodge the Portuguese from Luanda and other footholds in Angola.

After about 1600 the situation became even more complex, when the Dutch began to interest themselves in central African affairs and the slave trade. Throughout the sixteenth century Holland had been ruled by Spanish kings (who also, during the same period, ruled Portugal), but it gained its independence in wars betweens 1572 and 1609. Protestant, anti-Spanish forces had driven Spain out of northern Holland during the 1570's and had built an energetic commercial system which was sending Dutch ships all over the world seeking to break the trade monopoly of Spain and Portugal; one area of great interest to these Dutch merchantmen was the western coast of Africa.

By 1622 Kongo had developed so many contacts with Dutch traders that it was clearly allied with the Dutch against the Portuguese, despite protests from Lisbon, Madrid, and Rome. This alliance was bitterly resented by the Portuguese settlers at Luanda, who had already begun to suffer economically from Dutch competition. The long tension between the Portuguese in Angola and the Mani Kongo became deeper, as the Kongolese monarch cleverly used Dutch traders, his Vatican mission, and his contacts with friendly Portuguese and Spanish priests to lessen the influence of Portuguese Angola in central Africa.

This complicated international situation, interwoven with the greed of both Europeans and Africans eager for the soaring profits of the slave trade, took a heavy toll on the political health of the kingdom of Kongo. At the same time that the Mani Kongo was cementing an alliance with Holland or Ndongo against the Portuguese in Luanda, one of his vassal princes might be secretly conspiring with the Portuguese to evade his authority by shipping slaves without his knowledge or approval.

As the years wore on, the complexity of intrigue by both Dutch and Portuguese grew more bewildering.

The situation within Kongo was made far worse by the confusion over the laws regulating succession to the throne. After Affonso I, it had been generally agreed that only the descendants of his two sonsand one daughter were eligible to become Mani Kongo. But with the passing of generations, the number of Affonso's descendants increased to dozens, then hundreds.

The governors of the six Kongolese provinces were appointed from the higher ranking infantes, as Affonso's descendants were called, as were the administrators of the many districts into which each of the provinces was divided.

By the early 1600's Portuguese titles were officially used by these successors of Affonso; so that there was a long and complex list of members of the noble family: princes, dukes, donnas, marquises, and knights.

As the number of descendants multiplied, the bickering among various claimants to the throne and their supporters also grew. Alvare II seems to have been the last monarch who was able to rule the country in comparative peace. After his death in 1614 the records show a rising number of struggles marking the ascension to the throne of each new king, as well as periodic outbreaks of rebellion by rivals after the king had been crowned. In both the ascension to the throne and the subsequent rebellions the numerous trading agents of the Dutch and Portuguese were incessantly at work, eager to gain allies from whom they could buy more slaves. Indeed, the armed conflicts within the kingdom produced more slaves, so that the European slave traders tended to benefit no matter who won.

In 1641 a new period opened in Kongolese history, stemming the tide of disorder and internal convict for a brief time. In that year Garcia II, the last of the great Kongo kings in the mold of Affonso and the two Alvares, ascended to the throne. In the same year a Dutch fleet occupied the Portuguese fortress and city of Luanda, sending its defenders feeing into the interior of Angola. Also, a large contingent of Italian Capuchin missionaries arrived in Sao Salvador, at Garcia's request, to expand the lethargic missionary and education program still being pursued by the kings of Kongo.

Garcia was more successful in restoring order within Kongo than any of his predecessors since the time of Alvare II, more than thirty-five years before, although he was forced to accept the secession of the province of Soyo as an independent participate for several years. With Dutch help, Garcia managed to maintain order during the 1640's and 1650's although rebellions threatened to erupt throughout his reign. His efforts to expand education and prosperity were only partly successful, however, because the kingdom was struck repeatedly by pestilence and famine. Locusts swept across many of the farmlands in 1642, 1643, 1654, and 1658, and an epidemic, believed to be of plague, resulted in the deaths of nearly half the population in the years 1655-57.

Despite locusts, disease, famine, and internal rivalries Kongo reached a peak of power during Garcia's reign, and for the first few years of his successor, Antonio I, who came to the throne in 1661. Italian, Spanish, and Portuguese missionaries preached and built schools, so that the number of literate, Christian Kongolese was greater than ever before.

Garcia made several attempts to curtail the slave trade, of which he wrote: "instead of gold and silver and other goods which function elsewhere as money, the trade and the money here are persons, who are not in gold, nor in cloth, but who are creatures. It is our disgrace and that of our predecessors that we, in our simplicity, have given the opportunity to do many evils in our realm. . . .

The Dutch occupation of Luanda in 1641 was welcomed by Garcia and the kings of most African states in central Africa, who had little cause to love the Portuguese. Both Kongo and Matamba, the powerful state in the interiors, forced alliances with the Dutch to fight against the Portuguese in other parts of Angola and won a number of victories over the Portuguese forces. But in 1648 a Portuguese fleet from Brazil forced the Dutch commander of Luanda to surrender, following which the Dutch withdrew, leaving their African allies to fight alone.

For the next few years the Portuguese in Angola concentrated their efforts on defeating Matamba, which was at the time ruled by the remarkable Queen Nzinga. Nzinga was from Ndongo, and had been queen of that state until she was driven out of Angola by the Portuguese. Settling in Matamba, she married into its royal family, accumulated a formidable army of Ndongo, Matamba, and Jaga, and continued the war against her Portuguese enemies. In 1656 she was finally defeated, and forced to sign a treaty by which she surrendered her rights to the throne of Ndongo and her lands in Portuguese Angola. With Nzinga eliminated as a serious threat, the aggressive Portuguese in Luanda turned their attention toward Kongo.

Between 1658, when Luanda mobilized a large army, and 1665 Luanda's agents developed to campaign of subversion and intrigue against Garcia II and his successor, Antonio I. In 1664 two Kongolese territories, Wandu and Ambwilu, were persuaded to renounce their allegiance to Antonio and accept the sovereignty of Portugal, and war ensued. In 1665 Antonio I was killed in battle, just as his army was inflicting a defeat on the Portuguese.

Following Antonio's death civil War broke out in Kongo, as rival factions battled to claim the throne. The Portuguese were fearful of intervening after their bruising contact with the Congo army in 1665, but finally, in 1670, they sent an army into Kongo. The army entered the province of Soyo, where it was almost totally annihilated by the count of Soyo. This defeat ended the threat of Portuguese invasion of the Kongo heartland, but by this time there was little need for outright Portuguese conquest; Kongo had ceased to be a unified Power.

Between 1665 and 1710 there was constant civil strife in Kongo, as rival kings based in Soyo, Mbamba, and Mpangu ruled parts of the kingdom and disputed the legitimacy of the others.

Battles were frequent, although no force was strong enough to subdue the others and reunify the country. To make the unhappy situation worse, the growing numbers of infantes, with their Portuguese titles, began competing for rulership of the provinces, then of the districts within the provinces.

In 1710 one Mani Kongo, Pedro IV, succeeded in eliminating rival claimants to the throne, but by this time Soyo had become completely independent of the kingdom and most of the provinces were wracked by conflict over leadership.

From 1710 0n, until the end of the nineteenth century when modern colonial rule was proclaimed over all of central Africa, Kongo existed in a condition, which has often been compared with that Holy Roman Empire in Europe during the Dark Ages. The idea of a national king existed, and was accepted by the people of the nation. This idea served as a cultural bond, keeping alive a spirit of the kinship and common custom. But no strong king appeared, able to raise an army, subdue rivals, and rebuild the national government.

The glory and the promise of Affonso's Kongo, and its pathetic struggles and gradual dissolution after the l650's, make a poignant story. A great African kingdom, united under a ruler of grandeur and vision, shone forth from the heart of central Africa as a revelation to Europe and as a symbol of the achievement of the Bantu civilization. Under Affonso and his successors, for a century and a half, a determined campaign was carried on by a number of worthy monarchs to utilize Christianity to educate the people, develop prosperity, and modernize the land. But their great effort, inspired by Affonso's dream, failed. It was a victim of many forces. The Portuguese and Kongolese alike, hungering for the wealth and power they could gain from the evil slave trade, battled ceaselessly against the forces of unity and progress led by the best of the Mani Kongos and their few Portuguese supporters.

In the end the land was devastated by the ravages of the slave trade and the struggles for wealth and power, and by pestilence and famine. Slowly the kingdom deteriorated into a country of bickering princes, then into a host of tiny chiefdoms, some with fewer than a thousand people, each led by one of the numerous infantes Who ascended to royalty because he was descended from Affonso.

Today the Kongo people still remember Affonso and the ancient days of glory with pride. Many still long for a new leader who can bring them together into a modern nation and resurrect the luster of the past. But history has made such a resurrection virtually impossible. There is no longer, a pretender to the throne. The Congolese people are uniting with a modern state, the People's Republic of the Congo, with its capital at Brazzaville; and the Portuguese colony of Angola, ruled from Luanda, where the Portuguese still cling to the foothold they first established in the sixteenth century. Yet the memory of the ancient past remains alive in the hearts of the Kongolese people, giving them a pride in their culture and in the achievements of their illustrious ancestors."

Today the Interlacustrine Region contains the state of Burundi, Rwanda, most of Uganda, and eastern Tanzania. Congo's western borders touch it, and its peoples influence the affairs of Eastern Kenya. The colonial conquest at the end of the nineteenth century created these modern states, but three- Burundi, Rwanda, and Uganda grew directly out of the ancient kingdoms that dominated the history of the region for many centuries.

The first Bantu farmers arrived in the Interlacustrine Region as early as A.D. 500 or 600, but they were not the first immigrants. The area was inhabited long before their arrival by other, very different peoples, and is in fact adjacent to the country in which mankind probably first appeared. The plains between the Great Rift and the lakes, today rather dry and uninviting but densely populated by vast herds of wild Animals, have yielded the most important evidence of human evolution in the world. At such famous sites as Olduvai Gorge, Olorgesailie, and the Lake Rudolph-Omo River area, in Tanzania, in Kenya, and in southern Ethiopia, anthropologists have found abundant remains of creatures that range from ancestral primates, living 40 million years ago, right up to modern man. From these sites have come the numerous remains of Australopithecus, Homo erectus, and other ancient ancestors of humanity.

In the millennium before the first Bantu farmers arrived, three groups were living in the Interlacustrine Region and in the lands adjacent to it. One group was ancestral to today's Pygmies, small bands of whom still live in Uganda, Rwanda, and eastern Congo. Making their living by hunting wild animals in the forested parts of the region, and by gathering wild fruits, seeds, vegetables, and insects, the Pygmies were ultimately affected so deeply by the incoming Bantu that they have long spoken only Bantu languages, and their own languages are extinct.

The second group was the Khoisan, who hunted and gathered wild foods in the drier plains. Their territory once stretched all the way from the southern tip of Africa to the Ethiopian highlands. In East Africa they were completely absorbed by the Bantu immigrants, although there are several small ethnic groups in Tanzania who speak languages that are thought to be of the Khoisan stock. These people, such as the Hadzapi, are racially similar to their Bantu neighbors today, but they still live mainly by hunting and cling to their own language.

The third group was the Cushites, a tall brown skinned people who were related to the peoples of Ethiopia and Somalia; their modern representatives include the Galla of Ethiopia and Somalia, the Somali, and the Sidamo of Ethiopia."[2]

The Fate of the Bantu Achievement:

The expansion of the Bantu civilization throughout Africa south of the equator, and the gradual creation of great states and empires, represents a triumph in the face of considerable odds. Yet between 1700 and 1900 many of the most notable creations of the Bantu-speaking peoples suffered a poignant decline, especially when faced with the growing influence of Western ideas and power. What were the hallmarks of the Bantu civilization, and what were the weaknesses that caused it to erode so quickly when challenged from the outside world?

The Bantu achievement was most marked in six areas of life: agriculture, metal technology, crafts, architecture, politics, and creative ideas in religion, philosophy, and oral literature. At first glance, the Bantu contributions in these areas seem commonplace when compared with those of such ancient Mediterranean peoples as the Egyptians, Sumerians, Greeks, and Romans. Yet when seen in the perspective of a vast, isolated inhospitable environment, very insulated from the rest of the world, they reflect a great strength of adaptability and creativity.

In agriculture the Bantu achievement was the ability to adapt a basic knowledge of plants, land cultivation, and soil conservation to a wide variety of soil and climate conditions-almost all of which were somewhat less than generous. The very earliest ancestors of the Bantu-speaking peoples who spread out from the Katanga cradle land were tenacious farmers. They knew how to acquire supplemental foods from fishing, hunting wild game, and gathering a large variety of wild fruits, berries, roots, nuts, and seeds. But they concentrated their efforts on clearing the land of trees and underbrush in order to plant their crops of millet, sorghum, peas, beans, and many kinds of leafy vegetables.

The soil in which the Bantu farmers planted their crops had to be prepared and tended with great skill and care. It was mostly covered with tough grasses, thick wild shrubs, and trees with very hard wood. Under this natural plant cover the fertile layer was thin and relatively poor in the humus and nutrients needed to produce a good yield. One or two years of planting tended to deplete this scant natural fertility. Years of rest were necessary so that the native weeds, grasses, and shrubs could reestablish themselves, deposit leaves and twigs which decomposed to introduce new nutrients into the topsoil, and restore a measure of fertility. In most areas the rainfall was light and unreliable. For a few months of each year rain fell, sometimes in heavy downpours, and the rest of the year was dry.

Adding further perils to agriculture were the many insects that destroyed crops and the plant diseases that ruined those crops that had not developed immunity to them. The tropical warmth of the climate and the unevenness of the rainfall combined, ironically, to create further difficulties in maintaining healthy crops.

Fallen leaves, weeds, twigs, and branches decompose, in every part of the world, then gradually sink into the soil to deposit chemical nutrients as bacteria continue to decompose them.

In most of tropical Africa the decomposition process is speeded up by the constant warmth, so that the natural nutrients form on or very near the surface of the soil. Heavy rains tend to wash away some of these nutrients before they mix thoroughly with the soil. Through the process known as leaching, more of these essential nutrients are also washed downward too rapidly through the topsoil, finally becoming deposited at a deeper level than is normally cultivated. Between the leaching and the washing away, it is very difficult for the soil of tropical Africa to build up and retain a reasonable degree of fertility.

The skills of the Bantu farmer gradually developed a pattern, which was the best under the circumstances: the shifting plot system. When the farmers slashed down the trees and undergrowth covering a plot, they burned them so that the ashes would add useful chemical elements to the soil. After planting and harvesting one or two crops, they would either rotate less demanding crops for another year or two or move on to another plot. The original plot would be left to nature for regeneration.

This system requires large acreages for each family and appears to be a wasteful use of land. Yet it is the only method that works in most African soils, until there is available the money and knowledge to add artificial fertilizers and to grow certain kinds of cover crops, which replenish the soil's fertility more rapidly than nature can do. This advanced kind of knowledge was not available to the Bantu farmers; it is a relatively new thing even in scientific Western agriculture.

In some areas the Bantu civilization went beyond its basic system of agriculture, when local opportunities offered. In parts of [Zimbabwe], Tanzania, and Mozambique lands were terraced to prevent the erosion of soil and to retain as much of the rainfall as possible. In the Interlacustrine Region and some of the neighboring highlands cattle dung was used to fertilize the crops, enriching the soil greatly.

Seen from the perspective of history and knowledge of the problems posed by the African environment, the Bantu civilization's agricultural accomplishments were impressive. Theirs was no land flowing with milk and honey, but the Bantu-speaking peoples used their knowledge of plants and the soil creatively and flexibly to earn the best living possible. Where local areas were better watered and more fertile, they developed the best ways of producing abundant yields. Where lands were more arid and less fertile, they grew crops as best they could, and then grazed herds of cattle, sheep, and goats to provide an alternate source of food. When necessary they fished and hunted. Although the pattern of making a living varied according to the bountifulness of the land they settled, they made the best possible use of it to expand, their population and live as comfortably as they could.

The ability to use metals was the second hallmark of the Bantu civilization. Scholars disagree on whether the knowledge of mining, smelting, and forging iron was independently discovered in Africa or was brought there from the Middle East, where it was known as early as 1500 B.C.

Whatever the origin of this knowledge, however, Africans throughout the continent used it to great advantage. The Bantu-speaking peoples used it, at least as early as the time of Christ, to make axes, hoes, blades, knives, needles, scissors, and many other tools. If they had not been able to make these iron tools, they could never have spread their agricultural way of life across central and southern Africa. Stone tools, however useful they may have been to more primitive hunting peoples, were not adequate to the tasks of clearing large fields of stout trees and shrubs, and cultivating the harsh soil.

The Bantu civilization was built almost as much on its mastery of iron as on its knowledge of agriculture. In every new area the men who understood metallurgy quickly located available iron deposits. They dug out the ore, built highly effective small furnaces, and smelted out the crude iron from the ore. With simple but efficient forges and bellows they were able to melt the iron, then fashion it into the tools they needed.

Where iron was more plentiful it was used for weapons as well as tools, although tools were considered more important when the supplies of iron were scarce. The basic skill in metallurgy was used, of course, not only for iron but also for copper, tin, and gold, if they were available.

However, they were rarely considered to be of the same value as iron. Generally they were used to make ornaments and art objects, or, when the opportunity existed, to trade to the outside world for especially valuable goods. Today the countries of [Congo], Zambia, [Zimbabwe], and South Africa are the richest mineral-producing countries in Africa, as they were in ancient times long before the Europeans came. Literally hundreds of thousands of ancient mines have been found within their territories. It was the lure of gold, silver, and copper that aroused Portugal's interest in Angola and Kongo. The gold and iron that were exported from the [Zimbabwe] plateau down to the sea at Sofala were the mainstays of the great Swahili trading cities, as well as the magnets that drew the Portuguese up the Zambezi into the lands of Mwene Mutapa.

In working all these metals the Bantu-speaking peoples showed a mastery of all phases of basic metallurgy. There were few deposits, other than those deep under the earth's surface, that escaped the keen eyes of their artisans and miners. Their metal tools were well shaped, with hard, sharp blades and points. When working copper and gold the Bantu craftsmen developed devices for making fine wire and paper-thin plate, as well as gold tacks and nails which were used to secure gold wire and foil to wooden statues. Handsome cups and bowls were hammered to exquisite smoothness for the use of the nobility.

Attractive beads, bangles, bracelets, necklaces, and belts were fashioned in iron, copper, and gold to adorn the wealthy and the noble.

Most of the Bantu-speaking peoples achieved a notable level of crafts: pottery, musical instruments, woven baskets, stools, gongs, cloth of cotton and bark, and intricately carved staffs and maces for men of position. Utilitarian objects for the common people were simple but attractive, and were carefully designed and made to serve useful functions.

For cooking and eating there were many sizes and shapes of pots, bowls, and pitchers made of clay. In areas where trees were plentiful, bowls for serving and eating were often finely carved in hard woods. Where soft stone was available, it was frequently used to make similar vessels, some of which were elegant in their clean lines and superb craftsmanship. Spoons and forks were made from wood, stone, or bone in great variety. Needles, scissors, and shears were generally made from iron. Well made, attractive combs and hair ornaments were fashioned of bone, shell, wood, or metal; depending on what materials were available.

For the nobility and the wealthy, considerable artistry was used in both ornamental and utilitarian objects. Pottery vessels with very thin but strong walls were made in graceful shapes and, decorated with lovely designs. Often they were carefully burnished and colored.

Masks and statues for religious and ceremonial purposes were intricately made, and were passed down from generation to generation as objects of veneration. Eating utensils and bowls were sometimes made from gold or copper materials much too precious to be owned by the commoner.

Little is known of the ancient crafts of weaving and spinning, although spindle whorls of clay, stone, and metal have been found in many graves and at the ruins of many towns. Animal skins, crude wool, cotton, coconut fiber, raffia, and bark were all used for making clothing. Again the clothing of the nobility was richer than that of commoners.

In several Bantu kingdoms threads of gold were spun into royal robes, and clips and fasteners of gold and copper were often used for the robes of the highborn.

Even though most Bantu-speaking peoples have left no great ruined temples and buildings as magnificent as those of Egypt, Greece, and Mesopotamia, their techniques of construction were meritorious. In most parts of their territory they found little stone useful for building purposes. Generally the only easily available material was earth, which, mixed with water and straw, hardened into a very suitable covering for houses. Houses built of this material were constructed around a wooden framework, and roofs were made of thatch from the tall grasses that grew on most of the African savanna.

The houses were simple but comfortable. They were able to withstand many years of the typical weather conditions of central and southern Africa. And since the agricultural rotation pattern required that villages move every few years, few of the Bantu peoples found it worthwhile to build houses that would last longer than necessary. The houses were often decorated with geometric designs, frequently painted or etched with colors made of mineral ores and naturally occurring chemicals.

In some moister areas, such as the Interlacustrine Region, the extremely tall grasses of the area were used as a prime building material. In Buganda, for example, grasses and reeds were commonly used to produce truly elegant houses. The houses of the noble and wealthy people were very large, often with rooms more than thirty feet across, and were light and airy because of the material used. In these areas the weaving of reeds and grasses was developed to heights of real artistry. In the houses of royalty between the Baganda and the Kuba, grasses were woven into intricate abstract designs. The first European visitors to see these houses were struck by their beauty. Even today, when few African craftsmen practice these ancient arts, tourists are quick to photograph the woven houses they find-not because of their novelty but because of the extraordinary grace and beauty with which they are made.

In those areas where stone was readily available, such as the [Zimbabwe] plateau and the northern parts of South Africa, the craftsmen of the Bantu civilization turned their talents to working in that durable material.

Eventually they were able to build the hundreds of temples, enclosures, and other structures that dot that region today, and are so impressively symbolized by the brooding ruins at Great Zimbabwe.

Apart from these great stone ruins, of course, no one will argue that the Bantu civilization has left the world an outstanding architectural legacy. But the construction of houses and the plans of villages and towns were functional and intelligently designed. Towns were laid out with care to take advantage of natural drainage and the contours of the land. In areas where defense was a problem they were surrounded by trenches or thick walls to keep enemies at bay. The streets were often broad and straight, and were bordered by fences. Neatness and cleanliness were considered important. For a people who moved often, and whose lands produced little surplus wealth, the Bantu craftsmen performed well.

Another hallmark of the Bantu civilization, which can be appreciated only by what one finds today, was its achievements in the intellectual and esthetic field. Apart from the Swahili, no Bantu people developed systems of writing prior to the arrival of the Europeans; hence we have no written record of their ancient poetry, philosophy, religion, myths, and folktales. From what has been learned since the European contact, however, it is apparent that their accomplishments in this area were worthy ones.

Every Bantu society produces bards who specialize in memorizing and retelling its accumulate lore or wisdom. The best of these bards can speak eloquently for days on the lives and exploits of their great kings. These oral histories have produced epic literatures that can be thrilling in their dramatic presentation. Each serves to preserve the morals and virtues of the society, so the storyteller may spend hours describing the qualities of the great kings of the past: their piety, their bravery, their wisdom, their generosity, their charity to the unfortunate, their mercy toward enemies, and their great concern for the welfare of their people.

In some Bantu societies, such as those of Burundi and Rwanda, the aristocracy for many generations has devoted itself to the development of poetry and oral literature. A gifted Rwandan poet can recite for hours graceful epic poems, which he has composed over a period of years, constantly refining and perfecting them. Every Bantu society has produced its sages, who are looked to for the clearest statements of that society's religious and philosophical beliefs. The sages of Kongo, for example, reveal systems of belief about God, man, and the world which are extremely complex and elaborate, and which are sometimes beautiful in conception. In great detail they tell about God and how and why He created man. They tell of God's purpose in creating the seasons, the sky, the mountains, rivers, waterfalls, and other things on earth. Every natural phenomenon is given an explanation: the stars, the moon, the sun, the tides, and the movements of heavenly bodies.

Just as al-Masudi was impressed, in the tenth century, by the Bantu orators he found on his visit to the Swahili coast, almost everyone who knows Bantu culture today is struck by the eloquence of its great speakers. The man who can speak gracefully and with dramatic expression is honored, and people praise him for his retelling of a national epic or his delivery of a good rhyme, a clever riddle, a popular fable, or a telling parable. Children's stories are told around the fires at dusk, usually by grandfathers or grandmothers who have special talent for entertaining and educating the young. The best of these older storytellers are never at a loss for a good tale that may send the children into peals of laughter or shivers of fear. Sometimes their stories contain moral messages, but some are purely for entertainment.

Of all the qualities of the Bantu civilization, the most vivid is that of its politics and government. The many kinds of government that the Bantu created during the two-thousand-year period of their settlement of southern Africa were elaborate and effective. They maintained internal peace and tranquility, at their best, as well as any governments in any part of the world. They produced leaders of enormous vision and political talent: Affonso, Changamire, Shaka, and Moshesh, to name only a few.

The systems of government, which the Bantu civilization evolved from region to region and group to group. But they typically were organized around a king who was believed to rule with divine approval, and often to possess semi-divine powers himself. His powers were great, and he had authority over almost all the affairs of his kingdom.

Yet there were safeguards against unjust actions by the king. He had powerful ministers and advisers around him, whose opinions counted when decisions were made. He ruled over a land in which local chiefs, heads of families, and councils of elders also had power. If he ruled harshly and unwisely, there were factions that might depose him, and this happened from time to time in the history of every Bantu kingdom. When he grew old or ill, he was expected to abdicate his throne so that a younger, more able king could provide the leadership.

The Bantu system of government could not, of course prevent occasional despotism; no system of government ever devised by man has been totally successful in guaranteeing that its rulers would be wise and just. But the Bantu peoples resented injustice and harsh rule as much as any people. When they found themselves ruled by a man whom they regarded as unfit, they could and did act.

One of the most powerful and forceful kings ever to rise to power within the Bantu civilization was assassinated by his brother and a faction of notables who resented his obsessive military campaigns and expenditures.

In all the governments of the Bantu people there was a measure of democracy, although it was a very different kind of democracy from that of modern Europe and America. There were rarely formal political parties and systematic votes. In each village and district, however, the affairs of the state were studied and discussed daily by the elders and the men of local power. They sent their views to the provincial rulers and the king's cabinet, so that the king could act in full knowledge of the views of his subjects. While Europe was still in the Dark Ages, and millions of serfs lived out their lives with no power to influence their rulers, there were Bantu states where peasants had opinions about government, and ways to register those opinions. A wise king listened to their views, while an unwise king disregarded them, sometimes to his own peril.

In all these areas the Bantu civilization distinguished itself in the face of handicaps and difficulties. If one compares the Bantu civilization with those of Greece, Rome, Western Europe, Egypt, India, and China, however, it seems at first glance to be a modest one. Its technology was effective, but it never reached the impressive heights scaled by these civilizations. In its oral literature, philosophy, and arts it may have been gifted and creative, but they were never recorded in writing or carried to the elaborate lengths found in these other civilizations. In the face of such comparisons, must we judge the Bantu achievement to be of a lesser order? Any civilization must be judged in terms of how well its people are able to seize the opportunities afforded by their environment. The Bantu-speaking peoples were faced with two environmental difficulties, which set insurmountable limits; yet they were able to achieve much in spite of these difficulties.

First, and very importantly, the lands of central and southern Africa have long been meager in their fertility, especially when compared with the enormously rich valleys of the Nile, the Indus, the Tigris, and the Euphrates. Not until the development of modern agricultural science has there been any possibility of wresting better yields from the soil than the Bantu farmers were able to produce. Even today Western-trained agricultural scientists and engineers are facing an uphill battle in the Bantu lands.

Second, the Bantu civilization was almost totally isolated from the great currents of thought and development, which swept the countries around the Mediterranean and enabled the peoples of Europe to rise from barbarism. Except for those who lived in the narrow strip of land along the Indian Ocean, no members of the Bantu society had any opportunity to interact with different peoples, to learn new ways of solving problems, or to develop new methods of making a living. Throughout the history of mankind isolation has been a handicap, especially in the fields of technology and industry. When one considers that virtually everything the Bantu civilization accomplished was from the efforts of its own people, without benefit of new ideas and challenges from the rest of the world, it again begins to appear impressive.

In the realms of life where individual talent seems to make the most difference, the comparison between the Bantu civilization and others shows less inequality. The music, dance, and art of the Bantu peoples are of high esthetic quality by any standard. Artists from Europe and Asia today feel awe and deep appreciation when they view the sculpture or hear the music of Bantu Africa. They recognize that the men and women who produced African art were inspired by the same deep feelings that move all great artists, and that they expressed those inspirations for the appreciation of all men.

In their social and political life, too, the Bantu people developed concepts and practices that command the respect of all. Their ideas of justice, of good and evil, of order among peoples, and of wide leadership were mature and intelligence.

They knew what human misery and degradation were, and they developed ideas and systems of government that helped, as much as any system could, to give each person a sense of dignity and worth. One of the great ironies of history was that the Bantu peoples often pitied or despised the Europeans who conquered them, because they felt that the Europeans had been unable to learn the great concepts of civilized behavior that the Bantu way of life regarded as natural.

For all this, however, there was a weakness in the Bantu civilization, which is best described as fragility. This quality grew out of the poverty of the land, and it made the Bantu civilization vulnerable to conquest and imposed change, once a stronger, more determined military and political force faced it from the outside world. Basically, this fragility was a simple thing: One man, by his hardest effort, could support only his family, with very little food or goods left over. He had little leisure time to speculate about new and better ways of doing things.

There were few surplus resources to support an elaborate court, a large army, a great class of priests and philosophers, and large cities where people were free to specialize in industry and other nonagricultural pursuits.

The achievements of the Bantu civilization were thus produced, as it were, part-time, for example, pottery was made by women when they had the time. Even the "art" of war, which the Bantu, like all civilizations, occasionally practiced, could not be sustained for long periods.

If men went to war for more than brief periods, the crops and the herds were neglected, and starvation could result. Only a few men and women were free from the daily task of making a living, and they constituted the government, the small police force or standing army, and the masons, artists, and metallurgists.

In arithmetical terms, the average Bantu farm family could produce enough, grain, vegetables, and meat to support themselves plus, at best, a tiny fraction of the amount needed to support a non-farmer. A family produced perhaps 101 percent to 105 percent of what is needed to live on.

In ancient Egypt a farm family, tilling the rich soil along the banks of the Nile, could produce perhaps 150 percent or 200 percent of what it needed, leaving a substantial surplus for the support of philosophers, nobles, priests, stonemasons, brick makers, artists, and administrators. In modern America a farm family can produce as much as 3,000 percent of what it needs; in other words, twenty to thirty non-farm families can live on the surplus produced by one farmer.

This means that the economic base of the Bantu civilization was extremely slim. Except in a few regions which had more favorable environments, such as the Interlacustrine area, the more important Bantu states remained small until a trade system had developed. Trade allowed the state to sell its small surplus of gold, copper, iron, ivory, or other products (including slaves at a later period) in exchange for more efficient tools, cloth, luxury goods, and firearms. With these products a king could not only enhance his prestige but could give valued rewards to those subjects and colleagues who served him.

Even where trade brought in this very helpful wealth, however, the economic base of society severely limited the size of the king's court, his administrative structure, and his army. If he attempted to build up a large standing army of more than a few hundred men, the chances were that there was not enough food to support them, without the commoners to provide more in the form of taxation than they were willing to contribute. One of the factors in Shaka's downfall was the dissatisfaction caused by the expense of maintaining the large, active army on which he built his state.

The result of this economically based fragility was that every Bantu state was limited in how widely it could expand, how many people it could assign to nonagricultural activities, and how large and permanent its capital could become. Once it had reached a certain size and complexity of development, its growth slowed naturally and necessarily. If there were no radical change in environment or contact with different peoples, this stage of development could last indefinitely.

Where new opportunities arose the Bantu peoples seized them readily. In the Interlacustrine Region, isolated though it was, they turned to intensive cultivation of the more fertile soil and produced surpluses, which were large compared with those of most of Bantu Africa.

As a result, the strength of some of the Bantu kingdoms was substantial, and there was continuing evolution and development in every area of life until the twentieth century and the wholly new challenges it brought. Along the Swahili coast the people absorbed the immigrant Arabs and their knowledge of the Indian Ocean world. The result was the creation of a series of prosperous cities, a bustling commerce with the outside world, the adoption of Arabic writing, and the building of a graceful civilization, which blended Islamic and African ideas. Most of Bantu African, however, possessed neither the fertile environment of the Interlacustrine Region nor the continuing contact with the outside world enjoyed by the Swahili coast.

A great question of history is how quickly and effectively the Bantu civilization might have used the influx of ideas, techniques, and materials from Europe to develop its potentialities to higher levels. This question is unlikely ever to be answered, unfortunately, because of the swiftness and totality of the European conquest.

The first contacts between Bantu Africa and Europe seemed useful to Africans, and they might have led, had they taken a different path, to the gradual absorption of Western science and technology within an African cultural framework. Kings of coastal states, who had the first opportunity to trade with Europe, gained a new and important source of income; this enabled them to strengthen their power and add to the effectiveness of their governments. Even far into the interior, in states, which had no direct contact with Europeans, participation in the new commercial system stimulated political development. The period of greatest growth in Mwata Yamvo, Mwata Kazembe, Lunda, Bemba, and other interior states followed their involvement in this trading pattern.

The European contact failed to promote growth and development over a longer period, however. As time wore on, its effects proved to be more harmful than helpful.

One injurious effect was the decline of African crafts in the face of competition from cheaper European manufactured goods. African spinning and weaving suffered so severely from the influx of cheaper cloth from Europe and India that they became extinct in many Bantu societies.

African iron technology suffered as well. In earlier times an African ironworker might have exchanged a good hoe blade for several pots, baskets of grain, or animals. European hoes were imported at much less expense, however; one ivory tusk or a leopard skin might buy several hoes of good quality. By the end of the nineteenth century many traditional crafts that had been hallmarks of the Bantu civilization had ceased to exist, and Africans were totally dependent upon Europe for many essential articles.

Another serious effect of the European contact was the heightened tensions and rivalries within African states, caused by struggles among various factions to control the trade. Kings whose power had traditionally been secure found their vassals conspiring with each other or with European agents to establish new trade arrangements that would evade the king's regulations and his taxes. Ambitious vassals or clan leaders were emboldened by avarice to attempt coups or revolutions in order to seize the throne. Even though many Bantu kings were able to contain these internal problems, they added to the kings' burdens and problems of statesmanship.

Similarly, the European trade intensified rivalries between kingdoms and led to more frequent wars. Since each African state was eager to have the most direct possible access to the European trade, some were willing to resort to war to improve or protect their trading position.

The longer the contact between Africa and Europe, and the more profitable the trade, the more willing Europeans became to intervene in African affairs directly. The sordid history of Portuguese intrigue and intervention in the affairs of Kongo, Ndongo, and Mwene Mutapa, and the seizure and destruction of many Swahili cities, show the lengths to which they were willing to go to insure profits.

In those areas of Bantu Africa where European colonists settled, the negative effects of the European contact were even more vivid. In South Africa the Dutch, and later the British, seized African lands as they expanded. They were, in the process, guilty of trickery, bribery, and outright theft, and they often killed Africans who protested or resisted. White settlement of South Africa was marked by almost constant warfare between the encroaching Europeans and the Africans whose lands they occupied.

Despite these destructive consequences of the European contact, however, much of Bantu Africa was little affected until the nineteenth century. Between about 1480 and 1880 European contact with Bantu Africa was limited to the coastlands, except for shallow penetrations into Kongo, Angola, and Mwene Mutapa and gradual expansion into the interior of South Africa. The mass of Bantu-speaking people in the vast hinterland of Africa knew little of Europe and were touched only indirectly by the African-European trading system.

In about 1880, however, this situation changed with lightning speed; between that time and 1900 Europe subjected all of Bantu Africa to colonial rule. This colonial conquest, and the subsequent period of European rule, brought the Bantu civilization under alien control and influence, which has only begun to disappear in the past few years as the new nations achieve independence.

In 1880 European nations, as a result of the rapid industrialization they experienced during the nineteenth century, were engaged in a fierce rivalry for access to raw materials and markets. The factories of England, France, Germany, and other European states needed large supplies of cheap raw materials and customers for their rapidly growing production of a wide variety of manufactured goods. Africa, except for its coastal areas, was the one large area of the world that remained outside the European economic embrace.

European exploration of Africa's interior had begun some years earlier; as early as 1800 in West Africa, and 1850 in Bantu Africa. Between 1860 and 1880 a steady stream of explorers, including David Livingston, John Speke, Richard Burton, and Henry Morton Stanley, traveled deep into the heart of Bantu Africa, mapping its waterways and landforms and bringing back reports about the people and the goods they produced. From the interior of [Zimbabwe] and Zambia they returned with evidence of mineral wealth. From the upper reaches of the great Congo River they reported large populations, mineral wealth, and vast lands suitable for producing valuable exports such as rubber and palm oil. From the Interlacustrine Region they brought news of great and prosperous kingdoms and a dense population living on fertile lands.

European traders and missionaries began to move into the African interior. European trading posts in the coastal areas began to grow in size, and their agents worked energetically to build a more extensive commerce with the peoples in the interior. Although Portugal dominated the coastal trading stations in most of Angola and Mozambique, and Britain was in clear charge in South Africa, other areas were open to agents from any European company that was interested in joining the competition.

This quickening exploration and commercial expansion was transformed into a scramble by European nations for legal control of African territory when King Leopold II of Belgium proclaimed himself ruler of a vast Congo Free State in 1883. Leopold was acting in a private capacity, as a businessman who headed an international financial combine, and he used the development of a central African commercial empire as a means of increasing his personal wealth and prestige. As king of Belgium, he was subject to political and financial restraints by a Democratic Parliament; as head of a private corporation, which claimed rights to the Congo, he could act with little constraint. This he did boldly and ruthlessly.

He secured recognition of his claims from a number of countries (of which the United states was the first) and asserted that his Congo territory included all lands drained by the Congo River system.

This proved to cover more than 900,000 square miles, or roughly one-third as much land as that of the United States!

Germany, rivaling Britain as Europe's most important industrial power, had no colonial possessions at the time. But it saw in Africa a chance to become a colonial power, which would give it international prestige as well as control of raw materials and markets. In swift succession it annexed East Africa; ((Tanganyika), Kamerun (now Cameroun), South-West Africa (now Namibia), and Togoland. Suddenly the scramble began. France quickly moved troops into western Africa, eventually winning international recognition as the ruler of much of northern and western Africa. Britain expanded its South African foothold into what are now Zambia and Zimbabwe and the territories that are now known as Botswana, Lesotho, and Swaziland. In East Africa it seized Egypt and the Sudan, then Kenya, Uganda, and Zanzibar.

In South Africa Britain stepped up its pressures on the Boer Republics of the Transvaal and Orange Free State. In 1898 the so-called Boer War broke out, and when it ended with British victory over the settlers of Dutch descent, in 1901, Britain was in legal control of the entire territory that later became the Union of South Africa.

These European seizures of Bantu Africa, between 1883 and 1900, were not accepted passively by Africans. Many African states resisted, and there was a tragic series of bloody wars in, Tanganyika, parts of the Congo, Cameroon, South Africa, [Zimbabwe], and Zambia. After European colonial rule was imposed there were numerous major rebellions.

The German-Herero wars in Namibia claimed some 75,000 African lives, nearly half the Herero population. The Maji-Maji rebellion in Tanganyika, in 1904-6, claimed more than 100,000 lives. In Zimbabwe the Matabele and Shona, previously hostile to each other, united in a massive uprising against British rule, and lost several thousand lives before they were defeated.

The most horrible suffering in Bantu Africa, however, resulted from the "development" of the Congo Free State by large forces of mercenaries, employed by private companies and the Free State government. Many Africans were forced at gunpoint to abandon their own farms in order to work on great plantations and in mines; those who remained on their own lands were required to produce specified quantities of rubber, cocoa, maize, palm oil, and other cash crops. Those who resisted - and many did -were imprisoned, fined, tortured, maimed, or executed.

Within ten years after the establishment of Leopold's government, horrifying reports, usually by missionaries, began to trickle out to the European and American public. But it was not until 1908 that the Belgian Parliament, influenced by protests from many parts of the world, removed the Congo from Leopold's control. At that time the Congo became a Belgian colony, administered by a government responsible to the Belgian Parliament.

Official Belgian investigations of Congo atrocities found that Leopold's agents had' been guilty of unbelievably ruthless and inhumane acts. Although it was impossible to assess accurately the number of Congolese who had died through these acts and the starvation that resulted from men being forced to abandon their farms, some authorities believe the figure may have been as high as 3 million. Large areas of the Congo were virtually depopulated by this barbaric campaign, which lasted from 1883 to 1908.

European colonial methods differed from territory to territory. In every territory African resistance to European rule or economic policies was dealt with sternly, although rarely with the brutality used in the Congo. Some features, however, were common to all colonial administrations.

First, Africans were required to acknowledge the sovereignty and ultimate authority of the European colonial government. Some colonial governments followed the policy known as "indirect rule," which used African traditional chiefs and village headmen to carry out government regulations. This was particularly true in the British colonies, although the Portuguese and Germans used indirect rule to a limited extent. In their colonies, however, the more usual pattern was to use European district administrators, backed by armed forces, to rule directly over the people. Under this kind of direct rule African chiefs and kings lost most of their power, and became figureheads whose main function was ceremonial.

Second, economic development was given high priority, since the main motivation in the colonial conquest was to gain access to raw materials and to open up consumer markets. Where minerals were found, companies were formed to exploit them. Important cash crops needed in Europe, such as rubber and cotton, were put into production and African farmers were encouraged (or sometimes forced) to grow them. When force was not used directly, Africans were persuaded to grow cash crops mainly by taxation. Usually a set amount had to be paid, in cash, by each male over sixteen. In order to obtain the money to pay his taxes, a man had either to grow crops for sale or to leave his farm and seek work in the mines or in the towns where Europeans were settling.

Third, little was done to aid Africans was done by missionaries, until recent years. Missionaries were encouraged by the colonial governments to provide schools, health care, and religious instruction. The reliance upon missionaries was so widespread that even today many of the independent African governments continue to welcome missionaries and to rely on them to supplement state education, medical services, and community development activities.

Fourth, the colonial governments paid little respect to African cultures and traditional values. Missionaries were encouraged to convert Africans to Christianity.

African religion was dismissed disparagingly as primitive paganism or animism that the outside world is only now learning that it is based on a Supreme Being and requires its believers to adhere to high moral and ethical standards. African marriage practices, such as polygamy, which were deeply ingrained in the society, were often made illegal if they differed from those of Europeans.

African traditional authorities, the chiefs and kings, lost much of their power in the colonial period. Even where there was indirect rule, the colonial administrators made the important decisions, and removed from office any African officials who were regarded as disloyal or obstructive. Gradually the ordinary African placed less and less faith in his traditional rulers and accepted the colonial government as the source of power.

Colonialism so eroded the position of African traditional rulers that they played almost no role in African government; with the coming of independence in the 1960's a new breed of African leaders, who were educated in European schools or who acquired power in institutions such as labor unions, were the only ones who commanded enough popular respect to govern.

The dominance of Europeans was so complete during the colonial period that it was difficult, even for many Africans, to perceive the good qualities of the Bantu civilization. Many outsiders, and a few Africans, come to believe that the Bantu culture would die, to be replaced by a basically European one. African culture was for so long portrayed as weak and bad, and European culture as strong and good, that it seemed true to many people.

It is now recognized that this view greatly over values the quality of Western culture and underestimates the strength and enduring values of African. The Bantu civilization, which took more than two thousand years to develop, is still very much alive. It is a force that shapes the lives of millions of Africans. It has been changed by colonial rule, and many of its institutions, such as the chieftainship, have been fatally weakened. But its underlying values have not been lost. They shape African views about God, family ties, authority and government, the nature of life, and artistic expression.

No one, not even the most eminent African scholars and philosophers, can predict what the new Bantu civilization of the future will be like. Many decades of enforced Westernization under colonial rule introduced new ideas and destroyed some of the old. Under colonialism the Bantu cultures were, in a sense, anesthetized and partially hidden under the veneer of Western cultural influence and government. With the gaining of independence by Africans, however, and the removal of Western constraints, the vital force of the Bantu civilization is beginning to assert itself.

Using Western science and knowledge, it is now rising again, to help Bantu-speaking Africans create a future for themselves which will be a blend of old and new, indigenous and imported.

Today the majorities of the Bantu people live in independent nations; ruled by their own leaders, free to begin the long task of reconstructing and modernizing the Bantu civilization.

The modern history of the African struggle against colonial rule, which resulted in independence for many Africans, suggests that the Africans of these alien-ruled countries will continue to seek the self-determination that their kinsmen on the rest of the continent have achieved. If so, then they will someday join other members of the Bantu civilization in building a new way of life that is modern, yet blends in the proud heritage of their ancient past."3

In 1994, in his presidential inaugural speech, Nelson Mandela told his fellow South African brethren after centuries of oppression at the hands of Europeans that:

"Our deepest fear is not that we are inadequate.
Our deepest fear is that we are powerful beyond measure.
It is our light, not our darkness, that most frightens us.
We ask ourselves, who am I to be brilliant, gorgeous,
talented and fabulous?
You are a child of GOD!
Your playing small doesn't serve the world.
There's nothing enlightening about shrinking so that other
people won't feel insecure around you.
We were born to make manifest the glory of GOD
that is within us.
It's not just in some of us; it's in everyone.
And as we let our own light shine, we unconsciously
give other people permission to do the same.
As we are liberated from our own fear,
our presence automatically liberates others."
Thus, South Africa began the difficult task of restructuring politically,
socially, and economically, in order to meet the demands of the Twenty-
First Century under new leadership!

CONCLUSION AND SUGGESTIONS

In summary, America is still divided along the "colorline." However, in the words of Dr. Jane Tollett, Psychologist, in Los Angeles. Ca., "We'd like to think that we've made progress." Well to some extent this may be true. But in all actuality perhaps the progress that she is referring to is on the Caucasian side of the "Colorline."

To be sure, people of color do suffer from many more vices here in America than do our Caucasian counterpart. For example, the unemployment rate among African American men is three times that of Caucasian men and African-American men make up less than 15% of the population as a whole. Of those employed, gainfully, salaries for performing similar jobs are comparatively less for African-American men than for our Caucasian counterpart. Moreover, an even more staggering amount of these statistics are relevant towards the African-American youth of our society. According to fellow South Carolinian, the Rev. Jesse Jackson, "America would rather spend millions of dollars each year housing African-American youth in jail and penitentiaries than spend half as much providing an education for African-American youth that would keep them out of jails or incarcerated."

In 1968, Martin Luther King, Jr., had suggested a "Guaranteed Annual income" as a means towards full employment, in order to close the gap between the "Haves" and "Have nots." But congress wasn't willing to hear of such a solution as they thought at that time. Thus, we have inherited the results of their own neglect in that respect and they have dismissed the poor as being: Incompetent, Inferior, or Insane.

"The root problem in African-American communities all across America is "Race," and the unjust and unequal distribution of our nation's wealth, power and resources. One race, the descendents of Caucasian-Europeans, seemingly have checkmated African-Americans efforts to improve themselves. Caucasians live in privileged conditions, with nearly 100 percent ownership and control of the nation's wealth, power, and businesses with access to all levels of government support and resources. Caucasian society has a monopoly of ownership and control in America.

This monopoly of control resulted directly from centuries of abusive exploitation and expropriation of labor of the darker race, African-Americans of African descent. Though African-Americans reside in the richest nation on earth, their standard of living is comparable to that of a third world nation. African-Americans own and control less than two percent of the wealth, power, and resources of the nation, so we have little control over our lives and the conditions in which we are forced to live.

Both the disparity between whites and African-Americans living conditions and inequitable allocation of resources are the centuries-old problems. They are a major legacy of the "Peculiar institution" called slavery. It was that social system that a white patriarchal society consigned African-Americans to live in the most inhumane conditions, doing the harshest labor, without just compensation. The dominant white society felt that by stripping the African slaves of their humanity, all of his worldly possessions, his personal freedom, and keeping him hopeless, that African-Americans would be forever noncompetitive and powerless. Needless to say, the dominant white society's experiment in social engineering succeeded. The living conditions of a people, enslaved or free tend to reflect their status and power within the larger society. Conditions of African-Americans are no more or less than what was planned for them centuries ago."1

In the inner cities of: Atlanta, Detroit, Chicago, St. Louis, Memphis, New Orleans, Houston, Newark, Charlotte, Denver, New York, Los Angeles; and all across America, the color line is, very much so prevalent. This division in color was prevalent in our workplaces and communities as we closed out the twentieth century, and even in our courtrooms, the pendulum of justice is often persuaded by the color of one's skin.

In the case of: Rodney King vs. the City of Los Angeles. Clearly, the Los Angeles Police Department nearly killed Rodney King, as seen very vividly on the video tape of the incident. Needless to say an "all white" jury found Sgt. Stacy Kuhn and six others of his white militia, masquerading as city officials and under the auspices of peace officers, or some para-NeoNazi and Ku Klux Klan psychotics with white supremacy motives, not guilty of excessive police brutality in the "all-white" community of Simi Valley, California, courtroom. This decision of "Not Guilty" by an "all-white" jury set off days of rioting, protesting, burning, looting, and several assaults in the "City of Angles" where numerous lives were lost in 1992.

Although subsequent trials were held, the so-called police officers involved, including Officer Kuhn, received minimal punishment for their acts of barbarianism and torture of Mr. King. The acts of the all white jury clearly demonstrate the division that exists among the races in this country. This jury would have never allowed six African-American police officers to totally beat mercilessly any white man like that and not reach a decision of guilty of excessive force and police brutality. Hence, because the victim was an African-American they chose to look the other way when clearly the evidence on the video tape proved otherwise; hence, resulting in mass chaos.

In the case of: 0. J. Simpson vs. The State of California, there was a clear case of how our U. S. Justice system has failed. The United States Constitution says that a person can not be tried twice for the same offense. However, in the case of Mr. Simpson, here exemplified how the statutes can be changed in order to reach the desired end.

Needless to say, the case of 0. J. Simpson, he was tried a second time for the same offense in a civil court in Santa Monica, Ca., and found guilty by an "all white" jury for the same offense that a predominately all African-American jury had found him innocent of and acquitted him. Although he had been acquitted of all charges in the criminal court of his alleged wrongful misconduct in the case involving Ronald Goldman and Nicole Brown Simpson and defended by attorney Johnny Cochran, prosecutors' attorney's literally pulled out their ropes, seating an "all white' jury, and virtually "Hung" him in their civil courts. Hence, this was viewed in the African-American community as a case of "Double Jeopardy"; in as much as trying a person twice for the same offense. In the African-American community this was viewed as a means of getting even with him even if it meant the misuse of the U. S. Constitution. This outcome left the African-American community wondering whether the U. S. Judicial system could really be trusted, which many seriously doubt anyway, or if the prosecutor's attorney's were just that clever in manipulating the outcome of the trial by ascertaining certain clauses and stipulations and requesting various amendments to the state penal codes that were already existing in order to achieve their desired end; which in this case was guilty. Whatever their means were, the bottom line is that here was a man found not guilty by a predominately "African-American" jury, and found guilty of the same offense by an "all-white" jury is further indication of the presence of the "Color-line" as it yet exist in the American society, and the division of the races as we closed the twentieth century.

As we looked at our evening newscasts and saw our Latino brothers being beaten down by white border patrol officers for trying to enter the land of their forefathers it was also evidence of the color line. While Caucasian immigrants enter this country illegally everyday, and over stay their visa's, and go unharmed, our Latino and others Spanish speaking people from Central America gravely suffered the affects of severe racism and discrimination today as well. Ex-senator Bill Bradley, D-New Jersey, made the statement as early as mid 1997, that the greatest threat of the United States in regard to over population, was not the borders of Mexico, but rather, from eastern and western Europe by Anglo people who overstay their visa's and subsequently get citizenship in the United States, and take away jobs from the natural born citizens of this nation. This inevitably leads us to further hopelessness and discontent with this capitalistic/democratic system of government and overall equality in America. Moreover, my brothers from Haiti who risk their lives on small crafts to come to these shores are turned around and sent back to that poverty stricken island. I ask you, whatever happened to those rhetorical words in scripted on the Statue of Liberty in New York, that says:" Give us your tired, your poor, your humbled masses yearning to be free?" Does not this apply to them, too?! If they were from Eastern Europe you would have received them with Roses!

Although the majority of white America probably won't accept this fact, or any other of these for that matter, but today the vast majority of the homeless and disadvantaged in American society are African-Americans in proportion to our size in the population.

This being the end result of centuries of oppression and racism is the staggering disproportionate number of African-American males and females who suffer from various forms of mental illnesses (including drug and alcohol abuse), which is related to years of racial discrimination and torment by the hands of our oppressor. We African-Americans are more often dismissed from the consciences of whites by being branded as inferior, incompetent, or insane.

More importantly, African-American people are still unjustly labeled as "lazy and shiftless," when we are in fact, still afforded meaningless and remedial labor opportunities that yet promote sub-poverty level wages and poor mental health, which leads to further interrelated violence and chaos. According to Dr. William Tutman, of the African-American Coalition For Justice In Social Policy, "To oppress a race, and then label the reactions as 'Mental Illness,' is not only morally wrong, it is criminal and fraudulent."

"The idea of race and the operation of racism are the best friends that the economic and political elite have in the United States. They are the means by which a state and a political economy, largely inimical to most of the U. S. citizenry, achieve the consent of the governed. They act as a distorting prism that allows that citizenry to imagine itself functioning as a moral and just people while ignoring the widespread devastation directed at African-American people in particular, but at a much larger number of people generally. Poverty has a Black face not in reality, but in the public imagination. Crime has a Black face-again, not in reality, but in the public imagination. And I use the word "public" without a race adjective because the operation of racism is so thoroughgoing that even those individuals who are its objects are not exempt from thinking about the world through its prism.

The United States is not just the domicile of a historically specific form of racial oppression, but it sustains itself as a structure through that oppression. If race - and its strategic social and ideological deployment as Racism-didn't exist, the United States' severe inequalities and betrayal of its formal commitments to social equality and social justice would be readily apparent to anyone existing on this ground."[2]

Racism is a phenomenon that is so interwoven into the fabric of this American society that it is practiced nowadays unconsciously. America is a society that for so long, and to a large degree today, thatwanted its' African-American citizens to feel a kind of hopelessness, inadequacy, shame, and guilt for being who we are. This is where we are even today at the dawn of the twenty-first century. The game is to make African-Americans and to a large extent, other ethnic groups feel included but not in possession of any of the benefits that comes along with being included in this American game thing.

I once read a passage written by the greatest Historian, Dr. W. E. B. DuBois, where he compared the situation that African-Americans are forced to live in here in America as "being in a transparent vacuum tube and the whites on the outside of the tube are looking in and seeing the smothering people desparately gasping for air within the tube and crying out for help.

But to no avail is the adequate help received in the tube, only further turmoil. At any rate, if we allow ourselves to buy into this feeling of inferior or inadequacy, thus holding ourselves out of the game, then we will have no one to blame but ourselves. Hence, we can not become victims yet again by this very clever ploy conducted genuinely by the oppressor in order to perpetuate a false sense of his superiority.

"I personally agree with the late James Baldwin in that "the South won't change because the whites there won't change. Furthermore, the rest of America develops its attitudes about people of color from what takes place in the south. Nevertheless, it is still very depressing and difficult to come back to America after having served in the Armed forces in an intelligence division as a Radarman aboard ship and expecting to be treated equally and respectfully; but rather only receiving the status-quo, racism, lynching, and more hatred. I guess it kind of further smashed the white ideology of African-Americans as inferior myth. Moreover, it really magnifies or amplifies just how ignorant and how asinine the oppressor really is. Now when the white power structure is confronted with the suggestion of a very one sided social and economic system of injustice, their immediate response is that everything is working "just fine." Well, in reality the correct response to this suggestion is that "yes, everything is working just fine for the white elite of this society." But where does African-Americans stand in this system that's operating "just fine." Well it was documented that at the close of the twentieth century the number of people imprisoned had surpassed four million. A grossly staggering disproportionate number of whom are African-American, and the cost will be over $40 billion a year, a figure that is reminiscent of the way the military budget devoured, and continues to devour, the country's resources.

"The problem of race and resources has been festering for hundreds of years, but has yet to arise as the core public issue in America. Whites have inherited the power and wealth of their ancestors through a social and economic infrastructure designed and weighted to the advantage of non-blacks. African-Americans have inherited a legacy of permanent poverty and powerlessness. African-American labor made the nation a strong, wealthy international world power, but nothing has proposed to seriously bring about remuneration, parity or fairness to African-American people. It is clear that African-Americans must solve their own problems and structure a national plan of action that puts their priorities first and foremost. Self-empowerment is the only road to economic parity and justice, but it requires the support of a national policy and plan of action."[3]

I believe that Dr. Randall Robinson's illustration of the plight of the average African-American male at the dawn of the twenty-first century is only too accurate of where we are as a people today. More importantly, I see our current status in America, socially, politically, and economically, as merely that which was prescribed for the son's of the former slaves. The white southern proslavers believed, "that once freed, slaves would be forced into direct competition with whites in an "Unequal Economic Struggle." Therefore, these inequalities in the fight for survival would be too much to bare for African-Americans and this inequality would "hurry them off into extinction."

"For the purpose of illustration, according to Dr. Randall Robinson, and unparallel, to be sure, let us picture one representative African-American individual whose dead-end "CRISIS" in contemporary America symbolizes the plight of millions.

At various times in his life he will likely be in jail or unemployed or badly educated or sick from a curable ailment or dead from violence.

What happened to him? From what did he emerge? Well! His Great-great grandfather was born a slave and died a slave. Great-great grandfather's labor enriched not only his white southern owner but also shipbuilders, sailors, homemakers, rope-makers, caulkers, and countless other northern businesses that serviced and benefited from the cotton trade built upon slavery. Great-great grandfather had only briefly known his mother and father before being sold off from them to a plantation miles away. He had no idea where in Africa his people had originally come from, what language they had spoken or customs they had practiced. Although certain Africanisms-falsetto singings, the ring shout, and words like yam, had survived, he did not know that their origins were African. He was, of course, compulsorily illiterate. His days were trials of backbreaking work and physical abuse with no promise of relief. He had no past and no future. He scratched along only because some biological instinct impelled him to survive. His son, today's African-American male's great-grand father, was also born into slavery and like his father, wrenched so early from his parents that he could scarcely remember them.

At the end of the civil War, he was nineteen years old. While he was pleased to no longer be a slave, he was uncertain that the new status would yield anything in real terms that was very much different from the life (if you could call it that) that he had been living. He, too, was illiterate and completely without skill. He was one of four million former slaves wandering rootlessly around in the defeated south. He trusted no whites, whether from the north or south. He had heard during the war that even President Lincoln had been urging African-Americans upon emancipation to leave the United States in mass for colonies that would be set up in Haiti and Liberia.

In fact, Lincoln had invited a group of free African-Americans to the White House in August of 1862 and told them "Your race suffers greatly, many of them, by living among us, while ours suffer from your presence.

In a word we suffer on each side. If this is admitted, it affords a reason why we should be separated."

Today's African-American male's great-grand father knew nothing of Haiti or Liberia, although he had a good idea why Lincoln wanted to ship Africans to such places. By 1866 his life had remained a trial of instability and rootlessness. He had no money and little more than pickup work. He and other Africans in the South were faced as well with new laws that were not unlike the antebellum slave codes. The new measures were called "Black Codes"and as John Hope Franklin noted in From Slavery To Freedom they all but guaranteed that: "The control of Africans by white employers were about as great as that which slaveholders had exercised. Africans who quit their job could be arrested and imprisoned for breach of contract.

They were not allowed to testify in court except in cases involving members of their own race. Numerous fines were imposed for sedition speeches, insulting gestures or acts, absence from work, violating curfew, and the possession of firearms.

There was, of course, no enfranchisement of Africans and no indication that in the future they could look forward to full citizenship and participation in a democracy."

Although some Africans received land in the south under the Southern Homestead Act of 1866, the impression that every ex-slave would receive "Forty-Acres and a mule" as a gift from the government never became a reality. Great-grandfather, like the vast majority of the four million former slaves, received nothing and died penniless in 1902, but not before producing a son who was born in 1890 and later became the first of his line to learn to read English.

Two decades into the new century, having inherited nothing in the way of bootstraps with which to hoist him, and faced with unremitting racial discrimination, Grandfather became a sharecropper on land leased from whites whose grandparents had owned at least one of his forebears. The year was 1925 and neither grandfather nor his wife was allowed to vote. His son would join him in the cotton fields under the boiling hot sun of the early 1930's. They worked twelve hours a day and barely eked out a living. Grandfather had managed to finish the fifth grade before leaving school to work full time. In as much as he talked like the people he knew, and like his parents and their parents before them, his syntax and pronunciation bore the mark of the unlettered. Grandfather wanted badly that his son's life not mirror his, but was failing depressingly in producing for the boy any better opportunity than that with which he himself had been presented. Not only had he no money, but he survived against the punishing strictures of Southern segregation that allowed for Africans the barest leavings in education, wages and political freedom.

He was trapped and afraid to raise his voice against a system that in many respects resembled slavery, now a mere seventy years gone.

Grandfather drank and expressed his rage in beatings administered to his wife and his son. In the early 1940's grandfather disappeared into a deep depression and never seemed the same again.

Grandfather's son, the father of today's African-American male, periodically attended segregated schools, first in a rural area near the family's leased cotton patch and later in a medium sized segregated southern city. He learned to read passably but never finished high school. He was not stigmatized for this particular failure because the failure was not exceptional in the only world that he had ever known.

Ingrained low expectations when consciously faced, invited impenetrable gloom. Thus, father did not dwell on the meagerness of his life chances. Any penchant he may have had for introspection, like his father before him, he drowned in corn spirits on Friday nights.

He was a middle-aged laborer and had never been on first name terms with anyone who was not a laborer like himself. He worked for whites and, as far as he could tell, everyone in his family before him had. Whites had, to him, the best of everything-houses, cars, schools, movies theatres, neighborhoods. African-American neighborhoods he could tell from simply looking at them, even before he saw the people.

And it was not just that the neighborhoods were poor. No, he had subconsciously likened something inside himself, a jagged rent in his ageless Black soul, to the sagging wooden tenement porches laden with old household objects-ladders, empty flowerpots, wagons- that rested on them, often wrong sideup, for months at a time. The neighborhoods, lacking sidewalks, streetlights, and sewage systems, had, like father and other African Americans, preserved themselves by not caring. Hunkered down, gone inside themselves, turning blank, sullen faces to the outside world. The world hadn't bothered to notice.

Father died of heart disease at the age of forty-five just before the Voting Rights Act was passed in 1965. Like his ancestors who had lived and died in slavery in centuries before, he was never allowed to cast a vote in his life. Little else distinguished his life from theirs, save a subsistence wage, the freedom to walk around in certain public areas, and the ability to read a newspaper, albeit slowly.

Parallel lines never touch, no matter how far in time and space they extend. They had been declared free-four million of them. Some had simply walked off the plantations during the war in search of Union forces. Others had become brazenly outspoken to their white masters to the end. Abandoned, penniless, and unskilled, at the mercies of a humiliated and hostile South, millions of men, women, and children trudged into the false freedom of the "Jim Crow" South with virtually nothing in the way of recompense, preparation, reparation, Or even a national apology.

It is from this condition that today's African-American male emerged. His social "CRISIS" is so alarming that the United States Commission on Civil Rights by the spring of 1999 had made it the subject of an unusual two-day conference. "This is a very real and serious and difficult issue," said Mary Frances Berry, Chair of the commission. "This "CRISIS" has broad implications for the future of the race."

The African-American male is far more likely than his white counterpart to be in prison, to be murdered, to have no job, to fail in school, to become seriously ill. His life will be shorter by seven years, his chances of finishing high school smaller-74 percent as opposed to 86 percent for his white counterpart. Exacerbating an already crushing legacy of slavery based social disabilities, he faces fresh discrimination daily in modern America. In the courts of ten states and the District of Columbia, he is ten times more likely to be imprisoned than his white male counterpart for committing the same offense. If convicted on a drug charge, he will likely serve a year more in prison than his white male counterpart will for the same charge.

While he and his fellow African-American males constitute 15 percent of the nations drug users, they make up 33 percent of those arrested for drug use and 57 percent of those convicted. And then, they die sooner and at a higher rate of chronic illinesses like AIDS, HYPERTENSION, DIABETES, CANCER, STROKE, and HEART DISEASE. Saddest of all, they have no clear understanding of why such debilitating fates have befallen them.

There were no clues in their public school system's education. No guideposts in the popular culture. Theirs was the "NOW" culture. They felt no impulse to look behind them for the causes."4

Many Caucasians today still view African-Americans as being expendable in the American society. Their perceived logic is that since their foreparents were slaves to them that this would perhaps make us today more inclined to accept a life of servitude as well. However, the new African-American would rather die standing on his feet like a man than to live a life of servitude on his knees. Many whites are still very much so racist and they practice it in their own subtle way. But perhaps we are all victims of this shortcoming to some degree because due to the severe treatment that my people have had to endure this makes me very sympathetic and partial to them as well.

Most emphatically, I only wish that we African-American people would stop fighting among ourselves, especially our youth. I believe that we should value each others lives and hold each other in the highest regard because of what we have had to go through as a people here in America just to survive and to not become extinct like what has been orchestrated for us.

We as African-American people should try and put forth a very cohesive attitude of solidarity to the general population. It is very asinine for us to fight each other over something as ridiculous as a red or a blue rag supposedly representing someone's "TURF" or member of a certain group. In the meantime, our oppressors are standing back looking and laughing at how stupid we are, which is their view of us anyway.

They take great pleasure in the lack of self-worth and self-respect that we have for one another, which was instilled in us during the "Peculiar institution" period known as slavery. While this society yet view us as "second-class citizens" and "three-fifths men," We must, nevertheless, view ourselves as in the way my brother and fellow South Carolinian Jesse Jackson so eloquently phrases it, as "SOMEBODY."

Historically, African-Americans have been "the last hired and the first fired" in regard to jobs in this economic system. This trend of economic discrimination still exists today as we enter the twenty-first century. Moreover, the color-line that Mr. DuBois spoke of at the turn of the twentieth century is made most vivid in the area of average incomes between African-American men and white men between the ages of 28 to 45 years of age. Here lies the parameter in which the African-American male has indeed suffered most severely.

Here lies the imprisoned, the disenfranchised, the overlooked, and the left out. Personally, I feel that the area of economic parity is where the shackles of slavery and bondage are still very much so in tact on our people in America. Moreover, I believe that this large gap in average income between African-American men and white men in America is yet a part of the greater plan of the oppressor's conscientious effort to keep him in a position of power and dominance via discrimination.

In the November 26, 2001 issue of the Los Angeles Times, the plight of a typical African-American male is depicted precisely. Asserting the challenges that jobless African-Americans faces, the column stated that: "As the economy continues to falter this fall, African-Americans have felt the affects more keenly than other Americans. The rate of African-American unemployment- at 9.7% nationally in October, up from 8.7% in September has for decades persisted at about twice the rate of White men. Economists and African-American leaders cite a range of factors: Discrimination, lower educational levels, the remoteness of job hubs from African-American neighborhoods, and over representation of African-Americans in low-skill and part-time jobs with little security. Even in the best of times, African-Americans suffer the nations highest unemployment rate. In bad times, they tend to fare worse still, losing jobs at disproportionate rates and remaining out of work longer than other Americans. "It happens in every single downturn," said Harry J. Holzer, a labor economist, minority employment expert and visiting fellow at the Urban Institute, a Washington, D. C., research organization. African-Americans, he said, "get laid off more frequently. Once they get laid off, they have a harder time regaining employment someplace else."

Latinos as a group also have higher unemployment rates than whites, but their jobless rate is lower than African-Americans. Now, as the African-American unemployment rate begins to climb sharply, some worry that paredback resources for the jobless could make this recession particularly painful for African-Americans. Many African-Americans are not eligible for unemployment insurance because they worked part time or short term jobs.

And those laid off from low-wage jobs are eligible for benefits, but at meager levels. Welfare reform, designed in a boom economy, has curtailed benefits that many low-income African-Americans previously relied on as a stand-in for unemployment insurance. William Spriggs, who directs the National Urban League's Institute of Opportunity and Equality, joined with other labor economists this month (November 2001) to sound an alarm about the nation's slide into recession, noting that October job losses were "especially devastating to the African-American community." "Because of the absence of the safety net, this could be the first recession where there is a much greater disproportionate impact on African-Americans," Spriggs said.

The toll is already visible at the South-Bay One Stop Business and Career Center, a job counseling facility in Inglewood, Ca. Workers there estimate that about 75% of their clients today are African-American, compared to 50% just two months ago, and the total number of people seeking help also is up.

The Los Angeles Urban League's job center have seen a 25% increase in clients this year, a jump attributed mainly to the 11th of September attack on the World Trade Center in New York related job losses.

The undeniable fact has been and continues to be that African-Americans are discriminated against in the work place," said John Mack, President of the Urban League, who also pointed to educational and skill disparities as well as the tendency of employers to lay off those most recently hired.

The economic boom did much to alleviate African-American unemployment. In late 1994 the national jobless rate dipped below 10% for the first time in twenty years, then fell further to an all-time seasonally adjusted low of 7.2% in September 2000. In a tight labor market, employers "were forced to hire unskilled workers, many of whom were African-Americans, single mothers, and immigrants," said George Mason University Economics Professor Willem Thorbecke. Some of the gains could be permanent, since the previously unemployed gained useful skills, he said. But the dynamics shift in down turns, when employers have a broader pool to pluck from.

Nationally, as African-American employment jumped from its lowest point this year of 7.5% in February to 9.7% in October, the rate for whites rose from its low of 3.6% in January to 4.8% in October. Statewide, African-American employment climbed from a low of 7.3% in February to 8.2% in October, while the rate for whites remained virtually unchanged, fluctuating from 4.7% to 4.8%.

Some steep barriers keep a segment of the young African-American male population out of the labor force altogether, or relegate them to dead-end short term jobs. Those barriers include high child support obligations, poor skills, a shortage of blue collar jobs and discrimination. The result: Young African-American men are less likely to be working today than they were twenty years ago, even as young African-American women have seen their overall participation in the workforce increase, most notable during the boom of the 1990's, said Holzer of the Urban Institute.

Many African-American men simply stop looking; join the ranks of the so-called discouraged workers who don't show up in monthly unemployment statistics. For African-American women, who have recently worked themselves off the welfare rolls in significant numbers, there also could be trouble ahead. Many landed in vulnerable service sector jobs and are facing layoffs. Recent research by Holzer and Michael Stoll, an assistant public policy professor at UCLA, showed that among welfare recipients seeking to enter the job market, African-Americans have the hardest time getting hired.

The other root causes of disparity was the differences in high school graduation rates- that changed significantly over time, Spriggs said, but the higher unemployment rate for African-Americans has remained stubbornly persistent.

Discrimination in hiring, however, is difficult to detect or prove. Although the Equal Employment Opportunity Commission policies prohibit employment discrimination, it tends to focus on existing employees, not perspective hires. Spriggs and others would like to see more of a focus on discrimination in hiring. They also offer a range of policy suggestions that they say could better protect African-Americans by strengthening the safety nets in times of recessions. Among those is unemployment insurance reform so more unemployed workers could qualify for benefits, and a proposal to stop the clock on welfare time limits until the economy improves.

But the deep-rooted problems must also be addressed, Holzer said. That means developing better job training programs and improving transportation to carry residents from minority neighborhoods to job hubs."[5] Perhaps in this way we can at the very least make an effort to try to close the gap between the have's and the have not's that is very distinguishable a in our society at the dawn of the Twenty-First Century!

Today, too, the oppressor is all about ridiculing people of color and essentially all people who are non-white. He feels that he has to go to any means to perpetuate his own existence and not become extinct, as well.

This is the only rational for the continued discrimination and extreme racism that is widely practiced yet in the American society today. 'Therefore, as we enter into the Twenty-First Century, people of color must be ever mindful that "JIM CROW" is not dead in America. He could be wearing a well-tailored three-piece suit and very well groomed. But keep in mind, that if you're feeling that you're inadequate in the view of his demand, then perhaps its because you're looking at the devil. Then, keep in mind the pains and sufferings of our people at the hands of the oppressor.

So, your question to me is why do I hate the oppressor? Well in the Book of Ecclesiastes in the Holy Bible, chapter 3 verse 8 says that there's "a time to love and a time to hate." Well just how much do I hate the oppressor? Well for every lash across the backs of my Great-Great-grandfather and mother's and other African-Americans backs during their 400 years of rape and genocide, I hate the oppressor a million times each. I can feel the pains of my people as they were worked to death in the cotton fields in South Carolina. I can imagine the constant fear of being lynched or raped.

In the Bible, in the book of Romans Chapter 9 verse 3, the Apostle Paul speaks of his pain for his people. He says: "For the hurt of my brother, Christ, I wish that I could take the punishment for him for that which he has been accursed. My kinsman who is of the flesh." Therefore, for all of my brothers, sisters, mothers, fathers, great-great grandfathers and mothers according to the flesh so am I hurt, and with sufficient justification. Moreover, this pain is too much to bare alone, so I'll leave it up to God to deal with the oppressor as he sees fit. Therefore, I'll leave it up to the Most High to recompense the oppressor with his mighty wrath. As for me I love the good; but I hate the Evil! But I'll forgive, but never forget! Because as Medger Evers said, when you hate someone, the only one you hurt in yourself, and the ones you hate don't know it and everyone else don't care.

Time and time again I've thought of leaving America for good. I personally believe that it is up to the people who are in majority to establish a better racial atmosphere within the society and to end discrimination and racism within that society. However, this ideal gesture is just that, ideal. Racism and discrimination in America will never end because as it is written in the Book of Proverbs in the Holy Bible in Chapter 26 verse 11: "As a dog returneth to his vomit, so does a fool returneth to his folly."

I have a great deal of respect for Africans who left this country for something better. Men such as: James Baldwin, William E. B. Du Bois, Henry 0. Tanner, Paul Cuffy, Marcus Garvey, Josephine Baker, and many others. For it is like the late Brother Malcolm X said, "The African-American in America is like "Sheep living in a den of wolves." Moreover, these great African-Americans left because they knew that they'd be better off in a country where they'd be looked upon as men and human beings.

Time and time again I have thought of leaving America for good as so many of my friends have. The only reason why I haven't left is the fact that my family is still alive here in this country.

Most importantly, I don't want to be more than a few hours away from them. However, if I should happen to out live them then I'm out of here. I remember when I was attending the university in North Carolina, and I had a roommate who was from Kinshasa, Zaire, in Africa. I asked him what was he going to do when he finished his education here in the U. S. and whether or not he would be staying here. He quickly assured me that he would not be staying here in America because in his words "I don't want to live here because I don't want to be treated less." As I reflect over the past and ponder my studies over the years I can't help but to think of some sort of retribution for African-Americans who are the descendents of the people who were slaves and those who were left out of the economic system because of the color of their skin. It has been a very long time in conceiving such a notion but finally some sort of repayment is at least being contemplated by members of various African-American communities.

"In May of 2000, more than 200 supporters packed Chicago city council chambers to hear powerful and heart-wrenching testimonies by African-American legislators, educators, activists and historians in a hearing to discuss reparations for the descendants of African-American slaves. Inspired by a resolution introduced on March 15 by Alderman Dorothy Tillman, a former organizer for Dr. Martin Luther King, Jr., the joint hearing of the finance and human relations committees shed light on 300 years of institutionalized slavery and the 100 years of legalized segregation. The hearing also exposed the continued cruel treatment and denial of opportunity to African-Americans, which historians and legislators believe have caused "Post-Traumatic Slavery Syndrome," impending the community's social, economic, and educational progress.

The committee passed Ald. Tillman's resolution-which supports H. R. 40, a bill introduced by congressman John Conyers (D) Michigan, calling for a commission to study reparation proposals for African-Americans.

The resolution now goes to full city council for discussion and possible passage. Similar resolutions have been passed in Michigan, Ohio, Texas, and Louisiana. "We built this country without any compensation. In fact, African-Americans built Washington, D. C., our nation's capital. They carried the marble on their backs and put each piece in place. Some died due to the saw-dust in their lungs. If you go to the capital, you would never know that we existed. Also, African children were used as child laborers during the building of New York,'" Ms. Tillman said. The NAACP, the National Conference of African-American Lawyers, the National Bar Association, the Council of Independent Black Institutions, the International Association of Black Fire-Fighters, the Association of African-American Psychologists and the National Conference of African-American Political Scientists also expressed their support for the resolution. Referring to slavery and its aftermath as the "BLACK HOLOCAUST," Ms. Tillman has estimated that 80 to 100 million Africans died from starvation and disease due to brutal treatment during the voyage to America and other regions.

She said that slave labor is the root of wealth and some of the finest agricultural products in U. S. History.

Dr. Claud Anderson, author of "Black Labor, White Wealth," and the President of the Harvest Institute in Washington, D. C., said the booming stock market today is the result of unpaid African slave labor. "Africans were producing 99% of the items listed on the stock market-shoes, clothes, iron, timber, rice, sugar, cotton,- and the higher the value of the slaves working on the products the more the price of the products went up," Dr. Anderson told the final Call. "People were hedging their bets based on the number of slaves working on those products. "WE must focus on real problems of structural economic inequity which means we even have to separate wealth from income," he said. Historian Lerone Bennett and Congressman Bobby Rush (D-ILL.) both agree that the starting point for healing is with an apology from the American government.

"Why has it been so difficult to get somebody high in this government to "Apologize" for slavery and to make "Amends?" "If you hurt somebody you have to compensate them," said Mr. Bennett, The editor of the Ebony Magazine. "People say they weren't here then. They were here in the oaths their parents swore in their name...that they freely resume everyday by accepting the illicit gains of slavery and segregation. They were here during sharecropping," he said, calling for a Mashall Plan for African-American communities and a GI type Bill for individual payments to African-Americans. "Reparations are payable when a crime against humanity has been committed," said Rep. Rush, a co-sponsor of the Conyers Bill.

"Certainly, we can all agree that 400 years of slavery constitutes a "Crime Against Humanity." "And those who commit a crime must make reparations." "Although we came in shackles, we came to these shores as members of human families and communities, with intact identities, abilities, traditions, and inspirations. All of this was damaged and destroyed at the hands of America. Beyond being forced to benefit others and having our bodies maimed, tortured, and broken, our language, culture, religion and human dignity was distorted, damaged, diminished, denied and/or destroyed.

We as a people were wronged by America," said Dr. Wade Noble, founder and past president of the National Association of African-American Psychologists and Professor of Psychology and African-American Studies at San Francisco State University. Dr. Nobles testimony was so gripping describing how pregnant African slave female's had their bellies ripped and their babies killed as they fell from their wombs simply to entertain white slave masters. Then Ald Carrie Austin revealed to reporters that her Grandfather was a slave in Rocky Mount, N. C. While trying to get social security for her father, the Alderwoman learned that he was listed as property of a plantation owner behind the owner's "most prized animals." She told reporters that her family moved north after her father stole a cow to feed his family and would have been killed if caught.

Ald. Tillman's ordinance comes three years after $7 million dollars were issued to the survivors of the 1921 Rosewood, Florida, riots and the recent acknowledgement that reparations are due to African-American survivors of the deadly 1923 race riot in Tulsa, Oklahoma.

Ald. Tillman noted the continuous reparations granted to native Americans for land stripped from them and to Japanese-Americans who survived WW2 internment camps. The U. S. Government also supports restitution to survivors of the Jewish Holocaust and the appropriation of land to the Aborigines taken by Australia during the 18th and 19th centuries. "The reparations movement (in America) is over 150 years old," said Dr. Conrad Worrill, Chairman of the National Black United Front and an economic commissioner for the Reparations Movement N' Cobra. What form and how it will take place is what we're discussing. It can be land, goods and services, technology transfers... That's why we need an organized body like N' COBRA, to think through what kind of reparations African people will receive in this country." The dialogue is just getting started but the potential is so great.," added Rep. Danny Davis (D-lLL.).

If we want to move to the point that all men and women are endowed by their creator with certain inalienable rights and among these are Life, Liberty, and the Pursuit of Happiness, it's hard to pursue happiness if you don't have the tools or the wherewithal, if I've got to feel that every time I make a move that I'm viewed a certain way because of my prior position of servitude or the way I wear my hair. "This is an opportunity for America to put on the table a different look of herself, and out of this can come a country we never dreamed of," and where everyone is included.[6]

As we witness the dawn of the twenty-first century, African-Americans are confronted with a "Crisis" that is just as paramount as any other that we have faced. According to Dr. Alvin Poussaint "The persistent presence of racism, despite the significant legal, social and political progress made during the last half of the Twentieth-century, has created a physiological risk for black people that is virtually unknown to white Americans. We call this post-traumatic slavery syndrome. Specifically, a culture of oppression, the byproduct of this nation's development, has taken a tremendous toll on the minds and bodies of black people. We see the increasing rates of black suicide in the United Stated-and the remarkable fact that blacks comprise less than 13% of the U. S. population but represent the overwhelming majority of those doing time in the nation's prisons for violent or drug-related crimes- as part and parcel of that oppression.

Yet in the realm of mental health treatment, where black's rates of clinical illness and depression afforded those of whites, the concerns of blacks have received a fraction of the attention afforded to those of whites by those in the research, policy, and political communities who hold the power to address these issues."[7]

Among black youth, ages fifteen to nineteen, the rate of suicide has more than doubled since 1980, rising from 3.6 to 8.1 deaths per 100 000 in 1996. For African-Americans between the ages of fifteen and twenty-four, suicide is now the third leading cause of death, behind homicides and accidents, according to the United States Centers for Disease Control and Prevention. The increase in black suicides between the late 1970's and the 1990's is dramatic.

Although it falls far below the radar of national public consciousness, the growing number of African-American suicides might be viewed as a trend in our society at the dawn of the Twenty-First Century. Economic stress, Depression, Self-Hatered, Racial Oppression, Hopelessness, and other self-destructive behavior, such as drugs and alcohol, provide a chilling glimpse into the taboo subject of African-American mental health and the increasing rates of suicide among African-Americans. Moreover, the diagnostic models - the suicide "warning signs" established and accepted by mental health care policyholders nationwide over the past fifty-years- have not always been effective in addressing the unique mental health concepts of African-Americans.

Also the documented high rate of homicide among African-Americans might be viewed as evidence of a peculiar kind of communal self-hatred, an especially virulent form of anger, self-loathing, and lost hope that leads to a devaluation of the lives of fellow African-Americans; and that same self-hatred may also lead to a devaluation of self, which can lead to life-threatening, self-destructive, or suicidal behavior. Similar dynamics of self-devaluation and hopelessness may account, in part for the high rates of alcoholism and drug addiction among African-American people.

Until the late 1960's, many hospitals and health care clinics throughout the South were segregated institutions where blacks received little or inferior care, if any, and less blatant de facto discrimination existed in the North as well. Because African-Americans were routinely refused acceptance at many hospitals, they were unable to receive early preventive care for curable illnesses and conditions. Due to segregation and discrimination, in the North as well as in the South, African-Americans often died from treatable diseases and illnesses. Further, many white doctors, nurses, and other staff at health care institutions of all kinds were openly racist, leaving African-Americans with no reason to trust a system that demonstrated little regard for the value of a black life.

The mistreatment that African-Americans were often exposed to during their limited contact with the health care establishment included instances of un-consenting African-Americans being used as research subjects in dangerous experiments; the infamous case in which white government doctors directed syphilis experiments on the unwilling African-American patients through the Tuskegee Institute experiment during the 1930's and 1940's is but the best-known example among many.

This lack of regard and dehumanizing treatment has fostered distrust, even a sense of paranoia and fear; many African-Americans believe that the virus that causes AIDS was deliberately introduced by whites to decimate the African-American and African population. The well documented high rates of heart disease, hypertension, and other stress related illnesses found in African-Americans are traceable in part to social factors, including most prominently the long history of blacks being required to endure racism, poverty, discrimination, and the lack of adequate health services-including mental health care-in America. Many white mental health practitioners conditioned by years of cultural stereotypes depicting African-Americans as leading emotionally uncomplicated lives-have trouble acknowledging depression in African-Americans.

Consequently, severe clinical depression is often under-diagnosed among African-Americans. More importantly, these clinicians, also conditioned by equally persistent images of African-American (males in particular) as being dangerous, threatening, and prone to paranoia-tend to over diagnose schizophrenia among African-Americans. Compounding matters, most clinicians find it difficult to accurately assess the risk of suicide among schizophrenia patients, particularly since those suffering from disorders now believed to involve chemical imbalances (manic-depressive illness, severe depression and schizophrenia) are often to delusions and hallucinations.

Mental health clinicians have been trained to look upon severely depressed patients as likely to provide early warning signs of suicidal thinking, but schizophrenic patients are not as likely to present clearly definable suicidal intention. Of course, even in severely depressed individuals, it is not always easy to predict or prevent suicide.

Among African-Americans, who in many instances have become accustomed to down playing outward signs of depression or suicidal thinking mental health petitioners must be prepared to employ a uniquely personal and sensitive approach to assessment and treatment. For African-Americans, the "language of depression" often varies from that which a white interviewer might be accustomed to recognizing: describing oneself as having "the blues" or "the aching misery," or as "being down" may indicate a severe depression that slips past an unsophisticated practitioner. And the fact that many African Americans do not seek help from mental health clinicians, or have been put off by previous contacts with insensitive ones, creates an access dilemma which makes the medical practitioner's role all the more crucial. Even when an African-American makes it as far as an initial consultation, there is no guarantee that the health care practitioner will be able to address his or her particular experience and succeed in pulling the patient back from the brink.

Overall, the intricacies of an individual's despair are a mystery. What is certain, however, is the need for mental health practitioners to be as aware as possible of specific cultural factors underlying the surface of a patient's immediate concerns. To "take the extra step" with African-American patients may require a focused understanding of the special burdens that many African-Americans carry."[8]

"We believe that all of these elements, particularly the obvious but rarely studied components like persistent stress and despair among African-Americans because of racism and the legacy of slavery, must be thoroughly examined. Obviously, many negative conditions have existed in the African-American community for centuries-including drugs, racial discrimination, firearms, and despair. We propose that never before has their particular combination existed in such a high stakes, powder-keg social environment, at a time in which racism often bears a seemingly benign, difficult face to recognize.

But in our collective history as a nation, with the exception of the native American Indians, no other population besides African-Americans has had to struggle harder for self-preservation, to withstand the hardships and low blows that life can offer. The need to bear up under centuries of cruel treatment has made African-Americans in some ways particularly resilient - and in some ways reluctant to admit personal vulnerabilities, especially where mental illness is concerned."[9]

"The relationship between African-American males, crime, incarceration, and suicide cannot be overlooked. Indeed, some investigators feel that the rage felt by African-American youth can manifest itself in either suicide or homicide. Homicide is the leading cause of death among African-American men, accounting for approximately one fifth of the deaths in late adolescence during most of the 1980's and 1990's. Suicide rates among young African-American males still lag behind the total homicide rate, but the suicide gap between young white males and young African-American males is narrowing. In the United States homicide among non-whites occurs from seven to ten times more frequently than it does among whites. In 80 to 90 percent of the homicides in the U. S., the victim and the offender belong to the same ethnic group. Some observers conclude that urban riots are a form of community suicide in which the loss of African-American lives and African-American owned businesses is far greater than the damage done to the white power structure.

Many clinical professionals assume that depression must be low in blacks simply because for so many decades the suicide rate of blacks was less than half that of whites. This raises questions, however, about the influence of history and cultural myths on investigators' thinking. If physicians generally perceive blacks as "happy" though downtrodden, what is the likelihood that they would identify depression in African-American patients if they saw it? Perhaps what looks like a twenty-year increase in black male suicide is as much a function of late-coming awareness of biases in the medical community and of improved reporting methods as it is of any cultural or psychological factors that might be propelling a true increase."[10]

"The findings of a Georgetown University study of statistics show that blacks suffer disproportionately from treatable illnesses due to a combination of factors including low income, poor access to transportation and health care information, and cultural resistance to the medical establishment.

In 1999, a partial list of health problems that negatively impact blacks in greater numbers than whites, and which could be ameliorated with early treatment, was telling. African-Americans were 70% more likely than whites to suffer from diabetes, a disease which increases the risk for cardiovascular disease and blindness. The mortality rate for African-American babies, at 14.2 per 1,000 live births in 1996, was nearly two and a half times that of white babies. The death rate for African-American men with cancer was nearly 50% higher than for white men, about 226.8 deaths per 1,000 while the mortality rate for prostrate cancer was more than twice that of white men, 5.5 deaths per 100,000.

By 1998, more than 50% of new AIDS cases nationwide occurred among African-Americans, as did 63% of new cases among those between the age of thirteen and twenty-four years old-and blacks, particularly the poor, have much more difficulty in accessing and affording AIDS treatments than do whites.

In addition, in August 1999, a U. S. Centers for Disease Control and Prevention report raised the alarm about the high mortality rate for African-American women in childbirth: during the nine years between 1987 and 1996, one African-American woman died for every 5,102 who gave birth, compared with one in 18,868 whites."[11]

"In an interesting dichotomy, however much African-Americans avoid the medical health care community, they are more likely than whites to be diagnosed with serious illnesses should they be evaluated by clinicians. In 1980, for example, African-Americans made up 12% of the U. S. population but represented more than 18% of all hospitalized admissions nationwide, including admissions to mental health and Veterans Administration medical centers according to a 1992 compilation of African-American health care studies.

In a larger cultural context, the widening minority health care gap is but one of several examples of how vestiges of white racism continue to infuse the African-American experience despite the well documented gains African-Americans have made during the twentieth century in education, income, and other indicators of prosperity. African-Americans still fall prey to white discrimination in housing, employment, and the criminal justice system.

Beginning in the 1980s, vociferous attacks on Affirmative action and public funding for programs perceived as "minority handouts" were launched by white conservatives supported by a small percentage of African-Americans, heightening the sense of oppression for many African-Americans. Moreover, the historic difference between what many whites consider to be black behavior (often stereotyped) and blacks' place in the social structure, and what blacks see as appropriate behavior on their part and their place in society, continues to be miles apart.

In 1993, an essay called "Rage of a Privileged Class" journalist Ellis Cose examined some influential and prominent blacks who experience psychological stress that they attribute to remnants of white racism. In the course of his research, Cose found that millions of blacks who have "played by the white man's rules" and are educated, productive members of society are nevertheless frequently discriminated against by whites in nearly every aspect of life. "Why would people who have enjoyed all the fruits of the Civil Rights Revolution-who have Ivy League educations, high-paying jobs, and comfortable homes-be quietly seething inside?" he asks.

"To answer that question is to go a long way toward explaining why quotas and affirmation action remain such polarizing issues; why black and white Americans continue to see race in such starkly different terms; and why solving America's racial problems is infinitely more complicated than cleaning up the nation's urban ghettos and educating the inhabitants-even assuming the will, wisdom, and resources (exist) to accomplish such a task."[12]

Blacks in the 1990s were not being paranoid if they looked around and saw a nation that was still not entirely free of white racist practices. During the last decade of the Twentieth Century, African-Americans experienced a bittersweet mix of high achievement (the proportion of middle-class African-Americans continued to increase; between 1967 and 1991, the number of African-American household earnings $50,000 or more per year grew from 5.2 to 12.1 percent, according to the U. S. Census) and vivid reminders of how far they still have to go to attain across-the-board equality with the white population. In 1993 top executives at Texaco, a major energy company, were caught on audiotape making racist jokes and scheming to keep black workers out of the management ranks; in the 1990's several national fast food chains were found to discriminate against blacks both as employees and as patrons; recently the government has found merit in a class-action suit filed by African-American farmers alleging discrimination by public agencies; and across the United States, taxis continue to avoid picking up African-American people, which causes considerable personal distress. In the minds of many African-Americans, continuing evidence of white racism and oppression diminishes many of the lifestyle gains African-Americans have made.

The 1990's were, after all, a time when once again police brutality became a life-threatening concern for African-Americans and Latinos in much of the country. It was a decade when law enforcement agencies around the United States came under scrutiny for racial profiling, the practice of detaining African-Americans or Brown motorists because of the color of their complexions, for nothing more than "Driving While Black"; (DWB) is the ironic phrase used by African-American citizens who had been through the experience; a decade in which an African-American was dragged to his death behind a white Neo-Nazi's pickup truck in Texas; a time when two New York City police officers were tried and found guilty of brutality after using a broomstick to sodomize a Haitian-American in a station house bathroom; a time when four undercover New York City narcotics officers were indicted (but later acquitted by a jury) after firing forty-one bullets at an unarmed African immigrant, killing him on his own doorstep.

It was also a decade when African-Americans and other people of color continued to be left out of medical research projects. For example, in 1994 only 1.6 percent of the National Institute of Health's $60 million research budget went toward studying minority health, according to Dr. Moon Chen of Ohio State University's College of Medicine.

For many African-Americans, the centuries-old fear of being tagged "crazy" by Whites, has, over the decades between slavery and the post-civil rights era, turned into a deep fear of admitting emotional distress even to themselves. To do so conjures deeply held fears about appearing inferior, weak, or defective to whites and to one's own community.

African-Americans and whites in equal proportion suffer from a widespread stigmatization of mental illness, and even considering the late 1990s phenomenon of lurid public professionals of the type found on some television talk shows and in other media, few Americans are eager to admit emotional problems for fear of being ostracized or discriminated against by the community at large or by friends, employers, and family members. In avoiding seeking regular medical check-ups and preventive treatments, however, individual African-Americans ultimately jeopardize the future health of the African-American population.

The growing "Crisis" of Depression, Self-Destructive behavior, and Suicide, among African-Americans cannot be effectively addressed until African-American political, scientific, and cultural leaders confront the stigma surrounding mental illness and begin encouraging African-Americans to overcome their historic trepidation toward the medical establishment and white physicians. At the same time, it is foolish to hold African-Americans solely responsible for mending their frayed relationship with the white-dominated medical and mental health care establishment. The Government, as well as private health care providers, must do much more to acknowledge the truths of history that lie at the bottom of many African-Americans distrust of the medical community, and they must work diligently and with innovative methods to make African-Americans feel welcome and secure in seeking medical care.

Any serious attempt to stem the rising suicide rates among African-Americans or close the minority health care gap must begin with honesty about our history as a nation and the complexity of the problems we face. The future mental health of America's African-American children depends on our ability to overcome the obstacles of that history in order to fulfill the nation's promise.

Among the dominant risk factors for suicide-depression, a previous suicide attempt, drug or alcohol abuse, emotional isolation, access to firearms, and hopelessness is a symptom that can be difficult to recognize or treat, but most clinical professionals agree that an individual who has lost hope for the future is greatly at risk for suicide or self-destructive, life-threatening behavior. Distinct from grief or the genetic and biological factors that can contribute to mental illness, hopelessness is a situational element that is frequently a strong indicator of clinical depression, and it is often linked to a sense of fatalism about the future. This can be particularly true for black youth mired in poverty-stricken communities.

Homicide is the leading cause of death for black men from ages fifteen to twenty-four, with a stunning homicide rate of 85 per 100,000 in this age bracket. This reality no doubt contributes significantly to blacks youths' feelings of hopelessness in general when considering their chances for a brighter future. Succumbing to feelings of hopelessness has also been linked to alcohol and drug abuse, and other forms of self-destructive behavior.

Throughout their time in America, African-Americans have drawn a sense of hope from spirituality and religion that positively affected their progress in this country. Unfortunately, today the involvement of African-Americans (particularly young males) in church life has declined. This has weakened a support system that has historically been crucial to African-American survival.

Any comprehensive exploration of African-American suicide and self-destructive behavior should include an examination of the social context, including those institutions that have fostered hope in the community.

Within the context of the increase in African-American suicide rates since the early 1980s, it is likely that a loss of hope has played a significant role. Indeed, whether it predates mental illness or results from it, there is growing evidence that for millions of Americans, hopelessness, including a sense of being trapped by ones circumstances, undermines healthy emotional and psychological development. Since an estimated 18 million Americans currently suffer from a clinical depression, it is clear to the average citizen that tragedies may result when individuals who have psychological or emotional problems lose hope.

The role of hopelessness in the history of American violence-as distinct from motivations related to racism or quests for power and money-is difficult to appraise. Yet it is likely that hopelessness, especially among lower socioeconomic groups, has contributed to an environment that allowed homicide and suicide rates to escalate during the 1980s and early 1990s.

And among African-American youth born after the early 1970s, feelings of hopelessness may be especially painful due to heightened expectations as a result of the Civil Rights Movement. Indeed, though diminished, institutionalized racism, particularly in the employment and economic spheres, has continued.

Further, the ascendance during the second half of the twentieth century of advertising-driven commercialism gave rise to an acquisitive ethos in many low-income African-American communities that led some youths to view material objects such as Nike sneakers and designer fashions as key elements of their identity and self-worth. The gap between desire and ability to pay for these expensive items may have contributed to a high level of hopelessness-related substance abuse, as well as to black-on-black theft and violence tied to an illegal drug economy.

American culture, in its romance with violence, has made legends of white gangsters and outlaws such as Jesse James, Bonnie Parker and Clyde Barrow, John Dillinger, and Al Capone. African-American gangsters were not romanticized until after the Civil Rights Movement (in movies like Superfly and Shaft), but since then, with the rise of rap, they have become cultural icons to whites as well as blacks. (The use of violence to control or overcome feelings of weakness can give individuals a sense of power, particularly if they feel Minimized and oppressed.

During the Black Militant Era in the 1960s and 1970s, Malcolm X and the Black Panther Party argued that for African-Americans to maintain their own self-respect they needed to strike back with violence in self-defense if they were attacked. And, many revolutionary-minded African-Americans felt that violence by the oppressed against the oppressor could be psychologically liberating."[13]

"When considering the high morbidity and mortality rates among African-Americans during the second half of the twentieth century-including those that result from violence and substance abuse-it is likely that hopelessness,-in combination with other risk factors such as depression, plays a significant role. It is estimated that a loss of hope and a sense of fatalism among many African-Americans is the key to explaining the rising rates of suicide, homicide, drug abuse, gun-related violence, add self-destructive behaviors. In short, it is likely that African-Americas, despite a historic rejection of suicide based on Christian indoctrination, are now experiencing a rise in self-destructive behavior that stems from social factors, including economic, educational and cultural elements."[14]

"To be sure, one might argue that the changing face of racism in America by the close of the twentieth century from overt and unmistakable devaluation and even hostility to more subtle and nuances but still racist attitudes and assumptions-has added a peculiar burden to the African-American psyche, an element of elusiveness that may compound feelings of isolation and frustration for many African-Americans. In addition, African-Americans living in poverty (30%) are much more likely to have low self-esteem and suffer a sense of powerlessness than African-Americans who have obtained middle-class status or who are more highly educated."[15]

The Surgeon General, David Satcher, noted in 1999, that hopelessness and isolation- two risk factors that are present in most suicides-may be a primary contributing factor for the high rates of homicide in the African-American community. But accurately gauging the level of isolation and hopelessness that tips the scales toward self-destruction is difficult. Until more is understood about the elusive psychodynamics underlying the victim-precipated homicide, suicide by cop, and fatalistic life-threatening behaviors, law enforcement officers, public health officials, and policymakers should adopt a compassionate stance, when establishing practices for managing mentally distressed individuals in potentially deadly situations."[16]

Most importantly, Dr. Satcher asserted in the August 2000 edition of the "Guideposts magazine," that: "my faith, my values, my hopes and dreams, these are the blessings that were so richly bestowed on me and that even today hold me in good stead.

Health, I believe, is a matter of wholeness-a wholeness of body, mind, spirit and community, a wholeness that is rooted in family and faith and equality. For all our advances in medicine, we still have a ways to go in bringing quality health care to all Americans, especially the children. Using a scripture given to him by his father from the Book of Proverbs: Trust in the Lord with all thine heart... and he shall direct thy paths." These, he said, has been his directives."[17]

"Above all else, we believe that the increase in suicide among young African-American males should be a wake-up call to the African-American community and to the public health officials. And there is plenty of evidence to show that in fact the suicide rate among African-Americans is much higher than statistics indicate because of a historic underreporting of suicide among the African-American population.

Our tasks, then, at the dawn of the twenty-first century, in attempting to help stem the tide of African-American suicide and other self destructive behaviors (including homicide) should include the following:

1). Make mental health clinics and practitioners more accessible and user-friendly to African-American clients. African-American people should be made aware, through educational programs and media outlets, that clinical depression can be treated with antidepressants and talk therapy. Treatment programs for alcohol and drug abuse must also be made available and accessible.

2). Remove the stigma from mental illness while simultaneously educating the African-American community to seek professional help in times of emotional crisis, particularly if they are depressed or irritable or have suicidal or homicidal thoughts.

3). Provide education and training to mental health practitioners to eliminate racist stereotyping and simultaneously promote the skills for delivering culturally competent care.

4). Use a public health approach to reduce the risk factors that heighten the likelihood of suicide, such as depression, psychotic disorders, alcoholism, drug abuse, and the easy availability of firearms.

5). Support educational programs in conflict resolution, anger management, and violence prevention.

6). Campaign for health insurance coverage for all citizens and demand parity in coverage for the treatment of mental illness under all insurance plans.

7). Continue, as a nation, to fight on all fronts-social, political, and economic - the racism and poverty that continue to damage African-Americans and others psychologically, and which perpetuate severe mental stresses in African-American communities already suffering from poor education and high rates of crime and violence.

Indeed, as the health status of all Americans improves, we can anticipate in this new century a decline in the heart-wrenching self-destructive behaviors that have been so damaging to African-Americans. Then perhaps, as the Reverend Jesse Jackson Sr. so eloquently put it more than twenty years ago, it will be possible for even the most disenfranchised Americans to "Keep Hope Alive."

On July 28, 1999, United States Surgeon General David Satcher, along with Tipper Gore, wife of Vice President Al Gore, announced a national plan to prevent suicide in America. Speaking at a White House press conference, Dr. Satcher said, "For every two people who die by homicide in this country each year, three people commit suicide. We must continue to develop a national suicide prevention strategy but we must also do a better job right now of taking steps that we know can work."

There are several unique features- including the history of slavery and segregation, and continuing racism and discrimination in America-combined with other risk factors such as depression, anger, drugs and alcohol abuse, and easy access to firearms to make suicide and self-destructive behavior particularly complex issues within the African-American community. Additionally, as the surgeon general has rightly pointed out, the stigma surrounding mental illness is particularly damaging to efforts to prevent suicide; this stigma, while not unique to African-Americans, is especially powerful among African-Americans."[18]

There lies yet another "CRISIS" that is strikingly painful Among African-Americans who are the victims of generations and generations of racism, discrimination, and poverty. The offspring of the people who were the victims of "History's Greatest Crime" now face the life ending threat of the disease of Aids and HIV. "HIV-Hepatitis Infectious Virus and Acquired Immune Deficiency Syndrome is an increasingly disturbing problem in rural Eastern Carolinas' counties, home to the states' poorest and least educated people. Healthcare workers say they are struggling to fight HIV/AIDS, which disproportionately affects blacks and, increasingly, young, poor black women. The disparity is staggering. In South Carolina, September 2002 reports say that African-Americans represent almost 80 percent of the more than 17,000 reported HIV/AIDS cases even though blacks make up about 30 percent of the overall population.

74a

"THE AMERICAN DREAM DOES NOT END WHEN IT COMES TRUE FOR YOU; IT THEN BECOMES YOUR RESPONSIBILITY TO MAKE IT COME TRUE FOR OTHERS."

Dr. David Satcher, M.D.
U.S. Surgeon General

In North Carolina, which is 22 percent African-American, blacks make up slightly more than 70 percent of about 22,000 cases. The reasons are complex and societal, and the solutions are difficult, health-care workers say.

In rural areas, patients are spread out over hundreds of miles. Many don't have cars to get to the doctor. They lack health insurance and education, crucial to understand and adhere to HIV's complicated drug regiment. And in many cases, patients keep their HIV status a secret for fear of being ostracized. Health care workers say the disease spreads quickly when people don't, and sometimes won't use protection (sexually).

"I guess it's denial," says Cathy Johnson, who tracks HIV infections in rural South Carolina. At a time when drugs are making it possible to manage HIV, health-care workers face mounting barriers. Among them:

1). Lack of money to help people pay for expensive HIV drugs. North Carolina's waiting list numbered 701 on August 5, 2002, the longest in the country, said a Duke University HIV social worker. South Carolina had a waiting list until last year, when it won an extra grant.

2). The threat of budget cuts in both Carolinas.

3). The lack of understanding among the general public about how the disease is spread and prevented. It is said to have deep frustrations on the part of health-care workers such as Johnson, who works in Orangeburg, Bamberg, and Calhoun Counties, South Carolina. The region between Columbia and Charleston has some of South Carolinas highest rates of HIV infection and is one of the poorest areas. "It's not getting any better," she said. "We average eight new cases a month. That's high for a rural area. For that eight, there's another eight out there. Its like a pyramid."

To properly state the "CRISIS" that African-Americans currently face in the Carolina's, let's look at the ratio's or disparity in relation to race makeup. African-Americans does make up an increasingly larger proportion of total HIV cases in the Carolina's. Consider this: In 1986, 155 white men in South Carolina reported having HIV- more than the number of infected black men and women combined. In 2000, 473 black men and 278 black women reported having the disease, but only 144 white men reported having HIV. In North Carolina in 2000, 63 in every 100,000 blacks had HIV compared to 5.8 in 100,000 for whites.

Bamberg County, S. C., is a case study of rural HIV. When HIV appeared more than 20 years ago, health care workers say many thought of it as a scary and exotic disease primarily affecting gay men in large cities. Bamberg shattered that image. In 1987, the community - then population 18,200- made headlines when an unidentified woman tested positive for HIV. When health officials asked her to list sexual partners, she reeled off 60 names. A concerned doctor called the local paper, which warned in a headline: "Horror of AIDS epidemic Hits Home." Thus began one of the Carolinas' first cases of AIDS panic. Residents swamped the county health department and local newspaper with calls trying to learn the woman's name.

It was kept confidential. Anxious wives begged local police officers to follow their husbands. Health officials set up an HIV clinic to serve patients in the Bamberg area - the state's first in a rural area. But tiny Bamberg still has the second-highest HIV/AIDS rate in the state. Richland County, home to Columbia, South Carolina's capital, is first.

Some theorize that HIV infections spread south along the Interstate 95 corridor, which runs through eastern North Carolina and South Carolina.

The interstate may provide more access to intravenous drugs and prostitution. By 1999, the Carolina's, Florida, and Mississippi had the most HIV infections in communities with fewer than 50,000 people, according to a North Carolina statistical report. Nationally, the number of people contracting and dying from AIDS, the disease caused by HIV, has dropped, thanks to drug therapies. But it has dropped more slowly in the South.

Health-care workers aren't sure why the south is the epicenter of HIV and AIDS. But they suspect it's related to poverty, lack of education, and the difficulty of finding adequate health care relative to other parts of the country.

Bamberg's median household income is $24,000, the second lowest in the state. Bertie county, in rural northeastern North Carolina, has the lowest median household income in the state at just over $25,000. It also has the highest HIV rate, according to North Carolina epidemiologist. Mecklenberg county, the largest county in North Carolina, ranks sixth. Ms. Johnson, of Orangeburg, South Carolina, calls the patients "The 'Uns' of the world":

The UN-employed, The UN-educated, and the UN-insured. Linda Ashley, who directs a clinic serving York, Lancaster and Chester counties in South Carolina, said the number of female clients has spiked in recent years. Just five years ago, fewer than 20 percent of her clients were female; it's now 49 percent, or 140 women. For example, between 1990 and 2000, the proportion of black North Carolina women with HIV jumped 50 percent, making women more than 27 percent of all reports. North Carolina had reported 22,000 cases as of 2001.

Care for many female clients is often more complicated than for others. "In most cases, she's heterosexual, she has a child, and she makes her decisions on how she can take care of her children," Ashley said. That means sometimes choosing between medicine and food. There's another force at work as well, said Trish Bartlett, a clinical social worker for Duke University's AIDS clinic. Many patients are diagnosed with HIV in other states and return to family homes in the Carolinas. She estimates almost half of Duke's clients were infected elsewhere and came home to North Carolina once they got sick.

That's what happened to Louise, an HIV patient from Orangeburg county who requested anonymity. Louise's family moved to New York when she was a child. A former drug and alcohol addict, Louise learned she was HIV positive during a stint in rehab.

The news sent her on a drinking spree that landed her by chance back home in Orangeburg. "God is good," she said. AIDS clinic workers found Louise, bedridden with tuberculosis and pneumonia. She weighted 80 pounds. That was 11 years ago. She sobered up and gained weight.

The virus is now almost undetectable. Louise stayed in Orangeburg where she has extended family. But she won't tell her relatives about her health. "My family is ignorant," she said. She told of when an HIV positive friend visited her relatives and used their bathroom.

When the friend left, Louise said her relatives said, "get out the Lysol and clean the bathroom." Louise's reluctance to tell her family is common, workers say. Small towns help residents when they are sick, but they also can shun people they fear.

Unlike crowded cities where clients can remain anonymous, healthcare workers say many small town patients fear getting help at the doctor's office. They might run into a friend or relative.

Rural HIV clinics and agencies keep their locations quiet, fearing patients won't return if someone finds out where they're going. Stacy Williams, a case manager based in Laurens, S. C., near Greenville, sometimes meets her clients in neutral places such as McDonald's or the Bi-Lo parking lot. "You will find some pockets of people who embrace (people with) HIV," she said. But the majority of clients haven't told their families they're HIV positive." AIDS education in rural towns is a sticky matter. The small-town south can be conservative, workers say, and some people don't want to talk about condoms and prevention. Residents are often shocked to hear AIDS isn't just a city problem. This lack of understanding is a big barrier to fighting rural HIV, Williams said. The disease spreads quickly in small towns where a few people can infect a large proportion of the community. In one small town where she works, Johnson said, two individuals are likely responsible for at least eight or nine recent cases. "It spreads like wildfire," she said.

Both Carolina's now have AIDS outreach clinics to bring care closer to rural patients. But the job is frustrating, and it's heart wrenching, said Ashley of York County. Staffers try to provide support, or even just a hug. "It's not unusual for a client to say, "You're the first person to touch me in months," she said. Clinic staffers in both states say they need more money to pay workers; more outreach clinics; and more help for patients to buy HIV medications, which can run a $1,000 a month. AIDS assistance comes mostly from the federal government, but it is administered and supplemented by the states. Funding is based on a complicated formula and how it is divided out is often a sensitive political issue. Health-care workers are further frustrated by the possibility of state budget cuts, which could affect the money used to supplement federal funds. "

It's horrifying," said Bartlett, who has lobbied state and national leaders for more money. "This is an infectious disease. It is a disease people continue to not understand the spread of. We are totally hindered in our efforts to stop the spread of the disease."

Is there any hope? Well, clinic workers say they don't know, although they've noticed some positive changes "I am beginning to see some churches talk about it," Ashley said. "But in the mainstream South? In small communities? I don't know. I wouldn't stake a lot of money on it."19

Finally, to ensure that one is doing all that can be done in order to achieve longevity in life, here are but a few possible suggestions, which has been offered. It has been suggested to keep in mind that simple things make a big difference; such as:

Getting adequate rest
Exercising
Eating balanced meals
Vacationing
Praying
Laughing
Enjoying music
Eliminating drugs and alcohol
Cutting back on caffeine
Having monogamous relationships
Practicing safe sex wherever applicable

More importantly, more and more men and women are recognizing the benefits of talking to a minister, social worker, psychologist or psychiatrist.

Another "CRISIS" that should be noted is the deadly Cardiovascular disease that afflicts so many African Americans at an alarming rate. This disease, which affects the heart and the blood vessels, is the nations number 1 killer. Hence, the death rate for African-American men is 46 percent higher than for white men according to the American Heart Association. Studies show that African-American men are 40 percent more likely to suffer from high blood pressure than white men.

African-Americans suffer strokes more frequently than any other ethnic group in America. Strokes occurs when a blood vessel in the brain is blocked or bursts. These "brain attacks" or "blowouts" occur 98 percent more often in African-American men than in white men, the American Heart Association reports. A major problem is that many African-American men ignore the symptoms, which includes: unexplained dizziness, numbness, trouble talking, memory lapses, and problems performing simple tasks.

Some prevention to these cardiovascular diseases are to check your blood pressure at least twice a year, stop smoking, controlling your weight, exercising, eating potassium- rich foods like bananas and fiber to soak up cholesterol.

Cutting back on caffeine, salt, eggs, and greasy foods such as fried chicken and fried fish. Baked dishes are healthier. Moreover, eliminate alcohol, illegal drugs, and cigarettes, which promulgates ill health. Again, too much fat can raise your cholesterol level, which should be below 200 milligrams per deciliter of blood.

The American Heart Association's figures shows that 47 percent of African-American men twenty years of age and older have readings that exceed normal levels and that one third of all African-American men are overweight. Sedimentary men have a 50 percent higher risk of high blood pressure and triple the death rate of fit men. Hence, with all of these biological, psychological, and social problems confronting us, we do not need to further promote early deaths among African-Americans by adding domestic spousal abuse, family neglect, or drive-by shootings and killings, in our neighborhoods with gang violence.

To be sure, for African-Americans entering into the twenty-first century in America, it should be looked upon as a definite return to "EDEN," and a fresh new start. And, in as much as racism is concerned, well, we know by now just who we are and from where we have come. Therefore, our plight is to accept the infinite possibilities that lie ahead for us and obtain all."[20]

Most importantly, I still believe in the power of the Most High, "GOD"! Moreover, I still believe that He will someday come here and "Right" this ship. I often wonder why is it that America is so concerned with stopping international terrorism from abroad while right here in America the Ku Klux Klan and the police has been terrorizing and killing my people for four centuries. My brother Fredrick Douglas was right about their "Hypocracy." Hence, lemons doesn't fall far from their trees either.

Also I believe that African-American people have able leadership who will continue to stand up for us and be heard. I believe that contemporary men like Mr. Kweisi Mfume President of the NAACP, Mr. Julian Bond- NAACP, Dr. Jessie Jackson and his humanitarian efforts and coalitions, Min. Louis Farrakhan of the Nation of Islam, Brother Al Sharpton and his crusades and Congresswoman Maxine Waters, will continue to "Complain Ceaselessly" and continue to agitate the consciousness of the majority. They will continue to fight for "Affirmative Action" in the face of these "Anti-Progressive" people like Strom Thurmond, George Bush, Sen. Lott of Mississippi, and a host of other shoe-shine boys, kitchen boys, and boot-licking Uncle Toms like Armstrong Williams, Larry Elder, and Clarence Thomas. I believe what Brother Jessie Jackson say is true in that we still have "Unfinished Business" here that must be attended to and resolved.

Hence, our fight for economic, social, and political justice and equality is far from complete in America as we enter this new century. However, our only hope is through the continued diligence as we stride toward this goal.

More importantly, men must stride toward getting to know one another, clearing away all presumptions, which breeds false illusions. If we are going to co-exist on Gods earth these are indeed dispensable.

Racism, Economic Exploitation, Greed, and War, are essentially the anemia's that persistently plague our society and world as a whole. Unless we can cure our diseases we will inevitably self-destruct. Moreover, much of the responsibility in curing the disease of racism will fall into the hands of our political leaders. However, this will be a tall order to fill when we still have people with the mentality of the late South Carolina Senator Strom Thurmonds' ideologies. The "Problems" that he refers to still is African-American people.

They still don't know what to do with us. I have an idea that Mr. Thurmond followers might be able to use for themself. Why not consider the son's of the victims of "History's Greatest Crime"-400 years of Slavery, Rape, and Murder, as "Human Beings", and begin making your reparations payments? Massa Boss!

The current rumblings in the Middle East are merely the "Reveling in Squander Mania" on the part of our present political leaders. In the face of failed domestic policy this is indicative of misdirected priorities. Primarily, all of their energy's should be directed toward the health, housing, education, and the well being of this nations elderly, poor and disadvantaged, hence, in order to fulfill the commitments, such as: Equal Housing, Equal Job Opportunity, Fair Work Wages, Better Education Opportunity, Health Insurance availabilities, and afford-abilities, etc., that was abandoned by conservatives like Ronald Reagan and George Bush, Sr. and congressionalist like the former and former senator Strom Thurmond (R-S.C.) followers and Jessie Helms (R-N.C.) and the former Sen. Lott (R) Miss.

Internationally, In order to break the gridlock between warring nations, i.e., Iraq, Saudi Arabia, Syria, Libya, England, and the United States, over what is essentially controlling that regions oil resources, the U. S. should focus more on trade agreements with countries like Nigeria or Angola that has a surplus of oil resources.

This will, in my opinion, ease some of the tensions of the proliferation of nuclear war in our time. Realistically though I'm pessimistic about America dealing exclusively with a Black Nation on equal terms.

Finally there's the issue of U.S. Military and economic support of the Israeli government in the Middle East. Here too, lies the misdirected priorities of the U. S. government. In my opinion, America should not be aiding the Israeli government, who supported the South African Apartheid Government with guns in order to keep the South African Blacks oppressed for centuries.

For example, an organization, MIFTAH, followed the money trail that has been literally given to the colonial government of Israel. Since 1987, the Israeli government had received $3 billion annually from the U.S.- $1.2 billion in economic aid and $1.8 billion in military aid. Since 1991 an additional $2 billion was given to the Israeli government for federal loans;- equaling $5 billion or $13.7 million / day, Other U. S. tax dollars include $ 1.5 billion (tax deductible) private donations from Jewish charities and individual donors. Consequential aid adds up to $8 billion, the largest amount of foreign aid "given" to any country. The aid given to the Israeli government comprises a massive 30% of the total amount of the U. S. Foreign Aid Budget. Israel is the largest recipient of U. S. foreign aid in the world. Moreover, since 1976 the total U.S. aid to Israel is a massive $81.3 billion. Hence, by 2005 the total aid to the Israeli regime is proposed to exceed $97 Billion, with no terms of repayment for such aid.

This is, in this U. S. veteran's opinion, showing a total disregard and an insult for the efforts of the many homeless U. S. veterans and their families who sacrificed their lives for this country, yet receive little or no reparation at all for their sacrifice. As the former president of U. S. Veterans Upward Bound, I'm calling for the immediate withdraw of aid to the Israeli regime and such funds be allocated for the staffing of VA Hospitals, who consistently complains of being short handed and can't meet the needs of veterans, eg., talk therapy, and individual counseling. Moreover, increased benefits for Disabled American Veterans are needed, by at least 20%!, and the amending of GI Benefits to veterans of the American Armed Forces and increased benefits for the widows/dependants of deceased U. S. veterans.

The billions of dollars given to the colonial government of Israel is merely an example of how whites around the world assist each other in oppressing non-whites. These funds should be used to make reparations and restitution to veterans of this nation wars and who made this a free society and to those who are the descendants of the victims of "History's Greatest Crime"-The American Holocaust, "African-American Slavery!" Peace!

In the aftermath of Barack Obama's election to the office of the President of the Uinted States in 2008, the first president of African descent, and the 44th American President elected, many racists resurfaced and resulted in acts of vandalisms and threats, which dimed the post election glow for many in America. Moreover, there were incidents of cross burnings and young school-children chanting "Assassinate Obama!," while Black figures were hung from nooses and racial epithets scrawled on homes and cars. Incidents like these around the country referring to President Barack Obama immensely dampened his post election glow of racial progress and harmony, highlighting the stubborn racism that remains in America. From California to Maine, police have documented a range of incidents ranging from vandalism and vague threats to at least one physical attack. Insults and taunts have been delivered by adults, college students, and second-graders.

There have been hundreds of incidents since the election, many more than usual, said Mark Potok, director of the Intelligence Project at the Southern Poverty Law Center, which monitors hate crimes.

In Snellville, Ga., Denene Millner said a boy on the school bus told her 9-year old daughter the day after the elections, "I hope Obama gets assassinated." That night, someone trashed her sister-in-laws front lawn, mangled the Obama lawn signs, and left two pizza boxes filled with human feces outside the front door, Millner said. Mrs. Millner described her emotions as a combination of anger and fear. "I can't say that every white person in Snellville is evil and anti-Obama and willing to harm or desecrate my property, because one or two idiots did it," said Millner, who is Black. "But it definitely makes you look a little different at the people who you live with, and it makes you wonder what they're capable of and what they're really thinking." Potok, who is White, said he believes there is "a large subset of white people in this country who feel that they are losing everything they know, that the country their forefathers built has somehow been stolen from them."

Grant Griffin, a 46-year-old white Georgia native, expressed similar sentiments: "I believe our Nation is ruined and has been for several decades, and the election of Obama is merely the culmination of the change. If you had real change, it would involve all the members of (Obama's) church being deported," he said. Change in whatever form does not come easily, and a Black President Is the most profound Change in the field of race this country has experienced since the Civil War," said William Ferris, Senior Associate Director of the Center for the Study of the American South at the University Of North Carolina: "It's shaking the foundations on which the country has existed for Centuries." "Someone once said that Racism is like Cancer," Ferris said. It's never totally wiped out; it's Only in remission." If so, America's cancerous remission lasted until the morning of November 5, 2008.

The day after the vote, hailed as a sign of a changed nation, Black high school student Barbara Tyler of Marietta, Ga., said she heard hateful Obama comments from White Students and teachers cut off discussions about Obama's victory.

Tyler spoke at a press conference held by the NAACP calling for a town hall-style meeting to address complaints from across the state about hostility and resentment. Another student, from a Covington Middle School, said he was suspended for wearing an Obama shirt to school November 5th after the principal told students not to wear political paraphernalia. The student's mother, Eshe Riviears, said the principal told her: "whether you like it or not, We're in the South, and there are a lot of people who are not happy with this decision."

Emotions are often raw after a hard-fought political campaign, but now those on the losing side have an easy target for their anger. "The principle is very simple," said B. J. Gallagher, A Sociologist and co-author of the diversity book, "A Peacock In The Land Of Penguins." "If I can't hurt the person I'm angry at, then I'll vent my anger on a substitute, ie., someone of the same race." 'It's as stupid and ineffectual as kicking your dog when you've had a bad day at the office." Gallagher said, "But it happens a lot." Around the nation, there were many indications that the cancer of racism had resurfaced out of remission. In Hardwick Township, N. J., a cross was burned on the front lawn of Gary and Alina Grewal, where they had placed a banner congratulating president-elect Barack Obama on his victory.

In North Carolina, four North Carolina State University students admitted to writing anti-Obama comments in a tunnel designated for free-speech expression, including one that said: "Let's shoot that (N-Word) in the head." Obama has received more threats than any other president-elect, authorities say.

At Standish, Maine, a sign inside the Oak Hill General Store read: Osama Obama shotgun pool." Customers could sign up to bet $1 on a date when Obama would be killed. "Stabbings, shooting, roadside bombs, they all count," the sign said. At the bottom of the marker board was written " Lets hope someone wins."

University of Alabama professor Marsha L. Houston said a poster of the Obama family was ripped off her office door. A replacement poster was defaced with a death threat and a racial slur. "It seems that the election brought the racist rats out of the woodwork."

A Black teenager was attacked in New York City with a bat on election night by four white men who shouted Obama racial slurs.

Black figures were hanged by nooses from trees on Mount Desert Island, Maine, the Bangor Daily News reported.

The president of Baylor University in Waco, Texas said a rope found hanging from a campus tree was apparently an abandoned swing and not a noose.

Racist graffiti was found in places including New York's Long Island, where two dozen cars were spray-painted; Kilgore, Texas, where the local high school and a skate park were defaced.

In the Los Angeles area, swastikas, racial slurs, and "Go Back To Africa," graffiti was spray-painted on sidewalks, houses, and cars.

Second- and third-grade students on a school bus in Rexburg, Idaho, chanted "Assassinate Obama" a district official said.

In the Pittsburgh suburb of Forest Hills, a Black man said he found a note on his car windshield with a racial slur and a vague threat: "Now that you voted for Obama, just watch out for your house."[21]

In response to these vicious and hateful assaults resulting in the election of Barack Obama to the office of President of the United States, it is evident that the nation is still very divided in some sectors in regards to color. At any rate, there is still hope in the hearts and minds of the majority of Americans of all races due to the evidence of the outcome of President Barack Obama being elected to the office of President of the United States of America!!

Reference Notes

Chapter 1: Legacies of Oppression

1). William E. B. DuBois, The Souls Of Black Folk, Blue Heron Publishers and Bantam Classic Books, New York, Toronto, London, Sydney, Auckland, 1903, 1989, pp.10
2). Dubois, Ibid. pp.2
3). Dubois, Ibid., pp.11
4). George M. Fredrickson, The Black Image In The White Mind, Wesleyan University Press and Harper Row Publishers, Hanover, New Hampshire, 1987, pp. 46-47
5). Fredrickson, Ibid. pp. 47-49
6). Fredrickson, Ibid., pp. 78-79, 90
7). Fredrickson, Ibid., pp. 154-159
8). Fredrickson, Ibid., pp. 91

Chapter 2: Philosophies and Predictions Towards Extermination and Extinction

1). George M. Fredrickson, The Black Image In The White Mind, Wesleyan University Press and Harper Row Publishers, Hanover, New Hampshire, 1987, pp. 154
2). Fredrickson, Ibid., pp. 155
3). Fredrickson, Ibid., pp. 155-156
4). Fredrickson, Ibid., pp. 157-158
5). Fredrickson, Ibid., pp. 158
6). Fredrickson, Ibid., pp. 160-164
7). Fredrickson, Ibid., pp. 121-122
8). Fredrickson, Ibid., pp. 103-105
9). Fredrickson, Ibid., pp. pp. 123
10). Edward D. Smith, Climbing Jacobs Ladder, The Smithsonian Institute, 1988, p.1
11). Burnside and Robotham, Spirit Of The Passage-The TransAtlantic Slave Trade In The Seventeenth Century, Simon and Schuster, New York, 1997, pp. 19
12). James Michael Brodie, The Lives And Ideas Of Black American Innovators "Created Equal," Quill William Morrow, New York, 1993, pp. 7

13). Randall Robinson, The Debt-What America Owes To Blacks,
     Plume and Penguin Books, New York, Toronto, London, Australia, 2000, p. 84
14). Velma M. Thomas, Lest We Forget-The Passage From Africa To
     Slavery And Emancipation, Crown Publishers, Inc., New York, 1997, pp. 2

Chapter 3: The European Transatlantic Slave Trade

1). Burnside and Robotham, Spirit Of The Passage-The TransAtlantic
    Slave Trade In The Seventeenth Century, Simon and Schuster, New York, 1997, pp. 19
2). Velma M. Thomas, Lest We Forget-The Passage From Africa To Slavery
    And Emancipation, Crown Publishers Inc., New York, pp. 5
3). Burnside and Robotham, Ibid., pp. 25
4). Thomas, Ibid., pp.4
5). Thomas, op. cit., pp.5
6). Burnside and Robotham, Ibid.
7). Julius Lester, To Be A Slave, The Dial Press, Inc., 1968, pp. 24-25
8). Thomas, Ibid., pp. 6
9). Thomas, Ibid., pp. 7
10). S. E. Anderson, The Black-Holocaust, Writers and Readers Publishing, Inc., New York,
     1995, pp. 48-53
11). Burnside and Robotham, Ibid., pp. 39
12). Ibid., pp. 34
13). Thomas, Ibid.
14). Burnside and Robotham, Ibid.
15). Lester, Ibid., pp. 27
16). Robinson, Ibid., pp. 24
17). Lerone Bennett, Jr., Before The Mayflower-A History Of Black
     America, Penguin Books and Johnson Publishing Company,
     New York, 1961, 1969, 1988, pp. 30-31
18). Isidor Paiewonsky, Eyewitness Accounts Of Slavery In The Danish
     West Indies-Also Graphic Tales Of Other Slave Happenings On Ships
     And Plantations, Fordham University Press, New York, 1989, pp. 1-2
19). Paiewonsky, Ibid. pp. 2-16
20). Paiewonsky, Ibid., pp. 19-36
21). Paiewonsky, Ibid., pp. 40-43
22). Paiewonsky, Ibid., pp. 45-57
23). Paiewonsky, Ibid., pp. 73

24). Paiewonsky, Ibid., pp. 72-75
25). Paiewonsky, Ibid., pp. 82-88
26). Paiewonsky, Ibid., pp. 92-95

Chapter 4: Slavery and The Old South

1). David Robertson, Denmark Vesey-The Buried History Of America's
    Largest Slave Rebellion And The Man Who Led It, Alfred A. Knopf,
    New York, 1999, pp. 11-26
2). William E. B. Dubois, The Suppression Of The African-Slave Trade
    To The United States of America, 1638-1870, Louisiana State
    University Press, Baton Rouge, Louisiana, 1965, pp. 9
3). W. E. B. DuBois, Ibid., pp. 12
4). Revolutionary Times, Black Arcade Liberation Library, January 1, 1970, pp. 4
5). August Meir/ Elliott Rudwick, From Plantation To Ghetto, American
    Century Series, Hill and Wang, Inc., New York, 1976, pp. 44
6). Lerone Bennett, Jr., Before The Mayflower-A History Of Black
    America, Penguin Books and Johnson Publishing Company,
    New York, 1961, 1969, 1988, pp. 49
7). Bennett, Before The Mayflower, Ibid.
8). Robinson, Ibid., pp. 49-52
9). Bennett, Before The Mayflower, Ibid., pp. 113-118
10). Bennett, Before The Mayflower, Ibid., pp. 44-45
11). Bennett, Before The Mayflower, Ibid.
12). Bennett, Before The Mayflower, Ibid., pp. 70-71
13). Julius Lester, To Be A Slave, Dial Press, Inc., New York, 1968, pp. 28-29
14). Bennett, Before The Mayflower, Ibid., pp. 72-73
15). Bennett, Before The Mayflower, Ibid.
16). Bennett, Before The Mayflower, Ibid., pp. 78-90
17). John W. Blassingame, Slave Testimony: Two Centuries Of Letters,
    Louisiana State University Press, Baton Rouge, Louisiana, 1977, pp. 24-25
18). Rev. C. Hope Felder, PhD., Professor of New Testament Languages
    and Literature, HOLY BIBLE-THE ORIGINAL AFRICAN
    HERITAGE EDITION-KING JAMES VERSION, Howard University,
    Washington, D. C., pp. 333-334

19). Kenneth M. Stampp, The Peculiar Institution-Slavery In The
Ante-Bellum South, Vintage Books and Random House, Inc.,
New York, 1956, 1984, pp. 81

20). Stampp, Ibid., pp. 85

21). Stampp, Ibid., pp. 82

22). Stampp, Ibid., pp. 84

23). Stampp, Ibid., pp. 80-81

24). James Mellon, Bullwhip Days-The Slaves Remember, An Oral History,
Avon Books, New York, 1998, pp. 178-182

25). Fredrickson, Ibid., pp. 14

26). Blassingame, Ibid., pp. 697-698

27). Blassingame, Ibid., pp. 371-373

28). Candie and Guy Carawan, Ain't You Got A Right To The Tree of Life,
The University Of Georgia Press, Athens and London, 1966, pp. 3

29). James M. Brodie, The Lives And Ideas Of Black American Innovators
"Created Equal", Quill William Morrow Publishing Company,
New York, 1993, pp. 17

30). Brodie, Ibid., pp. 27

31). Benjamin Quarles, Lincoln And The Negro, Da Capo Press, Inc., New York, 1962, pp. 35-36

32). Lerone Bennett, Jr., Forced Into Glory-Abraham Lincoln's White
Dream, The Johnson Publishing Company, Chicago, Illinois, 2000, pp. 36-44 *

33). Bennett, Forced Into Glory, Ibid., pp. 47*

34). Bennett, Forced Into Glory, Ibid., pp. 57-59*

35). Bennett, Forced Into Glory, Ibid., pp. 66-69*

36). Bennett, Forced Into Glory, Ibid., pp. 87-110*

37). Bennett, Forced Into Glory, Ibid., pp. 112*

38). Bennett, Forced Into Glory, Ibid., pp. 113*

39). Bennett, Forced Into Glory, Ibid., pp. 119*

40). Bennett, Forced Into Glory, Ibid., pp. 125*

41). Bennett, Forced Into Glory, Ibid., pp. 126-127*

42). Bennett, Forced Into Glory, Ibid., pp. 248-254*

43). Bennett, Forced Into Glory, Ibid., pp. 257-259*

44). Bennett, Forced Into Glory, Ibid., pp. 271*

45). Bennett, Forced Into Glory, Ibid., pp. 272*

46). Bennett, Forced Into Glory, Ibid., pp. 273*

47). Bennett, Forced Into Glory, Ibid., pp. 282-283*

48). Bennett, Forced Into Glory, Ibid., pp. 286-287*

49). Bennett, Forced Into Glory, Ibid., pp. 298-300*

50). Bennett, Forced Into Glory, Ibid., pp. 309-310*

51). Bennett, Forced Into Glory, Ibid., pp. 328*

52). Bennett, Forced Into Glory, Ibid., pp. 330-334*

53). Bennett, Forced Into Glory, Ibid., pp. 337*

54). Bennett, Forced Into Glory, Ibid., pp. 338*

55). Bennett, Forced Into Glory, Ibid., pp. 341*

56). Bennett, Forced Into Glory, Ibid., pp. 342*

57). Bennett, Forced Into Glory, Ibid.*

58). Bennett, Forced Into Glory, Ibid., pp. 350-353*

59). Bennett, Forced Into Glory, Ibid., pp. 359*

60). Bennett, Forced Into Glory, Ibid., pp. 361*

61). Bennett, Forced Into Glory, Ibid., pp. 363-364*

62). Bennett, Forced Into Glory, Ibid., pp. 381-382*

63). Bennett, Forced Into Glory, Ibid., pp. 384-387*

64). Bennett, Forced Into Glory, Ibid., pp. 391-396*

65). Bennett, Forced Into Glory, Ibid., pp. 399-406*

66). Bennett, Forced Into Glory, Ibid., pp. 410-417*

67). Bennett, Forced Into Glory, Ibid., pp. 430*

68). Bennett, Forced Into Glory, Ibid., pp. 434-435*

69). Bennett, Forced Into Glory, Ibid., pp. 452-465*

70). Bennett, Forced Into Glory, Ibid., pp. 531-540*

71). Bennett, Forced Into Glory, Ibid., pp. 542-549*

72). Bennett, Forced Into Glory, Ibid., pp. 552*

73). Bennett, Forced Into Glory, Ibid., pp. 554-555*

74). Bennett, Forced Into Glory, Ibid., pp. 563-566*

75). Bennett, Forced Into Glory, Ibid., pp. 569-573*

76). Bennett, Forced Into Glory, Ibid., pp. 574-575*

77). Bennett, Forced Into Glory, Ibid., pp. 578-581*

78). Bennett, Forced Into Glory, Ibid., pp. 586*

79). Bennett, Forced Into Glory, Ibid., pp. 587-589*

80). Bennett, Forced Into Glory, Ibid., pp. 594-600*

81). William E. B. DuBois, Black Reconstruction In America, 1860-1888, Simon and Schuster publishing co., New York, London, Toronto, Sydney, Tokyo, Singapore, 1935, 1962, pp. 383

82). Alphonso Pinkney, The Myth Of Black Progress In America- "Black Equality In White America," Cambridge University Press, Cambridge, Mass., 1984, pp. 167

83). John Hope Franklin, From Slavery To Freedom- A History Of Negro Americans, McGraw-Hill Publishing Co., New York, St. Louis, San Francisco, Auckland, Bogata, Caraccas, Hamburg, Paris, London, Sao Paulo, Madrid; Fortieth Anniversary Edition, 1988, pp. 226-227

84). DuBois, W. E. B., Black Reconstruction-1860-1888, Ibid., pp. 171

85). DuBois, W. E. B., Black Reconstruction-1860-1888, Ibid., pp. 167

86). August Meir and Elliott Rudwick, From Plantation To Ghetto,
American Century Series, Hill and Wang Publishing co., New York, 1976, pp. 166-173

87). Deirdre Mullane, Words To Make My Dream Children Live-"A Book
Of African-American Quotations," Anchor Books, Doubleday
Publishers, New York, London, Toronto, Auckland, Sydney, 1995, pp. 124

88). David Levering Lewis, W. E. B. DuBois- Biography Of A Race-1868-1919,
John Macrae Books, Henry Holt and Co., New York, 1993, pp. 321

89). Lewis, DuBois- Biography Of A Race, Ibid., pp. 322

90). Fox Butterfield, "All GOD"S CHILDREN"- The American Tradition
OF VIOLENCE, Avon Books, New York, 1996, pp. 49

91). Lewis, DuBois-Biography Of A Race, Ibid., pp. 251

92). Pinkney, Ibid., pp. 56

93). Butterfield, Ibid., pp. 61

94). John Hope Franklin, African-Americans And The Living Constitution,
The Smithsonian Institution Press, Washington, D. C., London, 1995, pp. 31

95). Butterfield, Ibid., pp. 46-49

96). James M. McPherson, The Abolitionist Legacy: From Reconstruction
To The NAACP, Princeton University Press, Princeton, NJ., 1975. pp. 304

97). Butterfield, Ibid., pp. 49

98). Butterfield, Ibid.

99). John Lewis, Leon Litwack, James Allen, Hilton Als,
Without Sanctuary-Lynching Photography In America, Twin Palms
Publishers, Santa Fe, New Mexico, 2000, pp. 29

100). Butterfield, Ibid., pp. 50

101). Butterfield, Ibid., pp. 51

102). Butterfield, Ibid., pp. 57-58

103). Butterfield, Ibid., pp. 61

104). Mullane, Ibid., pp. 122-124

105). Russel L. Adams, Great Negros Past And Present, African-American
Publishing Co. Inc., Chicago, Illinois, 1963, pp. 248-250

106). Adams, Ibid., pp. 112

107). Lewis, Ibid., pp. 330

108). William E. B. DuBois, The Souls Of Black Folk, Blue Heron
Publishers, Bantam Classic Books, 1903, 1989, pp. 3

109). DuBois, The Souls Of Black Folk, Ibid., pp. 2

110). C. Vann Woodard, The Strange Career Of Jim Crow, Oxford
University Press, Inc., Oxford, England, 1974, pp. 67-69

111). Mullane, Ibid., pp. 122-124

112). Mullane, Ibid.

113). Michael Lee Lanning, The African-American Soldier, From Crypus
Attucks To Colin Powell, Birch Lane Press Books, Carol Publishing
Group, Secaucus, NJ. 1997, pp. 251

114). Lewis, Ibid., pp. 556

115). John Hope Franklin, The Color Line-Legacy For The Twenty-First
Century, The University Of Missouri Press, Columbia and London, 1993, pp. 36

116). Langston Hughes and Milton Meltzer, A Pictorial History Of The
Negro In America, Crown Publishers Inc., New York, 1956, 1953, pp. 248-250

117). George M. Frederickson, The Black Image In The White Mind,
Wesleyan University Press, Harper Row Publishers, Hanover, NH., 1987, pp. 272-273

118). Hughes and Meltzer, Ibid., pp. 264-267

119). John Lewis (Congressman), Without Sanctuary, Ibid., pp. 27-28

120). Herbert Shapiro, White Violence And Black Response- From
Reconstruction To Montgomery, The University Of Massachusetts
Press, Amherst, Massachusetts, 1988, pp. 200

121). Mullane, Ibid., pp. 122-124

122). Bennett, Before The Mayflower, Ibid., pp. 298

123). Bennett, Before The Mayflower, Ibid., pp. 299-301

124). DuBois, "The CRISIS," April 1, 1933, pp. 1

125). Hughes and Meltzer, Ibid., pp. 299

126). Carawan, Ibid., pp. vii

127). James Baldwin, NOBODY KNOWS MY NAME-MORE NOTES OF
A NATIVE SON, Vintage Books, Vintage International, A Division of
Random House, Inc., New York, 1961, pp. 67-71

128). John Hope Franklin, The Color Line, Ibid., pp. 38

129). William H. Chafe, Raymond Gavins, Robert Korstad,
REMEMBERING JIM CROW- African-Americans Tell About Life
In The Segregated South, The New Press, New York, W. W. Norton
and Co., Inc., New York, In Association with Lyndhurst Books of
the Center for Documentary Studies of the behind the Veil project
of DUKE UNIVERSITY, 2001, pp. 1

Chapter 5: The Civil Rights Movement

1). Lerone Bennett, Jr., Before The Mayflower, A History Of Black America, Penguin Books and Johnson Publishing Co., New York, 1961, 1969, 1988, pp. 315
2). Bennett, Before The Mayflower, Ibid. pp. 313
3). Bennett, Before The Mayflower, Ibid. pp. 314
4). Bennett, Before The Mayflower, Ibid. pp. 319
5). Pat Waters, Down To Now, Pantheon Books, New York, 1971, pp. 83
6). Bennett, Before The Mayflower, Ibid. pp. 322
7). Taylor Branch, Parting The Waters-America In The King Years (1954-1963, Touchstone Books, Simon and Schuster, Inc., New York, London, Toronto, Sydney, Tokyo, 1988, pp. 415-416
8). Branch, Ibid. pp. 283
9). Bennett, Before The Mayflower, Ibid. pp. 322-323
10). Stephen B. Oats, Let The Trumpets Sound-The Life of Martin Luther King, Jr., Mentone Books, New American Library, New York, 1982, pp. 171-172
11). Branch, Ibid. pp. 283
12). The New York Times, June 10, 1963, pp.20-c
13). Waters, Ibid. pp. 110
14). The New York Times, Ibid. pp. 29-c
15). The New York Times, Ibid. pp. 19-c
16). Emma Gelders Stern, "I Have A Dream", Alfred A. Knopf, Inc., New York, 1965, pp. 191
17). Stern, Ibid. pp. 193
18). Whitney M. Young, Jr., "To Be Equal," McGraw-Hill Publishing co., New York, 1964, pp. 55
19). Wallace Mendelson, "Discrimination", Princeton Hall Publishing co., New York, 1962, pp. 6
20). Michael Harrington, "The Other America," Penguin Books, Baltimore, MD. 1962, pp. 48-49
21). Oats, Ibid. pp. 252-255
22). Oats, Ibid. pp. 256-257
23). Lotte Hoskins, "I Have A Dream"-The Quotations Of Martin Luther King, Jr., Grosset, Dunlap and Droke House Publishers, Inc., New York, 1968, pp. 115-116
24). Hoskins, Ibid. pp. 115
25). Hoskins, Ibid. pp. 1
26). Stern, Ibid. pp. 198
27). The New York Times, Ibid. pp. 19-c
28). Peter Goldman, Civil Rights: The Challenge Of The Fourteenth Amendment, Coward-McCann, Inc., New York, 1970, pp. 13

29). Oats, Ibid. pp. 363
30). James Haskins, The Life And Death Of Martin Luther King, Jr.,
Lothrop, Lee, and Sheppard Co., New York, 1977, pp. 98
31). Hoskins, Ibid. pp. 146
32). Haskins, Ibid. pp. 98-99
33). Michael Lee Lanning (Lt. Col.-Ret.), The African-American Soldier-
From Crypus Attucks To Colin Powell, Birch Lane Press Books, Carol
Publishing Group, Secaucus, New Jersey, 1977, pp. 255
34). Jack Rummel, Malcolm X- Black Americans Of Achievement, Chelsea
House Publishers, New York, Philadelphia, 1989, pp. 256
35). Alex Haley, The Autobiography Of Malcolm X, Ballantine Books,
New York, 1964, 1965, 1999, pp. 172
36). Haley, Ibid. pp. 174-187
37). Haley, Ibid. pp. 195
38). Haley, Ibid. pp. 198-199
39). Haley, Ibid. pp. 202-206
40). Haley, Ibid. pp. 208
41). Cornell West, RACE MATTERS, Vintage Books, Random House, Inc., New York, 1993,
pp. 136-137
42). West, Ibid. pp. 151
43). Goldman, Ibid. pp. 96
44). Goldman, Ibid. pp. 109
45). Goldman, Ibid. pp. 113
46). Lanning, Ibid. pp. 255
47). Lanning, Ibid. pp. 257
48). Lanning, Ibid. pp. 252
49). Lanning, Ibid. pp. 278-279
50). James M. Washington, A Testament Of Hope-The Essential Writings And Speeches Of
Martin Luther King, Jr., Harper-Collins Publishing Co., New York, 1986, pp. 245-252
51). Robert Jakoubek, Martin Luther King, Jr.-Civil Rights Leader, Chelsea
House Publishers and Grolier Incorporated, Danbury, Connecticut, 1989, pp. 134-137
52). Oats, Ibid. pp. 246
53). West, Ibid. pp. 157-158
54). "JET MAGAZINE," A Johnson Publication, June 8, 1987, pp. 14
55). The Los Angeles Times, November 30, 1996, pp. A-18, A-20
56). The Los Angeles Times, April 3, 1998, pp.1 & pp. A-16

Chapter 6: Conflicting Religious Beliefs and Practices

1). Arthur Koestler, The Thirteenth Tribe-The Khazar Empire And
Its' Heritage, Random House, New York, 1976, pp. 13-22
2). Koestler, Ibid. pp. 38-40

3).   Koestler, Ibid. pp. 45-46
4).   Robert Marshall, Storm From The East- From Genghis Khan To Khubilai Kahn,
       The University of California Press, Berkley, and Los Angeles, California, 1993, pp. 120-121
5).   Koestler, Ibid. pp. 90-91
6).   Koestler, Ibid. pp. 21
7).   Koestler, Ibid. pp. 59-60
8).   Koestler, Ibid., pp. 60-61
9).   Koestler, Ibid., pp. 63-73
10).   Koestler, Ibid., pp. 80-81
11).   Koestler, Ibid., pp. 159-161
12).   David Robertson, Denmark Vesey-The Buried History of America's
       Largest Slave Rebellion And The Man Who Led It, Alfred A. Knopf, New York, 1999, pp. 16
13).   Koestler, Ibid., pp. 16
14).   Rudolph R. Windsor, From Babylon To Timbuktu- A History Of The Ancient Black Races
       Including: The Black Hebrews, Windsors Golden Series, Atlanta, Georgia, 1969, pp. 33-35
15).   Windsor, Ibid., pp. 83-87
16).   Windsor, Ibid., pp. 115-116
17).   Windsor, Ibid., pp. 120
18).   Windsor, Ibid., pp. 122-125
19).   Windsor, Ibid., pp. 129-131
20).   Windsor, Ibid., pp. 132-134
21).   Windsor, Ibid., pp. 146

Chapter 7: Origins, Cultures, and Customs

1).   E. Jefferson Murphy, The Bantu Civilization Of Southern Africa-
       A History Of African Civilization And Understanding Africa,
       Fritz Henry and Whiteide Limited, Toronto, Ontario, Canada, 1974, pp. 1-59
2).   Murphy, Ibid., pp. 133-134
3).   Murphy, Ibid., pp. 220-251

Chapter 8: Conclusion

1).   Claude Anderson, Ed. D., Black Labor-White Wealth, The search for Power And Economic
       Justice, Duncan and Duncan publishers, Inc., Edgewood, MD. 1994, pp. 10
2).   Wahneema Lubiano, The House That Race Built- Black Americans, U.
       S.Terrain, Patheon Books, New York, 1997, pp. vii
3).   Anderson, Ibid., pp. 27

4).   Randall Robinson, The Debt-What America Owes To Blacks, Plume Books, New York, Toronto, London, Australia, 2000, pp. 209-214

5).   "The Los Angeles Times," November 26, 2001, pp. A-1 & A-13

6).   "The Final Call," May 9, 2000, pp. 7 & 25

7).   Alvin F. Poussaint, MD. and Amy Alexander, Lay My Burden Down- Suicide And The Mental Health "CRISIS" Among African-Americans, Beacon Press Books, Boston, Massachusetts, 2000, pp. 15-16

8).   Poussaint, Ibid., pp. 12-17

9).   Poussaint, Ibid., pp. 19

10). Poussaint, Ibid., pp. 59-61

11). Poussaint, Ibid., pp. 78

12). Poussaint, Ibid., pp. 80

13). Poussaint, Ibid., pp. 80-90

14). Poussaint, Ibid., pp. 96-97

15). Poussaint, Ibid., pp. 103-104

16). Poussaint, Ibid., pp. 127

17). "GUIDE POST," August, 2000, pp. 14

18). Poussaint, Ibid., pp. 156-159

19). "The Charlotte Observer," September 2, 2002, pp. 1A & 4A

20). BET WEEKEND- SPECIAL SOUL BROTHERS ISSUE, New York, June 1977, pp. 14-15

21). The Daily News, Sunday November 16, 2008, pp. A22

Selected Bibliography

Adams, Russell L., Great Negroes Past and Present, African-American Publishing Company Incorporated, Chicago, Illinois, 1963.

Andersen, S. E., The Black Holocaust, Writers and Readers Publishing, Incorporated, New York, 1995

Baldwin James, Nobody Knows My name, More Notes of a Native Son, Vintage International, Vintage Books, A Division of Random House, Inc., New York, 1961.

Bennett, Lerone, Jr., Before The Mayflower, A History of Black America, Pengum Books and Johnson Publishing Company, New York, 1961, 1969, 1988.

Bennett, Lerone, Jr., Forced Into Glory, Abraham Lincoln's White Dream, Johnson Publishing Company, Chicago, Illinois, 2000.

Black Entertainment Television Weekend, Special Brother's Issue, New York, June, 1977.

Blassingame, John W., Slave Testimony: Two Centuries Of Letters, Louisiana State University Press, Baton Rouge, Louisiana, 1977.

Branch, Taylor, Parting The Waters-America In The King Years (1954-1863), Touchstone Books, Simone and Schuster, lnc., New York, London, Toronto, Sydney, Tokyo, 1988.

Brodie, James Michael, The Lives and Ideas Of Black Innovators "created Equal," Quill William Morrow, New York, 1993.

Burnside and Robotham, Spirit Of The Passage, The Trans-Atlantic Slave Trade In The Seventeenth Century, Simon and Schuster, New York, 1977.

Butterfield, Fox, All God's Children-The American Tradition of Violence, Avon Books, New York, 1996.

Chafe, William H., Gavins, Raymond, Koestad, Robert, Ortiz, Paul, Rittenhouse, Jennifer, Keisha, Roberts, and Waligora-Davis, Nicole, -REMEMBERING "JIM CROW"- African-Americans Tell About Life In The Segregated South, The New Press, In Association with Lyndhurst Books of the Center for Documentary Studies of Duke University, and documentary studies for the Behind the Veil Project, W. W. Norton & co., Inc., New York, 2001.

DuBois, William E. B., Black Reconstructions In America, (1860-1880), Simon and Schuster, New York, London, Toronto, Sydney, Tokyo, Singapore, 1935, 1962.

DuBois, William E. B., The Souls Of Black Folk, Blue Heron Press, New York, 1953.

The Final Call, May 9, 2000.

Franklin, John Hope, The Color Line: Legacy For The Twenty-First Century, The University Of Missouri Press, Columbia and London, 1993.

Franklin, John Hope, Frown Slavery To Freedom, A History Of Negro Americans, McGraw Hill Publishing Company, New York, St. Louis, San Francisco, Auckland, Bogata, Caracas, Hamburg, Paris, London, Sao Paulo, Madrid; Fortieth Anniversary Edition, 1998.
Fredrickson, George M., The Black Image In The White Mind, Wesleyan University Press and Harper Row Publishers, Hanover, New Hampshire, 1987.

Goldman, Peter, Civil Rights: The Challenge Of The Fourteenth Amendment, Coward-McCann, Incorporated, New York, 1970.

Guy and Carawan, Ain't You Got A Right To The Tree Of Life? The University Of Georgia Press, Athens and London, 1966.

Haley, Alex, The Autobiography Of Malcolm X, Ballantine Books, New York, 1964, 1965, 1999.

Harrington Michael, The Other America, Penguin Books, Baltimore, 1962.

Haskins, James, The Life And Death of Martin Luther King, Jr., Lothrop, Lee, and Sheppard Company, New York, 1977.

Hughes, Langston and Meltzer, Milton, A Pictorial History of The Negro In America, Crown Publishers, Inc. New York, 1956, 1963.

Jet Magazine, A Johnson Publication, June 8, 1987

Koestler, Arthur, The Thirteenth Tribe-The Khazar Empire and it's Heritage, Random House, New York, 1976.

LanningrMichael Lee (Lt. Col. Ret.), The African-American Soldier-From Cuscus Attacks To Colin Powell, Birch Lane Press Books, Carol Publishing Group, Secaucus, New Jersey, 1997.

Lester, Julius, To Be A Slave, The Dial Press, Incorporated, New York, 1968.

Lewis, David Levering, W. E. B. DuBois-Biography Of A Race (1868- 1919, John Macrae Books, Henry Holt and Company, Incorporated, 1993.

Lewis, John / Litwack, Leon F. / Allen, James/ Als, Hilton, Without Sanctuary - Lynching Photography In America, Twin Palms Publishers, Santa Fe, New Mexico, 2000.

The Los Angeles Times, November 30, 1996.

The Los Angeles Times, April 3, 1998.

Lubiano, Wahneema, The House that Race Built, Black Americans, U.S. Terrain, Patheon Books, New York, 1997.

Marshall, Robert, Storm From The East-From Genghis Khan To Khubilai Kahn, The University Of California Press, Berkley, Los Angeles, 1993.

McPherson, James M., The Abolitionist Legacy: From Reconstruction To The N. A. A. C. P., Princeton University Press, Princeton, New Jersey, 1975.

Meir, August and Rudwick, Elliot, From Plantation To Ghetto, American Century Series, Hill and Wang, New York, 1976.

Mellon, James, Bullwhip Days-The Slaves Remember (an oral history), Avon Books, New York, 1988.

Mullane, Deirdre, Words To Make My Dream Children Live- "A Book Of African-American Quotations," Anchor Books, and Doubleday, New York, London, Toronto, Sydney, Auckland, 1995.

The New York Times, June 10, 1963.

Oats, Stephen B., Let The Trumpets Sound: The Life And Death Of Dr. Martin Luther King, Jr., Mentone Books, New American Library, New York, New York, 1982.

Paiewonsky, Isidor, Eyewitness Accounts Of Slavery In The Danish West Indies-Graphic Tales Of Slave Happenings On Ships And Plantations, Fordham University Press, New York, 1989.

Pinkney Alphonso, The Myth Of Black Progress - "Black Equality In White America," Cambridge University Press, Cambridge, Massachusetts, 1984.

Poussaint, Alvin F., MD. / Alexander Amy, Lay My Burden Down, Suicide And The Mental Health Crisis Among African-Americans, Beacon Press Books, Boston, Massachusetts, 2000.

Quarles, Benjamin, Lincoln And The Negro, Da Capo Press, Incorporated, New York, 1962.

Revolutionary Times, The Black Arcade Liberation Library, 1970.

Robertson, David, Denmark Vesey, The Buried History Of America's Largest Slave Rebellion And The Man Who Led It, Alfred A. Knopf, NCW York 1999.

Robinson, Randall, The Debt -What America Owes To Blacks, Plume and Penguin Books, New York, London, Victoria Australia Toronto 2000.

Shapiro, Herbert, White Violence And Black Response, "From Reconstruction To Montgomery," The University Of Massachusetts Press, Amherst, Massachusetts, 1988.

Smith, Edward D., Climbing Jacobs Ladder, The Smithsonian Institute, 1988.

Stampp, Kenneth M., The Peculiar Institution-slavery In The Antebellum South, Vintage Books And Random House, Incorporated, New York, 1956, 1984.

Sterne, Emma G., I Have A Dream, Alfred A. Koph Company, New York, 1965.

Thomas, Velma Maia, Lest We Forget - The Passage From Africa To Slavery And Emancipation, Crown Publishers, Incorporated, New York, 1997.

Washington, James M., The Essential Writings And Speeches Of Martin Luther King, Jr., "A Testament Of Hope," Harper-Collies, New York, 1986.

Watters, Pat, Down To Now, Patheon Books, New York, 1971.

West, Cornell, Race Matters, Vintage Books, New York, 1994.

Windsor, Rudolph R., From Babylon To Timbuktu, Windsors Golden Series, Atlanta, Georgia 1969.

Woodward, C. Vann, The Strange Career Of Jim Crow, Oxford University Press, Incorporated, 1974

The World Book Multimedia Encyclopedia (TM) c 1996 525 W. Monroe Avenue, Chicago, Illinois 60661.

Young, Whitney M., To Be Equal, McGraw Hill Book Company, New York, Toronto, London, 1964.

Interviews

1). Mr. John Hatcher, President of the Ventura Chapter of the NAACP, EEOC director, Ventura, California. The Interview was held at the Port Huneme Naval Base at Port Huneme, California, 6 June 1991.

2). Mr. Hal Young, WW 11 Veteran (Tuskegee Airman 1943), the interview was held at the West Los Angeles VA Medical Center in Los Angeles, California, on 4 July 2002.

3). Mr. Bobby Murphy, Vietnam Veteran 1967, the interview was held at the   VA Medical Center in West Los Angeles, California, on 15 March 2001.

4). Mr. Robert W. Williams, Vietnam Veteran 1968-69, The interview was held in Santa Monica, California, on Thanksgiving Day 25 November 2001.

5). Mr. Ismael Bocar BA, Senegal, West Africa. The interview was held in my home on January 5, 2003, in Santa Monica, California.

INDEX

A

B

G

H

K

M

Minstrel Shows- 93-95

Missionaries- 16, 24, 153, 154, 347

Mississippi- 202, 209, 211, 214, 216, 220

Missouri Compromise- 91, 101

Monroe, James- 85

Montgomery Bus Boycott- 194, 195

Morocco- 273, 321

Mortality Rate/Statistics for African-American Infants/Women- 392

Moses- 26, 77, 91, 222, 261, 317

Mount Kilimanjaro- 14

Mount Zion AME Church- 295

Mozambique- 333

Muhammad, Hon. Elijah- 222, 224, 228- 230, 232

Mulattos- 9,234, 265, 270

Murphy, Bobby- 220

Music- 12, 25, 61, 364

N

NAACP- National Association For The Advancement Of Colored People- 155, 156, 167, 172, 177, 178, 199, 208, 403

Nation of Islam- 222, 231, 232, 403

National Association of African-American Psychologists- 386

National Bar Association- 386

National Conference of African-American Lawyers- 386

National Conference of African-American Political Scientists- 386

North Carolina A & T University- 193

Northrup, Solomon- 104

Ntinu, Wene- 344

Nullification- 170, 216

O

OAU- Organization of African-American Unity- 221

Obama, Barack H. - 405-407

Oliphant's Quarters- 257,259

Opthalmia- 45

Opium Wars- 226

Otis, James- 65

Oppression- 64, 105, 388

Oral Histories- 332

Orangeburg, S. C. - 199- 200

Original Jews- 321-326

Owen, Chandler- 174

P

Pagan- 225, 315, 317

Parks, Rosa- 193, 195

Paul, William- 71

Paine, Thomas- 26

Peculiar Institution- 382

T

U

X

PHOTO CREDITS

1). The AP/ Wide World Photos- Jack Rummel
2). Photo from Paiewonsky: Eyewitness Accounts Of Slavery
3). Photo from Paiewonsky: Eyewitness Accounts Of Slavery
4). Photo courtesy of: The New York Public Library, 4a). William L. Katz, Eyewitness
5). Slave Purchase Bill of Sale courtesy of: Samuel Tyrone Addison
6). Photo of "William Colbert"-The Reality of Slavery&The Cause of the War!
   Courtesy of: Lloyd Ostendorf
7). "The "Field Hand," Photo courtesy of: The Smithsonian Institute
8). Abolitionist Fredrick Douglas Photo courtesy of Dr. L. Bennett's "Before The Mayflower",
8a). George Beach, African-American Historical Commemorative Society, 2008
8b). William L. Katz, Eyewitness
9). Photo courtesy of: The Florida State Archives, 9a)William L. Katz, Eyewitness
9b). William L. Katz, Eyewitness, 9c). Katz, Eyewitness
10). Photo of Dr. W. E. B. DuBois courtesy of:The Moorland-Spingarn Research
   Center, Howard University, Washington, DC.
11). Photo of Booker T. Washington courtesy of: "Great Negroes Past and Present" (R. Adams)
12). The Men of the "Niagara Movement" Photo courtesy of: Langston Hughes
   and Milton Meltzer, "A Pictorial History of the Negro in America.
12a). William L. Katz, Eyewitness"
13). "Returning Soldiers" of WW1, Photo courtesy of: L. Hughes/Meltzer
14). Photo courtesy of: L. Hughes/Meltzer 14a). William L. Katz, Eyewitness
15). "The Silent Protest" photo courtesy of: L. Hughes/ M. Meltzer
15a). William L. Katz, Eyewitness
16). Lynching photos courtesy of: "Without Sanctuary"- Congressman John
   Lewis, Allen, Als, and Litwack
17). "The Shame of America" and Lynching Statistics courtesy of: L. Hughes and
   Milton Meltzer-"A Pictorial History of the Negro in America."
17a). William L. Katz, Eyewitness , 17b.) William L. Katz, Eyewitness,
17c). George Beach, African-American Historical Commemorative society, 2008
18). Marcus Garvey photo courtesy of: "Before the Mayflower" L. Bennett
18a). George Beach, African-American Historical Commemorative society, 2008
19). Mahatma Ghandi photo courtesy of: UPI/Bettmann News photo
20). Lynching photo courtesy of: "Lynching Photography In America"
   Congressman John Lewis, Als, Allen, and Litwack; "Without Sanctuary"
21). Photo courtesy of: Center for African-American Studies, University of California-Los Angeles
22). Photo courtesy of: Jet Magazine Press (1-27-03)
23). Photo courtesy of: AP/Wide world Photos
24). Photo courtesy of: AP/Wide world Photos
25). Photo courtesy of: Charles Moore/Black Star Press
26). Photo from: Langston Hughes/Milton Meltzer-"A Pictorial History Of The Negro In America"
27). Photo courtesy of: The Department of Archives and Manuscripts-Birmingham
   Public Library, Birmingham, Alabama

28).   Photo courtesy of: UPI/Bettmann News Photo

29).   Photo courtesy of: The Tennessean, Nashville, Tenn.

30).   Photo courtesy of: The Tennessean, Nashville, Tenn.

31).   Photo courtesy of: The Highlander Research and Education Center Archives

32).   Photo courtesy of: AP/ Wide World Photos

33).   Photo courtesy of: Charles Moore/Black Star

34).   Photo courtesy of: Charles Moore/Black Star Press

35).   Photo courtesy of: Taylor Branch-"Parting The Water's"

36).   Photo courtesy of: Dan/Sandra Weiner for Magnum, Inc.

37).   Photo courtesy of: UPI/Bettmann News Photos

38).   Photo courtesy of: Flip Schulke/Black Star Press

39).   Photo courtesy of: UPI/Bettmann News Photos

40).   Photo courtesy of: AP/Wide World Photos

41).   Photo courtesy of: The Library of Congress

42).   Photo courtesy of: Bob Henrique/Magnum Photos, Inc.

43).   Photo courtesy of: Fred Ward/Black Star Press

44).   Photo courtesy of: Moorland-Spingarm Research Center, Howard University

45).   Photo courtesy of: UPI/Bettmann News Photos

45a).   George Beach, African-American Historical Commemorative Society, 2008

46).   Photo courtesy of: UPI/Bettmann News Photos

47).   Photo courtesy of: UPI/Bettmann News Photos

48).   Photo courtesy of: O. L. Abel

49).   Photo courtesy of: UPI/Bettmann News Photos

50).   Photo courtesy of: UPI/Bettmann News Photos

51).   Photo courtesy of: UPI/Bettmann News Photos

52).   Photo courtesy of: UPI- United Press International & James Haskins

53).   Photo courtesy of: Magnum Photos/Philip Jones-Griffiths

54).   Photo courtesy of: The Washington Star Collections, The Washington Post

55).   Photo courtesy of: The AP/Wide World Photos

56).   Photo courtesy of: UPI/Bettmann News Photos

57).   Photo courtesy of: The AP/Wide World Press

58).   Photo courtesy of: Time, Inc.

59).   Photo courtesy of: Dan/Sandra Weiner, Magnum Photos

60).   Photo courtesy of: UPI/Bettmann News Photos

61).   Photo courtesy of: UPI/Bettmann News Photos

62).   Photo courtesy of: AP/Wide World Photos

63).   Family Photo courtesy of: Rosetta Boyd-Pendergrass

64).   Photo of myself taken in Tangier, Morocco-North Africa 1974

65).   Photo courtesy of: Jet Magazine Press 1987

66).   Photo courtesy of: The Los Angeles Times; Eric Glenn

67).   Photo courtesy of: L. Bennett, "Before The Mayflower"

68). The Chester News/Reporter

69). Photo courtesy of: Jamey O. Shepherd, Chester News/Reporter staff

70). Photo courtesy of: The Chester News/Reporter, J. O. Shepherd

71). Eyewitness Story by: J. O. Shepherd-News/Reporter staff writer

72). Photo courtesy of: The Los Angeles Times/Associated Press

73). The map courtesy of: A. Koestler-The Thirteenth Tribe

74). Photo courtesy of: R. Windsor-"The Ancient Hebrews"

75). Map courtesy of: Grolier Incorporated-1974

76). Cover artist/design by Meri Shardin-1974

About the Author

Mr. William B. Boyd is the former president of the Veterans Upward Bound Project based in Atlanta, Georgia, an active member of the Vietnam Veterans of America Service Organization, a member of the NAACP (National Association for the Advancement of Colored People), and a member of the Southern Poverty Law Center. He is a veteran of the United States Navy where he served as a Boatswains Mate and Radar Operations Specialist. He is a graduate of Chester Senior High School in Chester, South Carolina in 1973, and attended Central Piedmont Community College and Johnson C. Smith University. He has worked as a Design Engineer with Duke Power Company, a Bio-Medical Engineer for electroencephalography telemetry studies in the medical community, and as a Configurations Manager with Department of Defense sub-contractors. Mr. Boyd is currently self-employed, residing in southern California.